Slavery

NEW PERSPECTIVES ON THE PAST

PUBLISHED

David Arnold Famine*
David Arnold The Problem of Nature
James Casey The History of the Family*
Patricia Crone-Pre-Industrial Societies
James Fentress and Chris Wickham Social Memory
Ernest Gellner Nations and Nationalism
Ernest Gellner Reason and Culture*
David Grigg The Transformation of Agriculture in the West
Richard Hodges Primitive and Peasant Markets*
Eugene Kamenka Bureaucracy
Edward Peters Torture*
Jonathan Powis Aristocracy*
I. G. Simmons Environmental History
Bruce Trigger Sociocultural Evolution
David Turley Slavery

IN PREPARATION

Michael Adas Locating World History
William Ray The Concept of Culture
Merry Wiesner Gender in History

* now out of print

Slavery

David Turley

First published 2000

2 4 6 8 10 9 7 5 3 1

Blackwell Publishers Ltd
108 Cowley Road
Oxford OX4 1JF
UK

Blackwell Publishers Inc.
350 Main Street
Malden, Massachusetts 02148
USA

British Library Cataloguing in Publication Data
A CIP catalogue record for this book is available from the British Library.

Library of Congress Cataloging-in-Publication Data has been applied for

ISBN 0 631 16729 3
0 631 16731 5 (pbk)

Typeset in 11 on 13pt Sabon
by SetSystems Ltd, Saffron Walden, Essex
Printed in Great Britain by T J International Ltd, Padstow, Cornwall

This book is printed on acid-free paper.

Contents

Series Editor's Preface

History is one of many fields of knowledge. Like other fields it has two elements: boundaries and contents. The boundaries of history first acquired their modern shape in early modern Europe. They include, among other things, such basic principles as the assumption that time is divisible into past, present, and future; that the past can be known by means of records and remainders surviving to the present; that culture can be distinguished from nature; that anachronism can be avoided; that subjects are different from objects; that human beings are capable of taking action; and that action is shaped by circumstance. Above all else, of course, they include the assumption that history does actually constitute a separate field of knowledge that is in fact divided from neighbouring fields – not merely a hitherto neglected corner of some other field whose rightful owners ought ideally, and are expected eventually, to reclaim it from the squatters now dwelling there without authorization and cultivate it properly with the tools of, say, an improved theology or a more subtle natural science.

A prodigious harvest has been gathered from the field bounded by those assumptions. Making a tentative beginning with the humanist discovery of antiquity, gaining confidence with the Enlightenment critique of religion, and blossoming into full professionalization in the nineteenth century, modern historians have managed to turn their produce into an elementary ingredient in democratic education and a staple of cultural consumption. They have extracted mountains of evidence from archives and turned it into books whose truth can be assayed by anyone who cares to follow their instructions. They have dismantled ancient legends that had been handed down through the ages and laid them to rest in modern libraries. They have emancipated the study of the past from prophecy, apocalypticism, and other providential explications of the future. Pronouncements on the past no longer command respect unless they have been authenticated by reference to documents. Myths and superstitions have given way to knowledge of unprecedented depth, precision, and extent. Compared with what we read in older books, the books of history today are veritable miracles of comprehension, exactitude, and impartiality.

Success, however, has its price. None of the assumptions defining the modern practices of history are self-evidently true. The more they are obeyed, the less it seems they can be trusted. Having probed the realm of culture to its frontiers, we cannot find the boundary by which it is supposed to be divided from the empire of nature. Having raised our standards of objectivity to glorious heights, we are afflicted with vertiginous attacks of relativity. Having mined the archives to rock bottom, we find that the ores turn out to yield no meaning without amalgamation. And having religiously observed the boundary between the present and the past, we find that the past does not live in the records but in our own imagination. The boundaries of history have been worn down; the field is lying open to erosion.

The books in this series are meant to point a way out of that predicament. The authors come from different disciplines, all of them specialists in one subject or another. They do not proceed alike. Some deal with subjects straddling familiar boundaries – chronological, geographical, and conceptual. Some focus on the boundaries themselves. Some bring new subjects into view. Some view old subjects from a new perspective. But all of them share a concern that our present understanding of history needs to be reconfigured if it is not to turn into a mere product of the past that it is seeking to explain. They are convinced that the past does have a meaning for the present that transcends the interest of specialists. And they are determined to keep that meaning within reach by writing good short books for non-specialists and specialists alike.

Constantin Fasolt
University of Chicago

Acknowledgements

I am grateful for criticism and suggestions in response to earlier versions of portions of this book to members of the Cambridge American History seminar and audiences at meetings of the British Nineteenth Century American Historians group and the British Association for American Studies. I thank David Richardson, Michael Bush and Howard Temperley for inviting me to take part in informative and stimulating colloquia in London, Manchester and Norwich. The staff at Blackwell have been excessively patient in awaiting this book. Helen Rappaport has been a keen-eyed copy editor. Above all, I thank Kate for her urgings and Anna, Hilary and Celia for their occasional curiosity.

David Turley
December 1999

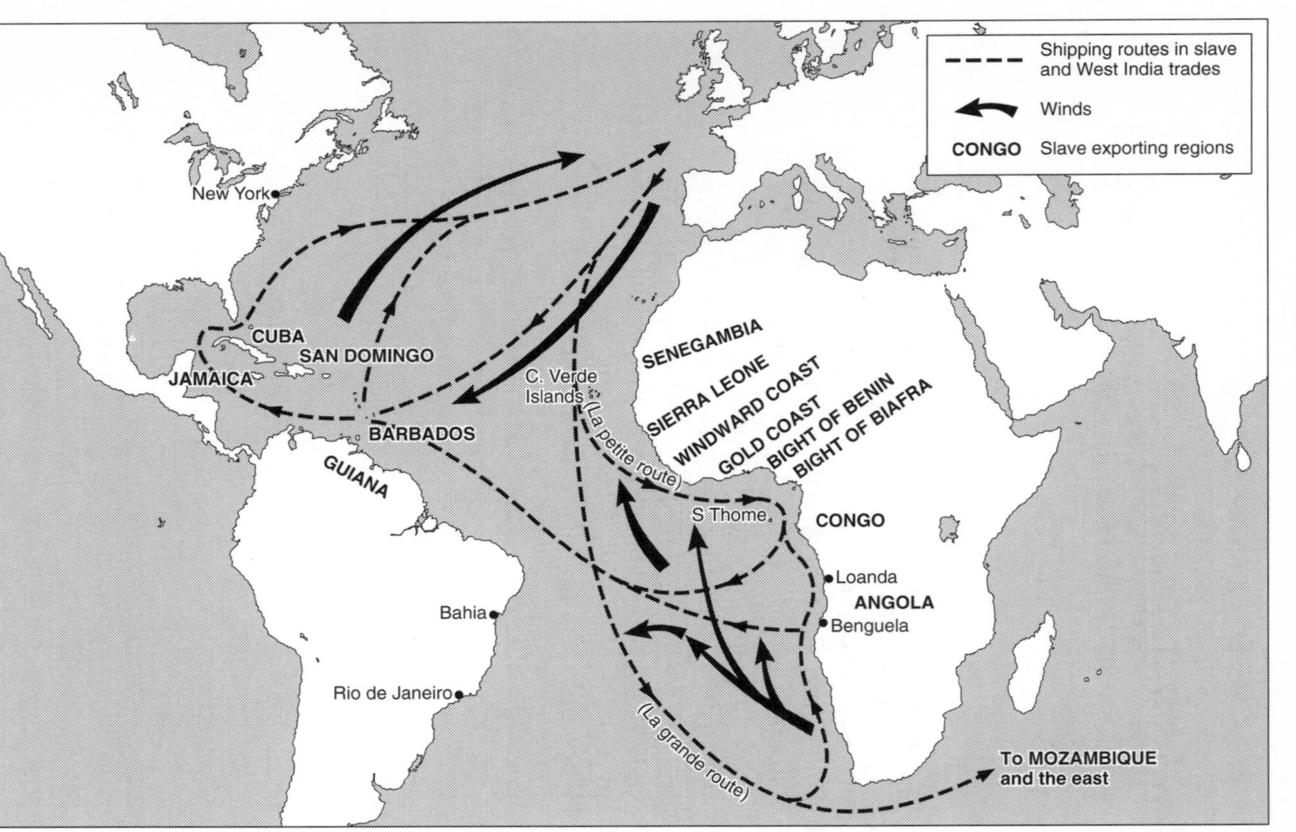

Map 1 The Atlantic slave trade, slave exporting regions and maritime routes (J. D. Fage, *An Atlas of African History*, 1958, Edward Arnold, p. 29)

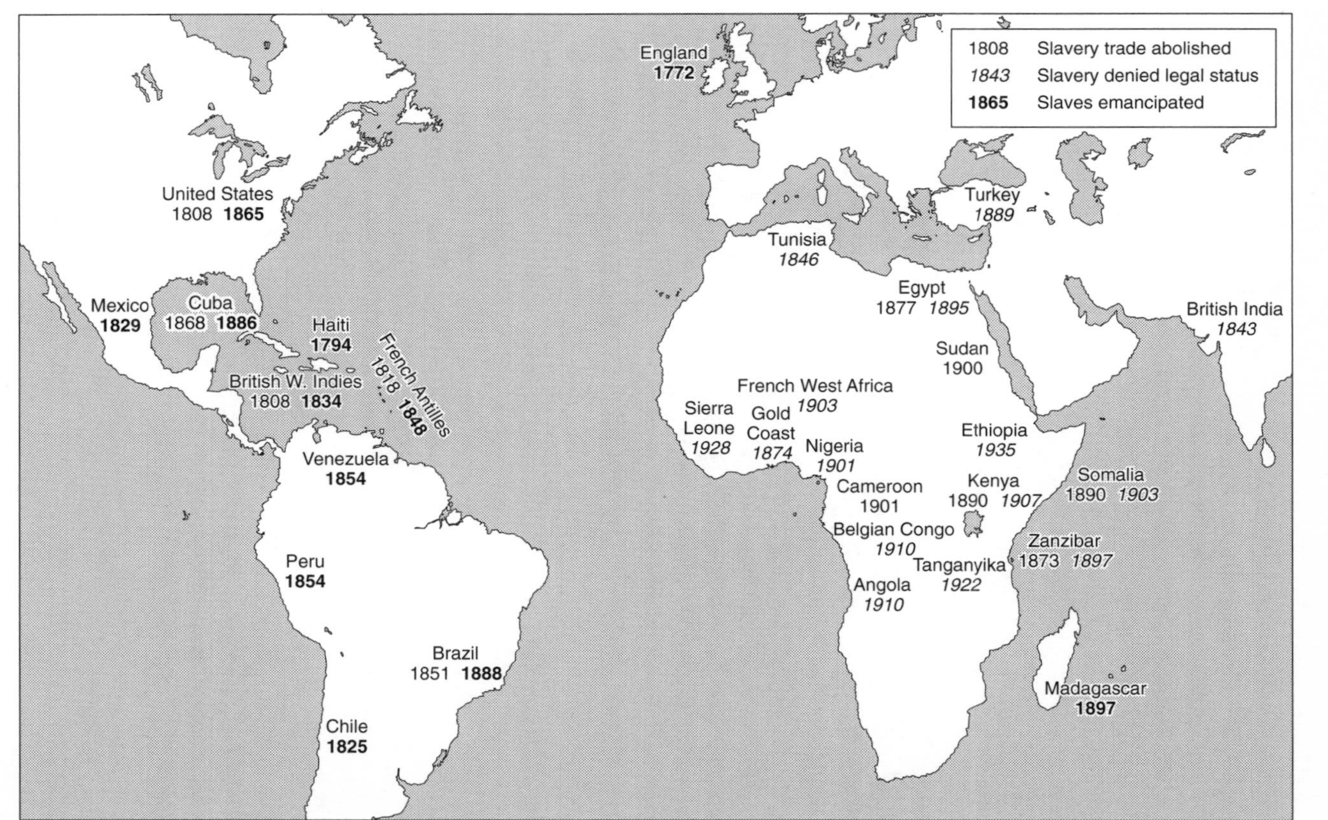

Map 2 Abolition of the slave trade and the emancipation of slaves (Patrick Manning, *Slavery and African Life: Occidental, Oriental and African Slave Trades*, 1990, Cambridge University Press, p. 154)

1

Approaching Slavery

Perhaps the most familiar image associated with slavery in many minds is of a figure of African descent bending over work in a field of sugar cane or cotton. It will require this whole essay to sketch the multifaceted character of the institution even in outline, but the popular image does provide two starting points from which to begin to understand slavery as an historical phenomenon. Certainly slavery has often been a system featuring a racially distinct subordinate group owned by, and working for, others. Most notably was this the case from the fifteenth century onwards in the Atlantic world where the enslaved population was increasingly drawn from sub-Saharan Africa. Moreover, as the worker in cane and cotton suggests, a major economic purpose in the use of slave labour in different periods of the past has been to engage in large-scale production of agricultural staples for markets often at some distance from the point of production. These systems of production and trade have been linked to various finishing processes. The ultimate product of the slave's labour in the early modern and modern Atlantic economy might well be a garment produced in a Manchester textile mill or a quantity of refined sugar in the kitchen of a New York household.

The geographical area from which this essay draws materials, however, comprehends Europe, the Middle East, Africa and the Americas. At various times and places within this vast region slave workers produced many items – sugar, dates, grain, tobacco, cotton, rice and coffee – along with some minor commodities, for sale in markets at the end of land and sea routes. The men, women and children who became slaves were themselves moveable commodities and, with what they produced, formed the substance of complex economic networks criss-crossing the Atlantic, the Indian Ocean, the Persian Gulf and both Saharan and sub-Saharan Africa.

Slavery, however, and the dilemmas it has posed for human societies, reaches back long before the time Europeans, making use of African labour, settled the Atlantic islands and the Americas. Any attempt at a synoptic account of the phenomenon must consider not only the geographical range within which slavery has existed but also the widely separated periods of time when it was historically present. The following discussion will make reference to pre-classical examples of slavery, the system in the Greek and Roman worlds, in medieval Europe and the earlier and later Muslim societies of the Middle East and Africa, with other instances in sub-Saharan Africa and the African racial slavery of the Americas.

A wider temporal and geographical purview reveals additions and qualifications that need to be made to the features of slavery indicated above. The racial distinctiveness of slaves has not proved to be an invariable historical attribute of slave systems. Almost universally, however, those imposing slavery have perceived their victims as in some senses apart and inferior. In the case of classical Attica, the Athenians were very reluctant to enslave other Greeks, or, if they did so, exported them outside the Greek world and became masters of non-Greek *barbaroi* instead. Usually these slaves were not particularly distinctive in physical appearance. On occasion even such 'ethnic' differences were lacking as a mark separating slaves from others. An eighteenth-century English observer in Senegambia, for example, noted the willingness of local people to enslave their own kind as a punishment for certain crimes. Once this had happened there was no doubt greater willingness to sell them off to European traders, but sometimes they were retained as inferiors in their own societies, of which they were no longer full members.

The central importance of race, ethnicity or criminality as sources of the perceptions of separateness and inferiority, seemingly necessary, though never sufficient, for the imposition of slavery on an individual or group, crosses time and space. But the fates of being a conquered enemy, or belonging to a different religious or cultural community, have also served historically, when other imperatives also operated, to mark out people for enslavement. Christians, Muslims and Jews have, at various times, felt justified in enslaving those not of their own faith or culture and have revealed ambivalence or opposition at the prospect of the enslaved then taking up their faith and eliminating part of the evidence of separateness. What all these different significations of distinctiveness and inferiority have in common is to be understood in relation to their outcomes for the enslaved. In creating 'outsiders', structures of difference and inferiority were deemed to legitimate the removal of all or most forms of protection provided by different kinds of communities or cultural groups for their members. Slaves, as the most inferior of outsiders, were exceptionally vulnerable to the exercise of their owner's power, and sometimes that of others, over them. Their theoretical defencelessness, a product of their virtual non-possession of any rights that had to be observed, has been subsumed in the resonant phrase of the historical sociologist, Orlando Patterson, as 'social death' in his *Slavery and Social Death*. The idea that slavery was the equivalent of death in being its replacement, though renewed in Patterson's work, itself has a long history. It is to be found variously in the Roman legal texts of Ulpian: 'Slavery is equated with death' and in the immemorial assumption that victory in warfare entitled the victor to impose slavery instead of death upon the vanquished. The expected absolute obedience and lack of rights of the slave were the consequences of his redemption from complete extinction.

Long temporal and wide geographical perspectives on slavery reveal also that large-scale agricultural production based on slave labour predates the modern Atlantic world, as in the slave-worked *latifundia* of late republican and early imperial Italy and Sicily. More important, however, it becomes evident how malleable slavery has been in fitting round the functional requirements of many different kinds of societies. Judged by the limited functions that slaves performed in American plantation societies – largely manual labour, artisan work and personal and domestic service – the range of activities they undertook and the positions they held in other periods and places was both great and startling. Slave artisans can be encountered from ancient Mesopotamia and Minoan Crete to the blacksmiths of the ante-bellum South of the United States; slave miners and industrial workers from the silver mines of Laureion in ancient Attica to eighteenth-century Minas Gerais in the Brazilian interior. But bondsmen could play much more exalted roles. Slaves took up uncommon, as well as common, household roles when the household itself was special. Slave members of the Roman imperial household, or *familia*, became administrators at the centre of the empire or powerful agents of the emperor in the provinces. Musicus Scurranus, for example, the slave of the Emperor Tiberius, took the office of *dispensator* or chief accountant of the Treasury in the province of Gallia Lugdunensis in the first century. Slave eunuchs acted as imperial advisers and officials particularly in the eastern Roman Empire and in medieval and later courts of Islamic rulers in the Middle East and Africa. Even general military command was within the grasp of talented and favoured slaves in both the ancient and Muslim worlds.

This glimpse of the variety and malleability of slavery indicates one of the difficulties in writing a synoptic account of the institution. Thus, in order to give coherence to the discussion, with due recognition of the range of the manifestations of slavery and its many contexts across societies and centuries, what follows will pursue three complementary themes, broadly conceived. These themes are the *structural location* of slavery within societies; the *experience* of slavery as registered both by the slaves and those seeking to control them; and, finally, *the ways in which slavery was reproduced and maintained* in different societies.

Broadly speaking, the structural location of slavery has been of two kinds. Firstly, slavery has been a visible but productively marginal feature of many societies. Often slaves were attached to households, family networks or lineages, a setting that provides the initial context for an analysis of the experience of this kind of slavery. The means of reproduction and maintenance of small-scale slavery were usually informal, requiring no organized system. These cases will be termed *societies with slaves*. Secondly, there have been societies containing substantial numbers of slaves working in agriculture and industry. The number of slaves, particularly as a proportion of the total population, was clearly relevant to the character of the overall social ethos. But numbers or proportion as such, even when they can be accurately established in particular cases, may not tell us very much. What must be the size of the slave part of the population before it decisively affects the character of the whole society? Alternatively, what degree of production must result from slave labour for it to be crucial? These questions are not susceptible to firmly grounded responses. In late eighteenth-century St Domingue in the French Antilles slaves were a majority of the labour force and produced the great bulk of commodities. In the nineteenth-century American South they were a minority of workers responsible for a majority of export commodities and a minority of other goods. Historians consider both societies to have been dominated by slavery but it is not clear purely from the measures of quantity what the categorization might mean. A structural approach, relating slavery to the social order, rather than extrapolating effects purely from quantitative estimates of population or production is likely to be more fruitful. Here three queries are relevant. Did the dominant group in the society depend for their freedom to rule on their control of the surplus generated by the slaves? How widely dispersed was slave ownership within the population as a whole? How possible, in social reality or perception, was it for individuals to rise into the slave-owning class? When the first of these questions can be answered positively the social ethos is likely to have been strongly influenced by slavery because of the power and generalized influence of the dominant group. If it can be concluded in response to the second and/or the third questions that a substantial element of the population was involved, then the ethos of slavery will have been that much more powerful. These cases constitute what will be called *slave societies*.

Refining the structural location of slavery further in both societies with slaves and slave societies means being alert to functions other than work that bondsmen and women might fulfil. They could meet the need for prestige or mark the status of the owner or accommodate sexual demands, all according to the various values and practices of the social and cultural worlds in which their owners moved. But when physical labour was a central aspect of the slave's function, and especially in slave societies, the structural location of slavery was crucially defined in relation to the accessibility, costs and social attitudes towards the different kinds of labour that were, or might relatively easily be made, available.

The other types of labour that have coexisted with slavery historically, and need to be distinguished from it, are of various kinds that may be envisaged as being on a spectrum between slavery and complete individual autonomy. The major forms span serfdom, debt bondage and legally free paid labour (whether paid by wages or in some other way). At the margins, the different types of labour could shade into each other when circumstances altered and only small differences of legal status were in question. But where slavery existed, its relations to the other kinds of labour shaped its structural location and changes in those relations charted the transition from a society with slaves to a slave society or a development in the reverse direction.

How, in general terms, are the kinds of non-free labour to be distinguished from each other? The problem of how to define slavery has generated a great deal of debate but it is proposed here to adopt a twentieth-century definition acted on internationally. Slavery, according to the Slavery Convention of the League of Nations (1926) is 'the status or conditions of a person over whom any or all of the powers attaching to the right of ownership are exercised'. This covers ownership of slaves on the part of individuals, corporate entities such as temples, the public or the state. The supposition also is that slaves remained slaves when loaned or hired to others. The fuller term 'chattel slavery' indicates that the slave was regarded, as far as was practicable, as an animate piece of property with the only limits to what could be extracted from him set by the individual's limitations of physical endurance and mental capacity. The slave's condition was also deemed to be heritable. In theory the slave was thus an extension of the will of another, without any rights needing to be recognized, lacking almost all formal acknowledgement of human worth and therefore all honour. He was the epitome of the degraded outsider.

Men and women occupying other non-free statuses have sometimes shared several of these conditions, but never all of them. In some circumstances, however, these statuses could evolve towards slavery. What were most important in indicating the extent of constraint attached to an individual's status were both personal and civic characteristics. For the individual they had to do with whether he could claim to possess property, the extent of influence he might exercise over his own mobility and labour time and how likely it was he might be permitted to marry and maintain a family. As a quasi-civic being his standing in the judicial process was crucial, as was the amount of recognition he might be accorded in religious, military and political activities. Any more precise generalizations are made difficult by variations over time and according to location.

Undoubtedly the most important non-free statuses in relation to slavery were serfdom and debt bondage. How to define serfdom has provoked almost as much debate amongst historians as has the parallel problem of the definition of slavery. The serf did share a number of characteristics with the slave. He usually worked on the land from which he was not free to move; he could not normally change his status; his condition was heritable and he was frequently regarded with scorn. Yet there were also significant differences between the likely conditions of serf and slave. Although the agricultural serf worked on land that was not his own, the terms of his situation were set by law and custom; in theory the services he had to render were defined and not limited only by what could be extracted from him. Even though in practice the terms of his service might often be the subject of conflict, and additional demands might be successfully imposed upon him, he normally had the advantage over the slave of not being able to be sold separately from the land he worked. His opportunities for marriage and family life were thus greater, he could organize the labour of his family so that they could provide for themselves and he received some recognition in law. The serf, in other words, was not normally an outsider. However harshly he was regarded or treated, he lived in a land where he was perceived as a native. Perhaps (using the term 'serf' without assuming the feudal system), like the Messenian helots under the power of Sparta, the serf was part of a whole community conquered by outsiders who stayed to rule. In contrast, the slave's conquerors more frequently carried him off to a foreign land; in the language of recent scholars the slave, but not the serf, suffered 'natal alienation'.

Debt bondage most often occurred when the person taking on a debt offered as collateral for the debt his own services or those of someone he commanded and, failing to meet the debt, had to provide services for the creditor. If the value of the services undertaken was either not set against the debt or the debtor was unable to get the extent of the services fixed – situations especially likely when the debtor was dealing with a socially more powerful creditor – then debt bondage ensued. There were cases when the creditor was probably not concerned primarily with repayment, or even with interest, but wanted labour services. Should the obligation be met, then usually the former debtor was able to resume his place in the community unhindered. If, however, the debt bondage had no evident termination, became permanent, then it amounted to enslavement. What started out as a defined and limited economic relation began to merge into a relation of lifelong social subordination sustained by extra-economic factors. The relation could be enforced on the next generation. When this occurred it amounted to an infrequent example of a member of a community undergoing enslavement at the hands of a member of the same community.

Paid, legally free labour, where an agreed amount or period of labour was contracted for a defined amount of compensation (whether in cash or some other form) might seem to have little in common with the other kinds of labour just discussed. But it is important to recognize that historically, and particularly alongside or in the aftermath of slavery, it has taken forms demonstrating that it cannot be understood purely as the polar opposite of slavery. In Ancient Greece work appropriate to a free man was defined less by the kind of work than the condition under which the work was carried on. In these terms Aristotle excluded wage labour as an activity for a free man. 'The condition of the free man is that he does not live for the benefit (or profit) of another.' Spanish immigrant labourers in Cuba, in the last decades of slavery after 1850, were paid for their work but shared many of the physical and disciplinary conditions of the slaves. Indentured labour, as amongst the Indians transported to the post-emancipation British West Indies and French Antilles, required the worker to commit himself to a particular employer for a number of years. Payment was accompanied by sacrifice of mobility.

Slavery as experienced by the slaves was in part framed by the tasks slaves performed as well as the size of the units that they worked on and of the group in which they worked. Since heterogeneity of function was perfectly compatible in slave societies with large-scale slave labour in agriculture or forms of industry, the variety in the range of slave experience related to function in a particular society could be considerable. The implication follows that there need be nothing automatic about any sense of commonality amongst slaves. Unless they deliberately sought to construct connections with their fellows they might share little with them but their formal status.

Attempting to understand, in a more rounded way, the experiences of all of those caught up in slavery requires a series of linked analyses. What were the interconnections between the legal and institutional features of slavery, the cultural and other resources that slaves brought to their situation and the social character and mental outlook of the slave owners and their agents? A study of the legal ordering of slavery offers opportunities for a comparison of how slaves and their circumstances were formally perceived at different times and in different places. The *Institutes* of Justinian, the medieval Castilian *Las Siete Partidas*, Muslim jurisprudence of the same period, the French *Code Noir* of 1685, the laws of the English Caribbean or the state slave codes of the American South in the first half of the nineteenth century provide such evidence. But reading prescriptive materials, such as laws, only has value in relation to the multiple experiences of slavery when combined with recognition of the ways in which the circumstances and behaviour of slaves and owners on the ground may diverge from the juridical conceptions of the system. When the Emperor Justinian issued his *Institutes* in 533 CE he followed the earlier traditions of Greek and Roman law in defining men and women as either free or slave. Yet a variety of conditions and types of labour, between slavery and freedom, existed in his dominions. The code, taking no account of these subtleties, was primarily a guide to the aspirations of the state and slave owners. Even leaving aside the variety of non-free statuses, with its implications for experience, the practical problems of legal enforcement were likely to promote judicial or legislative inconsistency or pragmatic accommodation to some of the slave's behaviour. He or she was a thing owned, a chattel, but as a human being was also capable of actions whose effects were to be taken account of; the slave could be an agent. From the point of view of law-makers or owners this was primarily a matter of management and control. In other words, the idea of the slave as simply an extension of the master's will had to bend to accommodate some recognition of the slave's consciousness and psychological needs. This was a process distinct in degree, but not fundamentally different in kind, from what was unavoidable in managing a free labour system. But at moments of crisis the harsh simplifications of the law continued to be a weapon for asserting the master's authority and thus partially constitutive of the experience of slavery.

However, the gap between particular local circumstances and the generalizing tendencies of legal rules and custom, or sometimes the simple fact that they could not be effectively enforced, could give space to slaves to influence their situation. The paucity of evidence in earlier periods, or its problematic nature in regard to slave attitudes and intentions, makes this aspect of the experiences of slavery difficult to write about with authority. But slaves' behaviour provides clues about their attitudes, demonstrating responses ranging from thankful acceptance to utter rejection of their situation. Their individual psychology and the cultural, family and possibly community, resources they might call upon were likely to have shaped significantly their day-to-day experiences of slavery and their predominant attitudes. Those attitudes also grew out of their recurrent unequal interactions with the master or other agents of authority, with other slaves and with groups not directly involved in the servile relationship.

How and with what success slavery was reproduced in any slave society was obviously important for the maintenance of the institution and therefore the relative balance of different forms of labour in the economy. But, equally significant, in combination with the way that slaves were distributed amongst different occupations between and within the main kinds of slave-based activity, the methods aiding the reproduction of slavery could have a powerful influence on the character of the overall social formation into which a malleable slavery fitted. Further, the ways in which slavery was reproduced and maintained at particular times and places both influenced, and were influenced by, the social character and outlook of powerful groups. Modes of slave reproduction thus fed back into the experience of slavery. The possibility of slave reproduction was not simply a matter of biology but of social and cultural circumstances governed by the attitudes of slave owners and slaves, the availability of men and women to be enslaved and the social and ideological features of dominant groups. In societies with slaves the reproduction of slavery over any great length of time was unlikely since there were no organized and routine operations by which sufficient reproduction could be generated. In slave societies reproduction through births to existing slave women was rarely sufficient to maintain slave levels. What means were adopted of supplementing the slave birth rate were crucial for indicating the relative significance of different social groups and the likely impact of their attitudes and values on the social whole. Warrior classes increased slave populations through warfare, or recurrent bandit-style raids on external peoples. Specialized groups of traders supplied labour through the development of an organized slave trade. In some societies a combination of methods were in operation. In each case there were likely to have been somewhat different effects on the ethos of a slave society.

All three of the aspects of slavery introduced in the preceding pages – structural location, experiences within slavery of slaves and their controllers and the reproduction of slavery – were relevant to the ways in which slavery came to an end and how much difficulty was involved in its ending. The structural location of slavery was pertinent in the sense of its relation to other kinds of labour available when the slave system began to erode, as in the later Roman Empire, or when its maintenance came into question in the modern period. How both masters and slaves had experienced slavery and what conclusions they drew from it, particularly through recurrent difficulties of management and peaks of slave resistance, helped shape their behaviour in response to more general crises in the slave regimes. The reduction or elimination of the provision of slaves, however they were obtained, could have a substantial impact on perceptions of the future vitality of slavery and stimulate slave owners to new courses of action. These major factors provide the starting point, the preconditions, for an analysis of slavery's demise. Together they indicate the limits of the possibilities for a progressive transition away from slavery as compared with the likelihood of a sudden rupture of the slave society. Each important case of the end of slavery, of course, constituted a historically distinct conjunction of circumstances affected, sometimes drastically, by the impact of contingent events. None the less, a general analysis of the *processes* leading to the end of slavery is possible and can fruitfully incorporate consideration of a number of alternative emphases that have emerged in the recent literature on the end of slavery.

This is particularly true of emancipation as it has developed since the end of the eighteenth century. Whatever the primary analytical framework integrating structural location, experience and the problems of reproduction and maintenance indicated about the likely sudden or gradual end to slavery, historians have tended to categorize the processes of emancipation in terms of a series of binary oppositions. This has been true despite the complexities of organized action against slavery through political or judicial authorities, social revolution or social reform movements operating at the critical moment in varying relations to government or judiciary. Either the end of slavery has come (usually), it is said, from above through actions of legislatures or courts, or (rarely) through an upsurge from below. These alternatives have been linked to peaceful (top down) as against violent (upsurge from below) change. Inserted in the historical literature in indirect relation to these bracketed binary oppositions has been discussion of the differential roles of committed elite reformers and of popular, but peaceful, antislavery movements in some cases and the absence of mass movements in others. The structures of political authority within the different slave systems and what slaves did towards achieving their own freedom also impinge upon the usual terms framing accounts of emancipation. Discussion of the role of ideas has focused on the relative weight to be attributed to the moral and religious critique of slavery as compared with the impact of the conceptions of liberal political economy on policy makers and public opinion. Of course, historians have also recognized that slave owners' mundane financial calculations of costs and benefits under the influence of changing notions about the ingredients of economic success played their part. Yet understanding how the various processes of emancipation unfolded, it will be argued in a later chapter, more often requires that these different emphases be seen not as alternatives and mutually exclusive but rather as subtly interwoven.

In the cases of emancipation, notably in Africa, that came 'late' in the modern period the relationship between empire and slavery assumed a more ambiguous form than in previous eras when territorial expansion both enabled and was facilitated by the provision of slaves. The 'new imperialism' from the late nineteenth century onwards was in part rationalized as a crusade against the trade in slaves inside Africa, to the Arab world and across the Indian Ocean. Yet the creation of stable colonial systems often required the collaboration of indigenous slave-owning elites and their provision for projects undertaken by colonial administrations of large amounts of sometimes slave labour. Both intentionally and unintentionally, therefore, the later phase of modern emancipation was long-drawn-out and morally tangled. Despite that, however, and despite the very mixed economic, social and political consequences of freedom for former slaves in the modern world, the presumptions of progress turned against slavery after millennia during which it went mostly unquestioned. In the twentieth century in consequence no significant society has depended on chattel slavery for the bulk of its labour or even substantially to supply the needs of its ruling class. 'Slave labour', whether accurately so termed or not, in the camps and gulags of recent totalitarian regimes has been accounted one of their distinguishing crimes. Even minor societies, when accused of retaining slavery, deny it, redefine it, make excuses or declare another emancipation. Though various kinds of non-free labour remain quite widespread, something historically significant has happened when an institution with such a long life reaches such a position. Slavery has become anathema in theory and to a considerable degree in practice.

2

Who Became Slaves, How, on What Terms?

Writers on slavery have long been lured by the prospect of being able to define the necessary conditions without which the institution could not have arisen. In recent times much the most discussed theory of the originating conditions of slavery has involved a refinement of propositions first prominently advanced at the time of European colonization in the early part of the nineteenth century. This tradition of writing on the political economy of non-free labour developed from Herman Merivale's Oxford lectures on colonization between 1839 and 1841 and Edward Gibbon Wakefield's projections of Australian settlement in the 1840s. It was resumed at the turn of the twentieth century, most influentially by the Dutch anthropologist J. H. Nieboer, and more recently, reflecting on Russian expansion to the East in the seventeenth and eighteenth centuries, by Evsey Domar. All these writers have worked on the assumption that land, labour and capital were the major factors of production in lands presumed to be largely 'empty', that is, setting aside usually widely scattered indigenous or local populations as irrelevant to economic development. Their writings, and sympathetic elaboration on them, have concluded that where land was plentiful but labour scarce and technology unlikely in the short run to be an effective replacement for labour, then settlement and economic development were shaped by the ratio between land and labouring population. Adam Smith had supposed that where there was a low man–land ratio in the colonial territory of a civilized country then that territory would 'advance more rapidly in wealth and greatness than any other human society'. But it has come to be recognized that economic advance in 'empty' land has occurred in distinctly different ways. Either it has happened largely through the emergence of independent farmers, forms of tenancy and with perhaps an element of relatively highly paid wage labour, or been achieved predominantly through slavery or serfdom. In the first set of cases, such as in Australia and the northern states of the United States, development could be steady. But in its earlier stages it was unlikely to attract large amounts of investment capital, or to need it, since production was likely to be of food and the by-products of stock rearing and mainly for subsistence and local markets. The linkage Merivale in particular made between plentiful land, relatively scarce labour and the outcome of forced labour, often slavery, arose from his focus on the production of a cash crop produced to satisfy an elastic demand in relatively distant markets. In these circumstances it was crucial to have a sufficient labour force able to be prevented from exploiting open land on its own account and thus preferably able to be distinguished from the rest of the population. This was economically feasible compared with a wage labour force held in place through high wages because investment capital to put into the slave labour force was attracted by the prospect of substantial profits from commodity production for an external market.

Yet in the circumstances considered by Merivale and other writers in the same tradition a low man–land ratio is a necessary but not a sufficient condition for slavery to emerge. In these terms Australia, Canada and the American North possessed the condition but were developed without slavery because they did not produce particular commodities for an elastic external market. When they did begin to produce such commodities – wool, grain – then the pattern of free labour had already been so firmly established as to be unable successfully to be challenged politically. Where slavery did become the major form of labour for production for external markets it rested upon the willingness of the state to maintain favourable laws, apply the threat or the use of force in support of property in slaves and allow the inflow of new slave labour. It will also become apparent from discussion below that other economic and cultural factors are likely to have been present. There has clearly been no *automatic* generation of slavery from low man–land ratios. Even as a necessary condition for slavery the low man–land ratio casts light on the emergence of some slave societies but says nothing about the generation of slavery in societies with slaves.

It is, however, worth considering further the relation of labour to land as it bears upon slavery. In parts of Africa where both land and population were comparatively plentiful, and especially where central authority was weak, cultivation was the province of family or lineage groups. If there were some slaves they were usually marginal to agricultural production. The LoDagaa of northern Ghana, members of a stateless community, existed largely without slaves. What few there were had probably sought protection from conditions of famine not far away or had been picked up as wandering strangers to work for a man who had no sons. Looking purely at the ratio of labour to land the tendency then was towards 'free' labour or to societies with (few) slaves. But the extent of commercial exchange or barter and the conditions of the political environment also require consideration. If the production of items for economic exchange called upon labour beyond that provided by family or lineage group, then stratification was promoted within the community through some working to produce a surplus for others. The consequent relations of production could include forms of unfree labour. Families and kin groups with the resources to take this initial step were progressively more distinguished from the rest of the community. The continuation of a relatively 'egalitarian' outcome in communities with plentiful labour on plentiful land depended also on the political environment. Only if there was comparative political stability in the surrounding area would weaker groups not be vulnerable to absorption by stronger, or the weaker themselves not seek protection from the stronger and thus avoid becoming subordinate to them. The LoDagaa were periodically raided for slaves by nearby states but without succumbing as a community.

When little land was available and labour substantial, the tradition of analysis associated with Nieboer would indicate a tendency to a system of cultivation controlled by landlords employing 'free' labourers or perhaps tenants, probably barely above subsistence level. Yet this was not necessarily the outcome, as the development of a small Caribbean island like Barbados suggests. An early phase of abundance of land settled by indentured white labourers and small farmers was succeeded by growing scarcity as cultivable land on the small island was divided up within the context of the emerging cash crop economy in sugar in the 1640s. The capital requirements of this kind of commodity production pushed many of the small farmers off the land and led to a concentration in ownership. Since increasing numbers of people had little or no land of their own it might seem they had little alternative but to work for others on harsh terms. It enabled their survival and did not contradict the landowners' assumed objective of profit maximization through sugar production for the European market. The outcome, however, was not a system of legally free European labour working under a rigorous regime, but African slavery.

Recognizing that displaced small farmers or ex-indentured labourers had some possibility of escaping the island, that some did get away to Jamaica and that the future flow of indentured labourers could not be guaranteed, these factors do not provide a sufficient explanation for the resort to slavery. This point is underlined by the recognition that building up a slave labour force required substantial outlays of capital and thus a choice not evidently initially cheaper than maintaining cultivation with a free labouring population, perhaps with somewhat enhanced wages. Apart from the freedom to act the landowners' political influence gave them, one other factor came into play: their knowledge of a population of 'outsiders' already identified as likely slave labourers and thus effectively permanently controllable. African slaves had been worked in plantation sugar production in the north-east of Brazil since the 1580s under the Portuguese and then the Dutch. They were therefore an aspect of the Dutch experience of sugar which, along with their technical expertise, made the émigré Dutch, driven out of Brazil as the Portuguese resumed control, so important in the early development of the industry in Barbados. Once more the ratio of labour to land proved not to be the determining factor in the labour regime that emerged, although landowners' *perceptions* of a potential shortage of labour probably contributed to the acquisition of slaves. In sum, the major variations in the relations between land, labour and capital as the factors of production cannot account on their own for the emergence of slavery. This is the case even in relation to slave societies, let alone societies with slaves where production by slaves was less important. Understanding specific cases of the appearance of slavery needs the integration of other significant factors: the role of the state and of law, the development of markets, the availability of people deemed fitted to become slaves. And, since men and women in part make their own history, the choices made by potential employers, based on their perceptions and attitudes, were also crucial.

In any event, exclusive focus on the relationships between the factors of production assumes that slavery emerged and functioned solely as an instrument for economic purposes. Not only was this not true in societies with slaves, it was not even always so in slave societies, where slaves could be used for other purposes in conjunction with production. There will be discussion in the next chapter of the milieux in which slaves were prized for the prestige they brought, the possession of power they signalled or the sexual access they provided. Nor are the factors of production that are central to the tradition of analysis we have been considering directly relevant to explaining the emergence of slavery in urban settings or in a corporate context such as attachment to temples in the ancient Middle East. There they might work as agricultural labourers to help maintain the temple and its priesthood but without there necessarily being a shortage of other kinds of labour.

Amongst the factors identified above whose various combinations led to the adoption of slavery, agreement within a community about who could properly be enslaved and brought in was fundamental. The next section of this chapter deals with who became slaves and on what grounds. How they became so was equally important because the means of reproduction were vital to shaping the major characteristics and ensuring the survival of any system of slavery. The final section attempts a survey of the formal religious and legal frameworks within which slaves were placed.

Slaves were 'outsiders', it has been argued, though who might be designated 'outsiders' could be quite complicated. The individuals seen as appropriately able to be made slaves were usually, though not invariably, seized as members of a vulnerable group. But in some cases it was precisely a wandering individual's perceived lack of existing membership of a recognized group that led to enslavement. This was probably one source of the few slaves of the LoDagaa mentioned earlier. It might indeed be the reason that an individual in a hostile world sought security in becoming a slave. In a similar situation were abandoned or 'exposed' children in ancient and medieval times, who were rescued from death 'through the kindness of strangers' but at the frequent cost of finding themselves in servitude to their rescuer. However, apart from their relative powerlessness, the characteristics as outsiders of groups or categories of people that made them appropriate victims of enslavement were extremely varied. Perceived as different, often inferior in important respects, and perhaps hostile to those who then seized them as slaves, their difference was constituted sometimes by one element and sometimes by a combination. One important distinction was expressed in terms of features associated in modern times with the concept of nationality: particularly the speaking of a common language. This seems to have been at work in the evident reluctance of the ancient Greeks to enslave Greek speakers, though it was a reluctance they sometimes overcame. Outsiders were also those with different cultural features in addition to language, or who were lacking in those cultural strengths deemed important. With their alien origins they belonged, in modern terms, to a different ethnic group. The different religious traditions shared an official distaste for enslaving fellow believers but often saw non-believers in a harsher light. Eventually, and notoriously, within Judaism, Christianity and Islam differences of skin colour, and particularly blackness and associated notions of race, were developed as marks of 'the other' amongst those who reciprocally grew in awareness of their own racial distinctiveness. All of these ways of seeing groups as outsiders, in other words, also solidified the perceiver's sense of the primary group of which he was a member. Yet, as was indicated in the previous chapter, sometimes those who could be construed as 'insiders' in relation to the operative categories of difference could be constructed as the equivalent of outsiders by virtue of infringing the norms or rules of the primary group. In the usual cases of crime or indebtedness this might be revocable, though circumstances could render it lifelong or even heritable. Thus the condition of being an outsider was not necessarily entirely based upon supposedly 'objective' features, such as language or colour, but was subject to the desire to interpret and impose the condition by those possessing the power to do so. The powerful could, and sometimes did, act in contradiction of cultural or religious norms in relation to a slave's 'objective' characteristics, such as his religious affiliation. Though the slave might have similar religious beliefs to those who reduced him to bondage, or become similar through religious conversion, the discretion of the powerful as to whether the slave should be acquired or retained in these circumstances remained significant.

Even setting aside these qualifications to the categories of people most likely to be made slaves, a survey of slavery in the ancient eastern Mediterranean suggests that the separation of outsiders as slaves from the rest of the society crystallized and became more definite over time. Foreigners as the main outsider-slaves only emerged in Greece in the sixth century BCE and in Rome from the fourth century BCE. In the earlier Mycenaean palace civilization, evidence from Pylos, Knossos, and to a smaller extent Mycenae and Thebes, suggests that, as in later classical times, there were both private slaves attached to particular masters and public or sacred slaves belonging to the gods. But in other important respects slaves in the Mycenaean period were less of a distinct group than were those in classical Athens. Slave unions with non-slaves appear to have been not uncommon and, although slaves probably had fewer resources than non-slaves, they received plots of land from prominent individuals or were assigned allotments from community land. It may be that the distinction between slave and non-slave was less important than the relative autonomy of both in relation to the palace authorities.

The 'foreign' or 'barbarian' origin of slaves in classical Athens probably developed as a result of the reforms carried through by Solon, traditionally dated to 594 BCE. Their effect was to crystallize the concept of citizenship by defining it in terms of a number of obligations and freedoms, including freedom from enslavement for debt, which emerged in parallel with the possibility of the citizen's active participation in the government of the city state. The gulf between citizenship and non-citizenship became so pronounced as largely to exclude even poor citizens from undertaking demeaning labour for others. Even hired free labour was regarded as a form of unworthy dependency and was probably not very extensive. After Solon, only in a small number of exceptional circumstances were citizens of Athens (and there were similar developments in other Greek states) liable to enslavement within their own state. One significant effect was the importation of slaves from outside, a process that also began to occur in other Greek states such as Chios, Corinth and Samos. The usual sources for barbarian slaves were Thrace (modern Bulgaria) Caria, Phrygia and other parts of Asia Minor, that is, outside Greek-speaking areas at some distance. In the classical era Greeks condemned the Cilician pirates of Asia Minor for seizing their fellow Greeks as slaves. There is also evidence of hostile discussion of the enslavement of whole Greek cities defeated in war, as in the case of Thebes when it fell to Alexander the Great in 335 BCE. The Greeks also felt an obligation to recover enslaved compatriots, whether through relatives arranging a ransom or the mediation or purchase back by a friendly city, actions meritorious enough to bring diplomatic credit in the Greek world. Miletus played this role in recovering enslaved Greek captives from Cretan cities that had engaged in piracy. Greeks undoubtedly manifested a strong sense of superiority to non-Greeks and, at least in the classical period, connected it to the freedoms they enjoyed in the city-state, the more secure and celebrated after the defeat of the Persians in 479 BCE. Barbarians as slaves embodied their inferiority in their status and at the same time, through their labour, helped sustain Greeks in the conditions of freedom that they believed justified their mastery.

The linguistic definition of who was Greek was crucial to their sense of cultural superiority expressed in the freedom of the *polis* or city-state because Greek was the instrument of *logos* or reason, the foundation for participation in public life. Those lacking *logos* thus required Greek masters to guide them through life. The linguistic distinction between Greeks and non-Greeks pushed to its extreme tended to become a distinction in nature (as in Aristotle) and thus both a description and justification of Greek enslavement of barbarians.

By no means all slaves were brought from a great distance to their 'houses of bondage', yet frequently the very strangeness of outsiders brought into slavery could often be the result of how far away their homeland was. Those who became their masters might never have encountered their kind before. Geographical distance facilitated social distance. The presumption of the captors was that strangers were likely to embody features justifying their continued subjection and, because of the distance from their homeland, were easier and more valuable to retain in bondage. Troops of the medieval West African state of Sonxai, for example, captured slaves from Kusata more than 1,000 kilometres away from their base. Once brought to the conquerors' territory successful escape by slaves to return home was virtually impossible and some accounts suggest that slaves came to recognize the implications of their enforced exile, encouraged through improvement in their treatment as they were taken further from their native land.

The slaves' cultural distinctiveness and social distance was also understood and acted upon in terms of their religious difference from their masters. The Torah forbade Jews to enslave Jews. Leviticus 25 required the Hebrews to take their bondsmen 'of the nations that are round about you'. After all, the Jews owed their continuing existence as a people to the escape from the Egyptian 'house of bondage'. Some of the bondsmen that they acquired were Canaanites, neighbouring peoples occupying land that Jehovah had promised the Israelites but also 'idolators' who had committed 'abominations'. However, obtaining gentile or Canaanite slaves was not always easy in ancient Palestine. When, in consequence, the Israelites did hold some of their own in bondage they were commanded, 'If thou buy an Hebrew servant, six years he shall serve: and in the seventh he shall go out free for nothing' (Exod. 21:2). Significantly these limits did not apply even in theory to the Canaanites or other unbelievers. Later Jewish tradition, expressed, for example, in the writings of Maimonides in the twelfth century continued to distinguish clearly between Jewish and gentile slaves in allowing that the latter could be worked rigorously even though in general the Jews were enjoined to treat slaves humanely. A gentile slave coming into Jewish ownership with the insistence that he should not be circumcised could be held for as long as the master desired and sold at any time to a non-Jewish purchaser. Other gentile slaves who became the property of Jews without this provision were to be allowed a year to contemplate conversion to Judaism and to undergo circumcision. If they then refused they lost all claim to preferential consideration and had to be sold abroad or to a non-Jew.

In the long medieval and early modern centuries of struggle between Christians and Moslems around the Mediterranean enslavement of enemies who were also unbelievers was recurrently and dramatically illustrated. The Christian baptism that signalled in Pauline doctrine the irrelevance of social hierarchy to the individual's standing before God was soon tempered in its social meaning by the association of Christianity with slave-owning respectable households from late antiquity onwards. The intellectual and ideological elaboration underpinning Christian slave holding will be treated in a later chapter; suffice it to say here that there was no incompatibility in practice between professing Christianity and holding Christians as slaves, especially, though not only, if they came to true religion *after* they became slaves. This was evidently the case in the parts of the Iberian peninsula left in Christian hands after the Moorish conquests of the eighth century. Christian slaves remained in Christian ownership as the earlier Roman and Visigothic system was continued. Yet opportunities to take Muslims as slaves were rarely set aside and were justified in religious terms. Christian masters of Muslim slaves were in a position to use their power to extend religious truth through enforcing conversion to the true faith on both slave and free Muslims. This was certainly true during the long *reconquista* by the Christian kingdoms of Muslim Spain. Since Christians contested a fluctuating military frontier with non-Christians, when they had the power they felt doubly justified in recovering territory from enemies also hostile to the faith. In the eleventh century, in what must have seemed a bitter reversal of fortune, 200 Muslims recently taken as slaves in the Christian capture of Avila were secured in chains and pressed into rebuilding the city walls. Especially from the twelfth century onwards most of the slaves who replaced the earlier Christian bondsmen were Muslims taken in warfare and by raiding into enemy areas. Such actions probably did little to encourage conversion to Christianity. Yet when a formal change of religious profession was achieved and 'Moors' became 'Moriscoes', Spanish rulers ironically continued to betray suspicion of the genuineness of such conversions even after the final expulsion of Islamic authority from the Iberian peninsula at the end of the fifteenth century.

Adherents of Islam were quite as willing to enslave their Christian foes as were Christians to subject them. But Muslim learned men also made absolutely explicit the prohibition on reducing fellow believers to slavery. The Iberian peninsula again furnishes examples in reverse of a militarized religious divide as a plentiful source of slaves. At the time of the initial Muslim conquest of Spain and Portugal in the early eighth century Christians' resistance to the invaders brought down on them the penalty of enslavement for women and children and usually death for the men, though acquiescence in Muslim rule often did not.

In the latter situation Christians kept their liberty and property, including any slaves that they possessed. But they were forbidden as non-Muslims to hold or purchase Muslim slaves and were compelled to sell any converting to Islam to fellow believers. By the late medieval period most slaves in Muslim Spain were seized in raids into the Spanish Christian kingdoms to the North.

However, as was also true of Jews and Christians, Muslims in practice did not always exempt co-religionists from bondage. In some Islamic areas of Africa at certain moments such transgressions provoked sharp cries of protest and on occasion fierce political reaction. Ahmad Baba, the Islamic scholar from Timbuktu, defined non-belief as the necessary, if not sufficient, basis for slavery in Islamic states. But in his 1614 treatise on the subject he lamented that the quarrels amongst Muslim rulers of the savanna states in West Africa led to the seizure and sale of free Muslims as slaves 'although their tongue is one and their language is one'. He saw their common Islamic faith as a commitment superior to the differences arising from membership of different polities. The only sign that this weighed in some respect with the rulers he criticized may be that they appear not to have allowed fellow Muslims to be kept as slaves but required that they be sold on to others.

At other times the purifying zeal of Muslim reformers produced more dramatic reactions. One of the energizing forces behind the assault of reformers against a number of states in eighteenth-century Senegambia was their hostility to the rulers' refusal to enforce Islamic law and traditions preventing the enslavement of and trading in the persons of free Muslims. The resulting renewal of the theocratic Muslim states of Futa Bondu, Futa Toro and Futa Jallon thus eliminated anti-Muslim or inadequately zealous regimes and through the *jihad*, or holy war, in turn reduced enemies of true religion to slavery. In other words, the power to make and enforce the definitions of marginality upon which slavery turned could operate as between different elements *within* a religious community, when one regarded another as betraying the faith, as well as *between* communities of different religious affiliations.

From the sixteenth to the nineteenth centuries slavery in the Americas was identified primarily with Africans whose physical distinctiveness their owners perceived as the outward sign of a nature fitted for slavery. The concept of races and their hierarchical relationships, and especially the supposition of the superiority of the white or Caucasian race and its rightful domination over the inferior and subordinate black or African race became fundamental in defining slavery in the Atlantic world. Yet the origins of the eventual seemingly unbreakable chain binding together colour, race and slavery, and consigning black Africans and their descendants in the Americas 'scientifically' to marginality and slavery, reach back centuries into the religious traditions we have been examining. Arguments and assertions relying on varieties of environmental influence and other ideas to be examined in a later chapter are also relevant here. But the connection across the centuries can initially be approached through following the deployment and elaboration of the biblical curse of Canaan. The curse of Noah upon Canaan and his line was uttered after God had sanctioned Noah's descendants to repopulate the earth after the Flood, the moment from which human difference and later inequality might be explained. According to Genesis 9, after the ark reached land Noah cultivated a vineyard and at some later point became drunk. His son Ham came upon him asleep and naked and laughed at him. He told his brothers Shem and Japheth who covered their father without looking at his nakedness. When Noah heard what Ham had done he cursed Ham's son Canaan declaring of him and his line 'a servant of servants shall he be unto his brethren'. If we set aside the extensive interpretative commentary amongst religious writers in the Middle Ages as to what precisely Ham had done and why his son Canaan should be punished, by that period Ham's sin and Noah's curse were widely thought to have generated slavery (and indeed medieval serfdom). But the initial version of the story did nothing to relate colour or race to slavery. That connection arose gradually over the centuries within the different religious traditions.

Within Judaism no doubt was entertained about Ham as the originator of slavery. But there was apparently very little before the eleventh century in textual commentary to associate him with black skin, although there were occasional hints of the connection in medieval Jewish travellers such as Benjamin of Tudela. Similarly in early Christian writings touching on Ham's sin links between black skin as a mark of race and the institution of slavery were equally sparse. Scholars have speculated plausibly that from the early Church Fathers onwards the metaphoric contrast drawn between the darkness of sin and ignorance and the light of Christian knowledge, with its possibility of redemption, may have inflected Christian attitudes towards black Africans. But for a long time such notions were not integrated firmly with the story of Ham and anyway the contrast was of a very general and abstract character. Moreover, the significance of blackness could be reversed since bringing the heathen blacks to the faith was a measure of the success of Christian evangelism. It was within Islam that a more emphatic connection was made at a relatively early period between blackness and slavery. The Qur'an has nothing to say about Ham but no later than the ninth century there was a clear current in Islamic thought which both assigned colour terminology to particular peoples – 'black' meant the peoples of sub-Saharan Africa – and attached particular skills and aptitudes to different peoples. According to Lewis, in the tenth and eleventh centuries the language of colour and group characteristics merged with an ethnocentric vision which calibrated colour and group qualities with distance from the central Arabic lands of Islam. The curse on the descendants of Ham takes its place within this current when Muslims took it over and adapted it for their purposes from Jewish and Christian sources. Thus black Africans from south of the Sahara, in terms that were to echo down the centuries, were understood as unsophisticated but capable of great labour, possessed a sense of rhythm and were exuberant in manner. In contrast to other peoples they lacked the artistic and intellectual attainments of civilization and the skills to rule a state and excel in warfare. As characterized in the eleventh century writings of the scholar Sa'id al-Andalusi from Toledo, along with other barbarians on the northern rim of the civilized Islamic world, these southerners 'are more like beasts than like men'.

In the medieval Islamic world black Africans were far from being the only people to be enslaved. Yet in societies that recognized the possibility of using slaves in a variety of ways many Africans were thought to be best employed in physical labour. It is true that as Arabs got to know black Africa better they made distinctions between different peoples; for the purpose of acquiring concubines in particular there was an evident preference for Nubians, Ethiopians and other Nilotic peoples as against the despised Zanj, usually identified as people from East Africa. The distinctions of colour and race, however, overrode in the minds of Arab Muslims in some instances the faith they shared with Africans. In 1391–2 the black king of Bornu in northern Nigeria wrote a letter to his fellow Muslim, the sultan of Egypt, recounting the destruction Arabs had brought to his country. Above all he complained that 'they took the free people among us captive, of our kin among Muslims . . . they have taken our people as merchandise.'

Christian deployment of invidious distinctions based on colour and race, in part expressed through an association of Ham with Africa, gained strength from the time of the Portuguese trade in slaves from West Africa in the fifteenth century. As Europeans began to colonize the Americas they possessed a mindset attuned to colour and race difference as a basis for slavery. But they were also inclined to distinguish Africans as more suitable slaves than the other racially distinct people potentially available to them, the Amerindians or Native Americans. As will be seen in more detail in a later chapter, Amerindians were initially the victims of slavery; they were heathens often hostile to Christians as well as being different in colour and appearance from Europeans. But they did not belong to the irredeemable offspring of Ham. As early as the mid-1550s one English voyager to Africa recorded his conviction that Africans lacked all marks of civilization; they were 'without a god, law, religion or common wealth'. In the tones of earlier prejudice he connected this fundamental deficiency to their physical distinctiveness and their supposed similarity to animals. In the seventeenth century the Spanish creole scholars, Buenaventura de Salinas y Cordova and Leon Pinelo sought to legitimize the African slave trade to the Americas and slavery by invoking the curse of Noah – in their case against the Amerindians too. Dutch settlers at the Cape, and later in the interior of what became South Africa, used the story of Ham as a justification for their enslavement of the Khoikhoi. The curse maintained a pro-slavery life in the eighteenth and nineteenth centuries because it seemed to provide a justification based on the Bible for inequality expressed in racial difference after the re-establishment of human society in the aftermath of the Flood. Nor was the tradition of Ham incompatible with the taste for defining black inferiority and justifying racial slavery in the 'scientific' terms favoured by some in the pre-Civil War American South. The physician Samuel A. Cartwright concluded that Noah's curse was proved by African-Americans' physiological weaknesses that led to laziness and misery 'as if the revelations of anatomy, physiology and history were a mere re-writing of what Moses wrote'.

The most significant ways in which slaves have been defined as outsiders have therefore been as enemies; as foreigners/barbarians/an ethnically distinct group. Their marginality has also arisen from their being strangers from distant places, appearing as heathens or infidels and as belonging to a different race, perceived especially in terms of physical appearance, above all dark skin colour.

But, as has already been indicated, individuals and communities have not behaved completely consistently in the observance of these distinctions as the basis for slavery. Not only did war between states with a common religious faith result in the enslavement of fellow believers but civil wars led to similar consequences. Civil conflict in Nupe in the 1850s arising from *jihad* promoted large-scale slave settlement inland beyond the Niger Valley through the use of prisoners of war. These slave-prisoners were culturally similar to their conquerors and, in contrast to ethnically and culturally distinct slaves drawn from south of the Niger who were treated more immediately as commodities, as part of their terms of servitude they paid tribute to individual notables. If they failed to do so then, despite being cultural 'insiders', the conquered could be sold away to merchants.

Three particular conclusions seem pertinent in relation to different notions of the outsider as a necessary basis for slavery. Clearly the importance of particular distinctions varied greatly according to place and time. Although there is some debate on the subject, differences of colour or race seem to have mattered relatively little to the ancient Greeks, but 'otherness' in terms of ethnicity and language counted for a great deal. Secondly, outsiders who could be defined in relation to more than one significant distinction were likely to be particularly vulnerable to enslavement. Enemies in war who also held to a different religious faith had small chance of escaping slavery when they were captured if they escaped death. Yet the process of acquiring slaves could also override characteristics uniting enslavers and their victims, such as contiguous place of residence, a similar culture or the same religious profession. Such instances illustrated, thirdly, that the power to define who was marginal, and thus who could be enslaved, sometimes became its own justification and was not always tied to stable markers of difference and inferiority. The authority of the powerful either allowed them to brush aside any awareness of their contravention of accepted practice or, as in intra-Muslim warfare and enslavement, to present their enemies as being not true Muslims at all. As redefined enemies of the faith there was no constraint on their subjugation.

Whatever the basis for slavery, once individuals or groups had acquired that status they were considered degraded and shamed figures and became the objects of contemptuous language. Free men underlined the slave's degraded status. The aspiring Roman orator was taught to avoid 'servile' gestures such as raising his shoulders. The slave was compelled to undergo dishonouring rituals, such as when prisoner-slaves were displayed before the populace during Roman triumphs. In Anglo-Saxon England the starving man compelled to sell himself into slavery in return for food placed his head between his master's hands and received a billhook or ox-goad. The Roman agricultural writer, Varro, refers to the master's power to name the slave afresh, a right also exercised in other slave societies. Symbolically this distanced the slave from his previous life and acknowledged the master's total possession of him. In the re-naming insult could be piled on injury when the name given to the slave indirectly referred to the master's standing (Felix) or the stereotypical red hair of the slave (Rufio) or linked the humble slave to one of the gods (Dionysus). In American cases some names mocked the slave's lack of power or perhaps suggested a parallel with a pet animal (Caesar). In African kin-based communities the slave was often given the clan name of the master just as the American slave, later known as Frederick Douglass, was initially called Bailey after his owner's family. The Imbangala of Angola staged a naming ceremony for slaves enacting protection for them as dependants but only after they had taken a medicine supposedly eliminating their original communal ties and removing them from the oversight of ancestors. But slaves as well as masters could be conscious of the symbolic significance of naming; it therefore became an issue of resistance and will be considered in that context in chapter four.

Particularly in societies where it could not be assumed that slaves would be recognized because they were physically distinct from the rest of the population they were likely to be deliberately distinguished by other observable marks of status. In ancient Babylon the slave's position as a chattel required, like any animal, that he have a property tag attached. There and in other ancient Middle Eastern societies it took the form of physical branding, perhaps with a hot iron, tattooing on the wrist, or an attached tablet. The symbolic significance of the marks was emphasized in the ceremony accompanying manumission in Babylon; a gesture of wiping the forehead was made as city officials proclaimed, 'You are cleansed.' In ancient Palestine a slave might have his ear pierced with an awl. American slaves were sometimes compelled to wear masks or clamps on their jaws to prevent them eating dirt or otherwise harming themselves. Having to wear fetters was common amongst slaves in classical antiquity especially in the mines and they might be further distinguished and degraded by half-shaven heads. This and other kinds of prescribed hairstyle were features of slavery elsewhere and at other times. Slaves among the Ashanti had to wear a particular kind of clothing and eighteenth-century South Carolina masters unsuccessfully undertook to regulate their slaves' clothing. In many instances, for example in Greece and the Caribbean, slaves did wear an identifiable form of rough clothing but more from lack of alternatives than as a result of prescription. There are also examples of restrictions on the personal decoration permitted to slaves.

The kinds of symbolic dishonour and degradation surveyed above implicitly take the form of treating slaves in the manner of beasts or children as an expression of their marginality. Some of the language for and directed to slaves extends the point, even if one should be wary of only understanding words in their root meaning and of ignoring the variety of terms available in relation to slavery at any time and place. One word in classical Greek for a slave was *andrapadon* 'four-footed.' In Roman terminology the legal language for the slave – *instrumentum vocale* – associated him both with livestock – *instrumentum semi-vocale* – and inanimate tools – *instrumentum mutum*. The language directed to the slave as child – *pais*, *puer*, boy (it would be possible to list parallel terms from Arabic, Syriac and other languages) – has already been referred to.

The processes making individuals and groups who were sufficiently marginal and inferior into slaves need more exploration. The organization and, frequently, the violence that they entailed reflected the insertion into social orders of various kinds of external elements who then had to be moulded to the demands of their new situation. Whether we are referring to seizure in war or raiding, slave trading and sale, the acquisition of abandoned children or self-sale, unless these processes continued over considerable periods of time then slave populations were not likely to expand or even be maintained. The main reason for this was that, with the one important exception of the United States in the first half of the nineteenth century, and a few more debatable and limited exceptions, no slave society was able to sustain its population of slaves from natural increase alone. It should, however, be noted that in some societies with slaves where no regular system of replacement had been established maintenance of numbers through slaves-born-in-the-house was possible, even necessary. However, taking the example of a major slave society, there appears little doubt that with the end of the military expansion of the frontiers of the Roman Empire after the Emperor Trajan in the second century slave labour grew scarcer and probably more expensive. The lack of captives was insufficiently compensated for through the commercial trade in persons; they were, anyway, primarily drawn from the stabilized frontier regions and thus fewer in number. Natural reproduction, despite recommendations from the agricultural writer, Columella, that female slaves giving birth be rewarded with bonuses, did not meet the shortfall. Not only were tough material conditions a factor but slave owners' lack of interest in encouraging slaves to reproduce, though it was not universal, may have been influenced by the considerations Xenophon had advanced earlier in the fourth century BCE. He noted that slave mothers were unable to work for some time around the time of birth, that there was a high level of child mortality amongst the slaves and that the development of blood ties could encourage solidarity in the servile class.

The usual insignificance of natural reproduction in developing slave populations can be further clarified by examining the American case and comparing some of its features with aspects of slavery elsewhere. As Xenophon's comments indicate, slave reproduction was as much a social and cultural as it was a biological phenomenon. It depended not only upon the fertility of slave women but equally upon the attitudes of slave owners and slaves, the availability of partners and the more general conditions of slave existence. In the case of the United States the flow of slaves into the country via the external trade from the West Indies and West and West Central Africa was officially brought to a close comparatively early, in 1808. We might suppose therefore that American slave owners had little alternative but to encourage their slaves to procreate and that, unlike other master classes, they were successful at it. The evidence points to a less straightforward story, however. The natural increase in the slave population in the American South was discernible before as well as after the abolition measure of 1808. Indeed, knowledge of that increase may have helped reconcile many slave owners to the measure. The area that became the United States in 1776, however, absorbed perhaps no more than 5 per cent of the number of Africans transported across the Atlantic between the sixteenth century and about 1870. Given that for much of that period and to most locations in the Americas the demand was for workers capable of long and heavy manual labour, the result was a striking predominance of males in the Atlantic trade. That in turn depressed the birth rate amongst slaves in many communities, particularly in the Caribbean and Brazil, thus necessitating more male-dominated imports of slave workers. But the modest size of the external trade to British North America and the United States had the effect of producing a less unbalanced sex ratio amongst slaves there than elsewhere. And this was true even before the end of the external trade. This divergence also reflected the voracious demand in the sugar cane-growing areas of the plantation zone in the Americas for young male labourers to undertake the peculiarly arduous tasks that the crop required, much less significant in the United States outside Louisiana. As it matured the Cotton Kingdom in the South developed a more balanced labour force in terms of sex and age than was true in sugar areas. The creole, that is American-born, proportion of the slave population in the United States rose and more slaves survived in a disease environment to which they had adapted without being subject to diseases brought in from Africa by fresh slaves.

Even after these favourable circumstances have been taken into account it might still be asked whether the United States was also exceptional in its slave system, in that the master class successfully encouraged natural reproduction through an explicit policy of good treatment. The issue of treatment will be dealt with more fully in a later chapter but the now general scholarly conclusion can be noted here that in material terms most southern slaves were able to do more than merely survive. So far as the treatment of infants, young children and nursing mothers was concerned, so vital to maintaining or increasing numbers, it is possible to find evidence from elsewhere, for example from the plantations of Sokoto in northern Nigeria in the nineteenth century, where circumstances seemed much worse. In Sokoto Hogendorn has found that the young slave children were often gathered under a tree at the edge of the fields where their mothers worked and could only be fed with the infrequent permission of a guard. At Gumbu, a Soninke town on the edge of the Sahara in present-day Mali, a similar practice prevailed and if children were troublesome they were on occasion buried up to their necks in sand, supposedly to keep them quiet. Generally American slave women appear to have been able to feed their infants quite regularly and sometimes away from the fields. Slightly older children, at least on the larger units, were fed by old women whose job it was to do so. All of this points to the advantageous features of the system in the American South that produced the exceptional outcome of a natural increase in the slave population. But it does not necessarily testify completely to the merit of the slave owners. At least part of the cost of successfully raising slave children was borne by the slave parents. They made contributions to their own family diet and living conditions to varying degrees and masters had no compunction in beginning to extract value from children by the age of eight through having them perform simple tasks.

Even granting that in some respects, compared with some other slave societies, aspects of the slave society of the South facilitated slave population growth, this falls short of concluding that superior treatment was a major factor in the natural increase of the slave population. If that were the case, as Klein has pointed out, compared with Caribbean territories where natural population decrease was the norm, it would be expected that there would be a lower age of menarche and a higher age of menopause amongst southern slave women as compared with Caribbean slave women. But there is no evidence that this is so. Southern slave women do appear to have given birth more frequently than their Caribbean sisters and, although there was a higher rate of infant mortality amongst blacks than whites, enough children survived to add significantly to the population. It has also been suggested that greater frequency of conception may be related to different cultural practices in relation to breast-feeding. In the American South slave women probably weaned their children at an earlier stage and were thus more likely to conceive again more rapidly. Yet even if the master had to invest his share more frequently in raising the slave children he was able to begin to cream off the value they created more often.

Even the one outstanding instance of a flourishing slave society resulting from the natural increase of the slave population therefore fails to point to the masters' attitude in regard to slave treatment as the major factor in population growth. Although slave mortality and life expectancy in slave societies were worse than for different categories of the free population, in part because of the nature and amount of their work, they did broadly follow those of free people. They were subject to the same disease and climatic environments as other members of the society. The likelihood of a reasonable rate of natural reproduction amongst the slaves was also related to the age structure of the slave population and to the sex ratio. But although a preponderance of males was likely to have a depressing effect on the natural reproduction of slaves there was no guarantee that a preponderance of female slaves would have the reverse effect. The surplus of women could well provide concubines as partners for free men and thus add children to the free or likely-to-be-free rather than the slave population. Even when this was not so the imbalance in favour of women meant that their relations with men would more likely be transient. There is evidence in the merchant towns of the Upper Zaire in the late nineteenth century that this was a peculiarly difficult context for motherhood, with women feeling vulnerable without the adequate support and protection to be expected from stable social networks. However similar the impact of the natural environment on free and slave people, the slave woman without protection was more subject, or feared that she was, to the wanderings and upheavals of an unstable social and political environment. Despite the balance in favour of women the result amongst such river communities was a low birth rate and resort to methods of abortion. These other factors influencing the context of reproduction obviously had more general application. Nor could the fertility of female slaves within a certain age range be taken as a given. Levels of nutrition affected fertility, and nutrition in turn depended on the balance between the master's provisioning, that is, supply of foodstuffs to the slave and the slaves' freedom and capacity in producing or finding food for themselves or in bartering and trading for it. These, it will be argued in chapter four, varied significantly but, we can conclude on this point, hardly ever led to a diet healthy enough to guarantee a high birth rate and low child mortality.

The insufficiency in almost all slave societies, and no doubt in some societies with slaves, of slave supply through natural reproduction made other forms of supply crucial. The reduction to slavery of captives taken in war is found from the earliest times. The Sumerian terms for male and female slaves indicated that they were foreign captives presumably taken in war. Babylonian inscriptions from the time of King Rimrush of the dynasty of Accad indicate that most war captives were killed on the battlefield but that whoever was spared was enslaved. The Hammurabi Code assumed enslavement of war captives and in Neo-Babylonian times Nebuchadnezzar used war captive-slaves on public works such as fortifications, roads, irrigation works and temple construction. Later, in Syria and Palestine, clashing city-states equally regarded skilled artisan-slaves as a valuable form of war booty. Similar incidents might be related from the Greek world. War in the last two centuries of the Roman Republic was a major source of slaves but that continued to be true into the second century of the Empire. The historian, Josephus, for example, mentions the large number of captive-slaves from the Jewish War of 66–70 CE. Long after a war was over the defeated might be required to supply slaves regularly as a tribute. A famous, and long-lasting, example was the annual levy of Nubian Christians to Islamic Egypt beginning in 652 CE and continuing for six centuries. Arab conquerors imposed similar tributes on rulers in Iran and Central Asia. As in the Arab cases, so elsewhere warfare resulting in the large-scale reduction of men and women to commodities paralleled the construction of military and state organizations which in turn became the agencies for further reductions to slavery. According to al-Zuhri in the mid-twelfth century, 'The people of Ghana fight in the lands of the Barbara, the Amuna and seize the inhabitants as the others seized them in the past when they themselves were pagan . . . The inhabitants of Ghana raid them every year.' Political fragmentation or religious dissidence in a region fostered conditions then exploited through war and resulting in large-scale enslavement. This also happened in parts of West Africa in the seventeenth and eighteenth centuries. At times the rhythm of war followed by enslavement, as in the twelfth century, assumed virtually an annual pattern.

Smaller-scale raiding to secure slaves, mainly against peasant populations often in stateless societies and uncomplicated by other objectives of state, was even more common. Crossing frontier zones to attack groups beyond the sphere of regular control of the raiders was a very significant form of slave supply. In the sixteenth and seventeenth centuries the Portuguese in Brazil, particularly from São Paulo, launched attacks against 'cannibal' Amerindians of the *sertao* or arid backlands. Some estimates of the total number of Indian captives in the two centuries run as high as 350,000 and, if anything like accurate, mean that these overland captive-slaves constituted more than half as many as the Atlantic-borne African captives taken to Brazil in the same period.

The equivalent of raiding when carried out at sea was, of course, piracy. This too could be a substantial source of slaves. Probably the most notorious pirates in the ancient world operated in the eastern Mediterranean and came from Cilicia in Asia Minor. Their victims added to the flow of slaves in the Mediterranean world over a long period. As early as the second century BCE they sold on those they had captured to Roman merchants at Delos. According to Augustine, pirates still seized slaves off the coast of North Africa at the turn of the fifth century CE and sold them to itinerant slave dealers. The Roman authorities periodically acted against pirates in support of legitimate trade but at other times recognized the convenience of this source of slaves.

However, the acquisition of slaves through war, raiding and piracy did not in itself ensure that slaves reached those who wanted them. The emergence of lines of trade in human beings, both as an adjunct to violent seizure and as an aspect of more complex commercial networks, were indispensable to the effective functioning of slave systems of any significant size. As will become clear, this refers to the necessary inflow of new servile groups but one other concern dictated the development of a market in people. We have noted that strangers from a distance could easily be seen as outsiders and thus potentially as slaves. But not all warfare or raiding was carried on at a great distance from the warriors' territorial base. Captives from nearby might more easily escape and return home or, if retained, encourage a renewal of conflict on the part of their fellow countrymen. These circumstances prompted the sale of captives further away and perhaps the buying-in of replacements from a distance. Again scholars have noted instances in eighteenth-century West Africa, in Segou on the Middle Niger, for example, after a period of warfare between neighbouring states. The process of alienation, central to the meaning of slavery, thus required the trade for its completion.

Before discussing the historical elaboration of slave-trading networks it is worth saying something more about the consequences of the link between the violent acquisition of slaves and their trading as commodities. When warfare produced slaves rulers and their military commanders took a proportion for state and their own purposes. In many instances ordinary soldiers also brought back a captive, as in the wars of conquest of the Roman Republic in the first century BCE. At different levels of society there was then posed the problem about how best to use these outsiders. Maximizing gain from large numbers of war prisoner-slaves encouraged the rise of merchants dealing in human beings when they believed they could find customers. The balance of initiative shifted over time in some societies from the rulers and military leaders who disposed of surplus captives, to dependent merchants, to the merchants themselves. Their command of an extensive market could provide an additional reason for state warfare or independent banditry in order to profit from large-scale demand. The situation in eighteenth-century Dahomey illustrates the intertwining of 'state' and 'private' elements. The large demands of European traders on the Slave Coast to supply the transatlantic trade were sufficiently important for the second ranking official in the kingdom to take charge of dealings and trade with the Europeans. He also acted as viceroy of Whydah, one of the main slave-exporting centres. Initially the state kept a tight control on private African merchants in Whydah but gradually state officials ceased to sell directly the king's slaves acquired by military expeditions into the interior. Initially acting as agents of state officials, by the mid-eighteenth century private Dahomean traders brought slaves from the interior on their own account and state officials regulated prices and collected export duties. Ultimately, despite these official constraints, a wealthy elite of private traders emerged in the nineteenth century to act as advisers to the king on commercial policy.

Slave traders, whether acting on behalf of states or corporations such as temples, or whether as individual entrepreneurs, frequently did not have to rely on violent seizures for their human trade goods. Neighbouring population groups, when they did not directly exchange people for goods, might have a trade link them. Individuals or groups deprived of the means of livelihood through the impact of war, disease or famine, if they did not venture to sell themselves, could fall into the hands of traders who sold them to a master and at least provided them with the prospect of survival. This was a source of servile labour at least from the time of ancient Babylon and Assyria onwards. Abandoned children or orphans were a particular category within this aspect of the trade in slaves. At many moments, from the ancient Middle East through classical antiquity and the medieval centuries parents in desperate straits abandoned and exposed their children in order to survive themselves or to enhance the possibilities of those children continuing to live. Abandoned children sometimes died but often they survived when they were adopted and placed in lifetime service by those who rescued them. Labour power was not so plentiful in pre-modern societies that the value represented by the many potential years of work of a young child could be easily ignored. Their rescuers could enslave them, however, or sell them off. So extensive did this practice become at times that it posed issues of policy. As governor of Bithynia-Pontus Pliny consulted the Emperor Trajan about the quite general problem of settling the legal status of people living as slaves but claiming to have been born free, exposed as children and taken off into slavery. In the Christian Europe of the Middle Ages, sometimes either genuinely or in the guise of an oblation or gift to religious institutions, children were left at a church and subsequently sold or held in lifetime service at a monastery. Amongst the Sena of Mozambique some traders specialized in the kidnapping and sale of children, especially at the time of harvest when they worked hidden from others in the fields. They were often moved rapidly into an extended trade network. It was also precisely the experience of passing through the hands of a variety of middle men that the young Olaudah Equiano recounted in the opening chapters of his famous narrative telling of his seizure and removal from present-day eastern Nigeria in the 1750s. In theory, religious law could impose limits on how 'exposed' children were treated. In Muslim communities, unless it was absolutely clear that an abandoned, unclaimed child's parents were slaves, he could not be reduced to bondage. It was doubtful that this rule was consistently observed.

The distances covered by slave-trading networks, drawing in strangers, foreigners and *barbaroi* became extensive from an early date. Records referring to slave sales in Mesopotamia in about 2300 BCE imply the movement of captive foreigners from distant areas. Elements of the Hammurabi Code indicate a trade in slaves from Babylonia to external territories. At this period merchants probably dealt in slaves along with other commodities, rather than concentrating on chattels, because the number of slaves required was probably insufficient for a specialist business. Later, Greek slave-owners benefited from a more developed organization of the slave trade. Specialized traders who followed campaigning armies to purchase captives, dealt with pirates and negotiated with non-Greek states and cities. A number of large centres of the trade emerged through which barbarians were brought into the Greek world. They came from Thrace and Scythia to the north, Caria and Phrygia in Asia Minor, Syria further south and Illyria in the northwest. There were markets in proximity to all these areas, as well as on the main sea trade routes, in Chios, Delos, Corinth, Aegina, Rhodes and Athens. In Athens the slave market was held regularly at the new moon in a particular part of the *agora*. This developed system suggests that there was a substantial demand to be met. Thucydides reported that 20,000 slaves escaped from the countryside of Attica when, during the Peloponnesian War, the Spartans occupied a nearby fort and that they were able to deal with the fugitives by selling them to the Boeotians. Roman slave traders, like their Greek predecessors, followed armies to feed defeated enemies into the trading network. Sometimes this meant the sale of large bodies of people at the same time – the whole Alpine tribe of the Salassi in 25 BCE,

100,000 citizens of Ctesiphon after the city's fall in Rome's war against the Parthians.

As in Athens, the slave dealers in Rome carried on their business in a special location, near the Temple of Castor in the Forum. The trade in slaves into the Roman Empire continued even with the end of frontier expansion in the second century. It reached beyond the imperial borders, most notably to the western areas of the Black Sea and into the Caucasus, a region still being tapped, according to Procopius, in the sixth century CE. Traders developed similar long-term and long-distance routes across the western Sahara from at least the second century, and in the tenth century Ibn Haukal spoke of both black and white slaves in the Maghreb, neither group being native to the region. Of course the expansion of Islam in the early Middle Ages extended the lines of slave supply enjoyed by the core Arab lands of the faith. Once the populations were converted, however, traders had to look for new supplies beyond the borders of Islam. And later, slaves, often with special skills, were brought great distances from regions whose inhabitants were regarded with some respect – India, China, South-East Asia, Byzantium. Despised labourers, through the collaboration of European (particularly Venetian) and African traders were acquired from the Slav populations of Europe and the peoples of sub-Saharan black Africa. The Ottoman phase of Muslim expansion, as with the earlier Arab, initially accumulated slaves from conquered populations including Christian inhabitants of the Balkans. When the Turkish advance into Europe halted in the seventeenth century and direct acquisition of new European slaves became difficult the Ottomans also turned to the Caucasus, absorbing Georgians, Circassians and related peoples. For a period in the seventeenth and eighteenth centuries the Turkish lands also fed off the raids of the Tatar khanate based in the Crimea, whose warriors made incursions into eastern and central Europe, carried slaves off to the Crimea and then traded them to Istanbul and other Ottoman markets. This only came to an end when the Crimea was taken over by the Russian Empire in the 1780s. A peculiarity of the slave trade to Islamic countries, the need for a supply of eunuchs, also tended to lengthen trade routes and elaborate the commercial organization required. Islamic law forbade mutilation of the person so that eunuchs had to be found from outside Muslim territories – mainly from amongst Slavs and 'Ethiopians' but including Greeks, Africans, Indians and occasionally western Europeans. When necessary, the unfortunate slaves were subjected to surgery at the frontiers of Islamic lands.

Notoriously, Africa, especially in its vast sub-Saharan reaches, has been the continent most conspicuously the victim of slave trading over the centuries. In recent times a large amount of excellent historical work has been devoted particularly to the transatlantic trade from the sixteenth to the late nineteenth centuries, but also to the trans-Saharan, Indian Ocean and internal African trades. This has helped clarify why Africans were to such a great extent the victims of the slave trade. A necessary part of the explanation has already been given in the discussion of the links forged in the minds of medieval and early modern Christian Europeans, Jews and Arab and Persian Muslims between colour, race and slavery. But there were also a variety of more material factors at work. Recurrent conflict within Africa, some of it encouraged by outsiders, was a major source of a large pool of slaves available for trading. Africans were attractive trade goods for a variety of outsiders and for fellow Africans too. For those looking to supply the Americas the price of African slaves seemed cheap. War and raiding were relatively low-cost ways of gathering them together and costs of transport both within Africa and to the New World were modest. Before the nineteenth century only a limited market existed for potential agricultural slaves in Africa itself and low slave prices also perhaps reflected the low productivity of the hoe agriculture with which Africans were familiar. Africans also had a reputation amongst traders to the Americas of being more disease resistant, especially in tropical and semi-tropical regions, than either Amerindians or Europeans. So far as the Mediterranean, North Africa and the Middle East were concerned there had been a flow of sub-Saharan Africans across the desert and the Indian Ocean for many centuries. But the flow seems to have grown markedly from the seventeenth century onwards as other sources of supply, particularly around the Black Sea, became cut off as a result of Ottoman Turkish conquests. Later, once these trades had begun to wind down in the nineteenth century but the trading mechanisms within Africa remained in place, the availability of slaves whose price declined with the markets for them outside Africa became irresistible to other

Africans. They were seeking labour for economic production to replace profits from the external slave trades.

Though debate continues over estimates of the size of the transatlantic trade there is no doubt of its enormous extent – probably 10.25 million or a little more on the most sophisticated recent calculation. It had a number of distinctive phases that can be variously defined in terms of intensity of shipments, major carriers and main destinations in the Americas. The Portuguese, already having links to Muslim trade networks in the Maghreb, shipped their first cargo from West Africa in 1444 and in the early decades primarily supplied markets for domestic slaves in European households. They then began the supply of workers from Senegambia, the Gold Coast and the Bight of Benin to the burgeoning sugar plantations of the Atlantic islands in the later fifteenth century. About 1500 when they occupied São Tomé in the Gulf of Guinea, the island became their major centre of operations. Beginning in the early sixteenth century the Portuguese began to ship Africans directly to the Americas. Thereafter in general the sources of supply began to move east and south, though with some variation. In the 1600s, especially after 1650, the main areas of supply shifted to the west central coast and interior of Africa, principally the Kingdom of Kongo and Angola with some return to the Slave Coast at the end of the century. In the eighteenth century, post-1740, the Niger Delta and the Cross River within the Bight of Biafra assumed major significance as slave-loading points for European traders and there were temporary spurts of activity in other parts of West Africa, such as the Gold Coast. After 1850, with the end of the trade to Brazil, the transatlantic trade faded away, with the exception of a modest increase in the late 1850s. It came to an end by 1870.

However, slaving had remained substantial in the first half of the nineteenth century despite abolition measures by a number of states and the operation off parts of the West African coast of British and some other naval patrols officially intended as instruments of suppression. These factors influenced the nationality of traders left in the business, where they secured their cargoes and what their destinations were likely to be. In the opening decades of the nineteenth century trades to Brazil and Cuba remained open despite treaty restrictions and Portuguese, Brazilian, and Spanish traders in particular were protected by their officials in their eagerness to supply the market. Although they were still able to gain supplies from the coasts of west-central Africa beyond the possible attentions of naval patrols they also resorted significantly to Portuguese-dominated areas in south-east Africa. This happened notably after the end of the Napoleonic Wars, a moment marking the beginning of the concerted British effort at international suppression of the transatlantic trade. Governments and traders under British diplomatic and naval pressure did not miss its irony. Earlier the British themselves had been intensively involved in the trade. On recent calculations it is probable that the British carried at least 45 per cent of slaves shipped across the Middle Passage between 1700 and 1809. They emerged as the major carrier as, by the middle of the eighteenth century, the British West Indian islands collectively, with Jamaica to the fore, became one huge sugar complex. British traders, along with American colonial carriers, also supplied the tobacco and rice producers of the North American mainland colonies and secured the *asiento* or Spanish government licence to provide African labourers to Hispanic territories in the Caribbean and South America. The success of British slavers involved partially displacing the Dutch whose powerful merchant marine achieved dominance in the Portuguese sugar trade from Brazil in the early seventeenth century. Later they had temporary control both in Angola of a major source of slave labour and in north-east Brazil of slave-worked plantations and occupied a leading position in the transfer of Africans across the Middle Passage, including a share in supplying both Spanish and British territories. In the second half of the eighteenth century in particular the French became a large-scale supplier of slaves primarily to their own St Domingue which surpassed Jamaica as the leading sugar producer at the cost of a voracious consumption of brutalized African slaves.

The variations in natural reproduction in slave societies, combined with the extent of slave work and the length of time during which slave sectors of an economy continued to command investment in labour, together provide the framework for understanding the distribution of slaves over time through slave-trading systems. In the transatlantic system the link between natural reproduction and distribution is seen most clearly in the estimates for arrivals in North America. British North America and the

United States received only about 560,000 slaves out of an estimated total arrival in the Americas of about 10.25 million. This was despite slavery lasting about 300 years and being so extensively used that the slave population on the eve of the Civil War was almost 4 million.

In the many cases of natural decrease in the slave population distribution of fresh workers flowed to areas so long as economic expansion occurred. Thus arrivals in the British West Indies were greater earlier than in the French Antilles as Barbados became a sugar island. The two sets of colonies kept pace in their appetite for Africans between 1700 and 1780 and then the French market raced ahead as St Domingue grew furiously in the decade before the great slave revolt of 1791. The effects of the French and Haitian Revolutions and the emergence of new foreign sugar producers meant that French territories declined dramatically as a market until there was a modest revival in the 1820s. In contrast, arrivals in the British West Indies remained significant until the abolition of the slave trade in 1807. Similarly the upward curve of investment in fresh Africans through the slave trade was evident in the arrivals in Cuba as it became the major cane sugar producer in the post-Napoleonic period.

Beginning in the mid-sixteenth century by far the largest number of slaves flowed to Brazil. The best estimate is a little over 4 million in the 300 years between the 1550s and the 1850s. This was not only a consequence of the lack of natural increase amongst transported Africans or the decimation and unsuitability of Amerindian labourers. The Portuguese and Brazilians successively developed economic sectors based substantially on slave labour beginning earlier and continuing later than other slave-based activities in the Americas. As early as the 1580s north-east Brazil had become the main supplier of sugar to Europe and made use of perhaps 15,000 slaves. From the late seventeenth century slaves opened up and worked a gold and other mining economy in the interior in Minas Gerais and Goias. Taking off in the 1820s and 1830s, as sugar and mining faded, a boom in coffee production occurred in the south-central provinces centred on Rio de Janeiro and São Paulo. It is scarcely surprising that the Brazilians resisted enforcing treaty requirements against the slave trade until additional persuasion was provided by British naval intervention in 1850.

Development and reproduction of slavery through the slave trade was never without costs, whether or not they were greater for the trader than the warrior or raider who seized the slave directly and made use of him. Most immediately, however, the costs were borne by the slaves, at their highest in death during the course of the trade. No adequate calculations on mortality are possible for trades other than the transatlantic one. Comment on its extent and causes will therefore be restricted to the trade between Africa and the Americas, though no doubt some of the factors discussed are relevant to other trades. Focusing on the Middle Passage it is apparent that mortality rates on individual voyages varied widely. This appears to be true even when other possibly relevant factors such as voyage time, size of ship, port of embarkation, composition of the slave cargo and nationality of the shipper are accounted for. When very high mortality did occur on a particular voyage it is sometimes possible to pinpoint an unexpectedly long voyage (and thus a consequent shortage of food and water) or an outbreak of disease as the cause. However, over the centuries an increasing proportion of ships completed their voyages with a relatively low number of deaths. Voyages in the early seventeenth century registered on average 20 per cent slave mortality rates, but by the end of the eighteenth century the figure was below 10 per cent and by the 1820s many were coming in at about 6 per cent. Some of the illegal voyages in the last decades of the trade may have experienced a rise in the rate but not dramatically so. There was no significant difference in slave mortality rates according to the nationality of the trader but the areas or ports on the African coast from which embarkation took place did make a difference and length of voyage to American disembarkation may have accounted for part of the difference. The lowest death rates from a major area of embarkation were for those leaving west-central Africa, with the shortest voyage time, averaging on the most recent calculation 9.5 per cent for the whole period 1590 to 1867. At the higher end of the scale was the Bight of Biafra at 17.4 per cent and highest of all south-east Africa at 18.3 per cent over a shorter period but with the longest voyage times. Apart from voyage time the likely explanation for the differences in mortality rates appears to reside in local circumstances in and around the area of embarkation. Local disease environments and the extent to which they were different from interior environments, whence some of the slaves had been brought to the coast, were relevant. So too was the incidence of dearth and the disruption of material life by political and social upheaval, resulting in the weakening of those brought to the slave ships and their greater susceptibility to disease.

These considerations remind us that the transatlantic trade cannot be viewed in terms of the Middle Passage alone; acquisition in Africa and passage to the point of embarkation are also part of the picture. Once we turn to this aspect of the trade the crucial roles that some Africans played become evident. For much of the history of the transatlantic trade, with the significant exception of the Portuguese in west-central Africa, Europeans or their agents were not able to penetrate far into the interior to acquire slaves directly. They had to deal at the coast with rulers, their officials or African traders controlling the flow of slaves. It is impossible to know the rate of mortality amongst these slaves but the numbers enslaved with the intention of selling them to Atlantic merchants must have been significantly greater than the numbers embarked, let alone arriving in the ports of the New World.

Africans' engagement in slaving arose in part from their interests in developing a power base and acquiring labour in some relatively thinly populated regions; it was not purely the product of European demand and their willingness to satisfy it. Conflict amongst African states occurred for a variety of reasons. One result of conflict, however, was the common presence of slaves and this situation obtained even before European contact. Not even the kingdom of Kongo's use of Portuguese military services in the early sixteenth century was directed primarily to the gaining of slaves for the Europeans. In Kongo's campaign against Munza to the south in about 1513 the king and the Portuguese sent perhaps 800 slaves back to the capital. Some 510 were channelled into the Atlantic trade and at least 90 were retained in Kongo. But the king complained that the Portuguese to whom he had consigned management of this aspect had left him too few. He had not undertaken the military enterprise primarily for the slaves but he had not intended that the Europeans should be the main beneficiaries. That African states and African dealers were not simply reactive suppliers to European demands for slaves was also evident in the periodic decision of Africans to withdraw from dealing in slaves with Europeans while continuing to make use of slaves themselves. About 1520 Benin restricted the trade and closed off exports altogether in about 1550. Kongo behaved similarly at the turn of the sixteenth and seventeenth centuries and neither state seems to have been put under European pressure to resume.

The Indian Ocean trade in African slaves has received much less attention than the trade across the Atlantic but it was of longer duration and also huge in size. So far as European participants were concerned, although several powers were economically active in the region from the period of the breaking of the Portuguese monopoly in the seventeenth century, European trading in slaves from the East African coast and interior only took off from the mid-eighteenth century. Then the French, seeking to establish plantations on the Mascarenes, developed a substantial trade. But, if we leave aside the flow of Mozambique slaves across the Atlantic in the first half of the nineteenth century, Europeans did not play a dominant role in the Indian Ocean trade. It had existed for many centuries before Europeans were a presence in the Indian Ocean. Evidence of black slaves from East Africa traded to Alexandria dates from as early as the second century CE. By the ninth century large numbers of East African Zanj had been transported to the area around Basra where they had helped drain the salt marshes and build up date plantations. Before the new phase inaugurated by the French trade particularly to Reunion one sober estimate of the Indian Ocean trade from Africa puts the number of slaves shipped at about 5 million. Thereafter there was an intensification of the trade, especially in the nineteenth century, when over 2 million were transported, mainly to slave-owning societies in the Middle East to work in agriculture and pearl fisheries. Effective elimination of this trade, including its extension into the Red Sea, did not take place before the early twentieth century. Slaves from the interior of East Africa, a proportion then being shipped abroad, were in fairly plentiful supply by the nineteenth century since they were required for clove and sugar plantations on the Swahili coast and then on the Omani Arab-run estates on Zanzibar. Merchants collecting slaves from the interior, at least in the later centuries, were usually Arab-Swahili.

As has been implied in the consideration of the trans-Saharan, Atlantic and Indian Ocean trades in the preceding pages, there also existed over many centuries an internal African trade not restricted to providing people for the trades that took them out of Africa. The many African societies with slaves and the few slave societies that existed before European contact provided an impulse to relatively local or regional commerce in human beings. Commerce sometimes had to be sufficient to provide large numbers for limited periods, as in the Niger Valley empire of Songhay in the fifteenth century, where estates employing hundreds of slaves grew food crops both to sustain the army and for export. In later centuries, with the closure of the Atlantic trade, a larger pool of slaves remained within Africa with the effect of reducing their price. Yet, at the same time, in the nineteenth century many parts of Africa were drawn more closely into the international trade system as transport costs fell and cheap industrial goods became available for import. To take full advantage, however, African states and merchants needed to develop products that they could export – palm oil from West Africa is a good example – and that required a large amount of labour much of which was initially slave labour. Thus the slave base of the Sokoto Caliphate provided leisure and goods for the local ruling class and export products to be exchanged for luxury imports to the taste of the elite.

These different kinds of slave trades from and within Africa also provide evidence about the composition of traded slaves of a kind that is virtually absent for earlier trades. The Atlantic trade absorbed males over females at a ratio of about 2:1. The kind of labour required of slaves in the Americas, particularly in the phase of initial development of plantation systems, was deemed to require disproportionate male labour at the height of its strength. Later, as the creole proportion of the slave population grew, so did the female proportion and the significance of their role in plantation agriculture. In contrast, in the areas of Africa from which slaves were shipped across the Middle Passage most of the field work was traditionally done by women. In cultures with predominantly matrilineal kin systems there were also the advantages of numbers and future labour resources to be gained for kin groups by keeping women. A rough continental gendered division of labour thus occurred but it was not usually the result of Africans acceding to market pressures in the Americas. Other market pressures were operating too with the effect of reducing the flow of women into the transatlantic system. In addition to internal African market preferences for women and children in many (though not all) areas, the Muslim and Arab dominated trades to North Africa and the Middle East also gave a priority to women. A guess here would be that the ratio found in the Atlantic trade is reversed in the Muslim trade from the African savanna states, as female slaves were required for household tasks and as concubines.

There can be no doubt that the organization of the slave trade from Africa depended upon a complex series of interactions between Europeans, Africans (Muslim and non-Muslim), Arabs, Asians and creoles of various ethnic or racial mixtures. Indeed, many of those engaged in the business of slaving from early modern times onwards and denominated by a single ethnic tag were in fact *culturally* creole, whether so by birth or not, in that to do their business they became adepts at cross-cultural negotiation. In the transatlantic trade Europeans, such as the Portuguese in Angola, occasionally used their own force to raid for slaves in the interior. But mostly, as indicated above, they, and other Europeans on, say, the Slave Coast were dependent on African port officials, local rulers and Muslim and non-Muslim traders dealing with the interior for their supplies of slaves. Those interior traders themselves behind the Slave Coast were attached to established inter-regional commercial networks. The European outsiders as part of the operations of a state chartered slave-trading company such as the Dutch West India Company or England's Royal African Company or, more likely from the eighteenth century onwards, independent traders and representatives of mercantile partnerships had to deal primarily on African terms. The Portuguese and, briefly, the Dutch in Angola and then the latter further north also tried sending agents into the interior. But they still had to rely on Africans bringing slaves from other areas for trade and finding the commodities that the Europeans had on offer sufficiently attractive. With whom they dealt, as the discussion of Dahomey indicated, varied according to period and place. Where states were weak then groups of local merchants might assume virtual monopoly powers over the supply of slaves. This was the situation for a period in the interior behind the Bight of Benin. But individual traders were always liable to try to subvert restrictive arrangements on both the European and African sides and to introduce a more open market. In the last decades of the trade across the Atlantic both creole traders based on the African coast rather than in Europe and syndicates of Africans took a more prominent part in the trade. A notable late example was the *Pierre Soule* sailing from Benguela to Cuba in 1855 carrying 479 slaves and bearing the hopes of 48 local African and creole part-owners with it. The Indian Ocean trade depended upon broadly similar interactions. When the French became directly involved in the 1750s a proportion of their human cargoes was bought from Omani and Swahili merchants at Kilwa on the coast and in Zanzibar. Only the Portuguese in Mozambique to the south penetrated much into the interior and they were primarily concerned with the trade to Brazil.

Inter-regional or internal slave trades within large, single political entities constituted a variation on the slave trade as a major provider of slaves. The two major examples in modern history deserving of a brief comparison were the trades within Brazil and the United States in the nineteenth century. Both of them appear to have been relatively sensitive barometers of the differential conditions of slave-based economic development in different staples in the two countries. In both Brazil and the United States there was a limited internal slave trade in existence along with the external trade, but in both cases it became much more significant after the abolition of the external trade. There were other similarities. In both countries the main flow of the interprovincial and interstate trades was from more northerly, and in the American case also more easterly, regions of relatively declining staple production to areas requiring additional slaves because output of their staple was expanding. More specifically, slaves left the sugar plantations of the Brazilian north-east between 1850 and about 1885 to enter the coffee areas of the south-central region, particularly Rio and São Paulo. Smaller numbers were also carried north from Rio Grande do Sul to work in coffee, since a crisis in southern cattle ranching made their retention impossible. In the United States tobacco in the Upper South faded and some of the longer established cotton districts on parts of the Atlantic seaboard also became less profitable than newer areas of the Cotton Kingdom. Slaves flowed south and west to the black belt counties of the Mississippi Valley, especially from the 1820s onwards. These trades were of course making use of existing and not new slaves, yet they were vital to the reproduction of slavery in both countries. After the closure of the external trade coffee in Brazil, as well as cotton and, to an extent, sugar in the American South, depended on a continued flexibility in the location of the labour force. Transfer of labour into what were in effect frontier areas in both cases was necessary to feed the most dynamic economic sectors. Negative natural reproduction in Brazil and positive figures in the United States made no initial difference on this point. It is rather underlined by what we know, or can plausibly infer, of the composition of the internal trades. Though the Brazilian evidence is fragmentary it seems that the make-up of the internal trade through Rio contained a higher proportion of males and females of prime working age than did the slave population as a whole. The trade in the United States was also concentrated on a similar age group. The flow to the Brazilian coffee region and to Louisiana sugar was predominantly male, however, whereas the larger movement of traded slaves to the cotton lands involved roughly equal numbers of men and women. But the internal trade was sex specific where and when it needed to be. In coffee most planters were dependent on credit and many of them were substantially in debt throughout the decades of a significant internal trade. They needed workers but found the costs of wholesale importations from outside the region too much to contemplate. In consequence, they focused their purchases from the north on required artisans and appear to have gained field workers more cheaply much closer at hand. Since slave artisans were likely to be both male and creole this probably accounts for those features of the Brazilian trade as well as the fact that it was smaller in size than the American trade. Between 1850 and 1881 the upper limit of transfers through the trade was probably about 200,000. The best recent estimates of the interstate trade in the United States from the 1820s to the end of the 1850s suggest that perhaps 60 per cent of total interstate movements of slaves (i.e. including non-traded slaves moving with their masters) were traded. Total movements in these decades fluctuated between about 150,000 and 280,000 per decade; the conclusion is that there was a much larger trade than in Brazil. The larger trade consisted of a male-dominated New Orleans trade fitted to meet the harsh requirements of the sugar business and a greater flow, with a roughly equal sex ratio, into cotton. The total numbers and the presence of equal numbers of young women widely used as field workers indicate that the trade to the Cotton Kingdom was intended to provide the whole range of labour necessary for setting up cotton plantations. The sex ratio and age structure of the trade also imply that cotton planters anticipated taking advantage in the future of American slaves' reputation for natural increase, an expectation not open to the Brazilians. In the cotton states slave reproduction through the trade worked with natural reproduction to maximize labour resources in the region where they were most needed, when they were needed. Yet the costs falling on American planters purchasing through the trade were large. The price of prime field hands, male and female, rose steadily in the years before the civil war only falling as the political crisis of secession approached. In these circumstances the function of the internal trade could only be maintained so long as cotton or other staple commodity prices remained high and owners kept up pressure on their slaves to perform efficiently. This had implications (to be discussed later) for master–slave relations.

When long distance slave trades were established they were both crucial in bringing men and women into slavery and in maintaining slave systems. But slave trades also aided more extensive forms of economic integration. As Rome secured slaves from the region to the west of the Black Sea, the Caucasus and parts of the Mediterranean, the trade became part of more general commercial links. At different times the Romans exchanged salt and grain for slaves with Colchis on the Black Sea, wine with Gaul before the territory came under their control, and a variety of luxury goods with the tribes of the middle and lower Danube. Slaves were a component of a complex medieval trading network in the Mediterranean connecting the Middle East, the larger islands, Italian merchant communities, North Africa and the Iberian peninsula. In the seventeenth and eighteenth centuries the transatlantic slave trade was one aspect of a system not only tying together West Africa, Europe and the Americas but also, in the Arab horse trade across the Sahara to meet the military requirements of some African states, the Middle East as well. Cowries as a form of monetary exchange, military goods and luxury items such as textiles were all part of flows of imports from different directions in return for African slaves.

Regions particularly likely to yield up slaves were areas with no significant centralized political authority, both because they were apt to generate captives through conflict and further had little capacity to resist forces external to the region. If they were also in reach of well-organized states then their fate was sealed. This was the case for at least two millennia in the lands to the west, east and north of the Black Sea whose populations were drained by Rome, Arab Muslim states and then the Ottomans, all of whom were able to make use of convenient sea routes. Areas of Africa also fitted this pattern, particularly the Sudanese–Ethiopian borderlands over many centuries and parts of West Africa. During the era of the slave trade probably a majority of Africans on the Atlantic seaboard and in the immediate interior behind the coast lived in small political units rarely larger in area than a sizeable modern city. They were often fairly thickly populated on the Slave and Gold Coasts but less so in central Africa. Since the standing and wealth of individuals or lineages depended upon their control over people rather than land in a comparatively land-rich environment the temptation to acquire slaves was considerable. When the Europeans arrived on the coast any decision not to collaborate with them in securing slaves could and would only plausibly be taken by the few larger and more centralized states such as Benin or Kongo.

Much less important than warfare, raiding and the slave trade (though not insignificant) in the provision of slaves were the processes briefly outlined in the opening chapter that sometimes led to the bondage of an individual within his or her own society. These comprised parental sale of children; adoption; acquisition of exposed or abandoned children; self-sale; debt bondage that became debt slavery in some instances; penal servitude that could become permanent. Children as relatively powerless members of a family or community were vulnerable to forms of bondage resulting from difficult circumstances faced by those having authority over them. Records surviving from several societies in the ancient Middle East reveal the practice of parents selling young girls outright or conditionally in the form of sale-adoption. In the latter case, depending on the bargaining position of the parent, the terms of the sale could require the girl's marriage to the purchaser or a son or, less favourably, a slave of the household. In an example from a Nuzi document marriage was to a slave of the 'adoptive' father; if the slave husband died then the girl was to marry another slave and remain in her purchaser's household for life. Clearly the terms of any conditional sale-adoption were likely to be harsh if the sale was occasioned by family desperation or existing indebtedness to the purchaser. In this Nuzi case it led to an outcome indistinguishable from slavery so far as the girl sold was concerned. Sumerian texts indicate that adoption could also include infants of both sexes and adults in which service was provided in return for protection and sustenance. If, however, the adopted person seriously refused obedience then Sumerian law was harsh. 'If an [adopted] son to his father "you are not my father" say he shall cut his [front] hair, put a slave mark on him and sell him for money.'

For centuries, and especially from the later Roman Empire to about the eleventh century, children were more widely exposed and abandoned in the Mediterranean world and Europe than the modern mind can easily accept. There were examples too amongst African peoples. It seems that female children were disproportionately exposed. Poverty, some perceived physical defect in the child or gender preference were probably the main reasons for abandonment, but neither in Europe nor in Africa did anything like all abandoned children ended up as slaves. Yet those who rescued or acquired the children could claim to have saved them from death and did therefore sometimes impose slavery upon them. Even when this was not the result long-term service was often the outcome.

Self-sale into bondage, particularly a resort of strangers without kin or friends as a way of surviving in hard times, is also recorded from the earliest times. In Babylonian and Assyrian records sale prices are mentioned, but in a Nuzi case in which the person selling himself is clearly a foreign immigrant probably finding it impossible to earn a living the sale appears to be for food, clothing and shelter only. Self-sale as a result of poverty or insecurity clearly varied in intensity but was a significant source of domestic slaves in seventeenth- and eighteenth-century Russia. It was even alleged to have occurred occasionally amongst free blacks in the United States.

In all of these social processes involving forms of bondage

imposed internally upon members of the same society there is some element of ambiguity about whether there were limits of time or character to the bondage imposed, that is, whether the bondage amounted to slavery proper. In some cases of self-sale, for example, it was probable that service lasted as long as the life of the master but no longer. In instances of sale-adoption the marriage of a girl, or at least levels of care, were promised even though she was held to permanent service in a household. 'Adoptive' fathers only imposed the marks of slavery upon recalcitrant adopted individuals when things had gone badly wrong. None of these processes *necessarily* led to slavery but they could do so and quite often did.

A similar point has to be made about debt bondage and the holding of hostages or pawns and the possibility that they could be reduced to debt slavery. However indebtedness arose, in both the ancient Middle East and Greece default in repayment entitled the creditor to compulsory labour from the debtor or from the person he had pledged in his place. When the security for the debt was a person he was required to remain in the service of the creditor until the debt was paid off. Nuzi documents suggest that if the obligation had not been fulfilled at the death of the debtor then it became the responsibility of his children. In other cases, securing amounts of labour from the debtor rather than repayment of the debt was the point of the original loan so that a time-limited obligation to work, even if the original debt had been repaid, remained in place. The time limit could extend to as long as 50 years, amounting in practical terms to a life time. Assyrian codes also allowed treatment of pledges akin to that of undoubted slaves. 'If an Assyrian man, or an Assyrian woman, who is dwelling in a man's house as a pledge for his value has been taken [in discharge of the debt] up to the full value, he may flog [him], he may pluck out [his hair], he may bruise [and] bore his ears.' Broadly similar arrangements for service in response to unpaid debt were in place in ancient Israel and Rome. The use of pledges or pawns for debt, often women, was common in many parts of Africa and failure to meet the debt in full could amount to permanent enslavement for the pawn. The debtors and the pledges, free-born or part of a free kin group, in almost all of these instances found themselves moving into a form of bondage in their own society. In theory, and perhaps often in practice, this was not permanent but might become so. This danger in relation not to strangers but to fellow members of the community clearly provoked anxieties reflected in evidence in the Old Testament of a limitation on debt bondage for Hebrews of six years and in Athens by Solon's reform ending debt slavery for citizens. Other Greek states followed the lead of Athens. Yet reduction to slavery for debt remained possible for non-citizens, for example for metics (resident aliens) in various Greek states.

Debt bondage sometimes leading to a form of slavery was not restricted to, but was more likely to occur in, societies in which commercial transactions were relatively common and in which, in consequence, social differentiation had begun to develop. In societies with slaves it could be a significant source of slaves acquired individually and in the absence of a regular market in slaves. In slave societies it could, to a small extent, supplement other sources of slaves but the more organized and extensive a slave market was in existence then the more marginal debt slavery was likely to be. Debt slavery tended to disappear during the central centuries of Roman slavery and to be virtually invisible in the Americas – until slavery proper came to an end. Organized systems of slave supply, dealing in outsiders, also relieved the social anxieties that would accrue from the imposition of debt bondage on fellow members of the same community.

As a punishment for crimes forced labour of limited duration has historically been extremely widespread. It has even been a punishment meted out to persons of high status. Penal slavery, the reduction to labour for life as a punishment, has been less common because it was usually imposed only for extremely serious or capital crimes. Once again slavery replaced death as a consequence of actions placing the perpetrator in effect outside the community. It was a marked feature of Roman judicial practice but tended to take account not only of the seriousness of the crime but also of the social standing of the criminal. By the second and third centuries CE it was largely restricted to free men and freedmen of low status and to non-citizens as punishments, for such categories of people became less and less distinguished from those for the already enslaved. Reduction to a form of slavery was dramatized through the loss of property and of all rights over family and household and dissolution of any marriage. Above all a formerly free man, to be reduced to penal slavery, had first to have his citizenship taken from him; he was put outside the community and the state. Thereafter, as state slaves, penal slaves could be put to whatever work the state required and could be subjected to whipping and being put in chains. Penal slavery remained in place in Europe during the Middle Ages, though it was of no great numerical significance except sometimes in particular sectors, such as mining and the manning of galleys. Only in Russia during the expansion eastwards from the seventeenth century onwards did penal slaves play a substantial part in economic development. Overall, similar points may be made about penal slavery to those about debt slavery; in societies with slaves it contributed to the unsystematic maintenance of the institution but in slave societies it was, with rare exceptions, a minor supplement to other forms of slave reproduction.

Although slavery had to be fitted into a variety of social orders there were a number of broad similarities in the underlying principles of the legal frameworks that facilitated it. They provided the formal, though not necessarily the experiential, terms on which the institution was organized in relation to the larger society. In reality much was left to the slave master or his agent's discretion. This obviously applied to day-to-day management but also to the handling of behaviour and situations that would have led a free man into the judicial process or would not have been a matter for consideration by anyone else. In their quasi-judicial role sensible masters considered the slave as *both* a person and as property. And so did the legal systems within which owners were often able to strike the point of balance between humanity and property according to their own judgement. Very occasionally community order or other interests took priority over the master's wishes. The clarity of the slave's dual legal character, in the American expression *chattel personal*, in societies influenced by western juridical traditions became much more sharply defined from the time of certain conceptual developments in Roman law onwards. The Romans and those succeeding to their legal outlook understood that the law of nations that recognized slavery had to be maintained despite the fundamental assumption that freedom constituted man's natural state. The *dominium* or absolute control of the master over the slave, as also the concept of absolute property that the Romans developed, was justified, for example, in the Justinian Code of the sixth century. 'Slaves are in the power of their masters; for we find that among all nations slave owners have the power of life and death over their slaves and whatever a slave earns belongs to his master.' Much Roman and successor law was devoted to spelling out the implications of slaves as pieces of property but the assumption of freedom as man's natural state also left space for legal expression, stronger in some legal codes than others, of the slave's (incomplete) humanity. This was particularly striking in the thirteenth-century Castilian code *Las Siete Partidas* (*c.* 1262). Provisions recognized a master's or anyone else's killing of a slave as a serious crime and similarly the abuse or sexual violation of slave women or children. The slave was granted a right in his *peculium* or accumulated personal property, though this did not displace the master's ultimate right to whatever his slave possessed. Yet even if these legal prescriptions were acted upon (and there is some debate on the issue) Moorish slaves in medieval Spain appear to have been subject to a tougher regime under the slightly later Code de Tortosa (1272). The balance within the French Code Noir (1685) between acknowledgement of the slave's humanity and the master's control of his property was rather different, although both received recognition. Not only did the master have large areas of discretion but also punishments for particular offences were often severe and there were no clear limits to chastisement that might have given a modicum of protection to the slave. The French legislation offered no recognition to slave property however obtained and, in common with many other slave codes, the slave was not recognized as having any power to make contracts. But the recognition of the slave as a religious being meant that he had a partial access to religious sacraments and the master was required to ensure the bondsman's baptism even if not to permit regular worship. Eventually a customary right of self-purchase began to gain recognition in the French Antilles and, in so far as it was practised, cut across some of the dehumanizing features of the Code. The horrors of the last years of colonial St Domingue, however, do not suggest a humane legal order.

Slave marriages were not legally sanctioned at Rome although a sort of common-law marriage (*contubernium*) was encouraged, or at least tolerated. But it was under religious law and doctrine that the issue of slave marriage tested the limits of recognition of the slave's humanity. As with *contubernium* the question was not one of recognition of the union of slaves – almost all societies have given some recognition to slave unions. The issue was whether slave *marriage* acquired any special recognition not merely resulting from instrumental manipulation or utilitarian calculation by the owner derived from the slave as property. Under virtually all traditions of Islamic law it does not seem that the slave was free to choose to marry, but if he became a Muslim then he was able to do so provided he received his master's permission. Religiously sanctioned norms within the law shaped whom the slave might marry. The powerful Islamic notion of *Kafa'a*, broadly, the requirement of pre-existing equality of status between marriage partners, reduced the likelihood of slaves marrying across the line of freedom. This underlined the power of the master to compel slaves to marry in other cases and he could also require a slave to give up his wife. Male slaves might be permitted two wives and be allowed to divorce them. Despite variations in different Islamic traditions overall there was an uneasy attempt in slave marriage to blend some respect for the institution with the rights of the master over his property and a characteristic prime consideration for the male over the female.

In principle the slave was entitled to marry under the religious sanction of medieval Christendom, as indicated in the Church-influenced *Las Siete Partidas*. The Church requirement of slave baptism sometimes received the support of secular law such as in the Code Noir but there was a reluctance to translate this religious imperative into either law or practice in the Anglophone Protestant slave societies of the New World in the seventeenth and eighteenth centuries. By the nineteenth century in the United States, though slave marriages were still not recognized in law, the paternalistic ideological claims that some planters made about their relation to their slaves may, in some cases and in the service of consistency, have contributed something to the stability of slave unions. But only through its inflection of the ideology of paternalism was Christianity likely to have made much impact on masters' valuing of slave marriages, even as the slaves' own religious sense of the significance of marriage may have intensified their despair when owners broke up this most intimate of relationships. But whatever limited acknowledgements under slave systems were made of slave marriages they seem never to have extended to granting slave parents any formally recognized control over their children. Whatever forms the reproduction of slavery took masters had to assert as much control over it as possible and claim slave children as property.

The most evident expression in law of the slave as a piece of property was when he was literally commodified and legal requirements governing slave sales were established. From at least the period of the Hammurabi Code onwards clauses appeared in slave sale documents guaranteeing the purchaser against defects in the property bought – legally vulnerable antecedents, incurable disease, temple services yet to be performed. Something similar developed in the regulation of slave sales in Rome, entailing the seller providing information of the kind mentioned above (similar in character to regulations for the sale of cattle) but also about any previous history of the slave as a criminal, loiterer or runaway. Ironically, what was to be supplied at the moment of the slave's most evident construction as a commodity was detail of his human agency.

As law framed the more general conditions of slavery in prescriptive terms it had to negotiate the relation between property and humanity over the slave's criminal activity, activity against him that might be regarded as criminal and his standing as a witness of possibly criminal activity committed by non-slaves. In Ancient Greece, and in most societies with slaves and slave societies, slaves could neither bring cases nor have them brought against them in their own persons. Only their masters and other free persons could initiate cases. Yet, of course, slaves were recognized as human agents; not to have done so would have meant no redress for the person injured or the owner of property damaged. Thus the slave could be punished judicially for criminal acts but his master, of whom the slave was merely an extension, might be required to provide compensation to the injured party even though he had in no way sanctioned his slave's act. That the slave's act was against another slave made no necessary difference to his master's responsibility in principle since the injured slave's master had suffered damage to property. If a criminal slave was executed then his own master might receive some compensation from the state for loss of property as a result of his slave's human act for which the master was theoretically but not actually responsible. Evidence of the slave's difficulty of access to the judicial system in most societies was underlined by the resort of masters to private resolution of issues involving their slaves to avoid the complexities outlined above. It was perhaps most brutally clear in the rarity of the conviction of masters, or even their having to meet judicial charges, for the murder of a slave. An owner must be able to do with his own what he willed. When the slave became enmeshed as the object of the legal system he was almost invariably as perpetrator punished more severely than the free person and as victim saw his assailant, free or slave, punished less severely than if the victim had been free. That the courts were not for the slave as an inferior and outsider was also apparent in how he was regarded as a witness. He could provide evidence against another slave but in most societies only in exceptional circumstances against a free person, often after torture and then in crimes such as treason deemed sufficiently important to the community to override the usual assumptions about the worth of a slave's evidence.

This general survey of the law's treatment of slavery smoothes out the peculiarities of particular systems but tries to bring out the necessary recognition in law, despite the presence of slavery in very different kinds of communities, of the slave as both property and person. The 'personhood' of the slave was only very imperfectly recognized and protected against the master and others since legal systems gave priority to the master and his property interest. At times, however, the property interest was best served by partial recognition of the slave as a person, usually, but not always, to the slave's detriment.

3

Societies with Slaves and Slave Societies

The discussion so far has made use of, without dealing in substantial detail with, the terms 'societies with slaves' and 'slave societies'. However, a number of features have been indicated as characterizing these terms, thus beginning to fill out conceptually organized descriptions as the basis both for illuminating concrete historical instances and refining the concepts themselves. Broadly, societies with slaves have begun to emerge as making use of slaves for social and service purposes carried out mostly within households, including royal and aristocratic courts. Such households were often, but not invariably, set within kin networks or lineage-based societies. Only for kings and aristocrats resting on top of lineage systems (and they had other resources to draw on in addition to household or other attached slaves) was the extent of slavery sufficient in itself to permit a life without work. Other heads of households or elders of the lineage had to work or rely on some other resource apart from slaves. Not least was this the case because societies with slaves both lacked any regular method of replenishing slaves and, if they came to need them, were anyway in the process of transition to a slave society, whether or not they reached that stage. The political context of societies with slaves could be extremely varied but was unlikely to be purely cooperative and consensual since the social differentiation that the presence of slavery indicated was expressed in at least rudimentary political organization. In contrast, slave societies made use of substantial numbers of slaves for economic production through a labour force of outsiders. Control was exercised by means of more or less elaborate institutional structures embodying the power of the class of slave owners with the implicit threat of the use of organized force. As this implies, slave societies drew on relatively developed state structures for the purpose of maintaining social order, though slavery was a sufficiently malleable institution to fit with different forms of political system. The economic deployment of slaves occurred characteristically within plantations, stock-raising farms, mines and a variety of manufactories. Where the social lives of slaves impinged on the interests of masters the latter endeavoured to shape them. When they did not, slaves had some room to act for themselves individually or even as a community. Slave societies developed systematic methods for replacing and relocating slaves, predominantly through commerce in human beings. Thereby the social distance in slave societies between slaves and their masters was more emphatically underlined than in most societies with slaves.

The purpose of the rest of this chapter is to explore in more detail, refine and qualify the outlines of these two kinds of society by taking up a number of themes. Bearing particularly on societies with slaves, they are: the nature of household slavery; the complexities of slavery in kin- and lineage-based systems, including the extent of incorporation of bondsmen, and particularly women, over time and the possibilities of changes in slavery within such communities. Sketching some of the paths of transition towards slave societies, as slavery became a significant institution without achieving a dominant position in production, leads on to themes relevant to systems of the large-scale economic use of slaves. They include the juxtaposition of the slave-based system of production with other kinds and the conditions prompting a shift towards the dominance of slave production; the significance of the market, the range of slave occupations and the organization of labour in the development of slave societies will also be surveyed.

There are, however, a number of preliminary general points to be made about the structural location of slavery and the milieux in which it existed. Where slavery was primarily a household institution it was not necessarily always simply for a domestic or sexual purpose. Slaves carried on forms of household manufacture such as weaving. And even when household heads had control of sufficient family members or kin it sometimes suited them to use their slaves for agricultural labour. Such decisions were not only a matter of economic calculation or rational use of resources; there might be cultural reasons too. In some Christian households in late nineteenth-century Ethiopia, for example, the slave's outsider status meant that though he worked the land he had no claim on it, whereas family members and even hired labourers would have. Elsewhere it was the slave's outsider status that had to be preserved by preventing him from combining his labour with that on household or lineage land. Lineage-based societies had slaves attached to them in various ways, including connection to a particular household or membership of a subordinate lineage. Economic activity as well as other functions were expected of them, perhaps working beside full lineage members, though production was mostly for use and not sale and was not the prime purpose in owning slaves. Equally important, slaves performed a wide range of non-economic functions in some slave societies. The more complex the society, the less slaves performed multiple functions and the greater the division of labour *amongst* the slaves was likely to be (though the extent still varied markedly) as well as within the whole society. In sum, the distinction between economic and non-economic functions was found amongst slaves in both kinds of society though the balance was dramatically different in each. A few agricultural slaves could be found in the same society with slaves as enslaved servants, soldiers and others. During the central centuries of Roman slave society large numbers of agricultural slaves were present alongside slave administrators, concubines and advisers.

Very obviously, in societies with slaves where economic activity was not the main purpose of slavery, then the social relationships embedded in slavery, including slave production and its social relations, were a minor adjunct of other forms of social relationship and production. It will become clear, however, that these social relationships of slavery could be a source of tension. In the very terms of the definition of slave societies offered in the opening chapter both the system of economic production based on slavery and master–slave relations imprinted themselves on many aspects of the society as a whole. Yet they too always coexisted with other forms of production and social relationship. When slave systems were the dominant socio-economic mode how they related to other features of the social and economic order still posed problems of social and political harmony and defined areas of potential and actual economic conflict. These issues will be taken up partly in this and partly in the next chapter.

Any student of slavery will soon encounter historical instances of state-owned or public or corporate slavery. The 'Scythian archers' of classical Athens constituted a slave police force, numbering several thousands at their height, and public slaves were employed on public building and works in Greece and Rome. Corporately owned temple slaves in the ancient Middle East materially maintained the priestly caste without being dominant in the system of production as a whole; regiments of slave soldiers have acted on behalf of many states and rulers in different contexts. It is worth asking how these forms of slavery relate to the two kinds of society containing slaves around which the discussion has been organized. A little thought indicates that public slavery as a phenomenon can be accommodated within the present terms of analysis. The Scythian archers, for example, were simply a supplementary service within a slave society; they contributed to the state's role in the maintenance of order, if necessary through the control of unruly slaves. The fourteenth-century Muslim traveller, Ibn Battuta, in the societies with slaves of the western Sudan, encountered public slaves in court service and in mining who probably made up most of the slaves living in the societies. The presence of bodies of public slaves, and the relative absence of private slaves, did not in itself determine the kind of society they inhabited.

The final preliminary point about the location of slavery concerns its relation to technology. There has been a recurrent debate amongst scholars on whether slavery in slave societies has retarded technical innovation (the issue was irrelevant in societies with slaves because slavery was economically marginal). Improvements in technology and practical economic arrangements certainly occurred in slave societies. In the ancient world screw presses for wine and oil and rotary grain mills and the development of drainage systems for fields are examples; in late eighteenth-century America the cotton gin was invented, immensely improving the harvesting of cotton. Yet in no slave society was technical change a dynamic force. In these circumstances technology did not begin to *replace* labour and command an increased share of the investment of resources. What technical change could do in slave societies was *intensify* the use of slave labour. The rotating drum of the grain mill in the Roman world, in use from the second century CE, was worked largely by female slaves and for long hours. Eli Whitney's cotton gin facilitated vast numbers of additional slaves working and harvesting huge quantities of short staple cotton across the American South, a kind of production previously too difficult because of the problem of removing the seeds from the cotton. When technical changes helped *replace* slave labour then it was a sign (though not the simple cause) that the institution was in decline in those societies. The diffusion of the water mill in place of the rotary mill saved the labour of thousands in Western Europe. It was a halting and extended process, beginning between the sixth and eighth centuries, but the water mill became dominant between the ninth and eleventh centuries at the time that slavery was ending in the countryside. Similarly slaves had to do much of the breaking of the land themselves in the ancient world because of the inadequacy of animal harnesses. With the appearance and spread of the shoulder collar for horses, again coinciding with the decline of European slavery between the ninth and eleventh centuries, the power of the horse replaced the labour of many men in the fields. Thus, while technical changes in themselves neither extended nor reduced the use of slave labour, they could be a significant factor in both processes.

It is now time to turn to slavery within the households of societies with slaves. Domestic slavery in slave societies will be dealt with later. Many examples could be provided of the involvement of slaves within households at different social levels in both Muslim and non-Muslim Africa and in the Middle East over a long period. The courts of rulers and the civil and military staffing of their palaces, the households of warrior aristocrats, the trading compounds and houses of merchants, attachment to government officials and even learned men and teachers were all milieux in which slaves could be found. In many societies with slaves they were less likely to be part of a farmer's household.

When the household was a royal court or palace at the centre of a system of political power the roles and significance of slaves could take on certain paradoxical qualities. Slaves, precisely because of their status, often held positions of responsibility or influence in a palace system. These systems of rule were rarely 'rational-bureaucratic' in Max Weber's definition of the administrative order of the modern state. In other words, instead of a pattern of government of demarcated areas of responsibility carried on according to regular procedures and with delimited powers by officials deemed qualified, in Weber's phrase 'the ruler executes the most important measures through personal trustees, table-companions, or court-servants.' Slaves holding positions in a court or palace system, as complete dependants on the ruler, were fitted to carry out tasks he personally assigned to them and to 'shadow' the activities of other officials. They were carriers of the ruler's will rather than the more impersonal will of the state. As such they often challenged or displaced the influence or authority of aristocrats and other prominent individuals who might otherwise have expected to exert authority within the political system. The development of the power of the king amongst the Ashanti in the nineteenth century was based on the displacement of the authority of chiefs and traditional leaders by the influence of palace slave-eunuchs exercised through a corps of officials and sustained by a body of household troops. Political systems of this kind often fostered rivalry between royal and aristocratic kin groups or lineages in the form of collateral descent groups. When factionalism broke out slave-eunuchs and slave women, because they had no independent power base within a kin network or lineage, could well be the ruler's protection against kin-based intrigue. The safeguard was at times effective enough to cut the king himself off from sufficient information and contact with others outside the circle of slave retainers in the palace to make him more of a figurehead than an active ruler. Rulers distributed slave women to prominent figures to encourage their loyalty (at Muslim courts they could be from the harem) but equally significant was activity at the palace by slave women themselves. To accumulate sufficient influence without being associated with any of the competing kin networks led them to connect with other similar 'neutral' figures, usually other slaves or former slaves. They became partners of the corps of officials and armed retainers and were either used for the purposes of influence by elite figures within the lineages or interests outside the palace assumed them to be useful as ways of reaching the ruler and his advisers. Since who took decisions within the palace walls, and how they were arrived at, was probably opaque to outsiders, slave-eunuchs and other slaves were assumed to possess influence and this may have contributed to any influence that they had. At various periods of its history Dahomey was the paradigm case of these processes; there slaves, including women, held positions in the royal household mirroring the position of ministers although not strictly part of the household itself. They were present at ministerial consultations with the king, took part in decision-making at the council and discussions at other assemblies.

The rewards of loyalty in nineteenth-century Dahomey are apparent from information we have on the career of the female slave, Tata Ajache. She was born on the Nigerian border, captured as a child and raised as a female warrior in Dahomey. She fought well, killing a man and was rewarded. The king made her pregnant, although he and she both knew that female warriors had to avoid pregnancy. She refused to reveal who the father of her child was, despite strong pressure brought upon her. The king, recognizing her loyalty, raised her to the elite, gave her riches and provided her with two slaves.

The highest position a slave woman could reach in these palace-household systems of power was that of queen mother, an official designation rather than the indication of a biological relationship. By the time she attained it she had ceased to be a slave but often began her household career as a slave-concubine of some prominent figure. If she produced a child then it became free, and so did the concubine on the death of the master-father. She achieved her position on occasion from having assisted a candidate to the throne through her influence and alliances within the palace. The king was in effect her protégé and probably continued to pay close attention to her wishes. In Dahomey the queen mother ultimately assumed authority over religious cults whose influence was then directed to supporting the king's power.

We have been discussing special slaves who were part of peculiarly prominent households that rested for their material support on surpluses extracted through a variety of forms of production (some of it by slaves) and carried on away from the court or palace. The discussion has also highlighted, though in abnormally dramatic form, the significance of slaves within the shaping force of the dynamics of kin or lineage systems. This was equally the case at less exalted levels in many societies with slaves. Full lineage membership in theory not only brought responsibilities but claims on other members and a share in corporate resources. In reality, however, a variety of tensions arose between individual members and collateral groups in lineages. And conflict could arise between lineages. The possession and use of slaves were often central to these tensions and conflicts. We have seen that in societies with slaves bondsmen were unlikely to be very important in economic production except perhaps in a few limited sectors. But their attachment to lineages had other functions. The elders of lineages could only deploy resources and maintain influence in their communities if they held on to or increased the numbers that they controlled. The acquisition of some slaves to add to the number of full lineage members could prove important even if acquisition was problematic in other ways, to be explored later. Not least in importance was the prestige of the elders of large lineages on the village headman's council. It was also probable that the headman's position at the formation of a new village, perhaps as a consequence of the pressure of population on village resources or conflict between lineages, would fall to a senior member of the largest lineage. This could provide power over the allocation of village land and, as another source of income, possibly authority to collect taxes. Other things being roughly equal, the greater the size of the lineage the greater the wealth that tended to follow. This in turn was likely to attract more followers, including more attached slaves, to the lineage over a period. It should be remarked, however, that many of the societies of south-east and east-central Africa that manifested these tendencies in the pre-colonial period were small in scale and limited in levels of production.

When the prime motive for attaching slaves to lineages was to bring the political and possibly the indirect economic benefits of greater numbers, the consequence was also to provide the strength of more bodies for work. Production in lineage societies in many cases was largely for use with, at best, a small surplus for exchange. Attached slaves worked alongside free lineage members and often at the same tasks in, for example, farming or fishing, though some of them may have been pressed harder than full lineage members. There was more evident differentiation in some contexts where trade and not farming was the source of livelihoods. On the middle Zaire, in the trade conducted in large boats organized by trading companies and propelled by numerous paddlers, slave and free also worked together. The paddlers, however, tended to be slaves and the captains were free. Both slave and free women supplied food for the voyages and any surplus was marketed. But traders provoked tensions in the kinship structures of river society in seeking permanently to incorporate women and their children into trading companies by cutting across the obligations of the offspring of female kin members in matrilineal kin systems to maternal uncles and other kin. The alternative, to which the traders increasingly resorted, was to try to control the procreation of female slaves whose children, since they were strictly without kin, they could command unhindered.

In some instances of societies with slaves the structural reconciliation of the organization of slave work with the idiom and obligations of lineage eventuated in the emergence of subordinate lineages. Their slave members were grouped in domestic units but any surplus that they produced was sold by the dominant lineage corporately owning the slaves. Amongst the Ashanti individuals owned slaves but mostly they were group controlled. Members of a lineage collaborated to buy slaves and used corporate lineage access, for example to kola groves, to produce for the market. The dependent lineages of slaves by the early nineteenth century were clustered in separate slave villages near the capital and also produced supplies for the army and leading kin groups. There was clear potential in these developments for the growth of a full-scale slave society out of the society with slaves, provided that the market became sufficiently large and the supply of slaves (problematic in a society with slaves) could be maintained.

There were a number of characteristic tensions surrounding slavery in lineage-based societies with slaves. They were largely to do with marriage, control of children and the passage of property and, as in the preceding discussion of aspects of slavery in relation to kin and lineage systems, they can best be analysed in African societies. In patrilineal societies free males, whether they married free women, slaves or both, or took female slaves as concubines, were able to control their children and the passage of property between generations. In many communities, though not all, even marriage to a slave woman or fathering a child on a slave-concubine produced free children. Should a free man take many wives and concubines then he might start a new lineage segment. This was a reinforcement of the traditional order. Only if free and slave women were largely monopolized by older men already in control of substantial resources did dissatisfaction manifest itself amongst lineage cadets. Then the senior men in lineages, in asserting their power and prerogatives too evidently, brought on social tensions. Yet this control of women need not only apply to the leading man's own marriages and sexual relations. If he was exceptionally eager to maximize his control of people and property by keeping them within the lineage then he had to circumvent the normal logic of the kin system. He married his daughters to his own male slaves and thus maintained another generation and their capacity to produce wealth under his authority as a lineage head. This was, of course, because the male slave had no kin. The immediate cost to be set against this strategy was the loss of bride price from the kin of free potential husbands. More diffuse social resentments might arise as free women were removed from the pool of the marriageable, depending upon the balance in the community of young women to men wanting a bride. The lineage elder could also require a female slave to marry a member of his lineage or one of his male slaves, all with the intended effect of retaining as many children as possible.

Societies following matrilineal principles engendered tensions surrounding slavery in different ways. Free men marrying free women lost control of their children to the brothers or father of their wives and property passed through their wives' lineage not to their own sons but to kin on their wives' side. In these circumstances, more than in patrilineal societies, and evidently in west-central Africa and parts of east-central Africa, men pushed against the logic of the matrilineal system. They resorted to marrying or fathering children on their kinless female slaves or gave some of them to their male slaves; all of these offspring remained in the male's lineage. As was alluded to earlier, the economic rationale for this strategy was especially clear in the trading companies of the middle Zaire; their organization was effective because they were structured around a single kin network.

The analysis offered above of the tensions inherent in different kinds of kin and lineage systems and the engagement of slavery in them is generally accepted and has a good deal of force. But there are reasons to register doubts about some of the assumptions underlying the analysis and to qualify some of the conclusions. Firstly, the analysis assumes that marriage and kin strategies were precisely that – long-term calculations based on interest, completely governed by concern for the control of persons and property. The role of sentiment is hard to calibrate with other factors and too much stress on individual preference is misplaced in cultures that structured perceptions of the good and of interest in terms of the group. Yet this does not mean that the vagaries of sentiment did not play a part in marriage decisions even though the point cannot be clearly demonstrated. Secondly, the conventional analysis assumes a world dominated by active males in which all females were passive. There is no doubt that any room for manoeuvre that women made for themselves was small. But sometimes they must have been in a position, and this was true even of slave women, to try to influence the outcome of male decisions in regard to themselves or even other women. It was rational for both slave and free women to try to present themselves as convenient partners of free men rather than slaves and that for material reasons. To succeed was to make the free status of their children, and perhaps eventually themselves, more likely. The success of some women, including slaves, in advancing to influence and freedom at royal courts and in palace politics, suggests similar possibilities at a more ordinary level in the lineage system. Finally, it is clear that slaves were used to subvert the normal operations of both patrilineal and, more especially, matrilineal structures, but the extent may have been exaggerated. In patrilineal societies the immediately calculable loss of a bride price for a daughter may not have seemed worthwhile against the uncertainties of her future issue. The supposed resentment of a male in a matrilineal system against loss of command over his children and passage of property to his wife's kin must surely sometimes have been eased by his recognition that he derived benefits from the system if he had a sister who produced children. With these points in mind it is necessary to step back a little from an implicit portrayal of the operation of lineage-based societies and slavery in them as purely male-driven, relentlessly instrumental and utterly material in concerns.

However, the issue that has generated most recent discussion of kin-based societies with slaves is the extent to which the outsider status of slaves was blurred through tendencies toward their incorporation into lineages in what were often quite small-scale social worlds. This is to say that discussion has focused on the structural location of slaves in relation to kin systems and the extent to which the situation could change without the slave ceasing to be a slave. Miers and Kopytoff in the ground-breaking volume of essays that they edited on slavery in Africa (1977) used the concept of 'institutionalised marginality' to relate slaves to kin systems and to society as a whole. They were referring to the ways that slaves were accommodated in a society while their lack of rights was underlined. In their view kin systems such as those in most of Africa with a continuing imperative to absorb people, i.e. 'open' kin systems, meant that over time, perhaps several generations, slaves were often integrated into a kin system while remaining marginal to the society as a whole. Their generalized identity as a slave thus did not disappear; they continued not to belong. At best, over a period they became 'half-strangers'. Critics of this position have emphasized the continuing outsider character of slaves and thus the incompatibility of slavery and incorporation into kinship structures. If that were to happen, then the slaves were no longer slaves. Indeed it is argued that the worth of slaves lay in the fact that they could never become kin and could therefore be permanently exploited.

No simple resolution of this debate is possible but a number of points may be made. Firstly, by no means every kin system was absorptive, even in Africa, and certainly not in Asia, though Asian systems of slavery will be passed over in this discussion. Secondly, where they were absorptive, Miers and Kopytoff did not see the process of incorporation of slaves as dramatic because of the length of time it was likely to take. In addition they understood full lineage members to be both *in* the lineage and *belonging to* the lineage and able to be transferred to others or pawned in payment of a debt. This was no doubt particularly true of junior members of the lineage. Yet it surely remains necessary to distinguish this situation from the exercise of rights over outsider-slaves and their children. The potentiality was no doubt there for permanent enslavement in the range of treatment that could be meted out to junior kin. But slaves were already slaves and, as Miers and Kopytoff recognize, many slaves never began to move along the continuum from slavery to kinship. Thirdly, the issue of incorporation has to be understood in terms both of the structural differentiation of the position of slaves and the attitudes or sentiments that developed towards them in a variety of circumstances in small-scale social worlds. Marriage of slaves to free lineage members, or a slave woman becoming a concubine and producing children, resulted in a change in the structural position of the slave. The slaves were no longer, except in very grave circumstances, in danger of being sold on. Their children were likely to become free and so was the slave in Muslim societies – at the death of the partner if not earlier. As this suggests, it was rather easier for female slaves to be incorporated than male because of their reproductive role. On occasion the slave's movement through the process of incorporation could be symbolized in gestures or ceremonies reminiscent of practices for full kin members such as the shaving of hair and naming ceremonies. It is unlikely, though, that any unambiguous indication of 'free' status in the lineage took place. Slaves who had been part of a household for a long time or had been born in the house were perhaps in a better position to achieve shifts in relation to the kin through marriage or concubinage than recently brought in slaves. They were apt to be culturally more *akin* to their masters than strangers. The sheer familiarity of some slaves to their individual or corporate owners no doubt affected attitudes towards them even when they remained structurally marginal. 'New' slaves, if female, were liable to be put under the authority of senior wives who probably worked them hard and others, especially males, since they did not constitute a reproductive loss to the lineage, could be made available for ritual sacrifice. Whatever the degree of incorporation, if any, that individual slaves attained, however, the collective social memory retained knowledge of who had been a slave, even when individuals had moved beyond that status. And it had practical effects. Slaves of the Sena People of Mozambique who had acquired kin links through marriage, and in effect been manumitted, none the less encountered forms of discrimination. They could be allocated less desirable hut sites and plots of land and treated with an element of contempt. In serious social crises such as dearth they might even be in danger of being sold. Neither structural shifts in the position of the slave in relation to the kin network nor changes in attitude toward him or her entirely erased the degradation of the past.

The features of some societies containing slaves, though they were not slave societies, reflected at certain periods incipient or actual changes that made plain the separate processes that converged when a slave society developed. The creation of subordinate lineages in some societies was a step towards the organization of slaves for the purposes of production rather than social status or political prestige and influence, though they might be that also. These forms of subordination were located in both agriculture and commerce, as in the trading companies of the Niger Delta and the Zaire. They foreshadowed the primary use of slaves for economic purposes in slave societies. But in parts of Africa in the later eighteenth and nineteenth centuries they were also ways of containing a body of slaves in societies that had not yet developed the scale and kind of economic activities that required their organization for production outside the kin system. Had that kind of economic development occurred then the inhibiting features of the kin form and idiom, notably (and especially in Muslim societies) moral restraints on the sale of children or of partially incorporated slaves, would have been evidently frustrating to slave owners. Systematic supply of slaves was also possible before the full operation of a slave society. A trickle and then a small stream of African slaves flowed into tobacco cultivation in parallel with white indentured servants and small farmers in the Chesapeake region of British North America in what was a society with slaves until the 1680s despite the existence of an organized slave trade. Similar was the movement of slaves from the south in the nineteenth century to the edge of and into the Sahara where they performed domestic tasks in the camps of the Saharans and then worked livestock and cultivated date palms without a full-scale slave society developing. But once the system of slave supply was in place numbers could be increased rapidly as conversion to a slave society took place. Capital accumulation and, at least in modern slave societies, the development of forms of credit were necessary to the investment needed to foster a large-scale commodity producing slave system. But when capital was available its use did not always lead to slave societies. In the eighteenth and nineteenth centuries the extensive trade network dominated by Indian and Arab merchants and centred on the Indian Ocean, linking it to the Persian Gulf, the Red Sea and the Nile Valley, generated considerable profits. Yet they were initially (in the first half of the nineteenth century) not invested in sufficient amounts, with the partial exception of Arab money in cloves in Zanzibar before the 1830s, to bring about a wholesale transformation in the nature of production. Creating slave societies along the East African littoral was not good enough business; trading was too profitable to divert funds from it into production. Another area of the same region, the Persian Gulf, in the same period and involving some of the same groups, illustrated ways in which slave labour could be quite extensively employed without a slave society fully emerging. Omani Arab merchants supplied slaves to the Gulf to work in agriculture, shipping, military and commercial activity. But the very malleability of slavery, a recurrent theme of this book, told against the establishment of a full slave society. Bodies of slave workers were deployed to fill temporary shortfalls in labour in different sectors without transforming any of them. Where other kinds of labour performed adequately slaves did not penetrate. In the Gulf they were not associated with new or newly desired commodities and new markets.

Elsewhere those were often precisely the additional economic features that were integrally bound up with the maturing of slave societies. Not all the commodities were absolutely new to Europe but it was the elastic European demand for precious metals and staples such as sugar, rice, tobacco, coffee, indigo and cotton that was necessary for the development of slave societies in the Americas from the sixteenth century onwards. The early, failed economic history of Barbados in its search for a crop of sufficient quality to be marketable in Europe in the face of competition from other developing American regions, until it settled on the cultivation and processing of sugar cane, is instructive in this regard.

The general conclusion to be drawn then is that, because slavery was such a malleable institution, the employment of slaves in more complex societies than those based on the household or the lineage system was widespread. This did not mean that all such slaves were part of slave societies. Slave societies in their economic aspects, only came into being when there was a convergence in the same period and the same area of the separate factors outlined above. They can be listed as an organized system of slave supply, insufficient controllable and affordable labour of other kinds, resources of capital attracted to invest in the slave system and commodities able to be produced for which there was an elastic demand. The result was a major productive role for slaves.

When each slave society is examined more closely it proves to have its own peculiarities in the economic sphere and, to a limited degree, in the structural location of slaves in relation to the rest of the population. In classical Athens after Solon's reforms the slave-*barbaroi* that traders brought in were relatively cheap, costing perhaps the equivalent of the wages for half a year of a free artisan. Though waged work was not unknown, and craftsmen with particular skills or 'professionals' providing certain services had some status, the general labourer (doing work slaves might do) was regarded with contempt. They were probably not available in large numbers. Neither they nor other kinds of arrangement, such as tenancy, constituted a full alternative to slaves for many Athenians. There remains scholarly controversy over the extent of slavery in classical Athens but little doubt exists that substantial landowners, often members of the political and intellectual elite, made considerable use of slaves in agriculture as well as in their urban households. Discussion has focused more on how widespread economic use of slaves was beyond this class. Since most Athenians gained their living from the land and most of them were small landowners the issue is of some moment in relation to Athens as a slave society. While it cannot be demonstrated with certainty, it seems quite likely that the numbers of slaves present in the society cannot be accounted for simply as the agricultural slaves of the small number of large landowners and as urban domestics and miners at Laureion. If that were so, a substantial surplus would have had to be generated to feed a large body of agriculturally non-productive people. And it would have to have been achieved mainly by family-worked peasant farms. This seems unlikely. When we recall the relative cheapness of slaves and recognize that when the *hoplite* (the modestly prosperous farmer in military guise) went to war he probably took a slave batman with him, then quite widespread ownership of small numbers of slaves appears plausible. Moreover, the smaller farmers carried on mixed and seasonal agriculture – grains, olives, wine, fruit and vegetables and a few animals – requiring some phases of intensive labour probably beyond the capacity of the family alone. Even if some farm families did not have one or two slaves of their own they may well have had to hire one or two at times of pressure to supply the urban market. All this would suggest that the use of slaves in Athens was extensive and that the influence of slavery was quite pervasive. An important aspect of its pervasiveness seems to be registered in the sharp distinction that Athenians drew, particularly after Solon's reforms, between citizens and non-citizens. To repeat a point made earlier, not only were citizens thereafter almost never enslaved, and certainly almost never retained as slaves within Athens, but after that boundary was so sharply drawn ordinary Athenians more evidently behaved as active citizens of the *polis*. The rights and freedoms of citizens advanced as barbarian slavery and the second-class status of free non-citizens were entrenched. It was possible, but not common, for a slave to rise to the status of a freedman or woman. But the distinction between free citizen and slave was underlined in that the harshest kind of labour to which a man could be subjected in Attica was work in the silver mines at Laureion; it was confined to slaves or their temporary equivalent, prisoners. This line was less permeable than the free lineage member–slave boundary in many societies with slaves discussed earlier.

Within the overall structure of slave societies there were significant differences in the Roman case as compared with the Greek. The Roman Empire as a whole was not a slave society. In the first two centuries CE there were some slaves in rural society in the provinces and a greater proportion in provincial towns. But kinds of dependent labour other than slaves probably performed most agricultural work in the distant reaches of the empire. The core lands of the Italian peninsula and Sicily were the classic site of the large estates, or *latifundia*, worked with numerous slaves. It was here that other forms of unfree labour had disappeared. The elite expended their gains on good agricultural land and country residences not too far from the centre of power. Rome and the other urban centres within reach of the estates, and sometimes Roman military units, contained considerable numbers to be supplied with wine, food, leather and wool goods and many of them to be provided with state grain handouts. The towns were also the location of slave artisans, domestics and providers of a variety of services. The flow of slaves into the system came primarily from war and military expansion, beginning with the wars during the Republic that brought Rome control of Italy and then the Mediterranean. For much of the republican period war captives who became slaves were often relatively near neighbours of the Romans and this may have contributed to the tradition of the somewhat more porous boundary between free and slave in Rome than in Greece. As the Empire grew more extensive and heterogeneous so one method of encouraging political coherence in an increasingly unmanageable political structure was the extensive granting of citizenship. This was not primarily intended to benefit slaves but citizenship following manumission was, none the less, a discernible path followed by slaves who had held positions of responsibility. Their numbers, however, should not be exaggerated.

Initial development of the British Caribbean slave societies took place after the African slave trade to the Americas was already well established. Along with the Dutch, British traders began to be involved in it before they needed to carry supplies to their own territories. Early settlement and development of British islands in the first half of the seventeenth century was the product of the convergence of aristocratic and mercantile capital, maritime enterprise and intermediary creole settlers familiar with the economic and cultural interactions of the Atlantic rim. Returning to Barbados as our example, we note that before, and for some years into, the 'sugar revolution' of the 1640s white indentured servants (and convict and refugee elements) were more prevalent in the labour force than were imported African slaves. Once landowners had discovered sugar as a commodity with an expanding European market – having failed earlier with tobacco and cotton – then slaves rapidly became a majority of the labour force, smaller proprietors were pushed to the margins and labourers who had worked out their indentures departed for more promising climes. As the system matured slave owners, overseers and other whites providing necessary services for the sugar plantation economy constituted a small minority in societies numerically dominated by a mass of African and some locally born slaves. By 1750 in Barbados, out of a total population of just over 80,000, slaves numbered some 63,000 and whites almost 17,000. Although Jamaica's trajectory as a plantation slave society had only begun in the 1680s, at the mid-point of the eighteenth century it maintained almost 128,000 slaves out of a total population of 142,000. In 1830, late in the slave period, the contrast was even starker. The total Barbadian population was a little over 102,000 and, of the total slaves, numbered 82,000 and whites almost 15,000. At the same date the Jamaican population totalled

378,000 of whom 319,000 were slaves while only 19,000 were whites. In both territories the remainder was made up of free coloureds. Where owners and their associates formed such a small minority of the whole, and when the population balance within the group was heavily male, a mixed-race population early emerged. The white minority progressively came to need an intermediate stratum to perform some of the functions of the society, but it is striking for how long the mixed race or 'coloured' group that usually undertook non-field tasks remained slaves. They had the responsibility of being in charge of the organization of groups of other slaves around the plantation, or if they were male did skilled artisan work as, for example, carpenters, boiler-men and coopers; if they were women they filled senior household roles. But neither their colour nor their occupations enabled them easily to move out of the slave class. The artisans might move about since they were sometimes hired out to others for periods and lived away from the plantation and their owner. But clear evidence emerged in legislation of the fears of owners that these slaves experienced too much freedom of action in practice. Legislatures tried to enforce residence under the eye of the master. The extent of movement into the freedman class during the most expansive period of sugar production was very limited. When we return to the population figures of Barbados and Jamaica, we find in 1750 in the former only 235 free persons of colour and in the larger island just over 2,000. In the mid-1780s Barbados registered 838 freedmen (mostly of mixed race) and Jamaica, a decade earlier, counted 4,500. However, in 1830 the figure for Barbados had risen to 5,300 and for Jamaica to 40,000. This strongly suggests that only as the economic dynamism of sugar declined in these older British islands did the boundary between slave and freedman status become more permeable, especially for some of the mixed-race population. Then the larger freedman group was able to increase naturally. There was a marked contrast with the Hispanic Caribbean territories of Puerto Rico and Cuba. There freedmen and women were proportionately a larger part of both the free and total populations in the later eighteenth century but the reasons for this indicated that the economic factor was not all-powerful in accounting for the completeness or otherwise of the barrier between slave and freedman. Substantial white and free mixed-race populations (including some freed people), increasing naturally, existed before the chronologically late sugar (and to an extent coffee) revolutions took place in these islands. There was also more generous legal provision for slaves gradually to buy their own freedom, the system of *coartación*, adding to the numbers of freed people. But comparison of the balance of freedmen to slaves between the late eighteenth century and 1830, when the sugar boom was well under way, showed a dramatic shift towards slaves and allows supposition of a higher barrier between slave and freedman status. This is confirmed in evidence of the constriction, without complete closure, of the operation of slave self-purchase. Despite variations then, the structures of Caribbean slave societies underlined the separation of the slave stratum from the rest of society but indicated some white accommodation to mixed-race groups, rather than blacks, when economic pressures were less strong. At times of rapid economic expansion the boundary separating slaves from freed and free was more sharply drawn and took only minor account of differences of colour amongst the slaves.

The British North American colonies and then the United States in the nineteenth century provided some variations on these various aspects of slave societies but confirmation of the main structural features. Before the 1680s the Chesapeake was the scene not only of a mixed white and black working population but also of social, sexual and cultural intermingling even after legislation had begun to establish racial discrimination in law. Yet the shock of Bacon's rebellion in Virginia in 1676, drawing support from amongst both whites and blacks, and combined with the continued growth of the market for tobacco, constituted a turning point in the development of a slave society in the Chesapeake. Slaves had already begun steadily to assume the work of white indentured servants and after the rebellion the tendency accelerated. In the 20 years following the defeat of Bacon's 'Choice and Standing Army' about 3,000 slaves flowed into the Chesapeake. Then, in the last few years of the century, even more slaves flooded in than in the preceding two decades and double that in the first decade of the new century. Indentured servants, were anyway, more and more attracted to service and eventual grants of land in Pennsylvania from the early 1680s onwards and the absence of competing slave labour may have been an added attraction to them. Small farmers had also been moving on. At the end of the century about a third of all workers in tobacco in Maryland and Virginia were slaves and a higher proportion on some of the larger estates that the new planter class had consolidated. The work force in the staple crop sector was rapidly becoming both slave and African.

The creation of a slave society in the lowcountry of South Carolina illustrated that the experience of the impact of slavery in colonial North America was not, however, completely homogeneous. Almost contemporaneously with the opening up of the lowcountry from the 1670s onwards masters entered with slaves from Barbados, then received traded slaves from elsewhere in the West Indies and Africa. There was little parallel with the initial 'creole' phase in the Chesapeake of a society with slaves with a mixed labour force, predominantly small- and medium-sized properties and the production of a staple alongside other commodities. The main reason for this was the shift to the cultivation of rice (with some indigo and also hemp for naval stores) in the lowcountry already apparent at the end of the century. Cultivation was carried out on large plantation units, initially on well-watered high ground, but then along the difficult low-lying shoreline and river estuaries and interior marshes of the area. In these circumstances the rise to dominance of African slave labour was tremendously speedy. Conditions of work were so harsh and disease-ridden that they offered no attractions to European labour; native Americans were deemed inappropriate even when they were available and African slaves were perceived as hardier. In some cases they were valued for possessing knowledge and skills from their homeland helpful to mastering the techniques of rice production. At the time of the Stono Rebellion of slaves in South Carolina in 1739 the bulk of the labour force was slave. In many coastal districts blacks formed a demographic majority and, apart from a thin urban layer of light-skinned creole slaves who had had less opportunity than in the Chesapeake to establish themselves as a distinctive stratum, overwhelmingly they were of recent African origin. The accompanying processes are by now familiar. Large units for staple production were consolidated; what small, white farming class had already become established moved inland. An alien labour force, separated by colour signifying racial difference and inferiority to slave owners, and patently at this stage of their American experience culturally distant from them, was held at bay and disciplined. Slave society had arrived.

As to the line between slave and freedman, the American experience after the establishment of slave societies points to both regional distinctions and differences according to period in its permeability. Even at the moment of some increase in the movement of slaves out of slavery in the age of the American Revolution, the line based on race and signified by colour remained as sharp as ever and minimized the overall effect of an increased incidence of freedmen and women. The increased number of freed people was largely restricted to the Chesapeake or Upper South and was the product both of initiatives in self-purchase and manumissions on the part of masters registering the ideological contradictions inherent in slave owning in the midst of a struggle for liberty. Between the mid-eighteenth century and the first American federal census of 1790 the free black population in Maryland grew threefold and then increased by 200 per cent more up to 1800. In the neighbouring state of Virginia the free black population grew by perhaps five times in the course of the 1780s and more than doubled again up to 1810. Yet, even at the end of this process, in the Upper South as a whole free blacks comprised no more than 10 per cent of the total black population of the region. In addition, legislators imposed restrictions on freedmen and other free blacks to underline the point that they were not the equals of whites. Slavery maintained the whip hand too, in the sense that, to avoid isolation between hostile whites and the large slave majority amongst African-Americans, freed people associated with slaves and built joint community institutions with them. In so doing they reinforced white perceptions that there was little difference between the free and the slave amongst Upper South blacks and that they should be held at a similar social distance.

In the Lower South (lowcountry South Carolina and Georgia) in the same era there is even less evidence of slaves crossing the boundary into legal freedom, let alone social acceptance. The exceptions were a relatively small mixed-race urban group released by masters who were often their fathers or other blood relatives. But, in an environment of even more rooted hostility to any signs of African-American dissent than was the case in the Upper South, their only space for manoeuvre lay in patterning their lives on, and thus displaying their loyalty to, the white slave owners and non-slave owners alike. Some of the free coloured population achieved slave ownership themselves but the majority were confined to some categories of artisan work (in the face of white fears of competition) and provision of services. Overall, the few escaped at the cost of accepting that their own survival depended on the rigorous enforcement of the line between slave and free, reinforced by colour and cultural distance. This latter was rendered more visible and audible as the result of the importation of new Africans in the years before the closure of the foreign slave trade to the United States in 1808.

Despite the natural increase in the American slave population to which contemporaries were already alert, the closure of the trade from the West Indies and Africa was not conducive to any greater movement across the line between slavery and freedom in the first half of the nineteenth century. Indeed, the dynamic expansion of cotton production and its geographical spread to the west and south-west, with its voracious demand for extra slaves, indicates the opposite. Relatively liberal, though not generous, manumission regulations in the late eighteenth century gave way to more restrictive laws by the 1830s and, except for some areas in the border states between North and South, prohibition was virtually complete by the 1850s. It is tempting to link this restriction of flows out of slavery with the ending of flows in through abolition of the external trade. At any rate the effect of official elimination of manumission was partial compensation for abolition at a period of economic expansion. Structurally, therefore, slave society in most of the American South in the nineteenth century maintained a very sharp line legally between slaves and the rest of the society. It was made more enforceable through a colour code that tried to recognize only white and black. And, as will become apparent in the next chapter, the notion of racial difference fed ideological justifications bolstering the system. None of the slave societies whose structures have been outlined in the last few pages made it especially easy for slaves to pass over into the free category. But, structurally, the American system appears more closed than most. The extent of manumission in the earlier centuries of the Roman Empire should not be overestimated, but when it did occur freedmen were able to attain citizenship and could anyway, since they were usually not obviously distinct from the rest of the population, and could melt away when they had secured their freedom. None of this was true in the American case. In relation to Rome ancient historians have been inclined to argue that slave awareness of some limited permeation of the line dividing slave from free statuses may have had some stabilizing effect upon the slave society. This is not an argument that plausibly can be applied to the American situation. What the closed off character of American slavery meant for the stability of the slave society and its relevance to how slavery came to an end will be pursued later.

As earlier discussion indicated, societies with slaves, though often relatively small in scale, illustrated the extensive range of roles that slaves undertook. The balance of slave activities depended on the character and prominence of particular households or lineages. They ranged from royal advisers and 'queen mother', to sexual services, to soldiering, and to a variety of daily economic activities often carried out alongside their owners or free lineage members. Although the main body of slaves in slave societies worked economically as producers, to varying degrees in different slave societies they also performed other functions. There are three areas to be explored on this issue. What were the kinds of economic activity slaves characteristically engaged in and were there any peculiarities associated with slave occupations? What of non-economic functions and especially the significance of slaves holding positions of authority in civil and military spheres? Why was the range of slave occupations so much greater in some slave societies than others?

Large numbers of slaves working in agriculture have been central to slave societies. The cultivation of particular crops for distant sale was, of course, the main purpose of slave societies in the Americas and involved the range of commodities previously mentioned, but notably sugar, cotton and coffee. Slaves worked different staples in broadly similar circumstances far distant in place or time from the slave societies of the Americas. Zanzibar and Pemba exported cloves in increasingly vast quantities from the 1820s onwards. East African coastal plantations sold coconuts, oil seeds and some gum copra (for varnish). Much earlier the farms and *latifundia* of the ancient world were the source of olives, wine and meat and hides from livestock. Yet in the interstices of staple production slaves were also often responsible for foodstuffs to feed themselves and their owners as well as urban and other distant markets. Many of the larger agricultural units, or particular districts, in slave societies were more or less economically self-sufficient.

Widespread self-sufficiency in the agricultural sectors of slave societies also involved the use of domestic slaves and artisans in addition to those charged with overseeing slave work in the fields and elsewhere. Domestic work, usually done by female slaves, might well involve baking and making textiles or other household goods on top of household chores and personal service. In larger households there was greater specialization of function. In Athens the occupations included butlers, housekeepers, maids, doorkeepers, hairdressers and *paidagogoi* or tutors and attendants of male children. This, however, was small-scale compared with the grander Roman households. In the typical *familia rustica* or rural household Columella listed 35 separate named occupations (including field jobs). The size and complex organization of the urban household (*familia urbana*) could be as great. At one extreme the household of Livia, wife of Augustus, contained 50 separate named slave occupations. As extensive an array of slave domestic functions as this was only found at the top of a slave society that had reached a point of maturity. It is possible to illustrate the level of development at different moments of British Caribbean slave society through examining the character of its plantation households. In seventeenth-century Barbados, at the frontier stage of a slave society, it was reported that very few 'servants' were even permitted to enter the master's house. What this household might amount to is revealed in the inventory of goods of one such master, Matthew Gibson. He had four servants, but in addition was listed as having only a chest, a cracked kettle, two pots, several barrels, a sieve, a glass bottle and a pamphlet without covers. In contrast in late eighteenth-century Jamaica the planter, Samuel Long, owned two mansions. His Spanish Town house required a sufficient complement of domestic slaves to service a residence whose principal room was large enough to hold 60 chairs and seven tables. His slave domestic staff also probably reflected the emergence in Jamaica at that stage of a three-class, colour-based social order in that many of them would have been of mixed race. The size and complex structure of slave household staffs may have been exaggerated in the nineteenth-century United States and much of the domestic work on smaller plantations was probably done by slaves who also periodically worked in the fields. Undoubtedly, though, on the larger estates in the rice and sugar country something like the elaborate, hierarchically structured slave domestic staff of popular imagining, holding themselves at a distance from the field hands, did come into existence. That, as we shall see, had implications for the experience of a slave community. Most domestic slaves in most slave societies, of course, toiled in more modest households than this. But they were always a significant part of the slave body and with a distinctive experience of the institution.

Though agriculture, at least a major, large-scale sector of it, was at the core of slave economic activity in slave societies, manufacturing was also always a part of the picture. In Athens, in the substantial absence of a pool of free wage labour, the only alternative to owning or hiring slave workers in manufacture lay with the independent craftsman using family assistants. In the fifth century BCE most manufacturing took place in small workshops with perhaps up to ten slaves under the control of a master artisan. They might produce such items as pottery, knives, clothes or lamps. Larger-scale businessmen who did not work alongside their slaves sometimes owned bigger workshops. The orator, Demosthenes, was no doubt helped to pursue a public career with the proceeds of his inheritance from his father of two workshops, one of 32 cutlers and one of 20 couch constructors. The former slave, Pasion, owned a shield factory with 60 slave workers. There were substantial similarities in the workshop employment and organization of slaves in Italy, for example, in the production of the widely used pottery known as Arretine ware. At least two producers are known to have owned 60 slaves each and about 90 workshops have been identified in the vicinity of Arretium (Arezzo) where production began in the first century BCE. In these workshops, although the master may sometimes have worked alongside the slave, it seems unlikely that the slaves worked with free wage labourers. On occasion, however, and particularly on public works in the classical world, slave artisans such as carpenters and stonemasons do appear to have been fellow workers with independent artisans. The larger plantations throughout the Americas all had their complement of slave artisans, particularly carpenters, blacksmiths and stonemasons. They provided the added bonus to the master of hiring out fees and gave the slave a wider experience and some daily freedom of manoeuvre as he worked away from his home base. This was particularly true of artisans working in towns. In the nineteenth century, however, the workshop production of some kinds of agricultural implements and their better distribution may have lessened the need for slave artisan skills. This was certainly the case in parts of the American South. But slaves as groups also began to enter foundry or factory work or their equivalent, usually under the direction of whites but also sometimes working with them. They were part of the mixed labour force of the large Tredegar Iron Works in Virginia and integrated into South Carolina mills producing rough textiles for the southern market in the years before the American Civil War. In Cuba during the final generation of slave labour from the 1860s onwards, if the term 'industrial labour' is extended to control of steam-powered, mechanized processes in the most advanced sugar mills, then a core of industrial slaves emerged there too. There was, in other words, nothing inherent in the malleable institution of slavery to prevent its employment in an industrial context. The extent to which it occurred was a manifestation of the general character and problems of industrialization in a particular region, including the attitude of slave owners to industrial development, rather than the result of any peculiarity of slaves.

Mining in slave societies was not consistently carried on wholly by slave labour but slaves did form a major contingent of the miners. The largest individual holdings of slaves in Athenian society were the property of the biggest lessees in the silver mines of Laureion. When they were being most intensively exploited in the fifth century BCE a total slave labour force of many thousands may have been at work. The magnates Callias and Nicias made individual fortunes from the leases while contributing to the wealth of the state. Xenophon asserted that Nicias had 1,000 slaves hired out in mining. The slaves operated in every phase of the industry including management; a Thracian slave, Sosias oversaw Nicias's slave labourers. Many of the slaves themselves, to judge from an analysis of their names, were from eastern parts, including Asia Minor and especially such regions as Thrace and Paphlagonia where mining was an established industry. Slaves were a large part of the labour force in notorious Spanish mines in the Roman period whence stories of tens of thousands being employed have come down to us. A whole mining economy, growing with dramatic speed, was based on slave labour in the province of Minas Gerais in eighteenth-century Brazil. Although gold deposits were only discovered in 1690, by 1710 there were 20,000 slaves in the province and a similar number of whites. At the time of the first slave census in 1735 the slaves had passed the 100,000 mark. They worked complex sluice constructions and hydraulic machinery, even reconstructed banks and diverted rivers in addition to engaging in simple panning. When deposits of diamonds also came to light at the end of the 1720s large numbers of scattered small groups of slaves entered the region and in the second half of the century almost a quarter of a million slaves were involved in mining operations. The question presents itself: why were slaves so commonly and so extensively used in mining? There can be no definitive answer covering all the major instances. But two elements of an answer seem widely applicable. The physical conditions of mining were almost invariably extremely harsh. It is unlikely that sufficient voluntary labour could have been found. Since the lives of slaves did not usually merit much consideration, their deaths or incapacitation could be calculated to be worth the extraction of high-value precious metals and stones. But what was extracted was also usually of small bulk in relation to value. The potential for miners to cheat the mine operators was considerable so that, where it was possible, the toughest of disciplinary regimes was enforced. In theory, slaves rather than free men were the appropriate subjects of such a regime. In practice, in Brazil, away from the larger mining camps located close to known deposits, close controls often could not be imposed on slave prospectors. In consequence they negotiated to hand over fixed amounts of what they had found to their masters, paid their own costs and themselves profited from the rest. It is not surprising that masters accepted an extraordinarily high rate of slave self-purchase in the Brazilian mining areas and did not try to maintain the line between slave and free so long as the slave supply from other regions and the coastal ports continued.

When the master expected his slave to undertake merely brute physical labour he simply inducted him into it by gradually getting him to complete heavier and heavier tasks as he grew in strength. American plantation owners, for example, started children on weeding or gathering fuel at the age of seven or eight. As they grew older they did more and learned the limited skills they needed through observing their elders. But a slave's education in more specialized skills and knowledge was one of the functions provided through the master's household. Seneca tells the story of Calvisius Sabinus who, wishing to have slaves to entertain him or perhaps to be able to perform as tutors, had an outside scholar come to train a group of his slaves in memorizing Homer, Hesiod and the Greek lyric poets. Roman masters also ensured that some of their slaves, for business purposes, learned to read, write and calculate. In the agricultural sector of every slave society promising young slaves were set to learn useful ancillary trades, such as carpentry, as in effect apprentices of older slave craftsmen. Nor was the demeanour of an accomplished house slave to be discounted. In Georgia, just before the civil war, Charles C. Jones, Jr, wrote to his father, 'Will you please keep George, if convenient, with you on the Island, about the house as I do not wish that he should forget his training. I want him to acquire a *house look*, which you know is not the acquisition of a day.'

However they obtained the necessary knowledge, some slaves in the ancient world occupied positions far removed from physical toil. In Greece some possessed considerable commercial knowledge, acted as assistants to merchants and undertook commercial negotiations and business missions abroad. There were several instances of slaves becoming adept in banking practices by working with a master and then taking over the business on his death, in partnership with the widow. In Rome slaves, acting on behalf of their masters as financial agents, provided loans at interest. If they had sufficient resources they used the contacts they had established and also employed their own money as the basis for a banking business. Success in these areas was possible because the functions were necessary but were not thought appropriate to be performed by members of the elite. Yet they could expect their slaves or those owned by their friends to do what was required loyally and with discretion. If anything went wrong members of the elite might avoid being directly implicated. And slaves or former slaves who had served members of the elite well in business could expect recommendations from them to others. Cicero recommended several such former slaves to Sulpicius

Rufus, the governor of Greece, and requested particular favours for them.

More striking even than the commercial or financial activities of slaves were the public offices, sometimes the high public offices, they could hold. We have seen something of this in societies with slaves; it was also a feature of some slave societies. In Athens the slaves performing public duties were public or state slaves. Some of the tasks were menial – removing corpses from public places, keeping the roads in decent condition – and others were administrative and necessary to keep the machinery of government going. These included public account-keeping and guaranteeing the integrity of official standards of weights and measures. Yet, in the city-state in which citizenship was an active principle and the most cherished distinction of those who possessed it, these public roles were the responsibility of those who by their very nature were not citizens. What was the explanation? First of all, it is necessary to be clear about the kinds of offices the slave held in Athens. They were administrative and executive; they gave no scope for departures in policy not authorized by a magistrate or body of citizens. The precise characteristic needed for administrative tasks was the slave's social and political 'neutrality'; he could have no recognized attachment to any part of the body of citizens, he was therefore defined as belonging to them all. More pragmatically, this made the slave a useful watchdog over any magisterial corruption in office. Public slaves such as the police force of 'Scythian archers' were thought to be able to enforce the law and keep order on public occasions equitably. Slave officials also provided continuity of knowledge and experience in a system predicated on annual rotation in office. Given the nature of the city-state, however, the public offices imbued with recognised political authority had to be in the hands of citizens.

In the more autocratic political context of the early centuries of the Roman Empire the structural location of slave officials has to be understood differently, a difference directly related to slaves' access to high positions of great influence. The explanation will recall some aspects of palace slavery in societies with slaves. The slaves holding significant administrative offices did so because they were the emperor's slaves, members of his household, the *familia Caesaris*. Some of them looked after the emperor's property and private affairs, others formed the core of an imperial administrative staff. Their importance lay less in their official designation than in their closeness to, and possible influence with, the Emperor. They might hold junior pro-consular posts such as the governorship of a minor province, but never major political office as governor of an important province. They rather occupied significant positions within the household that had political implications. Imperial slaves and freedmen, for example, often acted as financial secretary and head of the imperial fisc or treasury. They were responsible for all the revenues accruing to the emperor and for overseeing expenditure on the army and navy, financing the often socially crucial distribution of corn and seeing that public works were funded. Their responsibilities, in other words, were not directly political but as agents of the emperor their work could have serious political consequences. Slaves also handled petitions and grievances addressed to the emperor and business to do with official correspondence. The imperial slave-officials were usually drawn from the more culturally advanced areas of the empire and in general conducted themselves competently.

Some of the reasons to be adduced for Rome's use of slaves in these important positions are similar to those relevant to Athenian society. The slave's lack of any social relations that had to be recognized, his entire dependence on the Emperor's favour, his lack of a fully separate legal personality made him, in theory, an objective instrument of rule who could yet have responsibility for consequences projected on to him. Because he had no interests in society separate from his master the administrative slave could be moved about, his duties altered, his work varied and still be expected to show utter loyalty. Although the reality must often have been less clear-cut than this suggests, these factors probably made for an efficient bureaucracy.

The exercise of such power and influence by a category of people so despised does, however, demand more explanation. There is an important difference between the situation in Athens and that in Rome in the early empire. The Athenian public slaves acted on behalf of the city and in support of the elected magistrates; the administrative slaves in Rome belonged to, and acted on behalf of, the emperor. The different political context tied the slaves to the imperial fortunes and the actions of an autocratic emperor and at times of political difficulty made them targets of hostility. Their position was therefore vulnerable not only because the emperor might dispense with them but because a new ruler might well identify them as a malign element. Claudius's successor brutally eliminated his chief slave administrators. These considerations emphasize the point that was particularly true in the first century of the empire: if there had been any real alternative to the use of imperial slaves in senior administrative roles it would probably have been taken. But there was not. The old Roman senatorial aristocracy and the equestrian order both manifested an ethic of service to the state, an ethic with a reverse side that regarded *personal* service (even to the emperor) as incompatible with honour. The kinds of posts filled by senior slaves were ones the upper class refused in favour of pro-consular roles. Only with the passage of many decades did this class hostility to personal service to the emperor decline.

In the later empire the court eunuch (a slave or sometimes freedman) emerged as a figure able to undertake some of the tasks earlier performed by slave administrators. They were perhaps even more closely tied to the emperor than their predecessors. Presumably from outside the boundaries of Rome, since castration was forbidden within the Empire, they were literally unable to generate familial and kin connections in Roman society. They were isolated from all links of loyalty except to their ruler. They could serve him well when he might be sceptical (with good reason) of his military commanders and the senatorial notables. Similar factors played a part in encouraging other rulers to make use of slave eunuchs in high positions, notably in Byzantium and numerous Muslim states in Africa and the Middle East, including the Ottoman Empire. Eunuch advisers, though no longer technically slaves, were to be found at the Turkish court as late as the end of the nineteenth century. Ironically, there is more than one historical instance of the usefulness of such highly placed slaves to rulers faced with the opposition of notables turning into a form of constraint. The more a ruler came to depend on eunuch and other slave advisers and bureaucrats, the more he was likely to encourage the hostility of the traditional political and social elite. He thus became the more isolated and relied more on his slaves than they on him. Their advice and influence over him sometimes translated into a measure of control.

This was even more probable as an outcome when the elite slaves included leaders of military slave units. From the perspective of rulers, slave military units with slave commanders had much to recommend them. The considerations that follow applied equally in societies with slaves and slave societies. Military slaves were supposed to owe exclusive loyalty to the ruler. Drawn from outsiders, they were specially trained and sometimes granted privileges not available to other slaves. The Ottoman janissaries offer a prime example. These military units came into being as the result of the carrying off of Christian children from subject peoples, often in the Balkans. Once removed from their native background they underwent conversion to Islam, received military training and developed a strong corporate identity. Their loyalties were transformed, focused and put at the service of the state. They, and even less elaborately organized slave military units, could extend the power of the ruler and the authority of the state without being constrained by any intermediate loyalties. Military slaves then could be a powerful instrument against recalcitrant aristocrats as well as being successful tax collectors and guarantors of internal political and social order. They performed these functions severally and in combination in many of the Sudanese states in the eighteenth and nineteenth centuries. They also had the frequent advantage of reproducing themselves through the military acquisition of more outsiders who were then inducted into the system. However, the requirement for military success of a strong corporate loyalty amongst the slave soldiers and their separation from the rest of the society often turned their loyalties towards their own slave commanders. The recurrent result was for slave generals to seize power. Mamluk sultans and emirs ruled Egypt, Syria and western Arabia for 250 years before the Ottoman conquest of the early sixteenth century, after they had initially acted as politico-military support for existing rulers. And they maintained their political and military grip for so long in part through the strict methods they used to reproduce their military units. They refused to incorporate their own locally and free-born sons but acquired recruits externally with the promise of the kind of future achievement of freedom that they had themselves experienced. They created a bond with and between the next generation of Mamluks by repeating the process of creating in outsiders a distinctive identity separate from the rest of the society into which they had been brought.

Slaves have acted in a military context in less spectacular ways.

In the slave societies of Athens and the Roman Republic military service was in both cases seen as a duty of citizens and normally barred to non-citizens, and certainly to slaves. They were permitted ancillary duties as orderlies and batmen to citizen-soldiers but only in military crises, when manpower was insufficient, do they appear to have fought. Slaves were part of the Athenian forces at Argusinae in 406 BCE and a component of Roman units in the desperate circumstances in the Punic Wars after the defeat and losses of Cannae in 216 BCE. Even so the connection between citizenship and the duty to fight for the homeland was felt to be so strong that slaves, who by their nature were outside the political community, were manumitted before they took up arms or promised freedom if they fought bravely.

Wars and civil conflicts have provided occasions when slaves have been given arms by one or more sides in the hope of gaining advantage. The War for American Independence from 1775 onwards saw both the British and the Americans prompt slaves to fight for their side and promise freedom to those doing so. Some of the promises were even kept. Slave forces were used in the struggle between the Portuguese and the Dutch over the sugar lands of north-east Brazil in the mid-seventeenth century.

We have already recognized that the larger the household containing slaves in both societies with slaves and slave societies, the more complex its organization. An almost axiomatic principle of organization was the distribution of tasks according to gender, though where the distinction was made separating male from female tasks varied somewhat from one culture to another. In general, but by no means invariably, male slave roles looked out beyond the confines of the household (they might be messengers or porters) and female roles were more domestic and often involved serving or assisting the free women. In such cases slave women could move outside the physical confines of the household when, as in Muslim communities, their mistresses rarely did but domestic duties required it. In some societies with slaves in the western Sudan the slave women engaged in the purchase of goods for the household or sometimes took household-produced goods to market. Normally also when slaves born in the house and slaves bought in were both present the former were more senior, in closer relations with their owners, sometimes sexual, and charged with overseeing the work of the purchased slaves.

When limited amounts of agricultural work were one of the functions of slaves in societies with slaves, the slaves often worked with their owners or free members of the family, thus ensuring supervision of their activities. As part of the maintenance of the household women slaves did much of the cultivation of food crops in societies with slaves. This did not exclude their provision of small surpluses for local marketing. The development of myths about the suitability of different ethnic groups for particular kinds of work may also have helped shape the organization of slaves. The development of general ethnic and racial stereotyping was traced in chapter 2; around the Islamic Mediterranean over several centuries stereotyping more precisely focused on occupations. Indians and Nubians, it was believed, best carried out domestic service and small-scale commerce. The Zanj from East Africa and Armenians had unskilled agricultural and industrial work as their province. Within the domestic sphere amongst women slaves Muslim owners also tried to exercise a hierarchy of ethnic preferences. Preferences also tended to express the owners' sense of status. Any prospective slave concubine or wife of a member of the social elite ought to be white; in the substantial 'middle class' Ethiopian partners were common. Other African women were deemed suitable for the heavier household work.

Similar ethnic preferences operated amongst this category of slave owner in relation to the more public business of soldiering and administration. The Egyptian Mamluk regime militarily and in the ruler's household was primarily made up of white Circassians of slave origin. Turks were also favoured as soldiers. Ethiopians were prominent in the lower ranks of the sultan's or emir's entourage.

The largely economic functions of slaves in slave societies were reflected in a multitude of occupations. The institution gave owners the power to structure what a body of slaves did in whatever way they wished. Yet in the major sphere of slave work, agriculture, their organization across time and cultures indicates some remarkable similarities. Roman descriptions of the mode of operation of the slave villa in the first century correspond strikingly in outline to our knowledge of the West Indian sugar estate in the eighteenth century and the American cotton plantation in the nineteenth. The body of slave workers was divided into largely unskilled field workers, skilled artisans and machinery operatives and slaves in charge of groups of their fellows or in a more general supervisory position. The field labour was usually carried out by gangs working as a group and expected to work for a span of time or meet particular targets or complete particular tasks. This latter way of organizing work, the task system, gave individuals and groups of slaves the opportunity to make time for themselves and was distrusted by some slave owners for that reason. It was, however, widespread in the South Carolina and Georgia lowcountry as well as in Brazilian sugar. Its relation to independent forms of slave activity will be explored in the next chapter. The popularity of the gang system amongst masters is not hard to understand. Columella favoured it in Italy because he believed that it encouraged slaves 'to compete with each other and also identify those who are lazy'. Later analysts agreed. The gang's driver had to set an appropriate pace and maintain their rhythm throughout the period of work; their work was planned and overseen from the level of the estate as a whole by the foreman or overseer. He might be either a free man or, sometimes (often in Italy) a trusted slave. Cultural biases sometimes inflected, but rarely completely determined, the organization of estate labour in relation to gender. With the emergence of slave-worked estates on a larger scale in parts of Africa in the nineteenth century gang labour was sometimes mainly female, certainly for the most labour-intensive tasks such as weeding the rice plants. Elsewhere and at other times both men and women worked in the gangs, though they might be separate gangs with different kinds of work estimated to require different amounts of strength or special aptitudes. Cane cutting was normally a male occupation. Some women slaves gained a reputation for a peculiar dexterity in picking cotton. Almost universally, however, they were largely excluded from artisan work directly related to production of the staple. Instead, in the United States in the later eighteenth century they contributed significantly to household manufacture, spinning and weaving of clothing, on the estates.

Lagging behind, or incompetence, or obstruction throughout the centuries often brought the lash and the manacle. Yet, over a long period, agricultural writers, and the same was true of many practitioners, saw a place for incentives as well as punishments. In the fourth century BCE, for example, Xenophon advocated rewards to slaves of extra rations, better clothing and shoes for good work, once the slaves had accepted the basic discipline of their position. Nor did he neglect the rather cheaper resort of praising the slave. In 1974, in the widely discussed *Time on the Cross*, Fogel and Engerman interpreted the role of incentives to slaves on American cotton plantations as being very effective. On Brazilian sugar estates favoured slaves were further encouraged with rum, presents, extra rations and privileges.

Inevitably, there were also some differences in the organization of slave-worked agricultural units over time and in relation to the commodity produced. The Roman villa, probably at between 100 and 200 acres in extent, was staffed by a moderate number of slaves, though we have no precise evidence on which to base the estimate of an average unit. It is possible, though, that some casual free workers were taken on at harvest time. But clear evidence of very large slave workforces in agriculture suggests that they are related to the production requirements particularly of sugar and rice rather than to the mixed arable farming and stock raising that was the characteristic Roman pattern. Investment outlay for sugar and rice included substantial amounts for infrastructure and machinery – the grinding and boiling technology and the other accoutrements of the sugar house in the first case, sluices and banks in the second. Planters believed that the expenditure was only worthwhile if they planted out a large acreage in the expectation of a large harvest. That in turn meant that they needed to employ a large body of slave workers, much more so than in cotton or tobacco production. Only a few specialist free workers were taken on in addition to the slaves. West Indian sugar plantations frequently employed between 300 and 400 slaves and the only slave owners in the American South with more than 1,000 slaves produced rice in the South Carolina rice swamps. Many cotton producers in the United States, by contrast, barely (if at all) scraped into the category of planter, conventionally defined as a person possessing 20 slaves.

One further question remains for brief consideration in this chapter. Why, given the malleability of slavery as an institution, did some slave societies none the less make use of slaves in many more ways than others? More pointedly, why did Rome use slaves in elite positions when, say, the United States did not do so? Even if we restrict ourselves to this single comparison a number of factors need to be taken into consideration. We have seen that slavery emerged as the basis of a society in part because there were insufficient alternatives either in other forms of dependent labour or amongst the free. The point continues to have force in regard to whether or not slave societies deployed slaves in elite positions. The resistance of the Roman upper class to 'dishonourable' personal service to the emperor has been noted. The specialized education that some slaves received fitted them for administrative work. And, in a political system that was marked by the expansion of the emperor's power during the period when elite slaves were most widely used, they had the further qualification of personal dependence on him. There was of course no lack of willingness on the part of southern planters in the United States to rule their societies, even if much of their power derived from the fusing of political office with social prestige and economic prominence rather than the elaboration of bureaucratic authority. The planters assumed the right to rule and in so far as their ownership of slaves contributed to their social and economic position then the slaves facilitated their owners' rule. This was virtually the reverse of the Roman position where slaves replaced slave owners in areas of authority.

Roman elite slaves existed along with the large number working in fields and workshops. The function of the ordinary slaves was to provide a sufficient surplus to allow their owners whenever possible to live a leisured life, some part of which might be devoted to an appropriate form of public service. Slave and other production also had to meet the material needs of the portion of the population without access to land to avoid the danger of social disorder, a danger ever present in the minds of Rome's rulers. Satisfying that market was a political and social necessity. Thus slave economic activity was extremely important to Roman society but its importance did not reside primarily in fostering slave owners' pursuit of profits in a developed market system. In the United States slave production was market-oriented for economic reasons. Planters were interested in profits, as were their creditors, though economic success also brought social prestige and perhaps political influence. The American slave economy was linked to a competitive international economic system whose mode of operation enforced on owners concern with material progress. Despite, therefore, the shared importance of slave economic activity in both Roman and American slave societies, the purpose of the slave presence in the United States was bound to be much more simply economic than in Rome. Where slaves exercised power in American society was in the economic sphere as drivers and overseers; they were trained for production and its management and nothing else.

Discussion of societies with slaves and slave societies in this chapter has been mainly in terms of their structural characteristics and their economic organization. But to grasp their nature more fully we must now move on to analysing the character of slave owners' power and how slaves handled it in the master–slave relationship.

4

Stability and Disruption

In considering how the existence of slavery in a society affected its stability or contributed to periods of disruption the analysis of the relations between the master or his agents and the slaves has to take a central place. We need to examine how slaves were treated, how they experienced their treatment and responded to it. But, unless great emphasis is to be placed on the temperaments and individual characters of masters and slaves, about which there is little that can be said, we must establish an initial larger framework.

The balance between slaves and others in the total population was a pervasive factor, though difficult to give precise weight to, in the amount of attention political authorities paid to regulating slavery. The extent and nature of the state's concern with slaves, even if enforcement was comparatively lax, may well have had some influence on the owners' behaviour. So too could the religious culture of the society. In slave societies where production for the market was a major reason for the scale of slavery, the changing state of the market for the main commodities increased or eased pressure on both masters and slaves. How widely slave ownership was spread in a society was relevant to the breadth of support the institution commanded, not only from owners but from those hoping to acquire slaves. How secure a society felt about slavery influenced the relative firmness with which the boundary between slave and free was policed.

Focusing upon the more immediate contexts of master–slave interactions, it is clear that the conditions of life surrounding a slave's particular occupation and especially the production requirements of different commodities could significantly affect the substance of the relationship. A further nuance as to occupation and production was provided by the gender of the slave. Whether a slave worked largely on his own, in a group or as part of a large body was relevant to his experience of the institution and to the form of regime the master sought to impose. So too was the proportion of 'creole' or born in the house slaves to others captured or bought in. To what degree a body of slaves was made up of an ethnic mix also carried influence. These factors were bound to affect the frequency of contact between master and slave, the degree to which the owner thought strong discipline necessary and the personal tenor of any exchange. How physically close to the master a slave was normally located is hard to overestimate in its impact on mutual behaviour and attitudes.

On the sides of both owner and slave, and depending on their level of awareness, what they made of the larger social framework and specific events or contacts was filtered through their more general cultural attitudes and assumptions. Sometimes in the case of articulate slave owners or writers on slavery the assumptions attained sufficient coherence to be termed an ideology that presented the institution as an inextricable part of life. How slaves responded to their experience and, in the broadest sense, to how it was represented to them, was shaped in turn by their cultural outlook. That outlook was shaped in ways that the historian may find almost impossible to recover. Yet because the slave was often mute, in the sense of leaving little direct evidence to be interpreted, is no reason to conclude that he was passive in the face of the owner's actions or conceptions. The cultural resources he possessed, in part perhaps derived, or in modified form passed on, from the external society from which he had been taken, offered the slave an initial frame for understanding what was happening around him and a possible prompt to action. Some of what did or did not happen was at such a basic level that slaves' attitude to it was universal. This applied to aspects of the physical and material provision and the treatment a slave encountered. How the slave responded to more complicated situations usually expressed pragmatic calculation about what would lead to the best outcome in the context of both the slave's own distinctive priorities and the power of the master. No doubt, in some cases, the master's power and the pressure of his implicit or explicit view of the world did shape the slave's deferential and accepting response. Slavery was safe in the hands of a proportion of slaves. Others probably came to share some common ground with masters as a result of frequent interaction and a sense that there was much that could not be avoided. But many others as individuals, members of a group and sometimes even communally, continued to see themselves apart from and oppressed in the master's world. They were the slaves who disrupted the daily routine by resisting, even occasionally revolting.

In societies with slaves where slave owners were only a fraction of the population and their concerns carried no special weight the exercise of political authority on their behalf was not a significant factor. Punishment for helping a fugitive slave escape or for harbouring him was certainly quite widely found, but it may be that this should be understood more as an aspect of the protection of property than concern over property in slaves as such. When fugitives themselves were punished the responsibility was left with the master. This points to the problem in slave societies where slave owners exercised much more authority of grasping the meaning of state action in relation to slavery. How was the power of the state that maintained the interests of slave owners, but which also in theory fully respected their autonomy in dealing with their slave property, able to intervene seemingly to protect slaves against their masters? The point here is not the conceptual one made earlier, that is, the registering in the legal codes of the slave as both property and person, but the engagement of the state in facilitating the management and social control of slaves. A number of enactments in the Roman Empire under Augustus, Claudius and then again late in the first century introduced regulation into manumissions. They possessed features, such as constraints on indiscriminate manumissions of the kind that had taken place in the late Republic, that might be interpreted as attempting to bolster social stability by repressing slave aspirations. But such regulation also curbed the elite slave-owning class that in the past had hoped for political profit from mass manumissions. Legal limits on both manumissions during the life of the owner and in testamentary grants of freedom required selectivity on the part of the owner and promoted diligence and conformity on the side of slaves hoping to meet the master's approval and gain their freedom. Additional legislation regularized the intermediate status of freedom without citizenship but pointed the way to the freedman becoming a citizen through service to the state, marriage and the raising of a family. The effect, whatever the intention, of state intervention was to promote stability as regards slavery on terms desired by imperial policy makers rather than in the more narrowly defined interests of the slave-owning class. But it existed alongside legal marginalizing of slaves and their liability to judicial torture when caught up in the law even as witnesses. Roman political authority on occasion sought to foster the more socially responsible side of slave owners but there was no danger of tipping the balance of power against them. Nor in the later empire was there much sign of the Church, in its close relation to the Roman state, altering through its influence either the treatment of slaves in law or general practice. Church Councils sanctioned flogging as a standard penalty and Church Fathers pronounced slavery a corrective of evil in the slave.

Initially it might seem that Spanish and Portuguese authorities in Latin America and the Caribbean presided over a system more attuned to reining in the slave-owning class. They drew on the *Siete Partidas* and Manueline Ordinances containing clauses recognizing that the slave had certain minimal rights. These primarily related to personal protection and the retention of personal property though with residual rights to the property remaining with the master. Slaves were also assured of their right of access to the sacraments. Yet gradually over two centuries in Hispanic America, as the economic sectors of sugar and mining became so important, the fit between the actions of the state in Cuba and Brazil and the concerns of the slave owners became closer. Stability came to be associated with the imposition of further constraint on the slaves. Self-purchase in Cuba was recognized and then restricted. Free people of colour who might well have emerged through such a process earlier were treated with judicial ferocity at the slightest suspicion that they might be involved with slaves in any form of dissidence. The words of the British West Indian planter-historian Bryan Edwards applied as much to Hispanic America in the nineteenth century as they had earlier to the territories of the northern European powers: 'In countries where slavery is established, the leading principle upon which the government is supported is fear; or a sense of that absolute coercive necessity, which leaving no course of action, supersedes all questions of right.'

Paradoxically, in the early nineteenth century the search for stability in the British Caribbean was no longer as dependent on state-induced fear as earlier. In the seventeenth century when the West Indian slave societies were taking off, and particularly in the eighteenth when several of them reached their largest slave populations, the threat of the use of force was the main guarantee of social order. All the major European powers kept naval forces and substantial garrisons of troops in the Caribbean both because it was an important theatre of international conflict with rich island pickings for the victorious and to meet the anxieties of planter classes about internal security. They frequently asked for more and lamented any withdrawals. They saw imperial forces as making up some of the margin between their own modest numbers and the much larger slave populations, a concern present even in Cuba (with its more numerous white and free coloured groups) by the late eighteenth century. Slave owners were most directly integrated into the machinery of local state power through their commissions in the militias. They organized them in their own local districts and filled them with their neighbours. As early as 1657 Richard Ligon, the planter-historian of Barbados, wrote of his conviction that the volleys that the militia fired so terrified the slaves that they dared not consider any serious action. All free men in the British territories were expected to query anything untoward in the actions and movements of any black and to take part in searches of slave cabins and pursuit of fugitives. The good citizen was the mobilized citizen. Penalties inflicted on slaves for offences against good order were extreme. They were most evidently so in the aftermath of suspected slave plots or revolts when large numbers of slaves might be killed or judicially executed. This ferocity was the product of fear and intended to instil fear. Yet the more slaves adapted to an American environment and could no longer be seen as completely alien Africans and the more they gained some sense of the liberal movements of the Age of Revolutions, the less such heavy reliance on preserving stability through pure fear seemed plausible or worked. All the post-Napoleonic revolts in the British territories – Barbados (1816), Demerara (1823) and Jamaica (1831–2) – were primarily creole upsurges. Imperial rulers grasped this more willingly than the slave-owning elites. Whitehall gained limited and grudging acceptance from them for a policy of amelioration intended to maintain stability through giving slaves a stake in a policy of movement rather than stasis. Abolition of that symbol of both authority and degradation – the whip – and a promise of eventual freedom following on from the earlier recognition of greater freedom of movement and the right to keep property and establish a family sketched a strategy of limiting conflict through partial incorporation.

The story of the role of state power in the nineteenth-century United States combined greater rigidity with greater aspiration, largely unsuccessful, towards humane regulation. In the decades before the civil war the legislators of the elaborated slave codes of the southern states had nearly 200 years of legal experience to build on. Colonial law makers had begun to define the subordinate position of black slaves and free blacks from the 1660s onwards. They drew up early slave codes in the last decades of the century and revised and extended them in the first half of the eighteenth century. At the beginning of the revolutionary era in the 1760s colonial law, especially in the more southerly colonies, assumed that all black people were to a greater or lesser degree unfree. After their survival of and recovery from the shocks given to the slave system during the Revolution southerners further developed legal restrictions to control a numerically and geographically expanding slave population in the first half of the nineteenth century. The tightening of limits on manumission in all areas with substantial slave numbers, except in the border states between North and South, has already been mentioned. The unregulated movement and meeting of more than a handful of slaves was forbidden, as were bondsmen's independent business dealings and their access to help in becoming literate. Not all of these kinds of restrictions, devised with some variations in the separate states, had much impact in the localities. But at moments of perceived crisis, perhaps during rumours of a slave plot, they could bear down heavily on the slaves. When local enforcement was required then both slave owners and even other local white non-owners were expected to join patrols, question African-Americans and scrutinize their doings.

With the establishment and operation of the new federal government at the end of the 1780s, the powers of the national authority reinforced those of the local state over slavery. The new framework for a national government made no explicit reference to what was later to be known as the South's 'peculiar institution' but the interests of slave owners were catered for in several ways.

Although opposition to the foreign slave trade was widespread the loss of slaves who had fled or joined the other side in the upheaval of the Revolution determined South Carolinians and Georgians in particular to secure guarantees for its continuation. Under the Constitution Congress was prevented from interfering with the trade for 20 years. Masters had a right to have runaways returned from other parts of the country and the constitutional provision for the use of federal force to put down internal disorder could apply, and was assumed by many Americans to be primarily applicable to, the suppression of slave revolts. Perhaps most important because of its continuing significance, slave owners also secured a built-in political advantage through the agreement of the Philadelphia Constitutional Convention to slaves counting as three-fifths of a free person in the population-based calculation of representation in the federal House of Representatives. This advantage was also indirectly registered in the number of members of the electoral college from slave states who were eligible to choose the president. For much of the period before the secession of southern states from the union in 1860–1 the slave-owning interest made effective use of this constitutional and political leverage, sometimes in alliance with other groups. One instance was the simultaneous admission to the Union in 1820 of the slave state of Missouri with the free state of Maine and the mechanism of the Missouri Compromise line for dealing with similar problems over the following generation. Another was the successful maintenance of the internal slave trade, whose significance for the expansion of slavery has been indicated, despite the demands of its opponents that it be abolished under the federal government's regulatory powers in the interstate commerce clause of the Constitution. Supporters of slavery hoped that Texas would be a huge new area for the spread of slavery, and believed that this was best secured through the annexation of Texas to the United States. Both were brought to fruition in 1845 and the following years through the efforts of politicians from the slave states collaborating with other expansionists. The intellectual culmination of the planters' use of their political leverage was in the constitutional interpretation identified with John C. Calhoun of South Carolina who argued that the whole of the national territory was jointly owned by the separate sovereign states that had come together to form the Union. This meant in his view, a view never generally accepted outside the South, that slavery could be spread legally even into areas from which it had been removed. Although their opponents exaggerated their effect and understood political processes too simply, the slave owners' use of their power in national politics brought the charge that they were manipulating the federal government through a 'slave power conspiracy'.

Beside recognition of support for maintaining the stability and growth of slave society from controls imposed and policies pursued by state and federal power, one strand of historical interpretation has also stressed the complementary significance of protective regulation. Restrictions were legislated on the operations of the internal slave trade in some areas in gestures towards keeping slave families together, or at least in preventing the separation of small children from their mothers. Slave code phrases dealing with standards of food, clothing and shelter for slaves were rarely very specific but quite generous in tone. Efforts in law and sometimes in action were made to curb the killing and other physical maltreatment of slaves. There is no justification for dismissing this body of protective law completely. But, if it can plausibly be argued that law intended to control slaves was only unevenly enforced, there is no reason to suppose that more humane intentions were any more effectively made a reality. The most articulate advocates of reform measures were often ministers of religion who, even if slave owners, may have been a little removed from the everyday calculations of their more secular neighbours. Even during the crisis of the war, when some southerners wondered if God was punishing them for their failure to reform slavery, the reformers admitted they could make no headway in securing the legal recognition of slave marriage and the integrity of the slave family.

Religious traditions do, none the less, require further consideration as to their influence on slavery in its various settings. We have indicated at earlier points that Christianity in the Roman Empire did not significantly influence the way that slavery worked. As a generalization needing minor qualifications that remains true in Europe in societies with slaves up to the time of expansion into the Americas. The Church Fathers' conviction of the collective sin of slaves, that is, that slavery was a penalty for sin and those in the state of slavery were somehow peculiarly guilty, remained powerful in the early Middle Ages. Their true redemption would come through penitence. They must, therefore, have access to the sacraments. That recognized, there were no moral or theological problems for ecclesiastical bodies continuing to own considerable numbers of slaves. They were indeed seen as sources of wealth that could be used to aid the poor. St Paul's return of Onesimus to his master, Philemon, was taken as justification for the Church to refuse sanctuary to slaves. It is true that pronouncements of Church Councils urged humane treatment of slaves upon their masters and recommended manumission as an act of great piety. There were stories in saints' lives of such manumissions but no sign that such example and the Church's pronouncements had collectively had a significant effect on the manumission of slaves. Most slave owners were not saints. Some slaves were in a position to buy their own freedom from secular masters and the Church sanctioned it. But slaves owned by religious institutions were part of God's patrimony and not to be given up. The first of two areas in which the medieval Church offered criticism of slavery as part of the social order was of the excessively harsh treatment of slaves; in the late seventh century a council instructed clergy not to mutilate their slaves. The second was in the trading of slaves by Jews and the sale of slaves into their possession and that of heretics. It is difficult to know here whether the concern was over the slaves or the possible advance of Judaism or heresy. Finally, there is Marc Bloch's famous argument that might be advanced about any period when slavery and Christian evangelism have coexisted in the same society. He suggested that the Church's recognition that the slave had a soul inevitably led the slave to see himself, and for others to see him, differently; he was a human being. That there may have been some change in the mutual attitudes of free poor and slaves towards each other as a result of the slow but cumulative Christianization of the European countryside is suggested by the apparent increase in their unions by the ninth century. This suggests that slaves were not quite such outsiders as they had been. It was a mark of the continued erosion of slavery in western Europe but not evidence of Christianity as a general emancipating force.

The century of the foundations of European expansion in the Americas and the opening up of a new arena for slavery was also the century of the Reformation and Counter-Reformation. Yet, if the sixteenth century was a new start for Europeans geographically in the use of slaves, and to a degree also in the balance of the economic activities in which they used them, Christian ideas and practices in relation to the emerging slave societies initially changed rather little. Spiritual freedom was what mattered to the Christian. As has often been observed, the virtues he admired, such as obedience, humility and resignation, when translated into the outlook of slaves in a slave society, could easily recommend themselves to a slave owner as helping to secure his property and stabilize his society. Christianity of course continued to preach the spiritual equality of all believers, but only small numbers of radical sectarians understood the promise of the Gospel in relation to God's future kingdom to have any significance for social distinctions in life on earth. Luther and Calvin both sternly inculcated respect for established secular authorities and for private property. Luther, as his fierce denunciation of the Peasants' Revolt of 1525 indicated, utterly repudiated any interpretation of Christian liberty in terms of political or social liberty and of God's kingdom as a socially reordered earthly kingdom.

Both Reformation Protestantism and Counter-Reformation Catholicism regarded non-Europeans as heathens who provided an opportunity for evangelization. Despite the possible advantages of having Christians as slaves, some European slave owners in the Americas, particularly in Protestant areas, were uncertain about allowing the baptism of their slaves fearing that they might find it difficult to justify holding fellow believers in bondage. So long as they kept to this position they gave no opportunity for religion to influence the social order of slave society. But ecclesiastical authorities, the Bishop of London, for example, as the Anglican prelate responsible for the British North American colonies, reassured owners. Baptism within slavery was part of the process of bringing about a settled life and religious values to people believed to have been living in ignorance and morally degraded circumstances. Christianization and slavery were compatible. In British America only in the eighteenth century did West Indian and mainland planters reluctantly permit the introduction of religion to their slaves. Both resident clergy and missionaries knew that they had to concern themselves with the spiritual redemption of the slaves and steer clear of any discussion of the conditions of servitude. In the British West Indies when missionaries gave the impression to slave owners that they had attacked slavery, as did Shrewsbury in Barbados and Smith in Demerara, their chapels were destroyed and they were driven out or imprisoned.

An influential line of historical interpretation, going back in its modern form to Frank Tannenbaum's *Slave and Citizen* (1946), argues that the Catholic Church in the Caribbean and Latin America launched itself earlier and more energetically into converting the slaves than did Protestants. Further, they were able to affect the lives of the slaves for the better and thus indirectly contribute to social stability. One early and striking achievement of religious intervention had ironic consequences. On the mainland of Spanish America under the *encomienda* system Indians were early bound as labourers to a Spanish master. The Church, particularly in the person of the Dominican friar, Bartolomé de Las Casas, turned against the brutal treatment of the bound labourers and developed a fierce religious critique of the European colonists. Initially Las Casas thought Africans an acceptable replacement when he persuaded the Crown to begin a process of regulation leading to the end of Indian slavery and the *encomienda* system. African slaves, however, were less successfully protected. The emphasis in the historical tradition represented by Tannenbaum was on the logic of the Church's protective action flowing from its recognition that the slave had a soul and a moral personality. But the evidence, for example, in Cuba was that a mild paternalistic slavery could not withstand the impact of a full-scale market-orientated plantation system. Whether representatives of the Church in Hispanic America were sufficiently numerous, concerned or well placed to influence what went on in mines and on plantations may be doubted. When the demands of Catholic morality and religiously influenced law were inconvenient and stood in the way of the extraction of extra profit, it is not evident that either owners or the state met these demands.

States with Muslim rulers regulated slavery in more or less detail in harmony with the main precepts of Islamic law. In very broad terms such regulation assumed that the maintenance of good order entailed excluding Muslims from enslavement and offering some possibilities to slaves. As we have seen, the infraction of the rule against making fellow Muslims into slaves was recurrent and provoked much moral anxiety amongst good

Muslims. Sometimes rulers acted to reverse such infractions, particularly if the victim was a prominent figure. During the seventeenth century civil conflict in the West African state of Borno resulted in the sale to North Africa of a young man named Medicon. When his whereabouts had been established as a result of the efforts of his uncle, he was redeemed. But his uncle was the ruler of Borno. Such initiatives were not common and certainly not on behalf of ordinary subjects. Slaves were encouraged to become Muslims even if they did not undertake all observances. When they did so they were protected from sale, at least to non-Muslims. Owners were also urged to make provision for manumission of their own slaves on their deaths and during their lifetime to provide humane treatment and reasonable material standards. Slaves who felt they had been badly treated might be able to secure from a *qadi* in an Islamic court a judgement that could secure his freedom. But it is unlikely that this occurred frequently. Neither political nor religious authorities in Muslim states, however, were in a position to ensure strict enforcement of Islamic law in relation to slaves. As ever, the extent of social harmony depended a great deal on the circumstances of slavery and how the class of slave owners and individuals responded to them.

In the survey of structural conditions bearing upon stability in slave societies it is necessary, finally, to note the impact of market conditions for the prime commodities. They were one of the necessary limits within which other pressures operated. Cuba provides an excellent example of a society launching headlong into capitalist development on the basis of slave labour, its trajectory shaped by the historical opportunity to dominate the world cane sugar market. The brief British occupation in 1763 stimulated a burst of development; Cuba produced annually 14,500 metric tons of sugar at the end of the 1780s. Within 15 years the total was 22,000 tons and thereafter, with only minor dips in the trend, it moved relentlessly upwards. By 1840 production was 161,000 tons, in 1850 almost double, in 1860 at 533,000 tons and in 1870 over 700,000 tons. Fairly continuous strong market conditions in terms of both demand and price up to the 1860s fostered good profits, especially for owners of larger estates. They encouraged the introduction of the latest techniques in production and led to heavy capital investment in service railways, steam-powered mills and, of course, large numbers of slaves. In such a context the pressures to extract the maximum from the slave and supplementary indentured and free labourers were powerful. Schemes to enhance slave productivity included turning estates over almost entirely to young male labour forces, thus depriving the slaves of any possibility of family life. Barrack life on the plantations was intended to cut off slaves from external distractions and so contribute to the intense pace of work required to keep the much more efficient modern mills operating to full capacity. The new Slave Code of 1842 imposed a tougher regime than the old and the colonial government manifested a generally more rigid attitude toward social distinctions and social discipline. Social tensions and signs of instability in response to these pressures in turn intensified attempts at social control. Individual and group flight, maroon activity and conspiracy all accompanied the booming sugar market.

Whatever the resources and initiatives of the state, the impact of religion on the social order and the problems posed by economic conditions, slave owners and those speaking in harmony with them were compelled to represent slavery as an appropriate institution for whatever part it played in a particular society. Their justifications were to themselves, to non-slave-owning elements in the society and, in creating a social 'common sense' about slavery, to the slaves. The assumed and implicit, perhaps more often than the express, ideologies in support of slavery formed the cultural clothing of power relations in slave society. The extent to which the rest of the population, apart from the owners, silently internalized or partially accepted or rejected them helped shape the balance of stability and conflict in the society. Implicity, men of power and wealth in any society assumed that both they and those beneath them deserved their respective positions. It is doubtful, for example, that many of the Athenian elite reflected on the situation of the barbarian slaves at the mines of Laureion. They were a 'given', a part of the accumulation of things in everyday society. Herodotus appropriately listed slaves along with other mundane objects and possessions in his writings. Since possessing slaves and making use of them were part of the accoutrements of power and wealth, then in many societies the powerful acquired and treated slaves almost without thought. The assumptions of such owners were implicit in their actions and rarely publicly articulated. But there were always philosophers, men of religion and social commentators who considered the social world more conceptually amd expressly developed ideologies sustaining slave subordination; the next section of the chapter deals with them. But, although their thinking cannot be simply reduced to ideas at the service of the power and wealth of slave owners, nor were their views on slavery abstract speculation completely divorced from the existing social order. From the classical world on questions were periodically raised about the normal justifications for slavery but they fell far short of rejecting the institution. Rarely before the second half of the eighteenth century in Europe and North America did thinking about slavery among educated social elites depart drastically from received intellectual traditions both about slavery and social hierarchy more generally.

On their least sophisticated level ideologies sustaining slavery consisted largely of a derogatory stereotype of the slave. Had the 'big men' who assumed that slavery was simply a part of their surroundings been pressed to say why a particular body of people should be slaves, they might well have responded in terms of elements of the stereotype. Indeed elements of a similar slave stereotype were found in many societies and recurred over many centuries. Aspects, though never the whole, of the slave stereotype were also widely applied to other despised groups, notably women and peasants, whose social distancing through stereotyping likewise enabled any harsh treatment in the course of their subordination to seem less troubling. Slaves' stereotypical characteristics were implicitly, and sometimes explicitly, set against those of the master. The slave was concerned with the material and sensual aspects of life – food, drink, sexual activity and other pleasures. His physical appearance and even physical movements were visualized as revealing his 'low' character because he was thought of as ugly (appearance could be described in racially derogatory ways); he ran rather than strolled and had a characteristic habit of hunching his shoulders. His concern with the material indicated that he was deficient in the moral sphere. Thus slaves were thought of as cowardly, dishonest, lazy and amoral when not downright immoral. They also tended to be stupid and ignorant; their main recommendation was their capacity for physical labour, though it had to be directed. Compared with the free man, and particularly the master, they were passive, lacked self-control and above all were deficient in the rational faculty and thus incapable of initiative, planning ahead and directing others. In other words, they were believed to lack the full attributes of humanity and were conventionally compared to animals or birds. Herodotus, speaking of a particular group of slaves, remarked, 'Their language [normally thought of as an especially human attribute] can not be compared to any other, but only to the cry of the bat.' The African Anyi people regarded the 'marriage' of slaves as needing no ceremony 'since they are like chickens and cocks who keep each other warm'. This sort of characterization of the slave was current not only in the ancient world and in parts of Africa but was found among Arabs and in the Jamaican and American stereotypes of Quashee and Sambo – lazy, deceitful and irresponsible, but also humble, docile and loyal.

Elements of the stereotype fitted into more elaborate ideologies of slavery. In Greece, compared with the reason, foresight and courage of the citizen of the *polis* the barbarian slave had only the capacity to perform tasks as directed by others. In explanation of this convenient circumstance the increasingly ethnocentric assumptions of Greeks in the fifth century BCE were related by Hippocrates and his followers to the human qualities fostered in the city state in comparison to barbarian monarchies. They also linked various qualities and their own superior aptitudes to climatic variations between countries. These arguments reached towards conclusions implicit in Plato and explicit in Aristotle; that slavery was a 'natural' institution. Those who were naturally inferior, that is, without the moral autonomy engendered through inner virtue to be able to take on the responsibility of making decisions for themselves, possessed slavish natures. What capability the slave had was only appropriately employed when directed to performing functions defined by others; the very character of being master or slave meant that the relations between them must be profoundly unequal. In Aristotle's words, 'Some are marked out for subjection, others for rule.'

This was a conception of the master–slave relation that was to be long lasting. It had two clear implications. The inner nature and the outer condition of the slave were congruent and it was compatible with ethnic and racial difference as a basis for slavery.

Probably in response to some discussion in the Greek world Aristotle acknowledged that not every individual in a state of slavery had only the capacities that properly defined him as a slave. But he apparently thought that this did not happen often and was simply a misfortune. More generally, Greeks thought that slaves were bound to benefit from coming into contact with a superior culture, though they would never attain equality. Greek and Roman Stoic, Jewish and early Christian thought all noted the same difficulty with the idea of the 'natural' slave but responded in broadly similar ways. When fate rather than nature reduced a person to slavery, if his inner nature was not slavish it did not matter. The kind of freedom that did matter was in the spiritual and moral realm; bondage of the body was of secondary concern. A slave might be truly free in spirit and a free man in bondage to his passions or to sin. These doctrines had little impact on slavery as an institution, and Christian preaching, if not Stoic discourse, spread the ideas more widely as Christianity also became the creed that increasingly defined the terms of elite respectability in the later Roman Empire. The substance of the thinking of Church Fathers on slavery gave even less attention to querying its justice. Though Augustine deplored the trading of slaves in North Africa we have seen that he regarded slavery as a penalty for man's sinfulness and, despite some differences of emphasis amongst medieval religious thinkers, that Augustinian tradition remained powerful. It was supplemented, as we have seen, by the widespread diffusion of the interpretation of the curse of Ham as the origin of slavery. Moreover, spiritual and earthly freedom were in different spheres of existence so slave owners could keep their slaves. They might indeed acquire more through a just war against heretics, infidels or pagans. At the beginning of European expansion to the Americas this frame of mind was strengthened by a revival of the Aristotelian doctrine of natural slavery as applied to Amerindians and to Africans. When Protestant evangelism belatedly turned its attention to slaves in the Caribbean and North America it automatically gave priority to the spiritual sphere. Additionally, until well into the history of slavery in the hemisphere, preachers and missionaries assumed that the best way to advance religion was to secure the cooperation of the slave owners. Catholic penetration of slave populations was certainly earlier and, as we shall shortly see, probably deeper, but priests had no greater concern than ministers to question the master's authority.

The idea that slavery was a natural state for some people made headway in the Muslim world. So too, in explanation of who the slavish people were, did the argument based on climate and the curse of Ham. Avicenna in the eleventh century lumped together Turks and others from the cold North with Africans from the hot South as natural slaves, a convenient conclusion since at the time many of the existing slaves in Muslim societies come from such regions. Islam was, however, a proselytizing religion and Muslim masters drew slaves into the religious community where they could hear the promise of reward in paradise for the loyal and obedient. In both kin-based and more individualized Muslim societies the religious environment encouraged the senior kin member and master to assume a patriarchal role in accord with the Qur'an's emphasis on the proper treatment of slaves along with parents, kinsmen and orphans. But as the slave was partly drawn into the kin or larger community through being given a religious identity he was also perceived to be a fictive kin member, or as carrying fewer religious obligations than the free man. These distinctions might only be partially obscured in time. In such circumstances the master's patriarchal role was expressive of the deep inequality imposed upon the slave though he received protection and attachment in return. What was striking during the rapid plantation development on the Swahili coast of East Africa in the 1870s and 1880s was the masters' attempt expressively to continue the quasi-kin or 'client' ideology of an earlier phase when the reality had become a tough gang slavery regime.

In parts of the Americas the broad parallel to these ideological developments was the articulation of the notion of planter paternalism. In the American phrase 'our families white and black' there is offered expressively the idea of the slaves as quasi-kin. As on the Swahili coast they were not kin and the inappropriateness of the trope to its object of reference is underlined when we recognize that there was no material base, no likely passage of goods or property to root such a notion of kin. Indeed when blood kin benefited it was as a result of the surplus extracted from the slaves. In these general circumstances of plantation slavery, paternalism's power to induce in slaves anything more than the existing acquiescence of relative impotence required at the very least a forceful articulation of the ideology by a more than usually conscious social class. The basic conditions for this to happen did not exist in some parts of the Americas. In French St Domingue and much of the British Caribbean in the eighteenth century the drive for sugar production not only pressed hard on the existing slaves but constantly required that their stock be replenished from Africa, thus necessitating the rapid seasoning of the new workers. This fast-paced, profit-conscious plantation world left little time for the expression, let alone the acting out, of social paternalism. Nor did the large slave majorities in the Caribbean populations and the large slave units in which they were organized on the sugar estates make it plausible that masters could know, or even pay any attention to, more than a small minority of their bondsmen. The imbalance in favour of the slaves provoked anxiety and the conviction that a regular display, and the occasional exercise, of force was the best way to keep order. A good proportion of estate owners, once they had made enough money to leave the islands, returned to the metropolis and thereafter prospered as absentees. There was no expression of a paternalist ideology to encourage good order in St Domingue or Jamaica.

The best examples of American slave societies that present themselves for analysis as arenas where planter paternalism was articulated are the sugar region of the Brazilian north-east in the nineteenth century and the American South in the generation before the civil war. A working definition of paternalism has to include the dependence of the slave upon the master, their mutual recognition of the relationship and, within that framework, an element of manoeuvre and negotiation on both sides, though always shaped by the unequal relation of power between master and slave. At its most sophisticated, as employed by Eugene Genovese in *Roll, Jordan, Roll* (1974), the concept explained relative social stability through acceptance of the planter's hegemony but in the subordinated slave's room for manoeuvre also acknowledged conflict without extensive confrontation. With this in mind, when we turn to Brazil we note the self-consciously 'aristocratic' lifestyle of the sugar planters whose display of luxury and leisure they might accompany with gestures of what they regarded as appropriate generosity towards some of their slaves. They were occasionally willing to act as sponsors for some slaves through such institutions as godparenthood. Slaves sought moral and material help for their children and other family members and masters gave it and mediated problems with outsiders, at least for some slaves to whom they may have felt some attachment. At the time of final Brazilian emancipation in 1888 the number of slaves having already received manumission from their masters was several times larger than those manumitted through purchase from funds set aside for the purpose under the gradual emancipation law of 1871. Yet this image of a benevolent paternalism in the sugar region needs significant adjustment. Firstly, the depiction of paternalism draws much of its material from the later phases of the slave-based sugar regime when the economy was less buoyant than earlier. The pressures to enhance profits were fewer. As to personal relations, there do appear to have been a significant number of sexual liaisons between planter family males and some of their female slaves but this did not always bring many rewards for the slave except that the master-father might become his own child's godparent. More generally, sugar planters were only going to be familiar with slaves whom they regularly encountered; they did not include most field hands. Repeatedly in the images of master–slave relations in traditional Brazilian writing on the subject we encounter the 'Mammy' or household retainer. The master's role as godparent was probably often restricted to these special slaves. Even so, in the later decades slaves turned more frequently to sponsors outside the master's family, including to fellow slaves or freedmen, seemingly wishing to solidify relations with fellow blacks rather than with their owners. Moreover, the manumission figures taken as an indication that the threshold between slavery and freedom could easily be crossed, and the conclusion that this in turn supports the characterization of the sugar planters as benevolent paternalists, are misleading. The flow of manumissions only became substantial in the later years of slavery. Masters might have a number of reasons for acceding to manumission but at a time of growing uncertainty about the system many allowed slaves to buy their freedom with funds they had accumulated or borrowed. Others agreed to their slave's freedom in return for their continuation in work for a number of years more. There is no doubt that mutual feelings of respect and regard did occur between masters and slaves in the Brazilian north-east and that planters had some basis for their sense of acting out a paternalist ethic in both its benevolent and sometimes its stern aspect to keep good order. Slaves did have some room for manoeuvre. But whatever equilibrium in personal and social relations was arrived at must have been precarious when many slaves were distant from the web of connections around the Big House and many others were recently imported Africans in a trade continuing until 1850. The limitations of paternalism as a reality contributing to social stability were sharply exposed in the nineteenth century in the recurrent revolts in and around Bahia and the large-scale slave desertions from the estates in the later years of slavery.

The influence of paternalism in the American South raises both similar and different issues. After Nat Turner's revolt in Virginia in 1831 there were no more slave rebellions, though there were slave plots. Individual slaves and small groups fled from the South but no large-scale slave desertions occurred until the civil war. During the 30 years from Turner to the start of the war the consciously developed ideology of paternalism was most fully expressed. These were the initial conditions for taking the argument for southern paternalism seriously. But the South was also a society permeated by the discourse of racism. The master underlined his social distance from the slave in terms that demeaned the body of slaves in such a way that it was then difficult for him to convey the element of regard supposedly present in the paternalistic relationship. We also recall in the earlier discussion of the structural features of slave societies that, during the same decades of the development of the ideology of paternalism, the South made more rigid the line between slavery and freedom. If slave loyalty was not to be cemented with the hope of manumission, then southern paternalism had to be peculiarly effective in its own austere terms. This must have been especially so given the pressures on the newer cotton planters of the black belt areas of the Mississippi Valley to take advantage of boom conditions in the later years before the war.

Southern political leaders and intellectuals certainly celebrated the orderly hierarchy of their society, proclaimed an ethic of responsibility toward the slave that complemented the rights exercised over him and spoke a language suggesting that they presided over an extended family. In their views of the slave they mingled the stereotypical traits of laziness and simple-mindedness with public conviction of his loyalty and reassurances that the slave appreciated their firm guidance of him. Southerners thus asserted, in an era when paternalism (whatever its influence within the region) was also in part a defence of the South from northern and international antislavery criticism, the superiority of their society over atomized and volatile free labour societies. Southern paternalistic slavery, they argued, joined the slave owners' interests with their duty and created a harmonious social whole. But there were other sides to the South. The South deployed paternalism as an ideological moral bridge over the great social distance between planters and most slaves. Michael Tadman's close survey of planters' papers in *Speculators and Slaves* (1996) has indicated how frequently mention of a few 'key slaves' recurs and how most slaves fail to appear. They are bound to have received much less consideration than the few whom the master encountered regularly in the household and in giving instructions for the running of the estate. Taking further the point that paternalism in language and practice had differential effects on slaves, it can be recognized that slaves' general conditions provided them with a yardstick for measuring the substance of paternalism. They also had other sources of values than the master in their lives and the extent to which they merged or conflicted with the master's views affected whether paternalism as ideology or practice stabilized or disrupted social relations.

The importance of the internal slave trade to the functioning of the American system has already been highlighted. At a more human level it affected the conditions of many hundreds of thousands of slaves. They experienced wrenching movement away from family and friends, lost the sense of a familiar place and had to adapt to new people and new conditions. Many of them deeply resented it. These were not conditions that allowed a settled paternalist framework containing limited negotiations to operate easily. Masters in relatively recently settled areas of the Cotton Kingdom (a large area in the 30 years before the war) were not presiding over a regularly functioning system. With traded slaves they had constantly to begin to establish and then try to maintain authority over slaves new to them. In this context paternalism was likely to be part of a strategy, no doubt often not articulated, aspiring to control but accompanied by some anxiety over securing stability.

Masters thinking of themselves as paternalists did not necessarily provide especially good material conditions for their slaves, except that the house slaves and those with management responsibilities were sure to be better provided for. But it is unlikely in such areas as housing, clothes and food that they were particularly poor providers. Moreover, in both the American and Brazilian cases paternalism as an ideology and in faltering practice developed primarily after the supply of fresh slaves through the external slave trade had been cut off. Pressures to at least maintain numbers told against poor material provision. Elsewhere in slave societies, so far as the master's provision was concerned, the situation could be much worse and it is hard to see that a paternalist planter class would have made much difference. In the British West Indies in the eighteenth century, at times when the region was caught up in imperial conflicts, the lack of food grown in islands with so much acreage devoted to sugar cane, combined with enemy disruption of supply ships, led to periods of severe shortage. Eventually masters welcomed slave initiative in starting up their own food provision on plots. Even non-paternalists recognized that there was a link between adequate food and other material provision and getting adequate work out of the slaves. No scholar, however, suggests that masters on a regular basis went out of their way to be generous, though the tactic of occasional munificence (at Christmas) could be used to encourage gratitude. But, as we shall see, material shortage was sometimes an element in slave discontent.

Recent scholarship on slavery in the Americas has interpreted slaves' provision of part of their own food as worth considerable attention. This is not only because of its contribution to their standard of living but also because of its variable relation to the individual slave's room for initiative and his master's attitude to it. It also bears upon what constituted the activities of a slave community. It adds an economic dimension to the idea of a slave community previously interpreted mainly as a set of cultural and religious values, beliefs and practices. Assessment of the overall role of the slave community is crucial to understanding the balance and functioning of slave societies. But if the point of entry into partially autonomous individual and community slave activity and its meaning is the slave's own 'informal economy' then it is worth looking at slave societies pre-dating those of the

Americas. Roman slaves too engaged in independent food production and care of their own animals. The agricultural writer, Varro, depicted many rural slaves as having livestock and Pliny pointed to their growing of fruit and vegetables in garden plots both to supplement provisions from the master and to accumulate a little money from selling the surplus. There is no evidence that masters frowned on this, but nor does it appear that these activities were communal. The situation was more complicated in some other slave societies; a brief comparison of Jamaica and the American South will bring out the issues of interpretation. As we have seen, in the West Indies scarcity had been limited through slaves resorting to plot agriculture. That was valuable, but in better times continued to have an advantage for the master in reducing his provisioning costs. Saturday and Sunday, not normally spent in the cane fields, the slaves used to work their gardens, and since they were assigned land on the slopes and in the gullies they brought into economic use land that was unsuitable for cane. So far this analysis would suggest that almost all the advantages lay with the master. But by the early years of the nineteenth century the 'informal economy' of the provision plots had developed in some ways beyond the control of masters. Multi-generation family groups worked the plots, sometimes with non-kin newcomers attached or perhaps in collaboration with another family. They not only supplied their own needs but produced surpluses bartered or sold at large Sunday markets, occasions for bringing people together from different estates and creating a communal sense. Jamaican planters were compelled to acknowledge this distinct slave sphere; they not only dared not undermine the 'informal economy', they accommodated to it in allowing inheritance of provision grounds from one slave generation to the next. A process that had begun as integral to the success of the sugar estates held out the promise, on the eve of emancipation in the 1830s, of an independent peasant economy based on kin and organized in community and village form.

The Jamaican form of plot production and sale marked the opposite end of the spectrum from what we know of Roman slave activities in this sphere, that is, as being purely individual or based on family. The American case was in between, with more ambiguous effects. In the Carolina and Georgia lowcountry the task organization of slave work gave the faster slaves time at the end of a work day as well as at weekends to grow food, tend livestock, make objects, hunt and fish. Time was more restricted in gang labour areas and the gang organization meant guaranteed provisioning by owners. But slaves still worked plots, though probably smaller in size than in the lowcountry, precisely because their basic food was provided and what they produced was pure surplus for exchange. The larger social meaning of this 'informal economy' for master–slave relations and the strength and character of slave community is glimpsed through a look at the element of exchange involved. Selling or bartering only with the master sustained the master's authority because he was the immediate source of the benefit the slave gained. He could also control the items he put into the exchange and sometimes held back items to be presented later as an aspect of his generosity. In contrast any exchange taking place off the plantation provided the slave both with an alternative market and some choice over what he took for consumption in exchange, thus reducing the master's control over this aspect of his life. Some evidence has come to light that to a limited degree exchange could involve the slave in a cash economy and thus gave him access to resources for further purchase. In the South slave production and exchange usually began as an implicit compromise with masters; the latter probably calculated that a little more flexibility was worth the satisfaction the slaves gained from the overall effect of greater stability. Mostly that is probably what the 'informal economy' amounted to. Yet when slaves, however infrequently, engaged in cash or barter transactions away from the plantation and outside the control of masters, then the relation of the slave's personal dependence on the master – the core of paternalism – was to a degree undermined. Nor was the work in the 'informal economy' an entirely individual or family activity. Slave families appear sometimes to have worked together, pooling resources and sharing profits. This may have strengthened kin links, real or fictive, and, where there was a sufficiently large body of slaves, enhanced community mutuality. Some of this slave activity was clearly surreptitious and a quiet struggle over the slave's time and the space he made use of recurred in places. But some slaves were clearly easing the constraints that slavery had imposed upon them. The consequences for stability, however, were uncertain. In one sense, gains of this kind for the slave were a small victory over the master's power. In another sense, however, these small victories ensured their own limitation; if control slipped too far, the master acted to reassert it. Above all, for sensible slaves, small gains ruled out large confrontations; they knew there was even more to lose.

To varying degrees in different slave societies there was then a material base to slave communities. Historians have more frequently interpreted them as cultural entities, partially bolstering slaves against the pressures of slavery. Such a view of slave communities can be reconciled with different views about the balance of acquiescence and resistance in slave societies. There is no doubt that, to a greater or lesser degree, (and the variation in the same society could be considerable) most slaves were culturally influenced by the world of their masters and other free people. But the defence of community, and kin within it, could not be a response to the structural circumstances of societies with slaves, whether slavery was located in households or lineage systems. There were not enough slaves for a community to form and the few attached to a household or lineage had little alternative except to think of improvement in terms of a move towards closer involvement with the family or lineage that owned them. In slave societies substantial numbers of urban slaves, in Rio de Janeiro for example, lived close to each other and met each other at the work place, in the streets and in cultural and religious activities. They formed a slave, or sometimes an ethnic, slave community in conditions more conducive to the establishment of a partially distinct identity than in the countryside. In the city the owners' surveillance was necessarily less persistent and if slaves were hiring out their time they had a good deal of freedom of manoeuvre in relation to their lives outside as well as in work. Historians, however, have written mostly about the struggle to build and defend a community through its constituent elements of culture, religion and family in the context of rural plantations. The extent to which distinctive slave cultural patterns existed depended upon the population balance between slave and free, the size of the slave unit, the mix of ethnic or national groups and the balance between born in the house slaves and traded slaves. How consistently masters pressed processes of acculturation upon the slaves through interference in their personal, family and religious lives also affected the balance in the syntheses of cultural elements that emerged amongst slaves.

The cultural formation of individual slaves is beyond recovery in any detail but those closest to owners adapted most to the pressure to acculturate. To fail to have done so would have been to lay themselves open to harsh treatment. Some slaves acted as 'cultural brokers' between masters and their fellow slaves. The Roman *vilicus* or farm manager and the African-American driver or overseer were examples. They did not merely see that work was done but could more generally smooth out understandings and secure behaviour that minimized conflict. Influence of this kind was no doubt mainly directed to shaping how the slaves conducted themselves but could occasionally be turned towards masters. As walking cultural hybrids the early 'creole' slaves in the Americas, already familiar with the complex cultural interchanges of the Atlantic rim, were also crucial intermediaries as labour forces later became more rapidly Africanized. There were also occasions when masters and slaves underwent similar cultural and religious experiences but it is probable that many slaves gave them a different meaning from their masters. The culture of slave communities consisted of both separate practices and meanings and different slave understandings of activities and experiences shared with masters as well as imitative activities and absorption of elements of the outlook masters pressed upon them. But, very importantly, new cultural syntheses emerged.

In the Americas the emergence of creole languages was an important indication of the development of a slave culture and a binding force in a slave community. Pidgin, derived from the dominant European language in different parts of the Americas, and the initial way slaves had of communicating with the master and with other slaves from different ethnic backgrounds, was the precursor of more elaborate creole languages. Creole combined words from African as well as European languages and a largely Indo-European syntax. Although many whites and mixed race people could communicate in the local creole tongue, they normally spoke the dominant European language; creole was the main way slaves communicated with each other. Where sizeable numbers of slaves from a single ethnic group were in contact, more likely amongst urban than rural slaves, then they were bound together through maintaining particular cultural traditions. More commonly new cultural syntheses resulted from the convergence of a number of processes. Many New World purchasers of slaves deliberately mixed members of different ethnic groups as a security measure. On the model of a creole language, the more general cultural outcome was adaptation to the American cultural environment, including European cultures themselves undergoing adaptations, in part as a result of encountering Africans. The slaves' African cultural traditions were, in varying degrees, simplified and transformed not only because in the American environment some elements were not functional, but also because of the need to forge common beliefs, or at any rate practices, for people of different origins. Nor, in the random gathering up of the slave trade, was there necessarily the specialist cultural knowledge simply to maintain traditions. Thus slave culture was neither homogeneous nor static, a truth compounded by further revisions likely to have occurred in the course of oral and imitative transmission from one generation to the next in the New World. If this outline of cultural change is at all accurate, however, it is clear that slaves operated on assumptions and possessed values that distinguished them from their masters, whatever practical compromises they had to make. Thus within plantation communities the masters' ascription of particular status to individuals was not necessarily sanctioned in the slave community. The conjuror adept with spells and roots, the midwife and the good hunter rather than, or in addition to, the driver gained the slaves' respect.

Religion in slave societies was an area both of personal experience and public significance. It brought together and gave coherence to groups of slaves, acted as a channel for owners to inculcate obedience and moral discipline in their bondsmen and demonstrated both the merging and conflict of different traditions. In Greece and Rome slaves were drawn into some religious cults and their ceremonies and excluded from others. They were present, probably largely as spectators, at family ceremonies and, in the Roman case, rituals in the Lares cult in the household. Emphatically slaves were excluded from rituals surrounding the deities of the city-state since these were only open to citizens; they attended the activities of other public cults as watchers and in the presence of free men. They were occasionally found in the more marginal eastern cults that slaves had perhaps introduced to

Greece but the main socializing role of religion was through the admission of some Greek-speaking slaves with their masters to the Mysteries of Eleusis. In general, however, in Greece religion does not appear very significant either as a discipline over slaves or as a way in which they could find some social space. Rome employed membership of religious cults in a much more positive way to socialize slaves and legitimate structures of authority. Existing and new slaves took part in the festivals for Mars and Hera and were connected to the wider society through sharing ceremonies of other cults with Roman citizens. Most explicit in trying to engage slaves in sanctioning the forms of authority over them was the cult of emperor worship instituted by Augustus and creating for slaves an asylum and right of appeal at Caesar's statue. But, while showing favour to the slave in this fashion, the Roman state as we have noted, was limited in its interventions in slavery.

The model of cultural change used to describe the cultural syntheses that evolved in slave communities in the Americas can also be applied to the pattern of slave religion in the same continents. The forms of slave religion stretched from the almost completely African amongst new imports to affiliation to white-dominated Christian denominations amongst creole slaves. The more African patterns of religion departed from European practices in their integration of dance and forms of music that sounded inappropriate to Euro-American ears. Since the less public slave religious activities were, the more fearful outsiders were of what their effects might be in provoking emotional excitement or even social disorder, and public authorities and owners tried to exercise some control. Eventually they acquiesced in efforts to make Christians of the slaves. In Latin America this was a commitment of the Catholic Church from an early stage, though with varying degrees of success. As late as the second half of the eighteenth century few serious efforts had been made at converting slaves in Protestant areas. Even where priests and missionaries made some progress they had to accommodate existing beliefs and practices and recognize that many of their converts also continued in their old ways in parallel to Christian worship. In many areas the churches also had to respond to new Africans entering through the slave trade. Though there were differences between the cults nearer the African end of the spectrum in slave religious life, and some were more open to external pressures for change than others, it is possible to indicate their main elements and what their appeal to slaves might be. They provided resources for dealing with the difficulties of daily life. Music and dance aided the literal reception of the spirits through possession of the worshippers, marking a temporary fusion of gods and man and a sense of exaltation. Divination or soothsaying was an attempt to understand the will of the spirits or ancestors so as to act in harmony with them and to foretell the future in a world over which the slave had little control. Some ceremonies dealt with important moments in the cycle of life – birth, death, marriage, the change of seasons – and linked the slave within his community to the spirit world and the past. Beliefs and practices involving charms and spells in the *vodun* of St Domingue and the *obias* of the Protestant Caribbean contributed to a sense of protection of person and property. Priests of the cults, as well as other slaves, had a healing role through knowledge of the properties and powers of herbs and plants. In Brazil and parts of the Caribbean the Catholic Church acceded to the pressures of slaves for symbols, forms of worship and expression through religious brotherhoods compatible with African religious traditions. So we find cults of black Madonnas, tacit recognition that slaves identified particular spirits with Catholic saints, and confraternities full of slaves and free coloureds in which it was by no means certain that orthodox Catholic piety was being advanced. This kind of cultural and religious synthesis was largely absent from state church- and planter-supported religious denominations in Protestant slave societies in the Caribbean and North America. And slaves themselves were less attracted to these churches than to the missions of evangelical Protestants suffused with religious zeal and sometimes willing to give slaves a role with some responsibilities in the life of the church. In the demographically dominant white world of North American slavery where the supply of Africans bearing their religious traditions was cut off quite early, strongly African cults were less prominent than in the Caribbean and Brazil, though not absent amongst isolated populations. But in the nineteenth century the Christian denominations most acceptable to African-Americans, the Methodists and the Baptists, allowed a great deal of leeway to local churches (and the emergence of separate black congregations). Local autonomy, even if whites kept an eye on their activities, enabled slave and free black worshippers to make over the traditions of religious enthusiasm in ways they found congenial. The instrumental preaching at slaves in white churches, intended to encourage obedience, probably carried little weight against these possibilities. Black Christianity and white Christianity did not turn out to be the same thing.

As an inclusive religion Islam promised to slaves who converted membership of a religious community and to future generations the possibility of freedom. Though masters might sell Muslim slaves, this did not meet with approval in many societies. But there could be limits to the benefits of the Islamic faith for a slave. On the Swahili coast of East Africa in the second half of the nineteenth century most slaves were drawn from the interior and social and cultural distinctions between coast and interior remained pivotal. Though slaves might become Muslims, learn the Swahili language and adopt coastal styles of dress, fellow Muslims' awareness of their inferiority was not forgotten. Partly in consequence, partly for the comforts of familiarity, interior slaves retained distinctive religious and cultural features. They tended, for example, to interpret central religious myths differently from masters. The latter stressed the creation of different categories of being whereas slaves focused on the irrelevance of status to the depth of faith and piety as the source of religious purity. Slaves engaged in dances from the interior and formed distinct social associations without seeing these as being in conflict with their Islamic commitments. In some respects they probably saw themselves as better Muslims than the elite and thereby reciprocated the sense of distance that their owners had towards them.

We have seen that masters, through their implicitly ideological practice and language, used variations of the metaphor of family and kin to both underline and attempt to bridge the gulf between masters and slaves in the interests of order. Slaves also showed that family and kin were often central concerns for them, not as components of social harmony but as the basis for tolerable survival. In the case of slaves kin might as often be 'fictive' as blood kin, given their vulnerability to family separations. Slave shipmates on the Middle Passage, if they were able to keep in contact in the Americas, regarded themselves as having a bond that was inherited by later generations. Where slaves were able to form a community on the plantation they used forms of address to each other indicating a sense of quasi-kin and often welcomed in similar terms new slaves separated from family and kin elsewhere. Extended family members and even neighbours also took part in 'co-parenting' of slave children. In the United States masters and overseers showed dislike of slaves' sense of extended kin on the plantation and sometimes threatened slaves' expression of it. Kin links potentially posed the basis for resistance and expression of them set an egalitarian sense of connection amongst slaves against the hierarchical harmony the planter intended in 'our family white and black'. Evidence from Brazil and the French Antilles in the nineteenth century of slaves' choice of godparents and names for their children suggests that the longer the plantation system continued and the higher the proportion of creoles amongst them, the more they withdrew from 'familial' relations with the master. Further evidence from the Americas underlines fairly distinctive patterns of sexual and family relations amongst slaves, some of them probably from cultural preference, others forced upon them by the masters' operation of the slave system and a source of pain and bitterness. Africans had fewer opportunities than creole slaves to form families but most slaves in American slave societies lived in family units, even though the lack of legal and church recognition of marriage meant that the families were the products of free unions. There were many such unions amongst the free population in Latin America, and in the Caribbean where the female might often be a slave. The slave divergence from the white pattern of regular marriage in North America was much clearer. The slaves did not tend to move directly to stable free unions but to engage in pre-nuptial sexual relations and after the birth of a child seek a partner for a continuing union who was not necessarily the parent of the first child. It is not clear what the origins of this pattern were, but it is unlikely to have been mere imitation of whites. Thereafter, where they could, slaves maintained a stable family life but parenting arrangements, though accommodating co-parenting, varied from place to place. In the British West Indies perhaps a half of all slave family households were mother-and-children. There was a markedly higher proportion of two-parent family households in the United States and Latin America, though in neither case should the disruptive effects of the internal slave trade, the major form of owners' interventions in slave family life, be underestimated. Disruption of their family ties was a significant reason for slave disaffection in all slave societies. Many slaves in kin-based societies with slaves in Africa either were partners in unions with full kin members or attached to other slaves in subordinate lineages and in close proximity to their individual or corporate owners. Even though slaves in these circumstances could be sold the likelihood of disruption and resentment was less. Some Muslim societies of Central and Western Sudan located slaves physically separate from owners in slave villages where slave families were, therefore, largely unsupervised though production was in the charge of overseers.

In relation to the theme of stability and disruption it can finally be asked, what was the significance of partially autonomous slave culture, religion and family life? The question is most acute where slaves were in a position to pursue collective and community activities and where the dimension of exchange within an 'informal economy' was possible. The pressures of slavery at some time in all slave societies could have broken slaves, and sometimes did. Slave suicides are one index of this. But mostly slaves endured, often fiercely and grimly, but sometimes with moments of individual and communal pleasure, joy in what they had been able to achieve for themselves and their families and through the sustenance of their relations with other slaves and sometimes with free people. It is hard to encounter such heroic endurance without attributing importance to the cultural and community resources individual slaves called upon. They were a little better enabled to withstand the demands of the system and compensate for the large areas of life over which they had marginal influence. A small minority made arrangements with masters allowing them to dispense with the support of fellow slaves. At the same time the compensations of culture, religion, kin and community probably imposed some constraints on overtly rebellious behaviour. When situations arose that slaves found peculiarly unjust, however, their sense of an identity in terms other than those imposed by the master could facilitate acts of resistance. At rare times of deep social and political crisis in slave societies the strengths and solidarity imparted through distinctive cultural and religious experience promoted revolt.

Every day many slaves, in ways that were of more disruptive effect and easier to accomplish in slave societies than in the more personal context of societies with slaves, resisted in small ways. Day-to-day resistance was similar across all slave systems because it was at a level that minimized risk. Owners complained of theft (often food), slow work, feigned illness, injury of farm animals, the breaking of tools, the seeming stupidity (but was it?) of slaves. They lamented, in effect, that slaves were not simply an extension of their owner's will. Their bondsmen, if successful in these minor forms of resistance, gained a little temporary relief from pressure. There were inner forms of resistance producing some psychological release for the slave, even if no discernible harm to the master. Slaves passed on rumours to the detriment of their owner, in Aesopian fables uttered pungent moral judgements on their situation, and ridiculed the overseer or master amongst themselves. They retailed fantasies of power over the owner as in the story amongst South Carolina Sea Island slaves of the gory effects on the master's wife of an invisible whipping that a slave conjured up at a distance. In these instances slaves revealed a consistent desire to distance themselves from personal dependence. However, in the East African Swahili communities already mentioned, slaves' resistance often constituted pressure for greater inclusion in religious activities and commercial exchange. Slaves working as porters in the caravans of the ivory trade, for example, refused to be bound to working only for their owners and traded on their own account. Some accumulated sufficient profits to buy slaves and further blur their social position through assuming patriarchal airs as their own masters did.

Acts of personal violence against masters or their agents were more directly and immediately threatening to the order of slavery. The most brutal revelation of how the master class saw the logic of personal slave violence occurred after the murder in 61 CE of Pedanius Secundus, the city prefect of Rome by one of his slaves. Under the law all other household slaves were to be executed so that if they had conspired they paid the penalty and if they had not they learned, and their fate set an example for others, that they must always protect their master. About 400 slaves were executed as a result of this single murder.

Flight was also a constant of slave resistance. Whatever circumstances provoked it, its objectives were of two distinct kinds:

slaves sought permanent freedom or they were implicitly negotiating a return to the master on slightly improved terms. Whether the hope of flight to permanent freedom was realistic depended on a number of conditions. How far away safe territory might be was an important consideration in the American case. Escape from the Upper South to free territory in the northern states or, preferably, to Canada to avoid the fugitive slave hunters, was more feasible than in the Lower South. There fugitives looked to improve their circumstances, as with the slave whom the naturalist, Audubon, met in the Louisiana bayous, who wanted to be reunited with his wife away from whom he had recently been sold. He enlisted Audubon as an intermediary with his present master to purchase his wife. In the ancient world reaching a recognized sanctuary for slaves was a possibility and occasionally brought freedom when the master, to save face, was able to claim to be responding to the wishes of the gods. The slave community could help sustain the many fugitives continuing to lurk at the edges of the area that they had deserted through providing food and passing on news affecting the fugitive's prospects. They might also betray him. Nor did slave owners give up easily on getting fugitives back. Cicero wrote letters to a distant provincial governor about one of his runaways reported in the governor's jurisdiction. Romans, like other slave owners developed a class of slave catchers and those aiding slaves to escape could expect punishment in all slave societies. All in all, flight often demanded considerable courage, cunning, good fortune and probably desperation if it was to have a chance of success, even when its objective was an improvement in conditions rather than freedom.

Collective flight constituted the phenomenon of *grand marronage*, the making of a community of maroons, a dangerous example to others from the perspective of the class of owners. The prime experience behind large-scale flight was probably harsh treatment but, for the outcome to be the creation of a maroon community, the fugitives had to be able to exploit terrain that was difficult of access for pursuers and could be made defensible against attack. Maroons therefore tended to sequester themselves in mountainous regions (Drimakos and his followers on Chios in the early third century BCE or Cudjoe in the Blue Mountains of Jamaica), forests (the Saramaka in the interior of Surinam) or swamps (American maroons in the Great Dismal Swamp on the

Virginia–North Carolina border). In the case of Brazil the huge open frontier behind the backlands served the same purpose. The need to have the means of economic survival within the area of the settlement was sometimes difficult to reconcile with a defensible position. Some maroons raised stock and food crops or fished and hunted but others relied on banditry and raids on farms and plantations. It was this kind of action, likely to encourage further *marronage*, that particularly provoked attempts at suppression from political authorities. To survive in such circumstances required effective organization of defences and intelligent leadership. The structure of communities varied but was frequently autocratic with a main leader sometimes terming himself a 'chief' or 'king'. This may well have been an African cultural imprint in the case of American communities. Cudjoe, the leader of the Leeward maroons in Jamaica, used his authority to organize his followers in companies under military captains. They trained them in using spears and small arms 'after the manner of the Negroes on the coast of Guinea'. Success could be measured in part by how long a community survived. Effective mobilization for defence and the creation of an internal economy worked for much of the seventeenth century to sustain the independence of Palmares in the interior of the Brazilian north-east. Ultimately those communities that struck a bargain with the authorities tended to outlast maroons in constant struggle with the outside world. Usually in return for not luring more slaves away, perhaps turning new arrivals back and refraining from depredations on the countryside, they were left alone. Supposedly Drimakos achieved this in Chios; the Saramaka closed their conflict with the Dutch through treaty in 1762; the Jamaican maroons came to a similar arrangement with the British in the mid-1790s. What were the objectives of the maroons? The simplest and major one was to live unmolested away from the system of slavery. Judging from late eighteenth-century evidence from Brazil, some short-lived communities were bases from which to carry on trade union-style negotiations for improvement of working conditions on the estates. Some features of maroon communities in the Americas had an African character and it has been suggested that, in addition to autonomy, slaves wanted consciously to restore an African pattern of life. Africans took part in maroon activity, but so did many creoles who had less reason to think in those terms.

The African population in a particular community was unlikely to have been drawn predominantly from one particular group so that the meaning of an African restoration is unclear. At best the case is not proved.

The most dramatic manifestation of disruption in slave society was, of course, the slave revolt. But the history of slave societies was not continuously punctuated by slave revolts. Nor is this surprising. A large proportion of a number of circumstances needed to converge before a slave revolt was likely. No doubt societies that had drawn and defended the line between slave and free most firmly were in some general sense more liable to explosion than societies where the line was permeable. But that characteristic on its own explains little. Scrutiny of a range of slave revolts suggests that other factors were important. As with maroons, rebels needed to be able to exploit suitable terrain for defence and regrouping. Not surprisingly there were often connections between the prevalence of *marronage* and the outbreak of revolts. A substantial slave majority in the population could give rebels a sense of confidence. The larger the proportion of foreign-born slaves, the less they were acculturated and the more alienated from the workings of the society. If, further, particular ethnic or nationality groups were heavily represented, then an important source of solidarity was present amongst the potential rebels. Organization of rebellion was aided in a slave system of large units of slave workers. In the Americas most slave revolts took place in sugar areas where units of the labour force were larger than in both cotton and tobacco. Particularly distant owners to whom slaves could feel no loyalty posed no conflicts of loyalty in slave rebels. The size and outlook on slavery of the section of slave societies that did not own slaves could be crucial at the point of a slave outbreak. But slave revolts also needed leadership; there had to be slaves unusual enough, or freedmen sympathetic enough, in their vision to command support. And that vision was in some sense informed by an ideology even though it may be impossible for the historian to recover much of it. Material distress and incidents of harsh treatment were usually part of the trigger for revolt. But slaves, or their leaders, had to sense an element of weakness or disunity in the slave-owning class or between it and other powerful groups in the political structure. At which point they would try to capitalize on such a situation, when at other times, perfectly rationally, revolt seemed suicidal.

This survey of potentially relevant factors in slave revolts provides help in answering a question that has exercised historians since serious comparative studies of slavery began. Why were slave revolts more frequent in some slave societies than others? If we compare the structural features of Roman slave society during the period of large-scale revolts in the 70 years after 140 BCE with classical Athens or other parts of Greece when no revolts on a similar scale occurred, what differences stand out? In Sicily and the parts of Italy where the two slave wars and the revolt led by Spartacus occurred there were concentrations of large slave units and many of the slaves, the product of some of the recent Roman wars of expansion were both foreign-born and in ethnic clusters. Eunus, the rebel leader in the first slave war in Sicily in the 130s BCE, was a Syrian and many of his followers were probably of the same origin or from Asia Minor. Spartacus was probably a Thracian as were other slaves in Campania and Apulia. Other elements in the revolt were Germans and Gauls and their common ethnicity no doubt acted as a principle of coherence, though it should be noted that in the later stages of the revolt there is evidence of divisions according to ethnic group. Many slave owners in the areas in revolt were also probably absentees for part, if not most, of the time and commanded little personal loyalty. Political and social conditions were also volatile with recurrent small-scale slave outbreaks and political factionalism. Apart from large slave units in mining, and a few in manufacturing, Greek slavery was made up of small groups of slaves widely distributed amongst the population and, although clearly distinguished from citizens and with little prospect of manumission, with some attachments to the master's household. Their lack of many freedman models may even have blunted their aspirations in contrast to Roman slaves who could observe more freedmen around them, some of whom became citizens.

When many of the other factors were in place, the timing of revolts often seemed to depend on perceptions of divisions within the master class or between it and other politically significant groups. With the most dramatic consequences this was the situation in St Domingue in 1791. During the course of two years of upheaval in France white slave owners had pressed for greater autonomy in the colony but had come into conflict with free coloureds, many of them also slave owners, demanding an improvement in their civil and political rights. Smaller white property holders had political differences with both of the other groups. Ideological currents in the French Revolution provided political factions and eventually leaders of the slave revolt with egalitarian slogans with which to exploit social and political divisions. A huge number of slaves, many of them recent imports from Africa and shocked into revolt by their sudden subjection to the harsh planter regime, rose against the divided classes above them. The slaves themselves gained solidarity from the spiritual and social force of their popular religion, *vodun*. The slave revolt that was transformed into the Haitian Revolution, and became the only successful mass slave revolt in modern history, also illustrated the difference that leadership could make. A series of leaders of the slaves, creole, often with a degree of education and culminating in Toussaint Louverture, with startling opportunism and switching of alignments amongst the contending factions, organized and led the slaves towards freedom.

Slave rebels had expectations of freedom, however those expectations had been aroused. Whether freedom had a different meaning for them at different periods has been a subject of debate amongst scholars. The most influential distinction drawn between slave rebels' objectives at different periods has been Eugene Genovese's in *From Rebellion to Revolution* (1979). Studying slave revolts comparatively in the Americas he saw the Haitian Revolution as pivotal. It marked, he suggested, a revolutionary drive to emancipation with the objective of destroying the whole system of slavery. It was an aspect of the bourgeois-democratic transformation of the modern world. Thereafter all slave revolts pointed in this direction. Previously slave rebels had sought individual and group freedom within the context of restoring conditions as near as was possible to those from which they or their ancestors had been torn. We know very little about the objectives of slave rebels in the ancient world but it is possible to interpret some of Spartacus's movements as directed towards escape from Italy, perhaps in the hope of the slaves being able to return to their homelands. 'Restorationist' objectives in maroon communities as models of what rebels might have wanted, as we have seen, were stronger in some cases than others. The influence of the Haitian Revolution on slave revolts in the Americas in its aftermath was considerable but not exclusive of other influences. While the case can be made for the Tailors' Revolt in Bahia in 1798 and for Gabriel's Revolt in Virginia in 1800 in terms of explicit political ideas, it seems important to understand other revolts in the first half of the nineteenth century in other ways. The revolt in Jamaica in 1831–2 was fuelled by religious zeal; it lacked the Jacobin dimension but did seek to overturn the system. The series of outbreaks in and around Bahia between 1808 and 1835 rested very heavily on the solidarity and alienation of Muslim slaves. If the Haitian experience was relevant here it was that memory of it contributed to the rebels' isolation.

5

The Contraction of Slavery

The purpose of this chapter is to discuss phases of contraction in slave societies and in doing so to provide a perspective over time on the waxing and waning of slave systems. We shall examine the movement of slave societies to societies with slaves, and the eventual virtual disappearance of bondsmen from the latter, through the example of the decline of ancient slavery and its relation to the feudal order in western and southern Europe. Next the focus will be on the factors and something of the processes involved in the freeing of slaves in the Americas, ultimately registered in generalized state action. Finally we shall consider the continuities and disjunctions between the ending of slavery in the Americas and its later and less clear-cut shrinking in the Middle East and Africa.

Slave societies in the ancient world only existed in some Greek states, in the central Roman lands of Italy and Sicily and perhaps parts of Spain. Elsewhere in Roman territory, during the centuries of large-scale agricultural slavery at the imperial core, slaves were largely restricted to domestic, artisan and official roles. Thus the Roman provinces were societies with slaves throughout their history. But, in analysing provincial societies with slaves and the slave society of the core, many historians until recently tended to see a fairly continuous decline in the number and significance of slaves from the third century CE onwards. They posited the virtual disappearance of slaves no later than the fifth century. Broadly, it was argued, other forms of dependent labour replaced slavery and those labourers gradually evolved into a feudal peasantry. In late antiquity, perhaps from the beginning of the fourth century onwards, the debt bondage previously imposed upon the least fortunate of the poor free classes became marginal. And this was because it became unnecessary. The general condition of the free poor throughout the extent of the Empire deteriorated and rendered that mechanism for increasing easily controllable and dependent labour redundant. The exactions of a late Roman imperial state that needed to maintain a huge bureaucracy and military machine in conditions of virtually permanent crisis were extremely oppressive. Free peasants, smallholders and free tenants thus sought the protection of, and became subordinate to, the more powerful landowning class. They were tied to the land they worked or leased back land that they had surrendered and paid their landlords in kind or cash, though probably rarely in labour services. These arrangements both met the production needs of landowners and the producers themselves but in addition provided a basis for satisfying the fiscal demands of the reorganized state from the time of Diocletian at the end of the third century onwards. Under these arrangements the collection of a poll tax was simplified. But while the toilers remained juridically free, revealingly, at the end of the fourth century the Emperor Theodosius I tried to establish that such *coloni* had to be regarded as 'slaves of the land to which they were born'.

At the same time, in the core regions where agricultural slavery was significant, the structures of exploitation began to alter. Masters reduced their outlays through requiring many of their slaves to provide for themselves. They placed them on blocs of land and then took from the slaves much of what they produced, perhaps retaining direct slave labour only on 'home farms'. This labouring class, part remaining legally slaves and some being manumitted but becoming clients of their former owners, worked in circumstances difficult to distinguish from those of the degraded free peasantry. This was true both in their relations of production with the master-landowners and the possibilities, however impoverished, that they now had of achieving a settled family life and labour. Eventually both servile and free *manses* (the holdings to which slave and free labourers were attached) were occupied interchangeably by juridically free and slave or ex-slave tenants. Thus, despite the fact that in some areas in late antiquity old-style agricultural slavery persisted, as did free smallholders, the view of ancient slavery in continuous decline draws its strength from evidence of a generalized subordination of rural producers that rendered the distinction between slave and free increasingly irrelevant. These economic and juridical tendencies pointing to the continuous decline of ancient slavery were reinforced, it could be argued, through actions of the slaves themselves in revolt and flight. Attachment to the land under the protection of the powerful was the basis, with the added impact of the Germanic conquests, for the development towards feudalism.

The story of the end of ancient slavery has been complicated, however, by increasing recognition that the barbarian invasions reconstituted the system of slavery. They extended it to areas that in Roman times had seen little of it and, in so doing, contributed to forms of economic revival in the early Middle Ages. On this view, slavery did not virtually disappear by the fifth century and was not confronted by any coherent form of antislavery in late antiquity. Nor, because of the undesirable status of labour for wages in these later, as in the earlier, centuries of the ancient world, was there a 'free labour' alternative to slavery. In the period after the barbarian invasions, paralleling the situation before them, the prominence of slavery was only diminished through a shift in the balance of the mix of kinds of labour from slavery towards other forms of dependent labour. Slaves were found in significant numbers on both church lands and the estates of secular notables in the early Middle Ages, both in the old lands of bondage in southern Europe and to the north in Gaul and Anglo-Saxon England. In summary, there was no linear decline in ancient slavery. In its old haunts it lasted until the late tenth and early eleventh centuries. In new areas to which it was more thickly extended in the early Middle Ages the institution continued in a small way into the high Middle Ages.

The invasions and the later conflicts of early medieval Europe revived slavery because they provided large opportunities for capture in warfare. This was true both of the defending imperial forces and the invaders who seized populations within the boundaries of the Empire and used them as slaves when they settled there. Later, Anglo-Saxons enslaved Celts and Celts each other. Similar opportunities were open both within Merovingian Gaul and on its frontiers with Brittany and Germany. It is therefore plausible to argue that many were enslaved in Western Europe between the fifth and the eighth centuries. The evidence of the legal codes of successor barbarian states to Rome has been taken to indicate that, particularly in the sixth and early seventh centuries, slavery expanded substantially beyond what it had been in the last two centuries of the Western Roman Empire. It has to be acknowledged that there has been considerable dispute as to whether the terminology of the barbarian codes justifies this conclusion. Did the *servi*, *mancipia* and *ancillae* found there mean the same as the *servi* of the earlier centuries of the Empire? The best argument for concluding that they did is that the overall picture of the status of these persons that we get from the codes conforms closely to the characteristics of slaves that have emerged in earlier chapters. There was also some urgency to the recurrent justifications offered by clerics and philosophers for slavery, suggesting either that there was a living institution to defend or, at the very least, that it was in danger of disappearing but was still of value to powerful social interests. Substantial parts of the barbarian legal codes from the sixth to the eighth centuries were devoted to the *servi* and others described in interchangeable terms. The articles reveal that they were regarded as 'tools with a voice' and were characterized in terms applicable also to animals. Similar rates of reparation were provided to the owner for an animal or a *servus* who had been stolen or killed. In indemnities to be paid for murder or injury *servi* and cattle were used interchangeably as units of account. Articles in the codes allowed the beating with many blows, mutilation and killing of the *servi* who were also subject to fierce punishment for sexual relations with women of free status. A woman whose husband had been reduced to slavery was permitted to remarry, as if her slave husband were dead. The categories of persons dealt with in the relevant articles could accumulate property but in law had no ultimate disposition of it, like the Roman *peculium*. Nor did they have recognized control of their children because marriages between such persons were not legally recognized. What we also know of treatment of the *servi* in practice confirms their status as true slaves.

Erosion of the institution, therefore, took place gradually, and with dramatic interruptions, over a long period. How and why did it occur? First of all, manumission has to be taken into account. Recognized processes led to the enfranchisement of the formerly servile and there were reasons for the processes to be used. Though some religious spokesmen defended slavery others saw the granting of manumission as an act of piety. In the

Auvergne Gerald of Aurillac ensured that at his death in the early tenth century 100 of his many slaves were enfranchised; he later achieved sainthood. Historians now see economic growth as a framing feature of agricultural production, if not of long-distance trade, after the disruptions of invasion, war and plague and thus evident from the seventh century onwards. This was probably not continuous everywhere but substantial amounts of extra land were brought under cultivation in many places. Crucially, more often than not, growth in agricultural production was the outcome of small landowners fiercely surviving by bringing fresh land into use. In contrast there is evidence of the difficulties that proprietors of large estates had in getting labour effectively performed. The consequence was the parcelling out of the estates into tenancies requiring few direct labour services and the development of colonizing tenancies on new land, at a distance from the landlord's 'home farm', based on rent in kind proportionate to the crop. The logic of these developments was manumission to provide the flexibility and, if necessary, the mobility for tenants to pursue cultivation in the best ways possible. As expansion occurred, particularly in areas that had lost population to plague, there was some shortage of labour. Seeking to maintain servile statuses in these conditions was even more difficult and only encouraged the more daring or desperate spirits to flee and be welcomed as free tenants elsewhere. Again the economic logic pointed to manumission.

Technical change too played its part in the unravelling of slavery. It is time to emphasize the other side of the argument made in an earlier chapter. Some changes in technique or instruments of production under slavery promoted intensification of labour exploitation. But when technical changes in effect took the place of labour, saved labour power, then some shift of resources away from relatively inflexible slave labour towards technical replacement happened. The point is underlined with the recognition that diffusion of the water mill, stressed in the discussion in the earlier chapter, occurred mainly through groups of free small landowners and tenants.

Far from the whole story is told, however, in stressing the pious or economically rational manumissions on the part of slave owners or the diffusion of technical change. As indicated above, individual slaves or groups took advantage of labour shortages to gain freedom through flight. But they sapped the system in other ways too, though not always to their own immediate advantage. Because, as we have argued, slave systems require reasonably effective state structures to maintain order, periods of breakdown in state authority tended to encourage forms of initiative towards freedom beyond day-to-day low-level resistance or individual acts of violence against the authority of the master or his agent. The 'wars of the Bacaudae' in the late third and mid-fifth centuries were examples in late antiquity of revolts of many slaves and free poor at a time of weakened state authority. They did not destroy slavery but probably resulted in the escape from it of some rebels. There were occasional slave revolts thereafter in the early Middle Ages: in the kingdom of the Asturias about 770 and in Gaul during the Norman invasions in the late ninth century. Slavery remained, but in the disorder of rebellion and its suppression slaves became free men. At times of disorder those fleeing bondage might form bandit gangs or 'maroon' groups. In the seventh and eighth centuries the rulers of Lombardy had to face raids by bands of fugitives who liberated slaves on estates. There, in Spain in the eighth century and later in Charlemagne's empire the size of the problem of slave flight was manifested in the ferocity of laws designed to check it.

Ideologically churchmen were to be found on both sides of what debate there was about slavery. That made little difference in the medium term. But the spread of Christianity amongst the populations of Western Europe did affect the relation of slaves to their free neighbours. Aspirations of the servile class towards freedom were intensified when slave and free alike came to recognize their commonality as souls before God, a development demonstrated in the growing number of unions between slaves and free poor between the seventh and ninth centuries, despite laws against them. This was yet further evidence of the difficulty of enforcing legal prohibitions on kinds of slave behaviour favoured by social and economic circumstances and desired by the slaves themselves.

All of these factors undermining slavery acted together to produce a final, cumulative crisis for the system, above all in its traditional heartlands in Southern Europe, between the mid-tenth and mid-eleventh centuries. In terms of the disappearance of mentions of *servi* in the sources, dates varied from the end of the tenth century in Latium to the early part of the eleventh century in Catalonia and the Auvergne to the mid-eleventh century in the Charente. Only in areas of Spain where the struggle of Christian and Muslim continued were groups of slaves likely to be maintained. Yet these developments were not smoothly integrated into the emergence of feudal serfdom. Most specialists in the period now argue that in the former slave regions of southern Europe there was a gap between the disappearance of references to slaves and signs of the new serfdom in the latter part of the eleventh century. This interlude when the peasantry was almost wholly legally free was relatively brief but was only overcome with the forceful imposition of the rule of lords from castled centres of power. This kind of rule entailed the lord's legal authority over peasants tied to the land as well as extraction of economic surpluses, supposedly in return for protection. In more northerly parts of Europe, where slavery had become more extensive with the establishment of the barbarian states than it had been under Roman rule, its disappearance was less complete. Seigneurial rule pressed down upon continuing groups of *servi* derived from earlier generations of rural slaves alongside the newer servile groups generalized under the term 'serf'. No doubt in the high Middle Ages they were a very small proportion of the total rural population. But in these cases there was a limited continuity between slavery and serfdom in medieval Western Europe.

The limited slavery in the late medieval cities of Italy and the Iberian peninsula, and perhaps to a small degree on the sugar estates of Cyprus, were a distinct phenomenon derived from the trade in people largely by Italian merchants with the Middle East and the Black Sea regions. The beginning of the shift in Portuguese sources of slave supply to West Africa virtually coincided with the exclusion of Mediterranean traders from the Black Sea coasts and interiors as a result of the Turkish capture of Constantinople in 1453 and control of the Dardanelles. This development, with the supply of African slave labourers to the sugar plantations of the Atlantic islands, provided a model for, and constituted the link to, slavery in the Americas.

Slavery was clearly important to the development of the Americas, though not everywhere. Thus societies with slaves were interspersed amongst the major slave societies of the hemisphere and added to the variety of contexts in which American slavery came to an end. The different degrees of attempted state management of slave systems and the extent of identification of imperial and national elites at different times with the interests of slave owners helped define the social and political space within which any antislavery impulses operated. To reverse the perspective, how successful such impulses were bore close relation to the amount of disunity between imperial and colonial elites or within imperial, national and colonial elites. Such divisions were sometimes expressed through, or actually arose from, divergent elite responses to popular engagement with slavery. Where this popular engagement was most important in its effect on the ending of slavery it took the form of popular antislavery movements, or popular political upheavals with an antislavery dimension, within imperial or national societies and also, crucially, of the mobilization of the slaves themselves.

European imperial powers in the Americas, at least until the later eighteenth century, saw their colonial territories there, in mercantilist terms, as sources of wealth for the metropolis and slave-based production as part of the generation of wealth. The successful resistance of colonial elites to mercantilist policy in British North America, Spanish South America and to a lesser extent in Brazil contributed to movements towards political independence but important sectors of the new national elites remained attached to slave labour and feared social upheaval. Most broadly they did so because, in addition to the social authority conferred by slave owning, for them slavery was the basis of agricultural staple production largely directed to external markets. Particularly with the removal of previously guaranteed imperial markets, and fear of removal amongst remaining colonial elites, this external economic orientation enhanced fears of loss in a competitive Atlantic economy. They assumed that avoidance of loss depended upon minimizing the costs of labour as a burden on the overall costs of production. Holding labour costs as low as possible, they were convinced, was best achieved through a supply of labour via the slave trade and production under a tightly maintained slave system. For the still-colonial Caribbean these conclusions were shared into the nineteenth century in sectors of the imperial governing classes.

But changing circumstances rendered such ideological certainties vulnerable. The contradictions between material change and the assumptions underlying unquestioned convictions first became evident in Britain and the northern areas of what became the United States. There in the eighteenth century rises in labour productivity became sufficiently evident to provoke new thinking about the economic workings of society. This was articulated most systematically in the writings of Adam Smith but also more popularly by Benjamin Franklin and Tom Paine amongst others. Evidence of rising production from labour led to the dawning thought that, rather than increased wages encouraging idleness and loss of markets, higher costs of labour, so long as they were moderate, were more than offset by growing output per worker. The labourer too saw the way to meet more of his wants through better wages. These ideas, developed in the writings of the liberal political economists, became diffused, especially in Britain and the northern United States, in the earlier part of the nineteenth century. The spread of the notion that production and prosperity advanced through linking work to feeding more and more of the wants that all individual men and women possessed, undermined the little that was left of the mercantilist philosophy. But now the critique of mercantilism took a more explicitly antislavery turn. Wealth was no longer defined in terms of its contribution to the strength of the state. The outcome entailed, at least in theory, the greater distancing of the state from most of the economic operations of society. And it removed the force of a major argument in defence of the slave trade and slavery earlier advanced by merchants and slave owners: that their operations maximized returns and provided mercantile resources that could be turned to such purposes as maritime defence within an imperial system. Loosening the state's involvement in economic life also rendered the exercise of state power in relation to slavery potentially much more open to contest. More directly, these new conclusions pointed to the likelihood that slaves too would be more productive workers and would generate more wealth if freed to do so. From this point of view the slave system, by removing from the slave all but what was required for him to maintain himself, actually worked against efficient labour and the spread of prosperity. The urgent expression of the pro-slavery argument in the nineteenth century was a consequence of this shift in the paradigm of economic progress. The more prominent place within the argument of assertions of the inherent racial inferiority of the slave sought to counter the idea of the universality of human wants as a stimulus to work if the labourer by his labour was able to fulfil them. It did so in presenting the slave as virtually a separate species in whom the normal law of increasing wants as a stimulus to labour barely operated.

Changing economic conditions and the ideas that accompanied them were not reducible simply to the effects of industrialization but did have the earliest impact on the impulse towards emancipation in Britain. By the decade of West Indian emancipation in the 1830s both antislavery activists and members of the government were convinced that the influence of wants would operate powerfully even on 'negro indolence'. The northern United States also moved in the same direction. During the era of the American Revolution and the early republic, where slaves were marginal to economic life and no great social prestige attached to owning them, legislative and judicial decisions were taken against slavery. Significantly this occurred, from Pennsylvania northwards between 1780 and 1804, in places and at the time when indentured labour and even apprenticeship were falling into disuse. In the context of the spread of *laisser-faire* ideas and of the establishment of republican political institutions self-ownership and the aspiration to economic autonomy fitted neatly with the ideology of civic freedom.

But beginning in Britain and North America the challenge to the slave trade and slavery also took on a moral urgency, and in the case of some antislavery advocates was their primary impulse. Morally speaking, in the writings of both French and Scots *philosophes* like Montesquieu and Francis Hutcheson the main charge against slavery was that it failed to promote human happiness and ran counter to the developing ethic of benevolence that required empathy with others. It was, in other words, a major obstacle to moral progress just as it was also beginning to appear as a barrier to material progress. The urgency about this arose from a changing sensibility in the interconnected religious world of the North Atlantic. Transatlantic Quaker connections from the mid-eighteenth century gradually translated the personal convictions of the American Quakers John Woolman and Anthony Benezet into antislavery commitment in Quaker meetings on both sides of the Atlantic. The parallel 'Evangelical International', fostered through links between the revivalism of the Great Awakening in the American colonies and the Evangelical Revival in Britain, encouraged acute moral anxieties. Some evangelicals expressed these through their horror at the sinfulness of slave trading and slave owning. Antislavery also emerged amongst educated and influential circles on the rational and liberal wing of Protestantism, amongst Rational Dissenters in Britain and then Unitarians on both shores of the Atlantic. Thus the economic rationale for antislavery was initially expressed most strongly in Britain and the United States where the state had withdrawn somewhat from the regulation of economic life. The religious and moral impulse against the slave trade and slavery was similarly early prominent in the same societies where religious pluralism and denominational competition amongst Protestants were most marked. Antislavery became part of a 'religion of humanity' based on the conviction amongst religious people that all human beings were a single family under God. It was their duty to bring about moral change in those whose sinfulness sustained social evils. Many reformers who targeted slave traders and owners of slaves also attacked liquor dealers and drunkards, advocates of war as an instrument of policy and the valour of the military life. They were convinced that to ignore the moral roots of social evils was to fail in their religious duty and to risk calling down the wrath of God on the community or the nation. That deep anxiety was at the root of the urgency of antislavery appeals in the early decades of the nineteenth century.

None of this meant, however, even in Britain and the northern states of the United States where popular antislavery movements developed, that there was a simple and direct relation between the existence of strong antislavery sentiment and the emancipation of the slaves. Despite the organization of mass petitions to Parliament and Congress, the development of networks of local societies to mobilize communities and the vast production and distribution of antislavery literature, there remained strong barriers to the ending of slavery. That was even truer in societies where popular political and religious mobilization against the slave trade and slavery did not occur, or only arose, as in Brazil, in the last years of the slave regime. There was no general decline in slave economies, or even of elite individuals owning bondsmen in societies with slaves. This conclusion covers both those societies where emancipation came supposedly peacefully (the West Indies,

Brazil and much of Spanish America) and where it was accompanied by violence (Haiti and the United States). The British West Indies at the time of emancipation in 1834 were less significant economically than they had been at the beginning of the nineteenth century at the time of the abolition of the slave trade. Even so, the newly opened up colonies of Trinidad and British Guiana had created a fresh frontier for slave-grown sugar. The decline of the sugar region of Brazil was compensated for in the expansion of the coffee area in the decades before emancipation. Cuba was the dominant cane sugar producer not merely in Spanish-speaking America but throughout the world in the middle years of the nineteenth century, at a time when the antislavery consensus was becoming internationalized. As the slave rebellion that became the Haitian Revolution began in St Domingue in August 1791 the French colony had experienced a period of dramatic expansion and vast inflow of slaves. However backward and 'barbarous' some of its critics regarded it as being, the American South grew in area and levels of production almost continuously in the generation leading to the civil war.

The abolition of the various slave trades, both for what they tell us about the achievement of economic and policy changes and in terms of their relation to later instances of emancipation, have to be understood within this context of the economic vitality of slavery in the Americas. As previous discussion has indicated, slave owners in the Americas as elsewhere were concerned about how to reproduce slaves and thus maintain the system. With the exception of the United States the external slave trade was the major mechanism of reproduction in American slave societies. How significant the effect of the abolition of the trade was in different societies therefore depended on how policy makers, and, in some cases, antislavery reformers, thought that enough labour could be provided in those slave societies. At the time of the British abolition measures of 1806 and 1807 both reformers and members of the government, for different reasons, hoped that the planters would see it in their interest to improve the conditions of slaves and stimulate an increased rate of natural reproduction. This was not the outcome and the failure of natural increase to occur eventually led to antislavery pressure that contributed to the British government's policy of required 'amelioration'. The intention was to bring about emancipation, though initially the government left the timing vague. The abolition of the foreign slave trade to the United States in 1808 took place when there was already evidence of long-term natural increase in the slave population and confidence in future numbers. The example of the Haitian Revolution thus convinced a southern president, Jefferson, and other southerners to support it. The reduction in the proportion of unacculturated Africans that this brought about, and the initial lessening of external criticism, could be seen as making slavery more secure. The production of Brazilian coffee and Cuban sugar imposed tough labour regimes and both experienced natural decreases in their slave populations. These industries particularly needed the slave trade and their governments colluded with mercantile and planter interests to sustain it, despite formal agreements with the British to reduce and then eliminate it. In Cuba especially, Spanish imperial authorities were mindful of the need to retain the support of local elites in their major remaining American territory, something they had failed to do earlier during the Latin American revolutions. Only direct British naval action brought the Brazilian trade to a close in 1850–1. Naval patrolling was never completely successful in relation to Cuba, but the cessation of the trade by the late 1860s resulted as much from rising costs as any change of mind as to the desirability of slave imports. The blows inflicted by abolition on Brazil and Cuba were therefore more damaging than elsewhere.

The more intelligent slave owners in both areas were alive to the likely impact of these developments and in advance of emancipation sought possible non-servile alternative labour on terms that gave them strong control of labour conditions and costs. If and when the slaves were also freed there was a favourable model of relations of production to hand. Brazilian coffee growers experimented with mixed forms of labour, including European immigrants, as early as the 1850s. From the late 1840s onwards the Cuban plantocracy began bringing in Chinese coolies and European immigrants. In both countries governments assisted in the process. In both the conditions of the imported were 'slave like'. The numbers of these alternative labourers should not be exaggerated but their significance in relation to slave emancipation was that they made its effects seem more calculable to slave owners and other segments of the political and social elites and gave some guarantee of continuing government consideration. The result was not that slave owners happily gave up their slaves but that there was less likelihood of them seeing emancipation as simply a catastrophe and of them going to the lengths of large-scale violent resistance. They had also absorbed the lesson of the American Civil War by the time of their own final emancipations (1886 in Cuba and 1888 in Brazil). Emancipation on much of mainland, formerly Spanish, America constitutes a variation on this. Except in a few regions the Latin American successor states were societies with slaves rather than slave societies and the upheavals of the revolutionary era further dislodged the institution from many places. Though the early republican era saw official proclamations of freedom in different countries these were primarily states registering the result of already advanced erosion of the institution. They did not arise from deep social or political struggles.

There were basic structural reasons why the process of emancipation in the American South had to be fundamentally different from those described above. Politically slave owners elsewhere in the Americas were more directly subject to external authority than in the South. Even in the British West Indies the imperial government could and did impose its will over local planter-controlled assemblies. But just as the decentralized character of the American federal system facilitated political and religious mobilization in the free states against slavery in the South, so the same arrangements gave slave owners greater political autonomy than elsewhere. Constitutionally slavery was understood to be largely a local institution under the control of governments responsive to the wishes of planters. Alternative forms of subordinate labour were not part of the southern system and owners controlling a slave population growing naturally and receiving a substantial inflow of slaves through the internal trade felt no need of any alternative. The non-slave population was demographically dominant except in a few areas throughout the South and the majority of whites without slaves defined themselves as sharply distinct from the slaves and oppressed free blacks. These were not conditions conducive to an evolution towards a free labour system. Emancipation in the United States was bound to constitute a sharp break with the past and, given their political and material resources and the planters' sense of presiding over a rewarding and distinctive social order, the break with the past was violent.

Clearly some experiences of emancipation were much more violent than were others. The prime examples of violence were Haiti and the United States. Despite their differences they have a number of features in common. The impact of the ideas and opportunities of the French Revolution on the different non-slave groups in St Domingue provoked conflict between them that was very evident to the slaves and their leaders. The struggle of sectional political interests in the United States prompted awareness amongst the slaves that masters need not be forever in control of their own house. Once conflict became sufficiently open slaves took initiatives that displayed their sense that they could become political and military agents in their own cause. In the Caribbean case they moved into massive revolt, found and responded to leaders, most notably Toussaint Louverture, and formed increasingly formidable military forces. They ultimately triumphed over European military onslaughts and completed the political independence of Haiti in 1804 as well as gaining their freedom. In the United States they were not in the same way numerically dominant but were able to push the issue of their freedom to the fore politically through large-scale flight to Union lines during the early stages of the civil war. Military and political leaders were compelled to respond to this changing situation on the ground and ultimately did so on the Union side by transforming the war from a struggle to preserve the Union to one that identified its preservation with emancipation. Logically this opened military participation to free blacks and escaped slaves though, unlike in Haiti, they remained a minority of the liberating forces and under the overall authority of whites. In both cases some sense of group cultural distinctiveness amongst slaves, more emphatic amongst the heavily African population of Haiti, was combined, at least amongst black leaders, with a language of freedom that expressed their deepest desires. The language drew respectively on Jacobinism and nineteenth-century liberalism and, together with their existential experience, produced the cogency of black intervention on behalf of their own liberation.

It is important to recognize, however, that the instances when emancipation was brought about through war constitute only one point on a spectrum of cases of the popular element in emancipation. Nor was violence entirely absent from other examples. Reference has already been made to popular reform movements against slavery and these intersected in various ways with action on the part of the slaves. During the American Civil War, as slaves through flight forced their attention on military and political leaders, so campaigning abolitionists articulated the hoped-for consequences to leaders and northern public opinion alike. A generation earlier in Britain popular antislavery pressure coincided with the outbreak of the slave revolt in Jamaica, allowing liberal politicians and reformers to clinch their argument that further upheaval could only be avoided by emancipation, a conviction that some white residents of the colony then held. During the last decade of Brazilian slavery the newly created mass abolitionist movement connected with a wave of slave desertions from the sugar estates flowing on southwards. The reformers then helped organize such desertions so that slavery had disappeared in some areas before the Golden Law of final emancipation in 1888.

It has been indicated in discussion of British West Indian emancipation that the coincidence of revolt and peaceful abolitionist campaigning was important. But there is an additional context of the abolitionist campaign that needs to be recalled. Popular antislavery enthusiasm in Britain did not become violent but it refreshed memories of outbreaks of violence that had accompanied the immediately preceding conflict over political reform in 1831–2. Earlier, at the time of the retreat of slavery in the northern states of the new United States, the decision of the Massachusetts Supreme Court in 1783 that ended slavery in the state has to be put in its context. The judicial decision followed a whole series of slave protests against their status that had run through the violent upheavals of the revolutionary years. And the court decision itself was explicitly based upon the revolutionary doctrine of the state constitution of 1780, that all men are equal. The court declared that this amounted to the abolition of slavery that should now be realized in practice. Obviously neither the Massachusetts nor the British examples are directly comparable to the violence of the Haitian Revolution and the American Civil War. None the less the context of violence, the memory of violence and the fear of more violence were relevant to these 'peaceful' cases of emancipation.

This is not the place for an extensive discussion of post-emancipation societies in the Americas. It is as well, however, to show briefly the relevance of some of the factors in slave societies to the later situation. Former masters, with varying degrees of success, tried to hold on to as much of the labour of the freed people as possible. They sought to enlist the power of the state on their behalf through the enactment of loosely drawn vagrancy laws, the imposition of taxes – the need for payment of which pushed the ex-slaves towards estate work – and efforts to keep the freed people out of the land market. Many of the former slaves were stubbornly resistant to these pressures but often ended up in some form of tenancy arrangement with landowners. When this did not amount to sufficient labour the former slave owners turned to alternatives in as tightly controlled conditions as possible. In Brazil and Cuba this meant the sort of worker already introduced before the end of slavery. In the Caribbean the imperial state helped out with programmes for introducing Asian indentured labourers who worked both alongside and instead of the former slaves. In the medium term there was a whole spectrum of social and economic outcomes. They stretched from plantation wage labour through forms of tenancy to peasant farming, migration to towns, work in developing industrial sectors and various combinations of these. And all within a changing international economic order that rendered plantation production of some staples less secure. This indicates that few former slaves experienced rapid material benefits from freedom. But neither that conclusion, nor the severe legal and social constraints that many of them encountered in their working lives, should disguise the fact that limitations were interlaced with some strands of choice. The former slaves could, to a degree, separate themselves out from other groups and hope to survive. Or they could seek client relationships with the influential on terms probably a little better than those of slavery. And notably in the United States for some decades, and to an extent elsewhere, former slaves became political agents with limited but diverse results. Emancipation in the Americas did bring some significant changes.

Slavery in the Middle East remained in many respects very different from the system in the Americas. Observing it in the nineteenth century, westerners often termed it 'mild' in implicit or explicit comparison with the institution in the United States.

This may often have resulted from comparing domestic slavery with the field labour of African-Americans. But it did little to advance the ending of slavery in the Middle East. In fact external powers found it difficult to have much influence over slavery within Muslim states in the region, such as the Ottoman Empire. The *sharia* recognized slavery and was therefore deemed by Muslim rulers also to regulate it appropriately. European powers had more leverage over the trade in slaves to the Middle East since it traversed political boundaries and was potentially subject to diplomatic arrangements or naval action. The British saw ending the trade from East Africa and the Horn to the region as part of their commitment to suppressing the slave trade everywhere. They obtained decrees from the Sultan of Turkey, the Shah of Persia, the Khedive of Egypt and local rulers in Africa and Arabia to make illegal the involvement of their respective subjects in the slave trade. The Brussels Conference of 1889–90 devised an international agreement to eliminate the African slave trade on land and sea. The major powers were able to dramatize the evils of the trade successfully and they had the force available to act on their policy, especially on the sea. The International Slavery Bureau that they set up under the Brussels Act virtually ended the slave trade between Africa and Arabia in the years 1890–1914.

There were two obvious points of attack for Europeans seeking to get their view of slavery acted upon. They could demonstrate sympathy for slaves from the region who sought their protection; in 1846 the bey of Tunis moved to allow the enfranchisement of slaves who wished it to prevent them seeking the protection of foreign authorities. European powers also claimed concern over the circumstances of Christian (usually white) slaves, particularly in the Ottoman dominions. The effect was limited because in the nineteenth century the numbers of Christian and white slaves from the Caucasus were much reduced. In the Ottoman case progress against slavery depended on the actions of the Ottoman government itself. Improvements in the circumstances of Georgians and Circassians in the 1850s in many cases constituted *de facto* emancipation and the Turkish authorities responded on occasion to the exposure of illegal trading in Africans by freeing and protecting them. Yet a number of states in the region only undertook a general emancipation between the two world wars and it was not until 1962 that slaves were officially freed in the Yemen and by royal decree in Saudi Arabia.

In some regions of Africa south of the Sahara there was a growth of slavery within lineage societies and some slave societies emerged in the later eighteenth and nineteenth centuries. Slave societies developed partly as a result of internal economic change and partly as a consequence of the need to compensate for the loss of the external slave trades as a source of wealth. The shift to 'legitimate' trades – palm oil and palm kernels for example – ironically sometimes led to production based on slave labour, not least because some of the mechanisms for generating slaves within Africa were still in place. Supply of other agricultural products, via regional trade within Africa and especially within the belt of savanna states, also extended slave-based production. South of the savanna states, in Asante for example, trading in slave products developed to the north as much as outwards to the Atlantic. Developments in the eighteenth and nineteenth centuries made the ending of slavery in Black Africa a more formidable problem.

There was no organized African antislavery impulse but practices of manumission and/or partial incorporation continued in lineage systems and in conformity with Muslim custom. If individuals were thought to have been unjustly reduced to slavery they were rescued and slaves being carried by traders through a community could be examined to determine the conditions and legitimacy of their seizure. European engagement with the ending of slavery in Africa was bitterly paradoxical in a number of ways. Struck by the horrors revealed by Livingstone, Cardinal Laviguerie's White Fathers and other European missionaries the 'new imperialism' at the time of the Partition of Africa focused, as the Brussels Conference indicated, on the elimination of the slave trade within and from Africa. The powers were slower to do much about slavery itself. The new colonial authorities imposed internal order and, in largely achieving it, reduced activities that had led to the acquisition of slaves. However, in the process the conflicts generated by European forces, as with the French in the Senegal Valley in the 1880s, promoted the enslavement of prisoners. Maintenance of order and the building of infrastructures required the colonial regimes to secure the acquiescence if not the support of indigenous elites. Their influence over local populations remained and they were the most likely suppliers of labour.

But many of them also had interests in slaves. Work on early colonial development projects was on occasion partly accomplished by slaves.

These paradoxical outcomes arose as a result of colonial officials' priorities that did not put the ending of slavery first. They also registered later European reflections on the policies and experience of achieving emancipation in their colonial territories elsewhere. The need to gain the collaboration of local slave owning elites was in part justified by the presumed mildness of the institution as compared with the American form and the forced labour in Portuguese territories that was increasingly exposed to public view at the beginning of the twentieth century. Securing a regular and sufficient supply of labour, and thus avoiding disturbing existing patterns of labour too much, whatever their nature, seemed a sensible policy to colonial officials.

The British in particular had also drawn conclusions from their country's earlier Caribbean and Indian experiences. They interpreted Caribbean emancipation as a substantial failure. Their criteria were the economic decline of the plantation system, which they believed resulted primarily from the failure to command a sufficient and reliable labour force, and the financial costs of the emancipation, including compensation to the owners. The Emancipation Act of 1833 had not applied to slavery in India but in the 1840s the East India Company had taken a different approach there. The policy was to act against slave dealing in a particular region, as the Europeans had begun to do in Africa, and then to proclaim that slavery had no legal standing in the area. The policy was rarely made widely known to slaves and they were therefore given no great encouragement to leave their masters. Nor was any compensation offered. The assumption was that existing relations of production would only slowly change and slavery would erode gradually. This avoided disruption both in relations with elites and in labour supply and was economical in financial and bureaucratic terms. Formally it met the antislavery standard. In practice it meant that the final release of slaves from their situation was uncertain in the colonies where the British and the French adopted this approach. Even the starting dates for the non-recognition of slavery were widely separated: 1874 in the Gold Coast, for example, but 1928 in Sierra Leone. In more remote areas the possession of human chattels persisted throughout the period between the two world wars. In Mauritania, a sparsely populated and undeveloped region where the institution was deeply rooted, the French proclaimed its loss of legal status in 1905. This was repeated at independence in 1960, and again in 1980, when international investigation discovered that it continued.

Whatever the attitude of colonial officials and indigenous elites in Africa, the slaves themselves, as in other regions, sometimes took a hand in achieving their own freedom. When they grasped that slavery was under some pressure they might negotiate improvements in their position, perhaps in the form of settlement on a bloc of land and the agreed division of its cash crops. Individuals and groups might simply leave, particularly if their place of origin was within reach. Most dramatically in the Banamba and Gumbu regions of French Sudan in 1905 a rolling wave of mass desertion, broadly similar to the phenomenon in Brazil, simply brought the system to an end.

As in the Americas, for most former slaves there was no immediate or dramatic change in their lives. Many remained dependent in some form or another on their ex-masters or some other local notable. Others became more tightly integrated into the former master's kin group. With varying results yet others trekked towards their home regions. Some attached themselves to Christian missionary communities and others ventured into peasant farming hoping to take advantage of the growing markets for commodity production. Where urban economies developed wage labour was a possibility, but so was unemployment. There were periods when the unemployed became a reserve army of labour and colonial authorities moved them on to work in harsh conditions elsewhere. Emancipation brought some choices but no guarantees.

Epilogue

One of the themes of this book has been the way that slavery has been able to be adapted to very different kinds of social, political and even physical environments. Slavery arose and was maintained in such historical circumstances as war and the development of markets and justified in terms of the 'otherness' and inferiority of the slaves. Unfortunately these circumstances have been historically recurrent. The very *malleability* of chattel slavery has made it difficult to eliminate entirely. The progress made against it since the late eighteenth century, in the vast areas from which evidence has been drawn in this discussion, has also depended on the conditions of a particular phase of history now past. Early modern European imperialism greatly expanded chattel slavery but later European imperialism was implicated in its retreat. The antislavery impulse, with its material and moral constituents, spread outwards and was carried to other parts of the world on the material, religious, political and military power of Western Europe and North America. The freedom with which this power has been exercised in relation to slavery has been reduced in the twentieth century, contributing to the fact that chattel slavery remains in some places and related forms of bondage are still quite extensive.

The case of a country like Mauritania – largely traditional in its social and economic practices, undeveloped, isolated and rarely noticed – has already been referred to. The resurgence of war between peoples who have historically been enemies and in the past have reduced each other to slavery has had similar effects in recent years. The southern Sudan is such a region brought to public attention as a result of the civil war between the Islamic government in Khartoum and the Christian black African inhabitants in the south of the country. The clearest evidence of the revival of slave seizure and slave trading from the 1980s onwards has been on the border between the black population of the southern region and the Arabs immediately to their north. Continuing conflict over grazing land and water in an area with a tradition of slaving and marked by religious difference allowed the civil war there to revive enslavement. This has particularly taken the form of Arab seizure of Dinka women and children, some of them from refugee camps.

Before we briefly consider the forms of antislavery activity in the present and the recent past, and the problems they present, two other questions arise as to the extent of slavery in the twentieth century. The first is whether it is appropriate, in relation to our discussion of slavery historically, to understand the horrendous circumstances of the people subjected to Nazi concentration camps and the Soviet gulag as those of slaves. Were these 'slave camps'? Some inhabitants of these camps were in part used for work under regimes of extreme compulsion. Those who controlled them perceived them as alien in ethnic, religious, racial or political terms. They usually had barely enough sustenance, if that, to survive and could not know what prospect they had of being released from these circumstances. Within institutions more 'total' than any plantation the victims of the camps sometimes showed sparks of resistance and made some little space in which to preserve their humanity. These characteristics of the lives of the inhabitants of the camps paralleled the situation of slaves. But there was one feature of many of these camps, central to our sense of the experience of a century that proclaimed its humanitarian successes against slavery elsewhere, that made their circumstances worse than slavery. Those people controlling slaves were interested in maintaining the system, in the reproduction of slavery. In the final phases of the Nazi regime the opposite was true in the camps. In the gulag also, although systematic extermination was not pursued in the same way, the regime was utterly careless of the lives of the prisoners. In this fundamental sense the camps of the totalitarian regimes contradicted the rationale of slavery and, to the modern mind, resulted in even more horrifying consequences.

What forms of bonded labour remain in the contemporary world in addition to the kinds of chattel slavery already quoted? Do they in practice represent a new expansion of a system that earlier in the twentieth century it was believed was progressively disappearing? What of the Filipino maids working for Gulf Arab families, or Thai country girls in a Bangkok brothel, or children in debt bondage in South Asia or Brazil? Recent investigations have also highlighted the sale of women for marriage and the acquisition of child labour through sham adoption. From the perspective of the day-to-day experience of the victims it matters little whether they are to be regarded as slaves or some other kind of bonded labourer. And, as we have noticed in earlier phases of history, the individual in debt bondage may never see the redemption of the debt. He or she is thus a lifetime slave. Yet in some contemporary cases the distinction between chattel slavery and other forms of bondage may still have significance. Let us take the case, much discussed in recent times, of the Thai peasant girl reduced to prostitution in the urban brothel. She is, in effect, bought from her parents by her employer. But the ostensible form of the transaction may be of a loan of, say, $2,000 to her parents. She is then obligated not only to work to pay for her keep but also to pay off the original amount handed over to her parents. Eventually she may cease to be thought suitable for the trade in sex and then may be cast aside. This is a brutally harsh outcome when it occurs, but the bondage has not been permanent.

That chattel slavery is no longer the primary problem is revealed by the extension in recent decades of the definition of the concerns of the League of Nations and the United Nations in this field. The international bodies became committed to the elimination of debt bondage, the sale of women for marriage and child labour in its various forms. But the fact that these issues are now the concern of a world body is both a gain and a loss. The end of slavery can no longer be so closely identified with the power and values of Europeans or Americans. Hostility to slavery at some level has become a universal consensus. But the problem remains of translating that into reality in a wide range of different circumstances. The main political barrier historically has been the attachment of rulers and governments to their independent sovereignties. In the first half of the nineteenth century the British, in their efforts to end the international slave trade across the Atlantic, found themselves frustrated as a result of the resistance of other powers to what they saw as British interference. When, however, after the Brussels Conference, the major European powers collaborated on the suppression of other slave trades they made substantial progress, not least because they could rely on force if they had to. But since the First World War the responsibility for dealing with the slave trade and slavery has fallen to international bodies. They have had to pay more respect to national sovereignties than did the major powers earlier. Moreover, neither the League of Nations nor the United Nations has had the physical force available that the powers had. Much additional information has been gathered on slavery and related forms of bonded labour. Committees of experts, operating with definitions of bondage under international conventions of 1926 and 1956, have met and made recommendations down to the present. Investigations leading to exposure of scandals in relation to bound labour have brought denials from governments, excuses or the declaration of another change in the law. The problem remains, perhaps to the extent of between 20 and 30 million people in some form of unfree labour. Chattel slavery may be largely an institution in the past but few are aware that so many are trapped in circumstances no less dehumanizing.

Select Bibliography

The journal *Slavery and Abolition: A Journal of Comparative Studies* is a rich site of analyses of all aspects of slavery. A general bibliography is: Miller, Joseph C., 1977. *Slavery: A Teaching Bibliography*. Waltham, Mass. This has been followed by a series of supplements by Miller et al. in *Slavery and Abolition*.

Books and Articles

Anderson, Perry, 1978. *Passages from Antiquity to Feudalism*. London.

Archer, Leonie J., 1988. *Slavery and other Forms of Unfree Labour*. London and New York.

Berlin, Ira, Barbara J. Fields, Steven F. Miller, Joseph P. Reidy and Leslie S. Rowland, 1992. *Slaves No More. Three Essays on Emancipation and the Civil War*. Cambridge.

Berlin, Ira and Philip D. Morgan, eds, 1993. *Cultivation and Culture: Labor and the Shaping of Slave Life in the Americas*. Charlottesville, Va.

Bonnassie, Pierre, 1991. *From Slavery to Feudalism in Southwestern Europe*. Cambridge.

Boswell, John, 1988. *The Kindness of Strangers. The Abandonment of Children in Western Europe from Late Antiquity to the Renaissance*. Harmondsworth.

Bradley, K. R., 1984. *Slaves and Masters in the Roman Empire. A Study in Social Control*. Brussels.

Bradley, Keith, 1989. *Slavery and Rebellion in the Roman World*. Bloomington.

—, 1994. *Slavery and Society at Rome*. Cambridge.

Bush, M. L., ed. 1996. *Serfdom and Slavery*. London.

Cartledge, Paul, 1985. 'Rebels and Sambos in Classical Greece: a Comparative View'. In Cartledge and Harvey eds, *Crux, Essays in Greek History presented to G.E.M. de Ste Croix*. pp. 40–6. London.

Cooper, Frederick, 1977. *Plantation Slavery on the East Coast of Africa.* New Haven, Conn.

Curtin, Philip D., 1969. *The Atlantic Slave Trade: A Census.* Madison, Wisc.

Davis, David Brion, 1966. *The Problem of Slavery in Western Culture.* Ithaca, NY and London.

—, 1975. *The Problem of Slavery in the Age of Revolution.* Ithaca, NY and London.

—, 1984. *Slavery and Human Progress.* New York.

Domar, Evsey D., 1970. 'The Causes of Slavery or Serfdom: A Hypothesis'. *Journal of Economic History* 30: 18–32.

Drescher, Seymour, 1977. *Econocide: British Slavery in the Era of Abolition.* Pittsburgh, Pa.

Eltis, David, 1987. *Economic Growth and the Ending of the Transatlantic Slave Trade.* New York.

Ewald, Janet T., 1992. 'Slavery in Africa and the Slave Trades from Africa'. *American Historical Review* 77: 465–85.

Finley, M. I., 1968. 'Slavery'. In *International Encyclopedia of the Social Sciences*, 14: 307–13. New York.

—, 1980. *Ancient Slavery and Modern Ideology.* London.

Fisher, N. R. E., 1995. *Slavery in Classical Greece.* Bristol.

Fogel, R. W., 1989. *Without Consent or Contract.* New York.

Fogel, Robert William and Stanley L. Engerman, 1974. *Time on the Cross: The Economics of American Negro Slavery*, 2 vols. Boston.

Foner, Eric, 1983. *Nothing But Freedom: Emancipation and its Legacy.* Baton Rouge, La.

Garlan, Yvon, 1988. *Slavery in Ancient Greece.* Ithaca, NY and London.

Genovese, Eugene D., 1974. *Roll, Jordan, Roll: The World the Slaves Made.* New York.

—, 1979. *From Rebellion to Revolution.* Baton Rouge La.

Glassman, Jonathan, 1991. 'The Bondsman's New Clothes: The Contradictory Consciousness of Slave Resistance on the Swahili Coast'. *Journal of African History* 32: 277–312.

Holt, Thomas C., 1992. *The Problem of Freedom: Race, Labor and Politics in Jamaica and Britain, 1832–1938.* Baltimore, Md.

Hopkins, Keith, 1983. *Conquerors and Slaves.* Cambridge.

Klein, Herbert S., 1978. *The Middle Passage: Comparative Studies in the Atlantic Slave Trade.* Princeton, NJ.

—, 1986. *African Slavery in Latin America and the Caribbean.* New York.

Klein, Martin and Claire Robertson, eds, 1983. *Women and Slavery in Africa.* Madison, Wisc.

Kolchin, Peter, 1993. *American Slavery: 1619–1877.* New York.

Lewis, Bernard, 1992. *Race and Slavery in the Middle East: An Historical Enquiry*. New York and Oxford.

Lovejoy, Paul E., ed, 1981. *The Ideology of Slavery in Africa*. Beverly Hills, Ca. and London.

—, 1983. *Transformations in Slavery: A History of Slavery in Africa*. Cambridge.

Manning, Patrick, 1990. *Slavery and African Life*. Cambridge.

McGlynn, Frank and Seymour Drescher, eds, 1992. *The Meaning of Freedom: Economics, Politics and Culture after Slavery*. Pittsburgh, Pa.

Meillassoux, Claude, 1991. *The Anthropology of Slavery*. London.

Mendelsohn, Isaac, 1949. *Slavery in the Ancient Near East*. New York.

Merivale, Herman, 1861. *Lectures on Colonization and Colonies*. London.

Miers, Suzanne and Igor Kopytoff, eds, 1977. *Slavery in Africa. Historical and Anthropological Perspectives*. Madison, Wisc.

Miers, Suzanne and Richard Roberts, eds, 1988. *The End of Slavery in Africa*. Madison, Wisc.

Mintz, Sydney and Richard Price, 1976. *An Anthropological Approach to the Afro-American Past*. Philadelphia, Pa.

Newsweek, 1992. 'Special Report: Slavery'. 119 (4 May). 8–15.

Nieboer, H. J., 1900. *Slavery as an Industrial System*. The Hague.

Patterson, Orlando, 1982. *Slavery and Social Death*. Cambridge, Mass.

Phillips, William, 1985. *Slavery from Roman Times to the Early Transatlantic Trade*. Manchester.

Roberts, Richard and Martin Klein, 1989. 'The Banamba Slave Exodus of 1905 and the Decline of Slavery in the Western Sudan'. *Journal of African History*, 30: 89–106.

Sawyer, Roger, 1986. *Slavery in the Twentieth Century*. London.

Schwartz, Stuart B., 1992. *Slaves, Peasants and Rebels: Reconsidering Brazilian Slavery*. Champaign, Il.

Scott, Rebecca J., 1985. *Slave Emancipation in Cuba: The Transition to Free Labor, 1860–1899*. Princeton, NJ.

Scott, Rebecca and Seymour Drescher, eds. 1988. *The Abolition of Slavery and the Aftermath of Emancipation in Brazil*. Durham, NC.

Ste Croix, Geoffrey de, 1982. *Class Struggle in the Ancient Greek World*. London.

Tadman, Michael, 1996. *Speculators and Slaves: Masters, Traders and Slaves in the Old South*. Madison, Wisc.

Thornton, John, 1998. *Africa and Africans in the making of the Atlantic world, 1400–1800*. Cambridge.

Turley, David M., 1991. *The Culture of English Antislavery, 1780–1860*. London.

Twaddle, Michael, ed, 1993. *The Wages of Slavery: From Chattel Slavery to Wage Labour in Africa, the Caribbean and England.* London.

Wakefield, Edward Gibbon, 1849. *A View of the Art of Colonization.* London.

Walzer, Michael, 1985. *Exodus and Revolution.* New York.

Wiedemann, T. E. J., 1987. *Slavery: Greece and Rome.* Oxford.

Index

Luria's Legacy in the 21st Century

Luria's Legacy in the 21st Century

Edited by

ANNE-LISE CHRISTENSEN, PHD
Center for Rehabilitation of Brain Injury (CRBI)
University of Copenhagen
Copenhagen, Denmark

ELKHONON GOLDBERG, PHD, ABPP
Department of Neurology
New York University School of Medicine
New York, New York

DMITRI BOUGAKOV, PHD
The Institute of Neuropsychology and Cognitive Performance
New York, New York

2009

OXFORD
UNIVERSITY PRESS

Oxford University Press, Inc., publishes works that further
Oxford University's objective of excellence
in research, scholarship, and education.

Oxford New York
Auckland Cape Town Dar es Salaam Hong Kong Karachi
Kuala Lumpur Madrid Melbourne Mexico City Nairobi
New Delhi Shanghai Taipei Toronto

With offices in
Argentina Austria Brazil Chile Czech Republic France Greece
Guatemala Hungary Italy Japan Poland Portugal Singapore
South Korea Switzerland Thailand Turkey Ukraine Vietnam

Published by Oxford University Press, Inc.
198 Madison Avenue, New York, New York 10016

www.oup.com

Library of Congress Cataloging-in-Publication Data
Luria's legacy in the 21st century / edited by Anne-Lise Christensen,
Elkhonon Goldberg, Dmitri Bougakov.
p. ; cm.
Includes bibliographical references and index.
ISBN-13: 978-0-19-517670-4 (alk. paper)
1. Luriia, A. R. (Aleksandr Romanovich), 1902–1977. 2. Neurologic examination.
3. Clinical neuropsychology. I. Christensen, Anne-Lise. II. Goldberg, Elkhonon.
III. Bougakov, Dmitri. IV. Title: Luria's legacy in the twenty-first century.
[DNLM: 1. Luriia, A. R. (Aleksandr Romanovich), 1902–1977.
2. Neuropsychology. 3. Psychophysiology. WL 103.5 L967 2009]
RC348.L87 2009 616.8′0475—dc22

2008049531

1 3 5 7 9 8 6 4 2

Printed in the United States of America
on acid-free paper

Contents

Disclaimer

Drs. Bilder, Goldberg and Podell have proprietary interest in The Executive Control Battery.

List of Contributors

William B. Barr, PhD
Chief of Neuropsychology
Departments of Neurology and Psychiatry
Langone Medical Center, New York University
New York, New York

Robert M. Bilder, PhD
Neuropsychiatric Institute and Hospital
Chief of Medical Psychology – Neuropsychology
Jane and Terry Semel Institute for Neuroscience and Human Behavior
Stewart and Lynda Resnick Neuropsychiatric Hospital
David Geffen School of Medicine at UCLA
Los Angeles, California

Dmitri Bougakov, PhD
The Institute of Neuropsychology and Cognitive Performance
New York, New York

Xavier E. Cagigas, PhD
Postdoctoral Fellow in Neurobehavioral Genetics & Neuropsychology
Consortium for Neuropsychiatric Phenomics Semel Institute for
Neuroscience & Human Behavior University of California,
Los Angeles

Anne-Lise Christensen, PhD, Dr. Phil. H.C.
Professor Emeritus
Center for Rehabilitation of Brain Injury (CRBI)
University of Copenhagen
Denmark

Connie C. Duncan, PhD
Clinical Psychophysiology and Pharmacology Laboratory
Center for Traumatic Stress
Department of Psychiatry
Uniformed Services University
Bethesda, Maryland

Elkhonon Goldberg, PhD
Department of Neurology
New York University School of Medicine
New York, New York

Allan F. Mirsky, PhD
Scientific Review Officer
Division of Extramural Activities
National Institute of Mental Health, NIH
Bethesda, Maryland

Luba Nakhutina, PhD
Department of Neurology
SUNY Downstate Medical Center
Brooklyn, New York
Psychology Service
NYU-Rusk Institute of Rehabilitation Medicine
New York

Kenneth Podell, PhD
Director, Div. of Neuropsychology & Sports Concussion Safety Program
Henry Ford Health System
Associate Professor, Full-time Affiliate
Department of Psychiatry and Behavioral Neurosciences
Wayne State University
Detroit, Michigan

George P. Prigatano, PhD
Newsome Chair of Clinical Neuropsychology
Department of Clinical Neuropsychology
Barrow Neurological Institute
St. Joseph's Hospital and Medical Center
Phoenix, Arizona

Jared X. Van Snellenberg, MA, MPhil
Department of Psychology, Columbia University
New York, New York

Tor D. Wager, PhD
Department of Psychology
Columbia University
New York, New York

Klaus R.H. von Wild, MD
Professor of Neurosurgery
Medical Faculty of the W.W.-University Münster
Director, kvw-neuroscience consulting GmbH
Münster, Germany

1

Luria's Legacy in the 21st Century

Anne-Lise Christensen

The common thread in this edited volume is to revive and extend Luria's original concepts and bring them into the present day. The volume has its roots in the 1975 publication *Luria's Neuropsychological Investigation* (Christensen 1975); a second edition, first printing followed in 1979 with a second printing in 1991, since which the text has been out of print. This chapter will mainly concentrate on the theories of A.R. Luria, their clinical application through the years, and the results that have been achieved.

The challenge to take up this work stems from a continued worldwide interest in the scientific theories of A.R. Luria, his work in science, and his methods in diagnostics and rehabilitation.

In recent years, neurosurgical and neuropsychological societies—among them European Multidisciplinary Neurotraumatology (EMN), the World Academy of Multidisciplinary Neurotraumatology (AMN), and the International Neuropsychological Society (INS)—have with increasing frequency invited presentations about Luria's work at their conferences. Inquiries have persistently been made from publishers in various countries wanting to obtain copyright for a translation of the publication and from individual professionals within clinical neurology or clinical neuropsychology looking for information. It all indicates that Luria's ideas and thoughts are still alive and his methods wanted and needed.

Such an interpretation gains some support in a 2008 publication by Taylor & Francis, *Textbook of Clinical Neuropsychology*, edited by Joel Morgan and Joseph H. Richter. A chapter in this book bears the title "Theories of Clinical

Neuropsychology and Brain-Behavior Relationships: Luria and Beyond," written by Daniel Tranel, who refers to a paper by Luria published in *Cortex* in 1964 and describing it as "a historical gem." Tranel correctly emphasizes Luria's conception of "the distinct ingredients that make up complex mental functions" and concludes that "Luria's contributions have survived, and perhaps even thrived, with the test of time, and contemporary students and scholars would do well to heed his techniques."

The influence of American neuropsychologists, especially of Arthur Benton, leads Tranel to comparisons between the Iowa–Benton method and Luria's investigation, which in fact reveal similarities, such as flexibility, variability, and continuous hypothesis testing, following models known from clinical medical practice. The main difference seems to be the use of tests. Luria developed tests based on his theory especially for the examination of the primary functions only to be able to analyze the components of the patient's reactions as thoroughly as possible. In comparison, the core battery of the Iowa–Benton method consists of the well-known standardized neuropsychological tests. Thus, the difference between the two approaches is often characterized as qualitative versus quantitative; however, the difference should instead be acknowledged as analytical, determined by the understanding of the individual components of the function at hand, rather than a measurement of abilities, quoting Reitan.

In context of the expansion of neuroscientific knowledge, combined with the development in neurosurgery and neuroimaging, and the need in the present day of an updated neuropsychological theory and new and adequate neuropsychological tools for testing and rehabilitating brain-injured patients, Luria's theoretical and practical approaches may be in the right position to fulfill these needs.

Luria's Neuropsychological Investigation: An evaluation method in cases of brain injury

Luria's Neuropsychological Investigation was initiated by one of Luria's principal works, *Higher Cortical Functions in Man* (Luria 1966), and its publication was supported and authenticated by A.R. Luria himself as proved in his foreword to the book (Christensen 1975, pp. 7–8):

> It is a pleasure to write a few words as an introduction to this little book.
>
> During the last decades, neuropsychological examination of patients with focal brain lesions has become one of the most important methods of localization diagnosis of brain injuries.
>
> It is obvious that the classic neurologic methods, evolved for investigation of the most elementary functions of the brain such as sensitivity, movements, tonus and reflexes, are insufficient for an analysis of the function of the most complex cortical zones. These zones—known as secondary or tertiary (alias intrinsic) zones of the cortex—and occupying a major part of the hemispheres—have to do with the organization of complex behavioral processes, e.g. gnostic and practical forms of activity, speech and the cognitive processes.

Thus disturbances in these complex functions can be diagnosed by methods which have little resemblance to the methods used in classic neurology.

Unfortunately, psychology has not yet developed a technique for the adequate evaluation of localized injuries in these zones. Current psychological tests are too complex and they can only provide an evaluation of some general levels of cognitive processes but they can hardly be of any use for a localized diagnosis of brain lesions.

It therefore became necessary to develop a new methodology for a neuropsychological approach to the problem of focal diagnostics of these complex zones.

This goal has entailed extensive and complicated studies not only of the symptoms of disturbances of higher cortical functions, but also *qualification of defects* and an analysis of the factors underlying these behavioral defects.

For the past four decades, we have attempted to develop such a technique. We started with a basic reconsideration of the concept of "function," which we considered as complex *functional systems*, and we tried to find ways to learn what each zone of the cortex contributes to the organization of these functional systems. This brought us to the assumption that complex behavioral processes are, in fact, not localized, but *distributed* across broader areas of the brain, and that the contribution of each cortical zone to the organization of the whole functional system is *very specific*. We must then assume that each local lesion of the cortex results in a very *specific type* of disturbance of these complex behavioral processes and the approach showed the necessity for a careful analysis of specific disturbances in the neuropsychological examination of local brain lesions or for diagnosis of a local brain injury.

All this is of great importance for neurology and neurosurgery, and we are sure that neuropsychological methods can indeed enrich the examination of the brain-injured patient and provide a more precise and early diagnosis of focal injury.

It must be emphasized that a most important role is played not only by the selection of proper methods, but also by an adequate *analysis* of the symptoms, i.e. a *qualification* of the symptoms achieved by these techniques.

This is the reason why we deeply appreciate the attempt of our friend and colleague, Anne-Lise Christensen, to give not only a description of the neurological technique we use for the diagnosis of focal brain lesions, but to describe the very complicated methods for evaluation of the symptoms found, i.e. the careful qualification of the symptoms which can have different psychological structures and different meanings with different localizations of the injury.

We hope this book will be favorably received by psychologists, neurologists and neurosurgeons and that the introduction of the neuropsychological methods of examination for local diagnostics of focal brain lesions may prove its importance.

(Moscow, October 1972, A.R. Luria)

Luria also contributed a newly finished paper, which he considered illuminating and appropriate to be the first chapter of *Luria's Neuropsychological Investigation*. The title of the paper, translated from Russian, was "Neuropsychology and the Study of Higher Cortical Functions."

The content of the chapter constituted an eminently adequate background for the presentation of this new and specialized method to fulfill the demands for early and precise diagnoses of local brain injury in modern neurosurgery. Its applicability has to a rather high degree remained eminent, fitting the newest theoretical knowledge and not being refuted by any new insight.

This first chapter of *Luria's Neuropsychological Investigation* deals with the insufficiency of neurology to examine especially the more complicated forms of mental activity and the inconsistency of direct localization of the higher cerebral functions: "If function, defined as the function of a specific tissue, is to be 'localized' in a specific area of the secretory system or the nervous system, 'the functional system' obviously cannot be 'localized' in a specific area of the cerebral tissue, but must be distributed *in a complete system (or in a constellation) of cooperating zones of the cerebral cortex and the subcortical structures.* By these means—and this is of extreme importance—*each of the areas makes a highly specific contribution to ensure the operation of the functional system.* . . . and if we are to make a local diagnosis of a brain injury—a diagnosis based on an analysis of disturbances of the higher cortical functions—we cannot merely state that a defect exists, but we must qualify the disturbance in a given function, i.e. carefully analyze the defect psychologically (or psychophysiologically)" (p. 17).

The diagnosis has to be based on an *analysis* of disturbances of the higher cortical functions, and this "qualitative analysis" is the task of "the new branch of science—neuropsychology."

It is by the development of methods for the "qualification of the defect" that "*neuropsychology* has become an important aid in the diagnostics of local brain lesions and furthermore has led to a scientifically founded theory for the rehabilitation of the complicated functions that have been disturbed by local brain lesions" (p. 18).

On the same page, Luria further claims that "the importance of neuropsychology is not merely practical or clinical. It also has a great importance for the advancement of the scientific *theory* about the very structure of the psychic processes, i.e. for the founding of a scientific psychology to answer the question of the inner structure of the psychological processes."

Luria's Neuropsychological Investigation was published as a text, a manual, and test cards, the text being founded on the overwhelming impression the reading of *Higher Cortical Functions in Man* had made on me (i.e., A-L.C.).

The background for the publication was the first-ever position as a clinical psychologist at a neurosurgical department in Denmark, at the University of Aarhus, in the early 1960s. The job requirements for this position included examinations of the general psychological and emotional states of patients; and level of consciousness, motivation, and intellectual and cognitive functioning integrated in a diagnostic proposal.

Following the progress of patients was considered very important; all kinds of stimulation enhancing the progress was measured by repeated evaluations.

The diagnoses of the patients in the department included all kinds of illnesses of the central nervous system, brain tumors, cranial trauma, spinal cord trauma, aneurysms, and others.

In the attempts to fulfill these requirements, an examination method was required that used a terminology congruent with the one used by the medical and nursing professions and a method that was rooted in knowledge about the brain and its functioning.

With this background, reading *Higher Cortical Functions in Man* felt like a revelation.

To implement the methods described by Luria in my own daily clinical use, I made a translation of *Higher Cortical Functions in Man* into my own language (Danish) and structured the complex contents into a form that provided an overview and secured a process as close to Luria's intensions as I believed possible.

It was not long before this advanced and comprehensive contribution to the clinical neurosurgical practice became accepted by the staff of the department, and with a growing appreciation; so much so, that a position as a neuropsychologist changed from being viewed as an interesting curiosity to a meaningful, even illuminating addition, which could be made use of by all professionals in the department and indeed by the patients and their families. Studies in 1954 at the Center for Cognitive Studies at Harvard and attending Jerome S. Bruner lectures (Bruner, Goodnow, Austin 1956) turned out to be helpful in understanding the cognitive functioning of the patients undergoing this kind of "investigation." The theories of cognition, the cognitive revolution, which I had become acquainted with, matched the ideas of Luria and Vygotsky.

In 1969, I attended the World Congress of General Psychology in London. Luria was invited as the keynote speaker and was present at the welcome reception of the congress as was Jerome Bruner, who was a friend of Alexander Luria. Bruner urged me to introduce myself to Luria and tell him about my psychological work in neurosurgery. I did so, and Luria reacted by saying:

> Why don't you come to Moscow?

I did not meet Luria again during the congress as unfortunately on one of the first days, he was struck down by a heart attack, which required hospitalization.

Standing in for him, Hans Lukas Teuber read Luria's paper "The Origin and Cerebral Organization of Man's Conscious Action" (Luria 1969).

A few months later, however, I received an invitation from the Soviet Ministry of Health. I left Denmark with some trepidation, strongly supported by Jerome Bruner, who encouraged me "to go and learn from Luria for however long it may take".

The visit became an everlasting experience.

Luria's laboratory at the Bourdenko Neurosurgical Institute

I was accepted into the group of neuropsychologists surrounding Luria, among them Elkhonon Goldberg, who was chosen by Luria to be my guide at the Bourdenko Neurosurgical Institute. Here he ensured my adaptation to the scientific atmosphere in Luria's laboratory, to get to know his collaborators, and to be acquainted with the work and the research being performed.

The experiences turned out to be manifold; after work, in the spirit of Luria's and Vygotsky's emphasis on culture, I was encouraged to visit museums and cultural surroundings around Moscow. During my 3-week stay, the mornings were spent following Luria on his rounds and later watching him examining patients while I sat in an armchair next to Luria's desk. Also, members of the psychological staff were present, all of it creating an atmosphere of providing information and support to the patient being examined. The instruction to me was to observe the patient's behavior and reactions as closely as possible. Luria explained his questions and commands to me in English, occasionally asking me about my impressions and interpretations of the patient's responses, and wanting me to come up with questions and suggestions for further illumination of my observations. In the evenings, dinner at Luria's home on Frunze Street was not unusual. The dinner was followed by a lecture, where elements from the day's work or topics of special interest were presented as introduction for discussion. When leaving, I was given reprints to read, fetched from the shelves of Lana Luria's pantry, which served as a storeroom for Luria's papers (Christensen 2002).

During this first visit, I presented Luria with my personal manual on the structure of his investigation, written in Danish; he looked at it and made the comment: "Of course it is a vulgarization! However, I have always wanted someone to do what you have done." He suggested that I translate the manuscript into English when back home and return to Moscow when this task had been accomplished. I did so and returned in 1973.

Elkhonon Goldberg was not around this time (Goldberg 2001, Chapter 2).

Luria read my manuscript, made corrections, and urged me to have it published with the words: "The world needs it."

My third visit to the Bourdenko Institute in Luria's lifetime took place in 1975, when my book had just come out. Luria welcomed me with appreciation in his characteristic way of showing joy and delight, coming all the way to the aircraft stairs to receive me. When I arrived, the Danish and Swedish neuroscientists Niels Lassen and David Ingvar had just left Moscow, leaving Luria's office full of early regional cerebral blood flow (rCBF) imaging posters (Figure 1–1), which he rightfully experienced as verifying his theory (Ingvar and Lassen 1978).

Luria followed the reviews of the publication closely, and it was in a letter from him that I learned about the critical review written by Reitan. Luria wrote, much in the same style in which he in his letters to me usually referred to both his own and others' publications: "By the way, have you seen the review of Reitan—it is not too bad." The review was published in *Contemporary Psychology* (Reitan 1976) and the title was "The Vulgarization That Luria Always Wanted." Reitan's main statement was that Luria's procedures for neuropsychological evaluation seemed

(a)

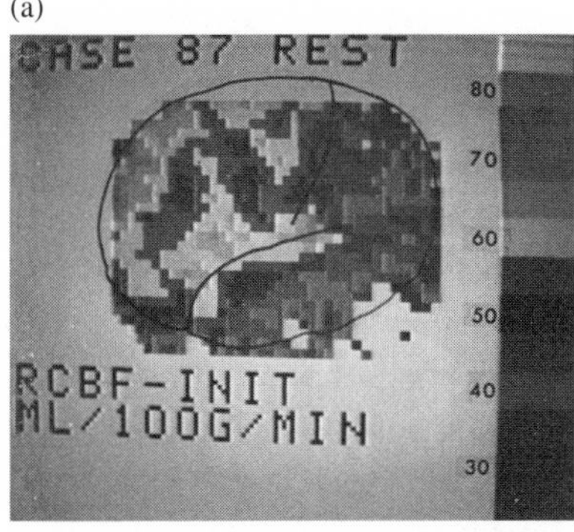

(b)

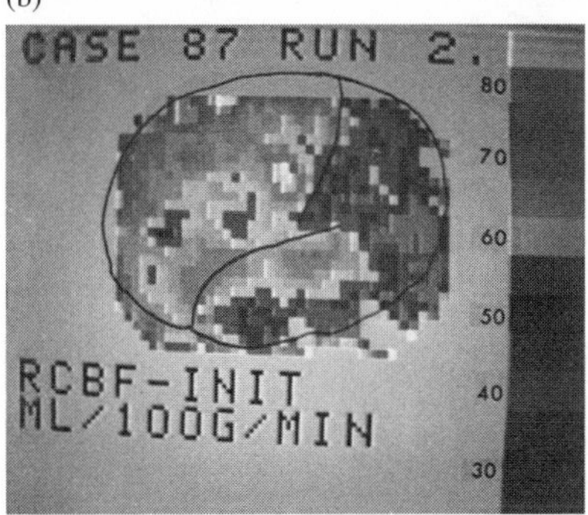

(c)

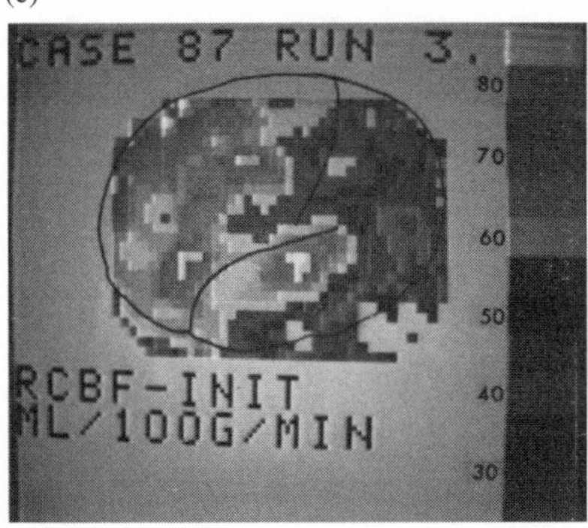

FIGURE 1–1. Examples of rCBF images hanging on the walls in Luria's laboratory, 1975: (a) rest flow; (b) citing the days of the week and the months of the year; (c) response to complex grammatical sentences.

to come closer to the conventional neurologic evaluation than to the psychological assessment as it is customarily performed in the United States. He further stated that Luria's neuropsychology "opens new paths to answer the question of the inner structure of psychological processes. Luria's approach is one in which he attempts to analyze the nature and interrelationships of deficits rather than measured abilities."

Progress of *Luria's Neuropsychological Investigation* (LNI)

The acronym LNI was soon used for the publication. It was welcomed by many, and translations were made into several languages: the first into Spanish in 1978 (University of Madrid), with a second printing in 1987; into German in 1980 ("Tüluc," initiated by Prof. Klaus Mayer, University of Tübingen); into Swedish in 1984 (Birgitta Stegmann, Karolinska University); into Japanese in 1987 (Prof. Nishimura, Osaka); and with special success into Zulu in 1999 (P. Msomi and S.G. Tollman, University of Natal). The advantage obtained was the culturally adaptable tasks.

However, in the United States, the LNI suffered the fate of becoming standardized as "The Luria Nebraska Neuropsychology Battery" (Golden, Hammeke, and Purisch 1978), which soon overshadowed the original publication. This confirmed the prophecy of Kolb and Wishaw (1990), who wrote a thorough review in *Fundamentals of Human Neuropsychology*: "Based on about 35 years of research by Luria and his colleagues in the Soviet Union, it is probably the most thorough battery available . . . ."

The principal advantages of Luria's battery are according to Kolb and Wishaw the following: "(1) It is based on theoretical principles of neuropsychological functioning, making the interpretation a logical conclusion of the theory, (2) It is thorough, inexpensive, easy to administer, flexible, and brief, taking only about 1 hour to administer, (3) It validates the actual behavior of the subject rather than inferred cognitive processes, thus making interpretation more straightforward."

However, the disadvantages of the Luria procedure were also presented: "(1) Scoring is subjective and is based on clinical experience. It is unlikely that a novice in neuropsychology or neurology could easily master the interpretation without extensive training. On the other hand, experienced neuropsychologists or neurologists ought to find the battery easy to learn. (2) Because the manual that accompanies the battery offers no validation studies, it must be taken on faith that the tests really measure what Luria claims they do. This criticism is the most serious, because most Western neuropsychologists are likely to continue to use psychometric assessment tools reporting validation studies."

In the standardized version of Luria's test procedures, Kolb and Wishaw's review contained a reference to Spiers (1981) "It is not the items, per se, but the manner in which Luria made use of them as a means of testing hypotheses concerning various abilities, deficits or functions, which is his method and his unique contribution to neuropsychological assessment. Consequently, the incorporation of items drawn from Luria's work into a standardized test should not be interpreted to mean that the test is an operationalization or standardization of Luria's method."

The statements about the LNI and the examples quoted in the various reviews indicated interest and acknowledgment but also a certain hesitation based on the fact that the analytic method of functions joined in systems was so far from the well-known, accepted, and usual psychometric approach. The *Zeitgeist*, or cultural tradition, in many countries was not as yet ready for an evaluation based on a theory as advanced as Luria's.

However, those who became knowledgeable about the method and made use of it believed that great advantages were obtained. An individualized, qualitative (replicable) approach was made available compatible with neurologic terminology and objective in nature: A method that allowed symptoms to be analyzed and combined into syndromes, where deficits and preserved functions were qualified. And perhaps most important of all, the procedure took place in an ongoing phenomenologic and dynamic interaction between examiner and patient, making full use of the feedback systems inherent in the theory, serving the patient's insight and possibilities for change and improvement.

At the same time, it also seemed possible to fulfill Luria's main goal, first expressed in *Higher Cortical Functions in Man* and later in a more elaborated form in *The Making of Mind* (Luria 1979): "to advocate for a new and close collaboration in brain injury, where a linking between (a) an emerging paradigm in qualitative, phenomenological neuropsychology (b) the improved techniques in neurosurgery and (c) the new trends in neuroscience can be promoted by the attempt to analyze, describe and understand individual functioning, and thus lead to fulfilling the main intention to reassure the best possible diagnoses and courses of treatment."

Currently, Lucia's legacy has gained renewed interest, supported by the still developing research in neuroscience—referred to and described by the contributors to this volume—which has confirmed and elaborated Luria's functional systems theory, closely related to the elaborated network theory of Joaquin Fuster (2003) and the Theory of Neuronal Group Selection (TNGS) of Gerald Edelman (2004). Edelman's theory consists of three tenets: (1) developmental selection and (2) experiential selection, both of which operate on repertoires of neural variants, and (3) reentry, a key process ensuring spatiotemporal correlation and conscious integration—a global brain theory explaining diversity and integration in the central nervous system. The insight provided by neuroimaging research has further illuminated and supported Luria's theories (see Chapter 3 in this volume).

On the whole through all the areas presented in this volume, support has been obtained for the updating of Luria's legacy with the purpose of reintroducing his methods into clinical work with brain-injury patients. New ways seem open to a deeper understanding of the dynamics in the mental functioning of patients, thereby serving to emphasize the role of the mind in the brain–mind relationship.

Interestingly, in the prefaces to *Higher Cortical Functions in Man* written in the 1960s, these same views were expressed.

Hans Lukas Teuber stated in his preface that

> Professor Luria's techniques, in their intent and in their application, are extensions of the classical neurological examination . . . that must be used in conjunction with, and not in its stead. In this way, the maximal benefit will accrue to the diagnosis and to an understanding of the roots of the difficulties.
>
> For it should be remembered that the central task of neuropsychology is always twofold: to help the patient by understanding the disease, in turn, as an experiment of nature, that if properly used, may provide us with essential insights into the physiologic basis of normal function . . . any contribution to neuropsychology attempts to tell us how the brain does work . . . by carefully observing how it sometimes does not.
>
> (p. xi)

The second preface written by Karl Pribram includes neuropsychology in the neurosciences, stating: "Luria has, with one well-aimed stroke managed to bring *Neuropsychology* back into the mainstream of scientific endeavor, while at the same time guarding the spirit and substance of the Soviet experiences in this area of science . . . ." (p. xv).

Higher Cortical Functions in Man is a documentary of bedside observations and experiments in the tradition of von Monakov and Goldstein—but the observations and the experiments are made in the image of Sechenov, Vygotsky, and Pavlov instead of Külpe, Brentano, and Wertheimer ("reflex organization is everywhere conceived of and shown to be a two-way street whose traffic pattern is built of feedback between the central nervous system and peripheral sensory and motor structures")—to which can be added: comparable to the perception–action cycle of Fuster (Fuster 2003).

The insight into the syndromes of difficulties the patient experiences provides possibilities for the neuropsychologist to initiate an interactive feedback process that can be closely linked to the planning of the most effective rehabilitation of the patient's cognitive, social, and behavioral way of functioning and thus create a strong and valuable connection between diagnosis and treatment.

The examination method as the basis for rehabilitation planning

As stated by Goldberg and Bougakov in this volume, little was known about brain plasticity and capacity for self-repair in Luria's times, and the trust in rehabilitation was sparse (Stein, Brailowsky, and Will 1995).

Rehabilitation, from the viewpoint of the Western world, had not obtained a strong scientific basis. Results had not been obtained that were considered sufficiently scientific on the one side, and on the other, mainly personal and social. As a result, agreement on the methods of assessment for building rehabilitation programs was not fully realized until the advent of Luria's theories.

Already in *Restoration of Function after Brain Injury*, Luria wrote about the problem of plasticity and the reorganization of functional systems, describing how, for example, temporary inhibition and removal of that inhibition could restore the function in its original form.

However, in most cases the damage sustained by particular areas of the cerebral cortex or by the conducting pathways is severe enough to cause a loss of the corresponding function.

> In such cases the fate of the disturbed function will be completely different and other methods must be used for its restoration. (Luria 1963)

Luria continues: "Since the neuronal structures of the cortex, once destroyed, are incapable of regeneration, restoration of the function of the affected system can hardly be expected, and it may be assumed that the brain lesion will cause irreversible damage to the complex psycho-physiological functions of the brain. This assumption, however, is quite unjustified."

Reconsidering the literature and current and newer animal research combined with developmental studies gives evidence of intensive reorganization taking place in functional systems such as perception, memory, and intellect, to a plasticity of operations of mental activity, which was characterized as its most important feature. Here Luria refers to Bernshtein having showed that a particular objective action (such as driving in a nail) is hardly ever carried out by the same system of muscles, except when it has become highly automatic. If the position of the body is changed very slightly, the striking movement will be carried out by a completely different selection of coordinated acts while the final object is preserved.

The higher psychological systems are characterized by an even more complicated structure. The theory of the various structural levels of the nervous processes, of which the current scientific knowledge is supportive, provides a background for the understanding of forms of compensation, replacement, or reorganization. Improvement in function has also been shown in cases where a specific movement is transferred to a new level of integration (i.e., examples giving rise to new ways in working with the patient in the rehabilitation process).

Luria's early work in a rehabilitation center in the Urals during the Second World War with patients who had penetrating gunshot wounds led to the development of goals and measures to (1) define precisely the loss of function associated with the specific brain injuries in various locations and (2) design rehabilitation programs resting on firm scientific ground.

These goals were adopted at the first European rehabilitation center, The Center for Rehabilitation of Brain Injury (CRBI), founded in 1985 at the University of Copenhagen. Several outcome studies from the CRBI have proved the efficiency of rehabilitation according to these methods and provided successful research and developed new methods in the combined diagnostic and rehabilitative work

(Christensen and Uzzell 1988, 1994, 2000; Christensen, et al. 1992; Christensen 1995; Teasdale, et al. 1997; Siert 2000; Svendsen 2006; Svendsen and Teasdale 2006; Schönberger, Humle, and Teasdale 2006).

The basis for the rehabilitation planning according to Luria (1963) is the qualitative description and the behavioral study of the interrelationships and coordination of functions. The primary aim of this qualitative analysis is to disclose the inner structure of the defect, as well as the intact functions in cases of brain trauma with destruction of cortical and subcortical tissue.

Luria distinguished between primary and secondary disturbances and developed a number of methods to help the patients. Observing the patients closely could reveal what he called "substitutive compensation," leading to reorganized functional systems, which could take place in two basic ways: in one, the same functional system is transferred to a new level of organization, which is referred to as "intersystemic reorganization"; the concept refers to the function being carried out on a more primitive, automatic level, or it can be transferred to the level of higher cortical processes (for instance, by employing speech, adding commands to each new step of the process). According to the latter type of reorganization, the patient can learn to rely on a different functional system: a type of compensation referred to as "intrasystemic reorganization." In both kinds of reorganization, "recovery" is brought about by the incorporation of some new afferentation into the disturbed functional system.

Here, Luria is referring to animal studies in which results have been described as relationships between functional systems and afferents. It has been proved that a functional system cannot exist without a constant afferent nerve supply. Each functional system possesses a particular group of receptors, which together form a specific "afferent field" ensuring the normal working of the functional system. The number of afferent impulses required for the working of any functional system decreases with practice, so that only a small group of receptors is in active use. One of these stands out as "the dominant receptor," and the rest remains in a latent state forming a reserve of afferent impulses for that particular functional system. The quickness and ease of reorganization that takes place within a system may be related to a rich supply of afferent impulses.

Characteristic of the rehabilitative process within Luria's theoretical system, the restored activity requires great effort and is carried out extremely slowly at first. The amount of effort reflects the degree to which the recovered function differs psychologically from the original function. The aid and direction of a therapist is usually necessary during the first stages of the recovery process. The therapist's role is to help the patients identify individual methods to compensate for the defect in mastering specific tasks. The training has to be guided and carried out systematically.

The theory and principles in *Luria's Neuropsychological Investigation* thus have provided the neuropsychologist with a background not only to get insight into the dynamics of the psychological functioning of patients but also to make it possible to qualify the disturbances caused by the brain injuries and thereby to support ways of reorganization meaningful for the cognitive adaptation of patients. The procedure of the investigation, hierarchically organized, including feedback and possibilities for change, based on the individual resources of patients and the culture of which they are part, at the same time influences motivation as well as the emotional state of the patients.

The aim of this presentation has been to provide the cornerstones for a basic understanding of Luria's theory. A reference to the theory of Joaquin Fuster, which incorporates neuroscience of today in a thinking that is very much in congruence with Luria's ideas, may serve as an example of an updating of the theory: "For an investigation to provide reliable results, it has to be performed in accordance with a theory, a theory where the notion is given up, that cognitive functions as perception, attention etc. are separate entities and separate neural substrates, but where a correlation is substantiated between a neural order and a phenomenal order, the isomorphism of cortex and mind, in the service of bringing us closer to an understanding of the natural foundation of the human mind. The accomplishment of these theoretical implications will make the neuropsychologist a most valuable member of the multi-professional team of the practical clinical work in brain injury" (Fuster 2003, pp. x, xi).

The clinical importance and the implications of Luria's work will be continued in the first part of Chapter 10.

References

Bruner, J.S., Goodnow, J.J., and Austin, G.A. 1956. *A Study of Thinking*. New York: John Wiley & Sons; and London: Chapman & Hall.

Christensen, A.-L. 1975. *Luria's Neuropsychological Investigation*. Copenhagen, Denmark: Munksgaard; and New York: Spectrum.

Christensen, A.-L. 1995. Functional Rehabilitation – European Perspectives. Editorial. *Helioscope* 5:2–3.

Christensen, A.-L. 2002. Lifelines. In: Stringer, A. (ed.). *Pathways to Prominence: Reflections of the 20th Century Neuropsychologists*. New York: Psychology Press, pp. 119–137.

Christensen, A.-L. and Uzzell, B.P. 1988. *Neuropsychological Rehabilitation*. Boston: Kluwer Academic Publishers.

Christensen, A.-L. and Uzzell, B.P. 1994. *Brain Injury and Neuropsychological Rehabilitation: International Perspectives*. Hillsdale, N.J.: Lawrence Erlbaum.

Christensen, A.-L. and Uzzell, B.P. 2000. *International Handbook of Neuropsychological Rehabilitation*. New York: Kluwer Academic Publishers.

Christensen, A.L., Pinner, E.M., Pedersen, P.M., Teasdale, T.W., and Trexler, L.E. 1992. Psychosocial Outcome Following Individualized Neuropsychological Rehabilitation of Brain Damage. *Acta Psychiatrica Scandinavica* 85:32–38.

Edelman, M. 2004. Wider than the Sky: The Phenomenal Gift of Consciousness. New Haven, Conn.: Yale University Press.

Fuster, J.M. 2003. *Cortex and Mind, Unifying Cognition*. New York: Oxford University Press.

Goldberg, E. 2001. *The Executive Brain. Frontal Lobes and the Civilized Mind*. New York: Oxford University Press.

Golden, C.J., Hammeke, T., and Purisch, A. 1978. Diagnostic Validity of a Standardized Neuropsychological Battery Derived from Luria's Neuropsychological Tests. *Journal of Consulting and Clinical Psychology* 46:1250–1265.

Ingvar, D.H. and Lassen, N.A. 1978. Cerebral Function, Metabolism and Blood Flow. News and Trends from the VIII International CBF Symposium in Copenhagen, June 1977. *Acta Neurologica Scandinavica* 57:262–269.

Kolb, B. and Wishaw, I.Q.1990. *Fundamentals of Human Neuropsychology*. Alberta, Canada: Worth Publishers.

Luria, A.R. 1963. *Restoration of Function after Brain Injury*. Oxford: Pergamon Press.

Luria, A.R. 1966. *Higher Cortical Functions in Man*. New York: Basic Books.

Luria, A.R. 1969. *The Origin and Cerebral Organisation on Man's Conscious Action*. An Evening Lecture to the XIX International Congress of Psychology. London: Moscow University.

Luria, A.R. 1979. *The Making of Mind*. Cambridge, Mass.: Harvard University Press.

Reitan, R.M. 1976. Neuropsychology: The Vulgarization Luria Always Wanted. *Contemporary Psychology* 21(10):737–739.

Schönberger, M., Humle, F., and Teasdale, T.W. 2006. Subjective Outcome of Brain Injury Rehabilitation in Relation to the Therapeutic Working Alliance, Client Compliance and Awareness. *Brain Injury* 20:1271–1282.

Siert, L. 2000. A Support Person Model: Maintaining People in the Work Market Subsequent to Acquired Brain Injury. *Brain Injury* 4:24–26.

Spiers, P. 1981. Have They Come to Praise Luria or to Bury Him? The Luria- Nebraska Battery Controversy. *Journal of Consulting and Clinical Psychology* 49:331–341.

Stein, D.G., Brailowsky, S., and Will, B. 1995. *Brain Repair*. New York: Oxford University Press.

Svendsen, H. 2006. *Long-Term Outcome Following Post-Acute Neuropsychological Rehabilitation: A Controlled Study*. Ph.D. Dissertation, Institute of Psychology and Center for Rehabilitation of Brain Injury, University of Copenhagen.

Svendsen, H. and Teasdale, T.W. 2006. The Influence of Neuropsychological Rehabilitation on Symptomatology and Quality of Life Following Brain Injury: A Controlled Long-Term Follow-Up. *Brain Injury* 20:1295–1306.

Teasdale, T.W., Christensen, A.-L., Willmes, K., Deloche, G., Braga, L., Stachowiak, F., Vendrell, J.M., Castro-Caldas, A., Laaksonen, R. and Leclercq, M. 1997. Subjective Experience in Brain-Injured Patients and their Close Relatives: A European Brain Injury Questionnaire Study. *Brain Injury* 11:543–563.

Tranel, D. 2008. Theories of Clinical Neuropsychology and Brain–Behavior Relationships: Luria and Beyond. In: Morgan, J.E. and Richter, H.H. (eds.). *Textbook of Clinical Neuropsychology*. New York and London: Taylor & Francis, pp. 25–37.

2

Neuropsychology and A.R. Luria's Concept of Higher Cortical Functions in the Beginning of the 3rd Millennium

Elkhonon Goldberg and Dmitri Bougakov

It has been three decades since Luria's passing. During this time, the neurosciences have enjoyed a great deal of interest and development. The last decade of the 20th century has been rightfully called the decade of the brain. Even though many mysteries of brain–mind remain undiscovered, with the arrival of new powerful tools and technologies to aid our research, we have accumulated a plethora of new findings. In the face of such rapid development of the field, it would be illuminating to take a survey of where ideas, theories, and clinical techniques put forth by Alexander Luria fit today.

A.R. Luria is rightfully considered to be one of the most prominent neuropsychologists of the 20th century; however, one of his greatest contributions is often overlooked. In Luria's times, there was a notable schism between cognitive science and neuroscience, and very little interaction existed between the two disciplines. As recently as the 1970s and 1980s, academic psychology was dominated by people who were not interested in the brain. A popular notion was that it was somehow possible to study cognition in isolation while leaving someone else to study how it is "implemented" in the brain. On the other hand, neuroscientists viewed psychology and complex behavior as too imprecise to be amenable to rigorous scientific examination. And even a generation after Luria, as recently as in the mid-1980s, the concept of cognitive neuroscience was not accepted by all mainstream neuroscientists. Presciently, Luria was one of the fathers of a discipline that now is commonly known as *cognitive neuroscience*. Even though the term itself was coined much later, Luria anticipated and created the kind of fusion of psychology and neuroscience that gained increasing prominence over the past few decades.

Luria was ahead of his times in his ability to think about the brain and about higher mental functions with equal depth. His ability to integrate the two traditionally disjointed domains into one culminated into *Higher Cortical Functions in Man* (1966)—one of the first monographs in cognitive neuroscience created long before the term itself was born. Without Luria, cognitive neuroscience would not be what it is today.

The advent of functional neuroimaging and the refinement of structural neuroimaging improved our understanding of the brain–behavior relationship and for the most part validated Luria's theories based on the lesion data. To this extent, functional neuroimaging tools corroborated Luria's foresight about the dynamic nature of psychological processes. More recently, certain aspects of Luria's functional systems theory of cortical organization have been refined and further elaborated both by those who explicitly continue his school of neuropsychology (Goldberg and Costa 1981; Goldberg 1989; Goldberg 1990) and by those who have independently arrived at a similar vision of the brain and cognition (Fuster 2003).

One particular extension of Luria's functional systems theory deals with hemispheric contributions to cognition (Goldberg and Costa 1981). In this theory, hemispheric differences are given a more dynamic explanation than that provided by the more traditional approaches. According to this theory, the nature of hemispheric specialization is better explained in terms of novelty/familiarity distinctions as opposed to material specificity (i.e., spatial vs. linguistic) or abstract properties (i.e., global vs. local) variables. Another major assertion of this theory is that hemispheric differences are dynamic as opposed to static. With an increased familiarity and experience with any class of cognitive tasks, the preponderance of cognitive control that is required to act upon such tasks shifts from the right hemisphere to the left hemisphere and from the anterior structures of the brain to posterior structures.

Another extension of Luria's functional systems theory can be seen in the relatively recent trend toward the refutation of the modular view of functional neocortical organization in favor of the distributed-emergent principle of functional cortical organization (Goldberg 1989; Goldberg 1990; Fuster 2003). According to Goldberg's *gradiental* theory, the functional organization of heteromodal association cortices is interactive and distributed. The heteromodal association cortex develops along the continuous distributions. In these distributions (called *gradients*), functionally close aspects of cognition are represented in anatomically close areas of the association neocortex.

Yet another theory of cortical representation elaborating on Luria's functional systems theory was put forth by Joaquin Fuster (2003). Fuster ascertains that cognitive functions do not have discrete cortical representation. In his theory, he introduces a re-iterant unit called *cognit*, which he proposes as a generic term for any representation of knowledge in the cerebral cortex. Cognits are dynamic structures that in neural terms roughly coincide with neuronal assemblies and the connections between the neurons. According to Fuster, cognitive functions are represented by information exchange within and between cognits, and different cognitive functions draw upon many overlapping cognits. The crucial tenet of Fuster's theory is that different cognits (neural networks) have identifiable cortical distribution but cognitive functions that use them do not, as different functions may rely on same or similar circuits.

In Luria's time, neuropsychology was primarily concerned with the studies of focal lesions. Recently, we have seen an expansion of neuropsychology into geriatrics, neuropsychiatry, and child/development psychology. We have witnessed the blurring of the borders between "diseases of the brain" and "diseases of the soul." If we look back to Luria's time, we can think of neuropsychology as being generic, treating all of humanity as one homogeneous mass, where distinctions are made between "average" norm and pathology. Now we are concerned more and more with the neuropsychology of group and individual differences, subtyping normality in a fractal fashion. Normal cognition is no longer thought to be a uniformed entity but more of a landscape of functions with peaks and valleys corresponding with individual strengths and weaknesses. In addition, we are discovering that there are differences in normal cognition that are related to age, gender, and hemispheric dominance. Armed with such knowledge, clinicians are better prepared to deal with the specifics of individual manifestations of the effects of brain pathology.

The thrust of clinical neuropsychological applications has also changed. With the advent and refinement of structural neuroimaging, use of neuropsychological methods has become less central to focal neuroanatomic diagnosis. Today, neuropsychology is particularly useful for fine cognitive analysis of neurologic disorders.

Neuropsychology also plays an increasingly major role in neurologic rehabilitation—the field that had allowed Luria to accumulate such a vast knowledge about the brain. More than 60 years ago, at the onset of World War II, Luria had found himself in charge of developing neurorehabilitative methods for the wounded soldiers. Through ironic serendipity, an abundance of penetrating gunshot wounds to the head had given Luria an opportunity to study mind–brain relations in a rigorous and systematic fashion. This opportunity had tied Luria to neuropsychology for the rest of his life and resulted in two books: *Traumatic Aphasia* (1970) and *Higher Cortical Functions in Man* (1966). Even now, these two volumes are considered neuropsychological classics.

Little was known about brain plasticity and capacity for self-repair in Luria's times. Consequently, Luria's approach to rehabilitation was based on the restructuring of functional systems. It was thought that similar cognitive products could be attained by recruiting and combining various cognitive operations in different ways, thus assembling equivalent, but differently composed, functional systems. More recently, we have witnessed an ever-increasing number of studies reporting the brain's capacity to renew and regenerate itself in animals, and more importantly in humans, throughout the life span (Goldberg 2005). What is exciting about these studies is that not only are they promising in terms of rehabilitation, but also they are opening new avenues for the prevention of cognitive decline. The notion is gaining increasing credence that by stimulating new neuronal proliferation and by strengthening synaptic connections through cognitive activity, it is possible to postpone the effects of aging on the brain and cognition and possibly even to delay or postpone the onset of various forms of dementia.

Another burgeoning application of neuropsychological procedures is monitoring the efficacy of cognotropic medications, in particular, medications designed to treat or prevent dementia. In addition, neuropsychological procedures help scientists to monitor for possible neurologic side effects of noncognotropic medications. Neuropsychological tests provide clinicians with a precise and reliable quantitative measure of pharmacologic success (or failure).

There is a growing convergence of neuropsychology and functional neuroimaging. Neuropsychological expertise is relied upon in the design of cognitive activation paradigms in functional neuroimaging studies. This is arguably one of the most significantly contributing factors for the true meeting of psychology and neuroscience, where neuropsychological tasks traditionally employed in the clinical setting are used to study normal cognition. To this extent, use of functional neuroimaging has been particularly illuminating in demonstrating the dynamic nature of cortical processes and thus supporting Luria's functional systems theory.

In his time, Luria was not a supporter of psychometrically rigorous tests and sided with what today is called the *qualitative approach* to neuropsychological diagnosis. In all fairness, Luria's aversion to quantification was more a reflection of his time rather than of geography—it was early 20th century rather than Russian. Lurian reliance on productive, nonquantitative signs and symptoms was not that different from the approach adopted by Kurt Goldstein in a chronologically comparable period but an entirely different cultural milieu.

Both Kurt Goldstein and Alexander Luria advocated use of what today is known as the qualitative approach. In fact, the dichotomy between "quantitative" and "qualitative" approaches is a false one, devoid of intrinsic contradiction. This is so because the "qualitative" approach is nothing other than an approach based on productive, positive symptomatology, which is eminently quantifiable. Today, we witness the necessary fusion of psychometric tradition with the qualitative approach in a new generation of diagnostic procedures that elicit productive signs that are then subjected to quantification (Goldberg, et al. 1999).

Since Luria's times, significant strides were made in elucidating and understanding the function of the frontal lobes, the brain structure that for the longest time was known as "the silent lobes" or even sometimes treated as (and often discarded as) a surplus of brain matter. Luria's clinical experience and foresight led him to recognize the importance of the frontal lobes in cognition in general and its preeminence in making the human mind distinctly human. He sometimes referred to the frontal lobes as "the organ of civilization." Luria's special interest in the frontal lobes is continued in his students' work and has inspired some of his students to develop a new generation of procedures better suited to examine the functions of the frontal lobes. These procedures reflect the current understanding of the role of the frontal lobes in cognition in general and their role in actor-centered, adaptive, nonveridical decision making in particular.

It is not widely known that Luria's becoming a neuropsychologist is more bittersweet serendipity than early career planning. Had Luria lived in a country where career choices were less dictated by the ruling party line and more open to personal preference, he would have probably continued pursuing his earlier interests in cultural psychology. Early in Luria's career, the brain was of relatively little interest to him. In fact, one of his first studies of brain damage was actually (admitted by Luria himself) a false start where he failed to demonstrate that the problem-solving skills are critically (and exclusively) dependent on language. At the time, Luria was interested in the relationship between the culture and the mind and how the knowledge externalized and crystallized in the culture becomes the personal, internalized knowledge of an individual. To this extent, Luria's early research was mostly developmental and cross-cultural in nature. However, cultural psychology fell out of favor with the Soviet state and, in order to pursue a viable scientific career, Luria was forced to adapt to the increasingly oppressive circumstances. It is then that Luria, already a full professor of psychology, went to medical school and subsequently began his groundbreaking work in neuropsychology.

Nonetheless, Luria' earlier interest in cultural psychology was not in vain. It had clearly helped him to become a visionary and a forebear of a new field of cognitive neuroscience. One can attribute Luria's success in facilitating the merger of neuroscience and cognitive science into a single cohesive discipline to a large extent to his thorough understanding of how the brain and the culture interact and to his dual training as a psychologist and a neurologist.

It is a known fact that Sigmund Freud and Alexander Luria corresponded. Similarly, it is known that Freud's early interests were in the study of how higher mental functions are affected in the face of pathology. Indeed, Freud is credited with the introduction of some widely used terms of neurology and neuropsychology (such as *agnosia*). Freud was a firm believer in the unity of the brain and the mind, but the science of the time did not have the tools to study the brain. On the other hand, much of Luria's career unfolded in the intellectual environment that was ready to be introduced to a new science. Nevertheless, there is a certain intellectual continuity that follows. In a way not obvious to many historians of science, the symbolic torch has been passed from Freud to Luria and, currently, to a new generation of neuroscientists.

It is in this tradition of intellectual continuity and in the spirit of the arrival of new diagnostic tools, accumulation of empirical knowledge, and theory that *Luria's Neuropsychological Investigation* has been evolving.

References

Fuster, J.M. 2003. *Cortex and Mind: Unifying Cognition*. Oxford and New York: Oxford University Press.

Goldberg, E. 1989. Gradiental Approach to Neocortical Functional Organization. *Journal of Clinical and Experimental Neuropsychology* 11(4):489–517.

Goldberg, E. 1990. Higher Cortical Functions in Humans: The Gradiental Approach. In: Goldberg, E. (ed.). *Contemporary Neuropsychology and the Legacy of Luria*. Hillsdale, N.J.: Lawrence Erlbaum Associates, pp. 229–276.

Goldberg, E. 2005. *The Wisdom Paradox: How Your Mind Can Grow Stronger As Your Brain Grows Older*. New York: Gotham Books, 2005.

Goldberg, E. and Costa, L.D. 1981. Hemisphere Differences in the Acquisition and Use of Descriptive Systems. *Brain and Language* 14(1):144–173.

Goldberg, E., Podell, K., Bilder, R., and Jaeger, J. 1999. *The Executive Control Battery*. Melbourne, Australia: Psych Press.

Luria, A.R. 1966. *Higher Cortical Functions in Man*. New York: Basic Books.

Luria, A.R. 1970. *Traumatic Aphasia*. The Hague: Mouton.

3

Where Culture Meets Neuroimaging: The Intersection of Luria's Method with Modern Neuroimaging and Cognitive Neuroscience Research

Xavier E. Cagigas and Robert M. Bilder

Much has changed in the world of neuropsychology since Alexander Romanovich Luria made his seminal contributions to the field more than three decades ago. The advent of neuroimaging has without question brought about the most revolutionary changes within our discipline since Luria's time. Though Luria had attempted to gain indirect access to the workings of the human brain *in vivo* through his *combined motor method* (Luria 1932)—an ingenious and innovative application of the technologies available at the time—functional neuroimaging has created a window into the working brain that Luria might not have imagined but in which he would surely take delight. Although these methods may not have been available to him, Luria nevertheless accomplished something extraordinary with his neuropsychological assessment strategies and concepts that modern neuroimaging is often lacking: a theory-driven approach that elucidates the intimate interface between the nervous system and the cultural–historical world that finds its synthesis in every developing human (Mecacci 1984 and 2005).

One can imagine what a tool such as functional magnetic resonance imaging (fMRI) would have yielded in the capable hands of someone like Luria, testing hypotheses to examine functional systems at work and to observe their breakdown in cases of pathology. Unfortunately, and we would imagine much to Luria's chagrin, modern neuroimaging research is often heavily driven by an atheoretical, data-driven process that desperately lacks a strong explanatory theory. Poldrack (2006) wrote a strong commentary on the frequent practice of *reverse inference* in fMRI research, which highlights the dangers of assuming uniformity across contexts and prematurely drawing inferences based on activation patterns alone. Poldrack states that at this time "it seems that powerful reverse inference awaits the development of a detailed cognitive ontology." Indeed, it is difficult to interpret the proliferation of neuroimaging studies, which demonstrate significant cultural variations in brain organization and function, without such a detailed cognitive ontology. It is precisely here that the mettle of Luria's contribution to neuropsychology is tested and emerges from the fire as a true cultural neuropsychology.

Neuropsychology has recently seen a reemergence in the interest of culture with the publication of three handbooks in cross-cultural clinical neuropsychology within the past eight years (Fletcher-Janzen, Strickland, and Reynolds 2000; Ferraro 2002; Uzzell, Pontón, and Ardila 2007). This rediscovery of culture, however, is not limited to the clinical sphere and has also reared its head in the world of neuroimaging research. Recent studies using neuroimaging have found cultural differences at behavioral, structural, and functional levels that are being attributed to differences in heightened experience within a particular skill set. As the post–genomic era unfolds, major efforts are also under way to determine the degree to which some population effects may also be explained by genetic variation that is sometimes confounded with cultural experience. This apparent multiplicity challenges the long-held doctrine of psychic unity, which experimental psychology has long operated under, but which Luria began to challenge early in his career with Vygotsky.

For example, a growing literature is consistently replicating the fact that early acquisition and continued persistent use of at least two languages not only affects a reorganization of the neural networks traditionally thought to subserve language itself, but also leads to a reorganization and enhancement of executive functions such as cognitive set shifting, flexibility, and inhibitory control (for review, see Halsband 2006). Similar long-term effects of reorganization have been observed in other groups that engage in chronic focused activities such as musical performance (Elbert, et al. 1995; Landau and D'Esposito 2006), taxicab driving (Maguire, et al. 2003), sorting mail (Polk and Farah 1998), performing mental calculations on an abacus (Hanakawa, et al. 2003), and more. Such effects were also prominently featured in a major theoretical work by Luria's student Elkhonon Goldberg, who hypothesized that the critical organizing dimension underlying hemisphere differences in brain function rested on the experiential acquisition and use of descriptive systems, including language and other "codes" (Goldberg and Costa 1981). Still other research has begun to put forth and test the hypothesis that the physical environment within which one is raised and regularly participates determines a person's preference for adopting either *ventral stream* or *dorsal stream* approaches to examining visual stimuli, and therefore, leads to the development of a particular cognitive style (Grön, et al. 2003; Chua, Boland, and Nisbett 2005; Gutchess, et al. 2006; Goh, et al. 2007; Han and Northoff 2008).

Whereas most neuropsychologists are comfortable with the fact that the cultural practices of literacy and education have measurable effects upon the brain, the idea that all systematic and organized human activity can shape and, in some cases, reorganize higher-order brain functions seems more difficult for some to accommodate. For Luria, on the other hand, the idea that organized cultural activities directly influence and maintain the functional organization of the brain was second nature.

From the very beginning, Luria was very much against a localizationist and modularist view of the brain (Luria 2002). Together with Vygotsky, he instead developed a theory that the brain itself was part of a functional system, which extended into the cultural–historical world. This *extracortical organization* readily observable in the environment was dynamically intertwined with the neural organization of the *working brain*. Luria came to believe that higher-order neurocognitive functional systems were formed by the brain's engagement of culturally organized activity in the real world. It was this insight that formed the cornerstone of Luria's dynamic conceptualization of brain function and provided a means of reorganizing or rehabilitating lost neurocognitive abilities due to brain lesions by reorganizing activities in the outside world (Luria 1963).

In Luria's view, the recursive interaction of the human brain with material human-made artifacts and people in a cultural world with historical origins is constantly re-created during ontogenesis to reorganize both the internal and external world of human beings. When viewed on a developmental scale, the social and the biological take the lead in constructing each other at different points in time. Neither the biological nor the social is a static entity that is acted upon by the other. Rather, when examining the functional systems that subserve higher-order cognition, reorganization in one plane leads to reorganization in the other making new things possible that were not possible in the previous configuration. This is the essence of Luria's neuropsychology, which was a heroic attempt to unify advances in neurophysiology with the sociohistorical approach to mediation. In essence, he carefully created a unit of analysis that was inclusive of both the internal and external worlds of humans, and even the space in between, by focusing his attention on the functional system—the constant interplay, in all its complexity, between the brain and the environment (Akhutina, et al. 2005). Luria's influence is duly noted in a recent paper that attempts to synthesize advances across the neurosciences with the theory of biological co-constructivism, which simply put is a reworking of Luria's original hypothesis in light of recent interdisciplinary evidence (Li 2003).

The ramifications of this theoretical framework for continued advancement in neuroimaging research are monumental in scope. The unit of analysis, therefore, becomes inclusive of the cultural–historical shaping that a person's brain has undergone prior to participation in a particular experimental task. As a result, specification of a person's cultural–historical background becomes as important as specification of a particular experimental task carried out in the scanner. Advances in statistical theory, also the result of technological advancement, such as the advent of hierarchical linear modeling and other such multivariate techniques, as well as developmental systems theory (Oyama 2000), allow for the possibility of beginning to analyze the greater cultural–historical context when studying individuals.

Luria's triadic organization of cortical areas (Luria 1969, 1973) also serves as a solid point of departure from which to begin the process of exploring the dynamics of brain function within a cultural–historical context. Imaging research has thus far confirmed that the greatest common activation patterns overlap considerably across subjects at specific points of convergence. These points of shared activation across subjects, not surprisingly, correspond with what Luria referred to as primary cortical areas. Modern neuroimaging studies have further illustrated the failure of strict modularity assumptions in more complex integrative and associative tasks, and current neuroimaging studies frequently employ analyses of functional connectivity (reflecting dynamically changing network engagement on an individual subject level both in "resting states" and during cognitive challenges) that can be considered formalizations of Luria's concepts (Rogers, et al. 2007). This work in fMRI is complemented by rapid developments in diffusion tensor imaging and methods for cortical tractography that may help provide a structural basis for, and statistical constraints upon, new models of distributed functional systems in the brain (Mishra, et al. 2007). Goldberg's extrapolation of Luria's ideas in his gradiental theory of cortical organization (Goldberg 1989, 1990), therefore, represents a powerful organizing framework for imaging researchers. These ideas are consistent with emerging evidence regarding the human brain's potential for remapping of cognitive representations after either brain damage or experience and highlight the "top-down" influences in cortical reorganization that reach even down to the primary cortical areas (Merzenich, et al. 1996; Mahncke, et al. 2006; Polley, et al. 2006). Goldberg's theoretical extension of Luria's work thus can help guide researchers in predicting where to look for cultural, experience-based differences and gives a reasonable account of why certain areas in the brain may be more amenable to environmental influences, including remediation strategies.

Leontiev, Luria's contemporary and a member of the original "troika," together with Vygotsky and Luria, also developed a theoretical framework that he christened *activity theory*, which was inclusive of the many layers that influence human activities (Cole and Engeström 1993; Engeström 1996). To date, however, this branch of thought has enjoyed little dialogue with the neurosciences but almost certainly influenced Luria's pioneering ideas. In short, Luria and the other two founding members of the cultural–historical school of thought attempted to create a metatheory that could guide research and help resolve what they called the "crisis in psychology," (Leontiev and Luria, 2005) namely the integration of the two psychologies originally proposed by Wundt: experimental psychology and Volkerpsychologie (Cole 1996; Cole, Levitin, and Luria 2006).

The problem of culture that neuroimaging is now bringing to the forefront has been present since the beginning of psychology, and certainly since the beginning of Luria's neuropsychology. The degree of sophistication and complexity needed to tackle this problem has historically discouraged many researchers from pursuing it in favor of a more incremental approach that attempts to somehow partial out the influence of culture. However, evidence from the field of cultural psychology and most recently neuroimaging seems to be forcing a return to the grand aspirations of Luria and his contemporaries to reintegrate cultural practices into cognition, or better yet to explore the hypothesis that neurocognition is a culturally constituted phenomenon.

The widespread availability of low-cost, high-throughput genotyping has led to a new framework for biological research that is focused on systematic analysis of phenotypes on a genome-wide scale and fostered the development of *phenomics* as a new transdiscipline (Freimer and Sabatti 2003). A genome-wide focus on neuropsychological phenotypes (cognitive phenomics; Bilder, et al. in press) essentially offers a modern translation of Luria's cultural neuropsychology. How do genes and the cultural–historical environment co-construct one another, and how is this imprint crystallized in the working functional systems of the human brain? A true dialogue among the neurosciences, of which neuroimaging is just one part, together with the metatheory proposed by Luria, which is inclusive of the cultural–historical world that the neurosciences are nested in, is closer than ever before. Luria's contributions and his refusal to separate the biological from the cultural–historical now provides a working theoretical framework upon which neuroscientists can deploy new technologies and yield a more fine-grained and inclusive understanding of neurocognition and its neural correlates in humans.

References

Akhutina, T., Glozman, J., Moskovich, L., Robbins, D. (eds). 2005. *A. R. Luria and Contemporary Psychology: Festschrift Celebrating the Centennial of the Birth of Luria*. Hauppauge, N.Y.: Nova Science Publishers, Inc.

Bilder, R.M., Poldrack, R., Parker, D.S., Reise, S.P., Jentsch, J.D., Cannon, T., London, E., et al. in press. Cognitive Phenomics. In: Wood, S., Allen, N. and Pantelis, C. (eds). *Handbook of Neuropsychology of Mental Disorders*, Cambridge, UK: Cambridge University Press.

Chua, H.F., Boland, J.E., and Nisbett, R.E. 2005. Cultural Variation in Eye Movements during Scene Perception. *Proceedings of the National Academy of Sciences of the United States of America* 102(35):12629–12633.

Cole, M. 1996. *Cultural Psychology: A Once and Future Discipline*. Cambridge, Mass.: Harvard University Press.

Cole, M. and Engeström, Y. 1993. A Cultural-Historical Approach to Distributed Cognition. In: G. Salomon (ed.). *Distributed Cognition: Psychological and Educational Considerations*. New York: Cambridge University Press, pp. 1–46.

Cole, M., Levitin, K., and Luria, A.R. 2006. *The Autobiography of Alexander Luria: A Dialogue with the Making of Mind.* Mahwah, N.J.: Lawrence Erlbaum Associates.

Elbert, T., Pantev, C., Wienbruch, C., and Rockstroh, B. 1995. Increased Cortical Representation of the Fingers of the Left Hand in String Players. *Science* 270(5234):305–307.

Engeström, Y. 1996. Interobjectivity, Ideality, and Dialectics. *Mind, Culture, and Activity* 3 (4):259–265.

Ferraro, F.R. (ed.) 2002. *Minority and Cross-Cultural Aspects of Neuropsychological Assessment*. Lisse, The Netherlands: Swets & Zeitlinger.

Fletcher-Janzen, E., Strickland, T.L., and Reynolds, C.R. (eds). 2000. *Handbook of Cross-Cultural Neuropsychology*. New York: Kluwer Academic/Plenum Publishers.

Freimer, N. and Sabatti, C. 2003. The Human Phenome Project. *Nature Genetics* 34:15–21.

Goh, J.O., Chee, M.W., Tan, J.C., Venkatraman, V., Hebrank, A., Leshikar, E.D., Jenkins, L., Sutton, B.P., Gutchess, A.H., and Park, D.C. 2007. Age and Culture Modulate Object Processing and Object-Scene Binding in the Ventral Visual Area. *Cognitive, Affective, & Behavioral Neuroscience* 7(1):44–52.

Goldberg, E. 1989. Gradiental Approach to Neocortical Functional Organization. *Journal of Clinical and Experimental Neuropsychology* 11(4):489–517.

Goldberg, E. 1990. Higher Cortical Functions in Humans: The Gradiental Approach. In: Goldberg, E. (ed.). *Contemporary Neuropsychology and the Legacy of Luria*. Hillsdale, N.J.: Lawrence Erlbaum Associates, pp. 229–276.

Goldberg, E. and Costa, L.D. 1981. Hemispheric Differences in the Acquisition and Use of Descriptive Systems. *Brain and Language* 14(1):144–173.

Grön, G., Schul, D., Bretschneider, V., Wunderlich, A.P., and Riepe, M.W. 2003. Alike Performance During Nonverbal Episodic Learning from Diversely Imprinted Neural Networks. *European Journal of Neuroscience* 18:3112–3120.

Gutchess, A.H., Welsh, R.C., Boduroglu, A., and Park, D.C. 2006. Cultural Differences in Neural Function Associated with Object Processing. *Cognitive, Affective, & Behavioral Neuroscience* 6(2):102–109.

Halsband, U. 2006. Bilingual and Multilingual Language Processing. *Journal of Physiology – Paris* 99(4–6):355–369.

Han, S. and Northoff, G. 2008. Culture-sensitive neural substrates of human cognition: a transcultural neuroimaging approach. *Nature Reviews Neuroscience* 9(8):646–654.

Hanakawa, T., Honda, M., Okada, T., Fukuyama, H., and Shibasaki, H. 2003. Neural Correlates Underlying Mental Calculation in Abacus Experts: A Functional Magnetic Resonance Imaging Study. *NeuroImage* 19:296–307.

Landau, S.M. and D'Esposito, M. 2006. Sequence Learning in Pianists and Nonpianists: An fMRI Study of Motor Expertise. *Cognitive, Affective, & Behavioral Neuroscience* 6(3): 246–259.

Leontiev, A.N. and Luria, A.R. 2005. The Problem of the Development of Intellect and Learning in Human Psychology. *Journal of Russian and East European Psychology* 43(4):34–47.

Li, S.-C. 2003. Biocultural Orchestration of Developmental Plasticity Across Levels: The Interplay of Biology and Culture in Shaping the Mind and Behavior Across the Life Span. *Psychological Bulletin* 129(2):171–194.

Luria, A.R. 1932. *The Nature of Human Conflicts*. Oxford, England: Liveright.

Luria, A.R. 1963. *Restoration of Function after Brain Injury*. Oxford, England: Pergamon Press.

Luria, A.R. 1969. *The Higher Cortical Functions in Man and their Disturbance in Local Lesions of the Brain* (2nd ed.). Oxford, England: Moscow University Press.

Luria, A.R. 1973. *The Working Brain: An Introduction to Neuropsychology*. New York: Penguin Books.

Luria, A.R. 2002. L.S. Vygotsky and the Problem of Functional Localization. *Journal of Russian and East European Psychology* 40(1):17–25.

Maguire, E.A., Spiers, H.J., Good, C.D., Hartley, T., Frackowiak, R.S.J., and Burgess, N. 2003. Navigation Expertise and the Human Hippocampus: A Structural Brain Imaging Analysis. *Hippocampus* 13(2):250–259.

Mahncke, H.W., Connor, B.B., Appelman, J., Ahsanuddln, O.N., Hardy, J.L., Wood, R.A., Joyce, N.M., Boniske, T., Atkins, S.M., and Merzenich, M.M. 2006. Memory Enhancement in Healthy Older Adults using a Brain Plasticity-Based Training Program: A Randomized, Controlled Study. *Proceedings of the National Academy of Sciences of the United States of America* 103(33):12523–12528.

Mecacci, L. 1984. Looking for the Social and Cultural Dimensions of the Human Brain. *International Journal of Psychophysiology* 1(4):293–299.

Mecacci, L. 2005. Luria: A Unitary View of Human Brain and Mind. *Cortex* 41:816–822.

Merzenich, M., Wright, B., Jenkins, W., Xerri, C., Byl, N., Miller, S., and Tallal, P. 1996. Cortical Plasticity Underlying Perceptual, Motor, and Cognitive Skill Development: Implications for Neurorehabilitation. *Cold Spring Harbor Symposia on Quantitative Biology* 61:1–8.

Mishra, A., Lu, Y., Choe, A.S., Aldroubi, A., Gore, J.C., Anderson, A.W., and Ding, Z. 2007. An image-processing toolset for diffusion tensor tractography. *Magnetic Resonance Imaging* 25: 365–376.

Oyama, S. 2000. *Evolution's Eye: A Systems View of the Biology-Culture Divide*. Durham, N.C.: Duke University Press.

Poldrack, R.A. 2006. Can Cognitive Processes be Inferred from Neuroimaging Data? *Trends in Cognitive Science* 10(2):59–63.

Polk, T.A. and Farah, M.J. 1998. The Neural Development and Organization of Letter Recognition: Evidence from Functional Neuroimaging, Computational Modeling, and Behavioral Studies. *Proceedings of the National Academy of Sciences of the United States of America* 95(3):847–852.

Polley, D.B., Steinberg, E.E., and Merzenich, M.M. 2006. Perceptual Learning Directs Auditory Cortical Map Reorganization through Top-Down Influences. *The Journal of Neuroscience* 26(18):4970–4982.

Rogers, B.P., Morgan, V.L., Newton, A.T., and Gore J.C. 2007. Assessing Functional Connectivity in the Human Brain by fMRI. *Magnetic Resonance Imaging* 25:1347–1357.

Uzzell, B.P., Pontón, M.O., and Ardila, A. 2007. *International Handbook of Cross-Cultural Neuropsychology*. Mahwah, N.J.: Lawrence Erlbaum Associates.

4

Cognitive and Motivational Functions of the Human Prefrontal Cortex

Jared X. Van Snellenberg and Tor D. Wager

When Luria published *Higher Cortical Functions in Man* in 1966, he was forced to concede that "... in considering the pathology of the frontal lobes we are dealing with a branch of modern neurology where the facts ... are still too few and often contradictory" (Luria 1966, p. 218). Nonetheless, based on clinical observation of countless patients with varying degrees of damage to frontal regions of cortex, Luria was able to differentiate between three broad regions of the frontal lobes with clearly distinguishable contributions to human cognition: the premotor division, the prefrontal convex division, and the mediobasal or orbital division (Figure 4–1). According to Luria, the central features of damage to these three regions are, respectively, "disturbance of skilled movement and a disintegration of complex kinetic melodies..., lack of continuous comparison between the plan of action and the results actually attained..., [and] gross changes in the affective sphere leading to disturbances of character and personality" (p. 293). Although this early presentation of frontal lobe function was, of necessity, extremely broad and nonspecific, it nonetheless anticipated the findings of modern work using both lesion data and functional neuroimaging techniques in healthy individuals.

Studies of brain-injured patients by Luria and others provided convincing demonstrations that different regions of the cortex are associated with different psychological functions. However, the question of how psychological functions map onto specific brain regions is a difficult one for a variety of reasons. One is that "functions" may be defined and categorized in a number of ways and at a

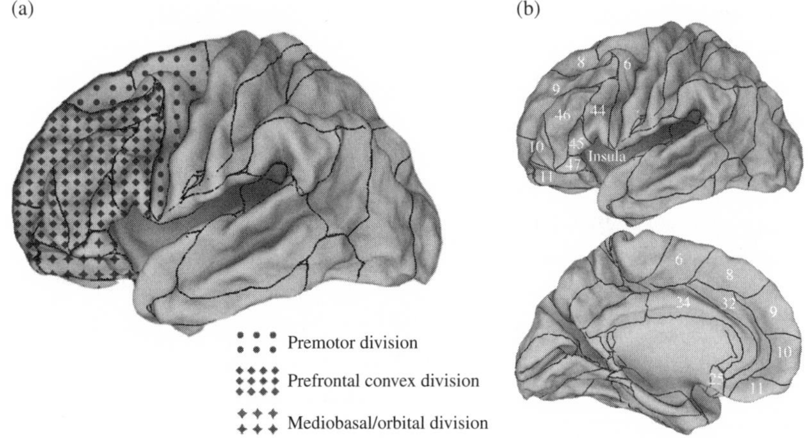

FIGURE 4–1. (a) The three divisions of human prefrontal cortex described by Luria (1966). (b) Brodmann's area labels for the lateral and medial surfaces of the prefrontal cortex (labels from CARET software; Van Essen, et al. 2001).

number of levels of generality. Finding semantic categories that "carve nature at its joints" is difficult because the natural ways of segmenting concepts in human language may not be those respected by the brain. For example, basic categories of emotion such as "fear," "anger," and "disgust" are easily recognizable as coherent concepts across cultures (Ekman, Sorenson, and Friesen 1969; Ekman 1992), but patterns of emotional alterations with brain damage (e.g., Hornak, et al. 2003) and brain activity in recent neuroimaging studies (Barrett and Wager 2006) do not seem to respect these categories. Luria argued that even "... such an apparently simple function as respiration is actually a complex functional system, effected by a differential dynamic arrangement of nerve cells belonging to different levels of the nervous system" (p. 25); thus, even in this simple example, the apparent function at the behavioral level (respiration) cannot be localized to a discrete brain region. However, in attempting to understand the brain, cognitive neuroscientists are searching for psychological concepts that best describe different areas of the cortex. A satisfactory description would ultimately associate particular cortical regions with specific "atomic elements" of cognitive processing that are used in different combinations across many tasks (e.g., in the Adaptive Control of Thought–Rational (ACT-R) model of cognition; Anderson, 1993).

Another issue that emerges is with assigning functions to areas of the brain based on experimental results from a single domain of study. For example, activation of dorsolateral prefrontal cortex (DLPFC; part of the prefrontal convex division described by Luria) in working memory (WM) tasks is commonly interpreted as reflecting active manipulation of the contents of WM (e.g., Rypma and

D'Esposito 1999; Smith and Jonides 1999; Curtis and D'Esposito 2003; Rypma 2006)—an interpretation of function made at the level of the cognitive domain under study. Although this is a very reasonable characterization, as we will show, activation of DLPFC (or at least portions of it) also occurs during studies of long-term memory (LTM), response inhibition, and task-switching (and quite possibly in other domains as well). Active manipulation of the contents of WM is not required in each of these domains, suggesting that the function of this region may be better characterized in other terms. An alternative characterization could be a more general function used in active WM maintenance and other cognitive control tasks, such as activation of task rules that provides context-dependent control over behavior (Asaad, Rainer, and Miller 2000; Miller and Cohen 2001), or alternatively the refreshing of information (Johnson, et al. 2005), which must be applied repeatedly and prospectively during WM maintenance and is also likely to be involved in maintaining task set in response-inhibition tasks. We return to these questions later in the chapter.

Despite the enormous amount of empirical research carried out on the functional organization of the frontal lobes since Luria's time, there are still very few frontal cortical regions whose functions can be specified with a high degree of certainty. One reason for this may be that a satisfactory characterization of function requires reliable information about the various kinds of task demands that do and do not produce deficits after lesions, or activity changes measured with neuroimaging, in a given region. In the example above, comparison of brain activity patterns across different types of tasks provided some basis for comparing alternative conceptualizations. In the remainder of this chapter, we continue along these lines and use evidence from meta-analyses of neuroimaging studies across a wide range of tasks to develop a synopsis of some of the current understanding of the functional organization of prefrontal cortex.

Meta-analyses

Meta-analysis of neuroimaging studies, particularly functional magnetic resonance imaging (fMRI) and positron emission tomography (PET), is an important tool in understanding functional brain organization that complements studies of patients with brain damage and other methodologies such as event-related potentials, transcranial magnetic stimulation, animal lesion studies, and intracranial recording. Ultimately, all of these methods provide a unique window into cognitive function, and each makes important contributions. An advantage of using meta-analysis to summarize neuroimaging studies is that there have now been hundreds of such studies published on similar tasks in a range of domains, and meta-analyses can identify consistent and replicable results across different laboratories, scanners, and study designs. Activation of a region in a single study does not provide strong evidence unless it is replicated across laboratories, and meta-analysis is a natural means of assessing replication. Meta-analysis also provides information on which regions are not active during task performance that cannot reliably be obtained from single studies. If a single study of LTM retrieval failed to find orbitofrontal cortex (OFC) activity, for example, this negative result would mean little: power in most fMRI and PET studies is extremely low when appropriate statistical corrections are used, and many scanner/pulse sequence combinations are poor at detecting activity in this region (Wager, et al. 2007). However, if no (or very few) studies of LTM ever find OFC, this provides stronger evidence for functional specialization.

A second advantage of meta-analysis is that results across many task domains can be compared, providing the ability to develop hypotheses about specific cognitive operations—like active maintenance, or refreshing—that are used to different degrees across many tasks. Because they synthesize all of the available functional neuroimaging work within a given domain, comparing the results of multiple meta-analyses across a range of domains can identify brain regions that subserve domain-general processes.

To date, our laboratory has produced meta-analyses of functional neuroimaging work across a number of domains relevant to the function of prefrontal cortex. Consequently, in this chapter we will use comparisons of these meta-analyses as a starting point for discussing potential domain-general functions subserved by different regions of prefrontal cortex, filling in these discussions with relevant lesion and animal work, as well as the results of individual neuroimaging studies where appropriate. The meta-analyses under consideration are of WM (Wager and Smith 2003), task-switching (Wager, Jonides, and Reading 2004), response inhibition (Nee, Wager, and Jonides 2007), LTM (unpublished data), and emotion (Wager, et al. 2003; Wager, et al. 2008). The meta-analyses use as data the spatial locations of peak activations, which are typically reported in neuroimaging publications for one or more comparisons between task performance and control conditions. Statistical tests are performed to locate consistently activated regions; that is, those regions in which many peaks across different studies are reported. In Figure 4–2, an example of this process is briefly presented for studies reporting peaks during WM tasks with an executive component. The testing procedure involves making a map across 200,000 or so "voxels" in the brain (sampled at $2 \times 2 \times 2$ mm resolution) of the number of studies that report peaks in the neighborhood (typically 10–15 mm) of each voxel, and using simulations to locate regions where reported peaks are clustered densely enough to distinguish the cluster from the background noise (peaks scattered across the brain with no apparent spatial pattern). These methods are summarized in the individual papers and in a recent paper on meta-analysis methods (Wager, Lindquist, and Kaplan 2007), and we do not review them in detail here.

To evaluate the extent to which regions in the prefrontal cortex are activated in multiple domains, we produced a set of conjunction images—that is, brain

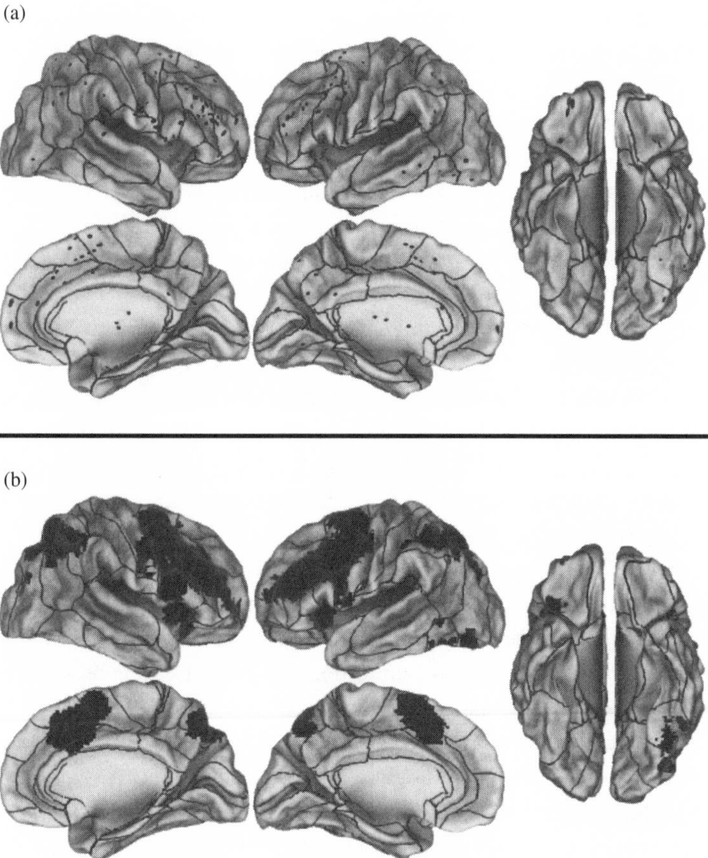

FIGURE 4–2. Example of how meta-analytic results are obtained in neuroimaging studies. Each of the points in (a) represents an activation peak reported in an individual study of executive WM. Spatial smoothing is then applied to each of these peaks, and statistical analyses are carried out to determine, for each voxel in the brain, whether there is consistent evidence for activation of that voxel across studies. The activated regions in (b) represent the areas of significant activation based on the peaks displayed in (a).

volumes of activated voxels that include only those voxels that are activated in a set (two or more) of analyses of interest—for each of the possible combinations of meta-analysis data sets. Because there is some degree of spatial variability inherent in functional imaging data, we expanded the activated regions in each of the meta-analyses by 2.5 mm in order to better detect regions of prefrontal cortex that are involved in multiple domains. Finally, we mapped each of these images onto surface renderings of the PALS atlas (Van Essen 2005) using Caret software (Van Essen, et al. 2001) to produce the figures presented throughout this chapter.

Meta-analytic data sets

In discussing the findings of these meta-analyses, it is important to be aware of the kinds of studies that went into each data set. We present data from two contrasts in the WM meta-analysis (Wager and Smith 2003): WM storage and WM executive. Identified peaks in the WM storage contrast reflect consistent activations across study conditions that require the maintenance of information in WM compared with a non-mnemonic baseline, whereas the WM executive contrast reflects activations across studies that involve manipulation of the contents of WM, continuous updating of the information held in WM (e.g., in an n-back task), or memory for the order of items in the memory set. Importantly, the WM executive contrast reflects only those regions that are significantly more active during WM executive tasks than during WM storage.

The inhibition data reported here (Nee, Wager, and Jonides 2007) reflect consistent activations across studies of the Stroop, flanker, go/no-go, stimulus–response compatibility, Simon, and stop signal tasks. Though a thorough description of each of these tasks is beyond the scope of this chapter, they all require either the inhibition of an already-initiated response (a paradigmatic case being the stop signal task, where in some trials a signal to inhibit responding is presented shortly after a stimulus that would otherwise be responded to) or the inhibition of a prepotent response, for example the Stroop task in which subjects must overcome the prepotent tendency to read words in order to correctly name the color the words are printed in. Importantly, in this latter set of tasks, it is generally presumed that the need to inhibit an already-initiated response also occurs, insofar as the prepotent response is likely to be initiated and later inhibited on at least some trials.

The task-switching meta-analysis (Wager, Jonides, and Reading 2004) included studies in which the contrast of interest reflected a condition in which participants had to change stimulus–response (S-R) contingencies in some prespecified way in order to perform the task successfully. This could include changes in the spatial location of stimuli that were to be responded to, changes in the dimension of a stimulus to which responses are to be made (e.g., shifting from responding based on stimulus color to responding based on shape), reversal or reassignment of response contingencies, or conditions in which the stimulus set was changed.

For the emotion meta-analysis (Wager, et al. 2008) we report on regions that show greater activation during the experience of emotion than during the perception of emotion (i.e., viewing emotional faces or scenes that are unlikely to evoke a strong emotional response in participants compared with conditions in which participants generate strong feeling states in response to stimuli of various kinds).

Finally, the LTM data set reported here is a preliminary analysis of 165 studies of LTM. Reported peaks reflect regions that are significantly active across this data set, which included studies of either encoding or retrieval (or both) of information from LTM compared with an appropriate baseline.

Hierarchies of prefrontal function

In the following sections, we discuss some putative functions subserved by specific regions of the prefrontal cortex, beginning with those regions activated in the broadest range of cognitive domains (across our meta-analytic data sets) and moving to those activated in the fewest domains, and finally discussing those regions activated during both cognition and emotional experience. We will then argue that the available data suggest that processing within the prefrontal cortex proceeds in an approximately hierarchical fashion, with posterior premotor regions maintaining specific S-R associations in order to direct motor behavior in a task-appropriate fashion, the inferior frontal junction (see later) establishing or switching between different S-R mappings depending on the current context, DLPFC engaging in top-down biasing of representations in posterior cortices, and anterior lateral prefrontal cortex involved in higher-order or subgoal processing. At the "top" of this network are the OFC and rostral medial prefrontal cortex, which assess the potential reward value of stimuli in the environment and, via the anterior insula and the dorsal medial prefrontal cortex, direct motivated cognition and behavior in a manner that maximizes expected reward. A list of the prefrontal regions discussed here, along with a brief description of their putative function and the meta-analytic data sets in which they are significantly activated, is presented in Table 4–1.

Common activations across cognitive domains

A number of regions were found to be active in all or most of the cognitive domains for which we have meta-analytic data, suggesting that each of these regions subserve a domain-general function that is deployed under a variety of task conditions. These results echo an early report by Duncan and Owen (2000) that a wide range of tasks, including WM, response conflict (e.g., Stroop), novel task learning, and tasks involving perceptual difficulty activated a common set of regions—dorsal anterior cingulate and mid-dorsolateral and mid-ventrolateral prefrontal cortex bilaterally—very similar to those activated in our analysis. We now discuss each of these regions in turn.

Dorsal Medial Junction

As shown in Figure 4–3, all of the included tasks show bilateral activation of a medial prefrontal cortex region, which we have termed the dorsal medial junction (DMJ) to refer to a collection of regions homologous to macaque rostral cingulate motor area (CMAr) and presupplementary motor areas (pre-SMA; Picard and Strick 1996) because it lies at the interface of medial Brodmann's areas (BAs) 6

TABLE 4–1. List of regions with significant activations in multiple domains

REGION	BAs	TASK DOMAINS							PUTATIVE FUNCTION
		LATERALIZATION	WM (s)	WM (e)	LTM	INHIBITION	SWITCHING	EMOTION	
Dorsal medial junction	6/8/32	B	X	X	X	X	X		Energization and motor preparedness
Inferior frontal junction	6/44/46	L	X	X	X	X	X		Task-setting
Inferior frontal junction	6/44/46	R	X	X	X	X			Task-setting
Posterior IFG	44/45/46	L	X	X	X		X		Task-setting
Posterior IFG	44/45/46	R	X	X	X	X			Response inhibition
Dorsal lateral PFC	46	B	X	X	X				Top-down biasing
Middle and anterior IFG	45/47	L	X		X				Semantic retrieval and selection
Rostral lateral PFC	10	B		X	X				Subgoal processing
Anterior insula	—	L	X	X	X		X	X	Directing cognition based on reward value
Anterior insula	—	R		X	X			X	Task-setting
Orbitofrontal cortex	11	L	X	X	X			X	Valuations of reward
Orbitofrontal cortex	11	R		X	X			X	Task-setting
Dorsomedial PFC	9	B			X			X	Generation and regulation of affect

Note: BAs, Brodmann's areas; WM (s), working memory storage; WM (e), working memory executive; LTM, long-term memory; B, bilateral; L, left; R, right; IFG, inferior frontal gyrus; PFC, prefrontal cortex.

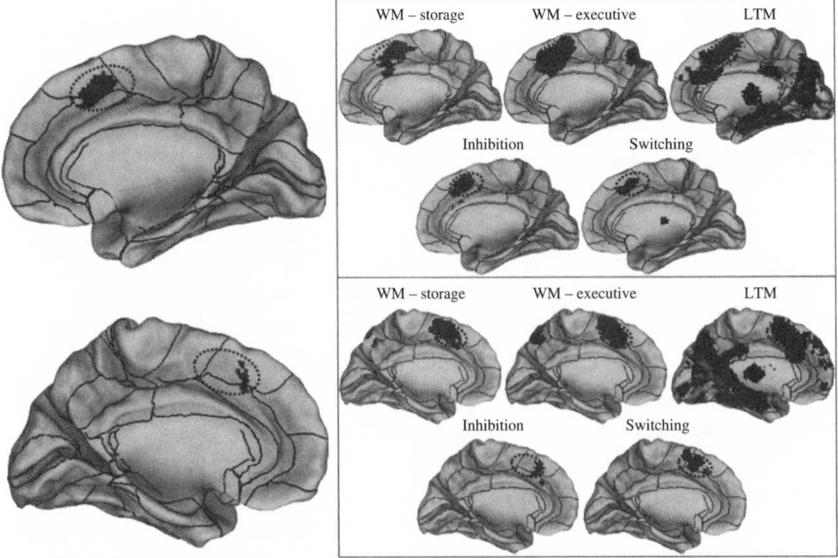

FIGURE 4–3. Conjunction images of the meta-analytic results for WM storage, WM executive, LTM, inhibition, and task-switching shown on the medial surface of the brain. Insets show the activated regions in each individual domain. The region indicated with a dotted line is the DMJ region discussed in the text.

and 8 and the dorsal portion of BA 32. Although activation of this area of cortex is frequently referred to as activation of anterior cingulate cortex (ACC) in the literature, we prefer the term DMJ because the data from our meta-analyses show that the activated region frequently includes a substantial portion of noncingulate cortex and typically only includes the most caudal portion of BA 32, a rather restricted portion of ACC (see Figure 4–3). Furthermore, when authors refer to ACC, it is frequently unclear precisely which area of the ACC they are referring to. Given that the region identified in our meta-analyses is consistently activated in WM storage, WM tasks that require executive processing in addition to "simple" maintenance, LTM, response inhibition, and task-switching, it is probably true that in most cases pertaining to cognitive tasks authors are referring to the same region of cortex identified in our meta-analyses.

It is beyond the purview of this chapter to enumerate the wide array of domain-specific functions that have been attributed to the ACC. Suffice it to say that activation of this region occurs in an astonishing array of cognitive tasks, and there does not seem to be general agreement about the functional role of this area of the brain. An early review of 107 PET studies (Paus, et al. 1998) examined a number of potential predictors of activity in this region and concluded that the best predictor of activation was "task difficulty." Indeed, the fact that it is activated in all of the cognitive tasks for which we have meta-analytic data strongly suggests that it plays a domain-general role in cognition that is deployed in a wide variety of situations.

One interpretation of the role of the DMJ consistent with the range of domains in which it is activated in our meta-analyses comes from human lesion work by Stuss and Alexander (2007). Based on behavioral data from patients with lesions in a variety of frontal sites across a number of cognitive tasks, these authors propose that patients with lesions of superior medial frontal cortex, which overlaps almost entirely with the DMJ region identified in our meta-analyses, exhibit a specific deficit in "energization"—the ability to refresh task-relevant perceptual and motor representations in the absence of specific cues. Observing that neural activity generally diminishes without continuous input, these authors propose that "in the absence of external triggers or motivational conditions to optimize responding, lower level perceptual or motor schemata would have to be energized or re-energized when activation becomes low . . ." (p. 904). Thus, energization, and consequently the DMJ, is essential for speeded, optimized performance in cognitive tasks where an attentional set facilitates performance.

There are a number of behavioral findings reported by Stuss and Alexander (2007) that are selective to damage in this region compared with damage in other regions of frontal cortex (and not predicted simply by the extent of lesion). First, patients with lesions in this area exhibit slower reaction times (RTs) but normal error rates in a range of RT tasks that vary in complexity, independent of fatigue or motivation to perform the task, and consistent with a difficulty in energizing or otherwise maintaining the preparation to respond. Perhaps most striking among these findings is the fact that patients with lesions in this area, but not other cortical areas, showed no RT benefit when a warning stimulus appeared 3 seconds prior to target stimuli, again suggesting a failure to energize cognitive resources relevant to the task at hand. In addition, patients with superior medial prefrontal lesions uniquely failed to produce a greater number of words in standard verbal fluency tasks in the last 45 seconds of the task compared with that in the first 30 seconds, suggesting that relative to other patients they were unable to maintain performance over time. Finally, these patients show greater RTs and many more errors in the incongruent condition of the Stroop task, a finding interpreted as indicating that the patients were unable to maintain the intended response.

The energization account of DMJ activity, which implies selection and strengthening of behavioral responses and/or their related task sets, may be contrasted with a conflict-monitoring account (Carter, et al. 1998; MacDonald, et al. 2000; Botvinick, Cohen, and Carter 2004), which implies only an indirect link to the control of behavior. Additional evidence for energization, as opposed to conflict monitoring, comes from studies that directly pit manipulations of conflict at the response selection stage against manipulations of conflict at preresponse selection (perceptual and semantic) stages. A growing body of studies has found that the DMJ region responds to increasing demand on response selection but not to other forms of "conflict" (Milham et al., 2001; Nelson, et al. 2003; Liu, et al. 2006). Other studies have found evidence that the DMJ can be recruited in anticipation of response conflict, before the target stimulus is presented, and that anticipatory activation is correlated with reduced interference (Stern, et al. 2007). As mentioned previously, the DMJ appears to overlap with both the CMAr and the pre-SMA in the monkey, which have strong connections to motor cortex and some direct projections to spinal motor neurons (Dum and Strick 1991), further supporting the argument that the DMJ is involved in higher-order contextual control and initiation of response selection. In addition, some researchers have reported that lesions of dorsal cingulate do not specifically impair performance on "cognitive control" tasks (Fellows and Farah 2005). These diverse types of evidence are difficult to explain with a conflict-monitoring account but are consistent with a behavioral "energization" account. Although the pattern of anatomic projections from DMJ strongly implicates motor control, the anatomic inputs to the DMJ also imply a role for incentive-based or motivationally based action selection. The CMAr receives input from a wide variety of limbic structures, including the rostral temporal cortices, insula, retrosplenial cortex, and OFC (Morecraft and van Hoesen 1998). In humans and animals, the pre-SMA appears to be particularly important for internally generated behaviors (Goldberg 1985; Passingham, Chen, and Thaler, 1989). Like the concept of internally generated actions, the energization concept implies that the activation of task goals or motor plans by DMJ is partly a function of incentive, which is consistent with evidence from primate studies linking the cingulate motor fields to reward-based action selection (Shima and Tanji 1998).

What is appealing about the energization account of the function of the DMJ is that it provides a simple explanation for why this region seems to be activated in nearly any task condition requiring greater cognitive effort. To the extent that a given task of any sort requires incentive-driven energization of response selection, the energization view predicts greater activation of DMJ. The ubiquity of DMJ activation in the cognitive neuroscience literature supports this view. Though positing that the DMJ subserves energization makes precisely the same predictions as a view that says it is simply involved in more effortful tasks, "effort" is not in itself a function and gives no explanation of why a particular brain region should exhibit greater activation in all cases of more effortful cognitive processing. The energization view put forward by Stuss and Alexander (2007), on the other hand, provides a neurophysiologic explanation for why recruitment of a discrete brain region may occur under such a wide array of task demands.

Inferior Frontal Junction

As shown in Figure 4–4, the only other region activated in all of the cognitive meta-analyses is the left inferior frontal junction (IFJ), so-called because it lies at

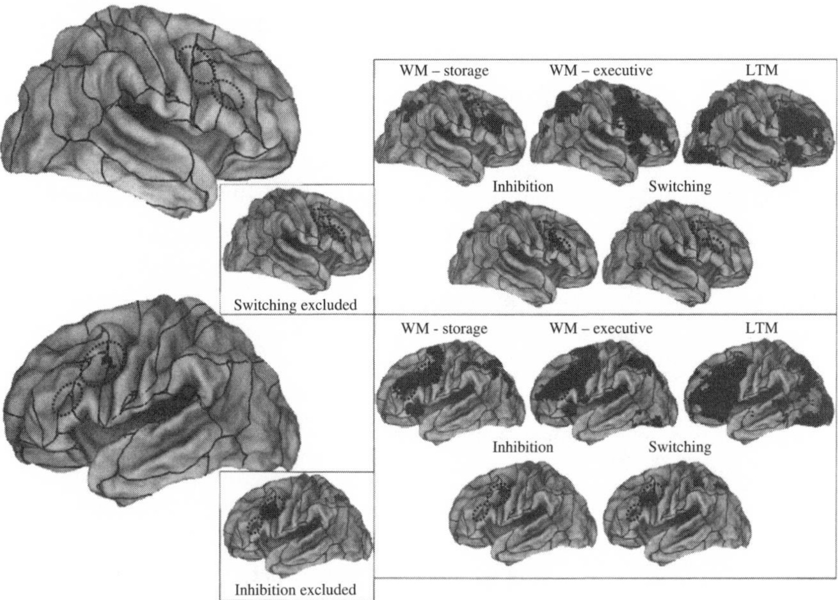

FIGURE 4–4. Conjunction images of the meta-analytic results for WM storage, WM executive, LTM, inhibition, and task-switching shown on the lateral surface of the brain. Insets show the activated regions in each individual domain. The anterior-most region indicated with a dotted line is the posterior portion of the IFG, and the more posterior and superior region is the IFJ.

the junction of the inferior frontal sulcus and the premotor sulcus, encompassing superior BA 44, posterior BA 46, and mid-lateral BA 6. In our meta-analyses, the right IFJ was active in all of the cognitive domains except task-switching (i.e., Nee, Wager, and Jonides 2007; Wager and Smith, 2003; Wager, unpublished data), whereas the left IFJ was active in each of these domains as well task-switching (Wager, Jonides, and Reading 2004). This region was also found to be active bilaterally across a range of task-switching, set-shifting, and S-R reversal studies, as well is in the left hemisphere in Stroop tasks, in a recent meta-analysis by another group (Derrfuss, Brass, Neumann, and von Cramon 2005). Finally, a recent study comparing different types of attention switching in the same individuals showed event-related activation of IFJ, especially in the left hemisphere, related to shifts both between objects and object attributes, and shifts between both visible stimuli and stimuli held in WM (Wager, Jonides, Smith, and Nichols 2005).

As alluded to at the beginning of this chapter, this region makes up at least a part of the DLPFC region proposed to subserve manipulation of the contents of WM. However, this interpretation cannot account for why this region is activated during response inhibition and task-switching, as well as in WM and LTM tasks that do not require manipulation of the contents of WM. Consequently, the IFJ must play some broader, domain-general role in cognition that is needed in each of these tasks.

Neuroimaging studies have demonstrated that this region is specifically active during the presentation of a cue that indicated which of two tasks the subject had to perform (Brass and von Cramon 2002), an activation that was later shown to be specific to task preparation rather than encoding of the cue (Brass and von Cramon 2004). In addition, in line with the meta-analytic results presented here, the IFJ was found to be active across task-switching, Stroop, and WM tasks within a single set of subjects (Derrfuss, Brass, and von Cramon 2004).

Human lesion work has also produced results consistent with the findings of neuroimaging studies described above, at least for the left hemisphere. Stuss and Alexander (2007) show that patients with damage in and around this IFJ region exhibit selective impairments in a number of conditions that can be best explained by a difficulty in establishing an appropriate task set: (a) false alarms on the first 100 trials, but not the subsequent 400 trials, of a complex RT task with five possible responses; (b) false alarms in a Stroop-like task; (c) false alarms, but not false negatives, in an RT task in which targets are a specific conjunction of three features; (d) difficulty establishing the correct response set in the Wisconsin Card Sorting Task, as indexed by an error after three consecutive correct responses; (e) false alarms in a word recall task; and (f) false alarms on a no-go task.

Consequently, both functional neuroimaging and human lesion studies have suggested that this region, at least in the left hemisphere, is involved in "task-setting" (Stuss and Alexander 2007) or "updating of task representations" (Derrfuss, et al. 2005). Although the details vary slightly, both of these interpretations propose that this region sets up S-R mappings in other cortical regions that facilitate appropriate responding based on the specific demands of the task (essentially the prefrontal cognitive control function proposed by Miller and Cohen [2001]), a putative function that is consistent with the broad range of cognitive domains that result in activation of this region in our meta-analytic data.

One issue that has not yet been fully resolved is whether this task-setting function is subserved specifically by the left IFJ or if it is subserved by the IFJ bilaterally, although the evidence seems to be in favor of some degree of left lateralization of this function. First, our meta-analytic data for task-switching failed to reveal activation of the right IFJ (Wager, Jonides, and Reading 2004), and although the meta-analysis by Derffuss, et al. (2005) did reveal activation of right IFJ, the activated region was substantially smaller than that observed in the left hemisphere. Given that task-switching paradigms should be a canonical case of task-setting, inconsistent activation of the right IFJ in task-switching suggests that the right IFJ is less involved in task-setting than is its contralateral homologue. Second, individual functional imaging studies typically find that left IFJ activation is more prominent during task-switching (Sylvester, et al. 2003; Wager, Jonides, and Reading 2005). In addition, whereas the initial report by Brass and von Cramon (2002) revealed cue-specific activation of both left and right IFJ in a task-switching paradigm, when they isolated the need to switch task set from simple presentation of the cue, only left IFJ activation was apparent (Brass and von Cramon 2004). Finally, and perhaps most tellingly, the behavioral task-setting impairments in lesion patients described by Stuss and Alexander (2007) were selective to lesions in the left hemisphere.

Right Posterior Inferior Frontal Gyrus

Another prefrontal region that is commonly activated in cognitive tasks is the posterior portion of the inferior frontal gyrus (IFG), specifically the region including mid-posterior BA 46, superior BA 45, and mid-anterior BA 44 in the right hemisphere (see Figure 4–4). This region is active during LTM (Wager, unpublished data), response inhibition (Nee, Wager, and Jonides 2007), and WM storage and executive tasks (Wager and Smith 2003), but unlike the DMJ and IFJ, activation of this region is notably absent during task-switching (Wager, Jonides, and Reading 2004). In perhaps the largest fMRI study of task-switching to date, we scanned 40 individuals chosen from a group of more than 250 to be either high or low in RT switch costs (Wager, Jonides, and Reading 2005), and IFG activity was inconsistent across switch types. Bilateral IFG activation was elicited by switching between objects held in WM, or between visible object attributes, but not when switching between attributes in WM or visible objects. One explanation is that some kinds of switch may have loaded more heavily on selection and/or inhibition among competing representations. In contrast, another study from our laboratory of three different tasks that place high demand on response selection/inhibition all showed right IFG, but not left IFG, activation (Wager, Sylvester et al. 2005).

An emerging consensus in the literature is that right IFG is related to late-stage (i.e., motor) response selection, whereas left IFG is more related to selection among semantic representations or concepts held in WM. Nee, Wager, and Jonides (2007) used a logistic regression strategy to examine the relation between selection demand at different stages of processing (stimulus, response selection, and motor execution) and brain activity in studies of cognitive control and found that stimulus-related selection demand and selection among verbal materials predicted left IFG activity, whereas late-stage demand for selection in response execution predicted right IFG activity. This dissociation is consistent with other recent syntheses that link left IFG with semantic selection (Poldrack, et al. 1999) and right IFG with motor inhibition (Thompson-Schill, et al. 1997; for review, see Aron, Robbins, and Poldrack 2004).

Other neuroimaging studies of response inhibition, particularly those that emphasize demand on inhibition of already-initiated responses, have also consistently demonstrated activation of the right IFG (e.g., Garavan, Ross, and Stein 1999; Rubia, et al. 2003), and response inhibition has been shown to be selectively impaired by damage to the right IFG in humans (Aron, et al. 2003). With this in mind, a plausible interpretation of activation of this region by LTM and WM storage and executive tasks is that these tasks also require both stimulus and response selection processes for their successful performance.

Common activations across memory tasks

Here we discuss regions of prefrontal cortex that were active in more than one of the three memory contrasts investigated in our meta-analyses (i.e., WM storage, executive WM tasks, and LTM) but that were not active in either inhibition or task-switching. Thus, regions discussed in this section likely reflect processes specifically related to holding information in mind or otherwise carrying out processing on that information.

Before discussing brain regions active in both WM and LTM tasks, it is important to consider the extent to which LTM and WM reflect truly dissociable memory systems. A nascent view in cognitive neuroscience is that WM actually reflects a reactivation of information stored in LTM (Ranganath and Blumenfeld 2005; Jonides, et al. 2008). Whereas the classic view that WM and LTM are distinct forms of memory is supported by numerous demonstrations of double dissociations in studies of patients with lesions of the medial temporal lobe (exhibiting selective LTM deficits), perisylvian cortex (exhibiting selective WM deficits), and the frontal lobe (exhibiting greater WM deficits), Ranganath and Blumenfeld (2005) have marshaled an impressive array of evidence that poses a serious challenge to the classic view. The LTM tasks used in these studies have typically required encoding of material that is semantically meaningful (e.g., words), whereas WM tasks have often required repeated short-term maintenance of material without semantic meaning (e.g., strings of letters or digits). Ranganath and Blumenfeld summarize a substantial amount of data showing that patients with medial temporal lobe lesions do exhibit severe deficits in WM tasks that use novel materials (e.g., trial-unique stimuli, rather than the same set of letters or numbers repeated a large number of times throughout the task), that patients with perisylvian lesions have deficits in LTM tasks if study items are not semantically meaningful, and that lesions of prefrontal cortex do not produce a specific deficit in either WM or LTM but rather interfere with cognitive control processes typically brought to bear in both types of task.

With these objections in mind, Jonides et al. (2008) review the available data on WM and present a neurobiologically grounded model that essentially proposes that the actual representations of to-be-remembered items occur in posterior cortical regions and are bound together or associated with each other to form a memory trace by the hippocampus, and that prefrontal cortical regions subserve control processes relevant to encoding and retrieval of this information as well as other aspects of task performance (e.g., attention and response selection).

Though a final resolution of this issue will ultimately incorporate evidence from diverse sources, and is not attempted here, we observed striking overlap between brain regions activated in both WM and LTM tasks in our meta-analyses, suggesting that both types of tasks use common brain systems, particularly in the frontal cortex. We discuss these commonalities below.

Dorsolateral Prefrontal Cortex

As shown in Figure 4–5, nearly all of BA 46 was active bilaterally during WM storage, WM executive, and LTM tasks, but as shown in Figure 4–4 this activation was absent during both task-switching and response inhibition (i.e., there was insufficient evidence for consistent activation across laboratories). It is important in considering this activation to keep in mind that our analyses of executive WM tasks used WM storage as a subtraction, indicating that BA 46 was active during WM storage but was significantly more active during WM tasks with executive demands. Furthermore, whereas BA 9 and 46 are frequently discussed as though they were a single region in the literature, our meta-analytic results clearly show activation in the majority of BA 46 that does not overlap at all with lateral BA 9. This strongly suggests that BA 46 plays a distinct role from BA 9 in cognition that is consistently associated with memory tasks. The reader should bear in mind throughout this section that the region of DLPFC to which we are referring is specifically the area activated in common across all of the memory domains investigated in our meta-analyses, namely BA 46, and does not include BA 9, which presumably plays a separate role in cognition that we do not address here.

The DLPFC has been the target of an immense amount of research and theory in the past several decades, a thorough review of which is not possible here. However, a number of authors working in various literatures have now proposed that one of the functions of this region is to activate task-relevant representations in posterior cortex, thus establishing a processing bias toward relevant material (Miller, Erickson, and Desimone 1996; Desimone 1998; Hopfinger, Buonocore, and Mangun 2000; MacDonald, et al. 2000; O'Reilly, et al. 2002; Curtis and D'Esposito 2003; Pasternak and Greenlee 2005; Ranganath and Blumenfeld 2005; Ranganath 2006; Jonides, et al. 2008). In WM rehearsal, BA 46 might serve to repeatedly reactivate or "refresh" posterior representations of to-be-remembered material (Raye, et al. 2002; Johnson, et al. 2005).

By this view, the representation of information in posterior cortices (e.g., semantic information in the temporal lobe, visual information in inferior temporal and/or occipital cortices, spatial information in parietal cortex, and so on) must be periodically refreshed so that it is not lost due to decay or interference. Demonstrations of delay-period activity of cells in primate DLPFC during delayed-match-to-sample are now classics in the field (e.g., Funahashi, Bruce,

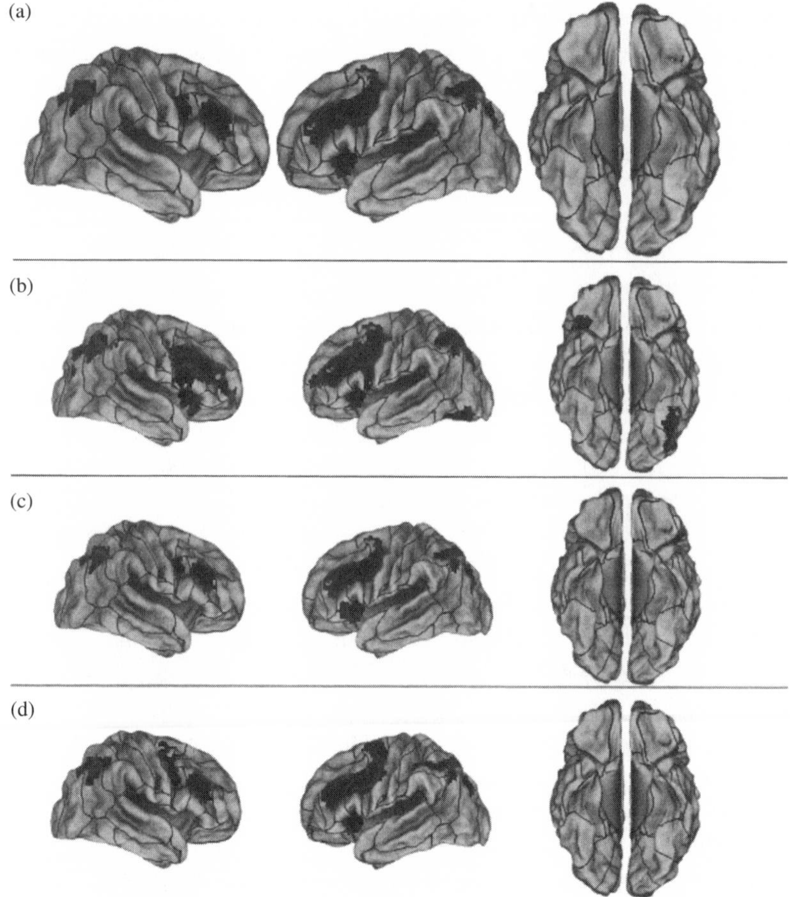

FIGURE 4–5. Conjunction images of the meta-analytic results for all of the memory domains investigated here, shown on the lateral, medial, and ventral surfaces of the brain. (a) WM storage, WM executive, and LTM. (b) WM executive and LTM. (c) WM storage and LTM. (d) WM storage and WM executive.

and Goldman-Rakic 1989; Fuster 1973), and whereas these findings were initially interpreted as reflecting the actual storage of information in WM in DLPFC (Goldman-Rakic 1987), this interpretation has been challenged by evidence that cells in posterior cortices are also active during the delay in these tasks and that delay-activity is consistently observed in cortical regions that are known to be involved in the perceptual processing of the stimulus features critical for task performance (for review, see Pasternak Greenlee 2005). Thus, in standard (visual) non-match-to-sample tasks, cells in inferior temporal cortex exhibit delay activity, whereas tasks in which the direction of motion of a visual stimulus must be remembered result in delay activity in area MT, somatosensory WM tasks result in delay-related activation of primary and secondary somatosensory cortex, and similar results have been found for auditory cortex and WM for tones (Pasternak and Greenlee 2005). However, the lateral prefrontal cortex, unlike posterior cortex, seems to be critical for maintaining representations over a delay period when distractors are presented, consistent with a role in refreshing posterior representations and making them robust to interference (Miller, et al. 1996). In another study, reversible deactivation of DLPFC (via cooling) disrupted delay-related activity in inferior temporal cortex during a visual WM task (Fuster, Bauer, and Jervey 1985).

This interpretation of the role of BA 46 is consistent with our meta-analytic data, in that one would expect that a brain region responsible for maintaining representations in posterior cortices would need to be recruited after retrieval of information from LTM (in order to keep the information online to guide accurate responding) as well as during the maintenance of information in simple WM storage tasks. Furthermore, relatively greater activation of this region can be expected in WM tasks with executive demands than in simple storage tasks, insofar as tasks that demand manipulation of information in WM presumably require the temporary maintenance of additional intermediate states in the transformation process (e.g., given the demand to alphabetize a set of four letters stored in WM, a series of intermediate states would need to be represented given that the subject is, presumably, unable to alphabetize the entire set simultaneously). In essence, then, manipulation of information in WM inherently creates interference and thus requires DLPFC. In this regard, it is worth noting that patients with lesions in this area have been shown to be particularly susceptible to distraction when performing WM tasks (Chao and Knight 1998).

Manipulation of information in WM requires additional scheduling and operating processes as well, which may require more anterior portions of DLPFC (e.g., BA 9 and 10), which we discuss later. Because simple "refresh" operations (Raye, et al. 2002; Johnson, et al. 2005) and simple selective attention tasks (Hopfinger, Buonocore, and Mangun 2000; Weissman, Warner, and Woldorff 2004) are sufficient to elicit BA 46 activation, we associate the region with elemental top-down biasing operations rather than with more complex processes.

If top-down biasing recruits BA 46, one can ask why it is not more reliably activated in task-switching and inhibition studies. Though both types of tasks require top-down biasing for successful performance, the control conditions in these tasks (e.g., nonswitch trials in mixed switch/nonswitch task blocks) are likely to recruit BA 46 as well. Thus, the top-down biasing view would not predict differential activation of this region in experimental and control conditions in many switching and interference-resolution studies.

In addition, it is worth noting that the Nee, Wager, and Jonides (2007) meta-analysis reported here also examined activated regions in several inhibition tasks separately (whereas we report only on those regions significantly activated across all the task types) and found activation of BA 46 in go/no-go and Stroop tasks. Based on an individual study (de Zubicaray, et al. 2000) that demonstrated longer RT and fewer errors, along with greater DLPFC activation, as the proportion of no-go trials in the task increased, Nee, Wager, and Jonides interpreted their DLPFC activation in go/no-go tasks as reflecting the deployment of greater control during a "response selection" phase prior to initiating a response. This interpretation is in line with the view of the role of DLPFC taken here, in that during the performance of a go/no-go task with a high proportion of no-go trials, an efficient strategy may be to devote extra processing resources to the stimuli themselves, which may require additional strengthening of representations of the stimuli in posterior cortices via top-down biasing by the DLPFC. Likewise, activation of the DLPFC by Stroop tasks is to be expected because the ability to respond correctly on incongruent trials specifically requires enhancing relevant representations and/or inhibiting irrelevant ones.

Finally, it is interesting to note that the putative roles of DLPFC and the IFJ as presented in this chapter have an intuitively appealing relationship to each other given their anatomic proximity; namely, that DLPFC maintains task-relevant representations in posterior cortices (whether these representations were retrieved from LTM or have been actively maintained since the stimulus presentation), whereas the immediately posterior IFJ sets up S-R mappings, or a "task-set," in order to produce the correct behavioral responses to stimuli. This raises the (admittedly speculative) possibility that stimulus information being maintained via top-down control from the DLPFC is passed from the DLPFC to the IFJ, which then influences the development of motor plans in the supplementary motor area (SMA) that lie immediately posterior to the IFJ. This foreshadows a view of prefrontal cortex function that posits an anterior-to-posterior gradient of hierarchical information processing that will be taken up in greater detail in the final section of this chapter.

Left Anterior and Middle IFG

Figure 4–5c also reveals activation of the left anterior and middle IFG, BAs 47 and 45 respectively, in LTM and WM storage tasks. Functional neuroimaging studies have demonstrated greater activation of this region of the left IFG under conditions that require greater controlled retrieval from episodic memory (Wheeler and Buckner 2003), greater selection demands on information retrieved from semantic memory (as discussed earlier in the section "Right Posterior Inferior Frontal Gyrus"; Thompson-Schill, et al. 1997), and the resolution of proactive interference in WM (Badre and Wagner, 2005; Jonides and Nee, 2006).

Recent evidence suggests that BA 47 and 45 make distinct contributions to the cognitive control of memory that are consistent with our meta-analyses as well as with the individual studies mentioned above (Badre and Wagner 2007). Whereas our meta-analytic data do not dissociate activation in these regions, Badre and Wagner argue that anterior IFG is involved in controlled retrieval of information from memory while mid-IFG is involved in postretrieval selection; that is, the selection of task-relevant features of a retrieved memory (assuming that not all of the information brought to mind during a recall attempt will be task-relevant), a view that we alluded to when discussing the role of right IFG in response inhibition. Critically, this same postretrieval selection mechanism is presumed to resolve proactive interference in WM tasks, and indeed activation of this region is correlated with behavioral measures of proactive inhibition (Badre and Wagner 2005). Thus, when a negative probe that was part of the target set on a preceding trial is presented (i.e., a probe in a WM task to which the correct answer on the current trial would be "no," but to which the correct answer on the preceding trial would have been "yes"), episodic information relevant to the preceding trial is automatically retrieved, and the participant must select between multiple active representations (of the current and preceding trial) in order to respond appropriately.

Anterior Lateral Prefrontal Cortex

As shown in Figure 4–5b, portions of BA 10, or anterior lateral prefrontal cortex (ALPFC), were active during both LTM and WM executive tasks. Although activation of this region was relatively limited in extent and largely lateralized to the right hemisphere, it is important to keep in mind that the sinus cavities generate susceptibility artifacts in the fMRI signal in frontopolar and orbitofrontal regions, leading to signal distortion and dropout in many studies (Wager, et al. 2007).

A number of theories regarding ALPFC function have been proposed that vary in their details, but all have in common the notion that ALPFC operates at the top of a processing hierarchy in cognition such that it performs operations on, or selects between, task representations in more posterior regions of the lateral prefrontal cortex, such as the DLPFC (Koechlin, et al. 1999; Christoff and Gabrieli 2000; Braver and Bongiolatti 2002; Koechlin, Ody, and Kouneiher 2003; Christoff and Keramatian 2007). Thus, activation of ALPFC is generally found during the performance of tasks that require subjects to generate subgoals (Koechlin, et al. 1999; Braver and Bongiolatti 2002) or to perform cognitive operations on internally generated information (Christoff and Gabrieli 2000; Christoff and Keramatian 2007), or in other words when processing needs to be carried out on the results of prior processing on task-relevant stimuli.

Such a high-level goal selection or subgoal system might play a role in optimizing performance in many tasks, which is a potential cause of ambiguity in mapping brain activity patterns to specific task types. For example, we have found task-switching–related activation of ALPFC, particularly when switching among multiattribute objects stored in WM (Wager, Jonides, et al. 2005). In addition, we have found that activity in right BA 10 is correlated with successful preparation for upcoming conflict in a Stroop-like task (Stern, et al. 2007). In the switching case, subgoals might be involved in simultaneously coordinating rehearsal of objects in WM and shifting tags for behavioral relevance from one object to another. In the conflict case, BA 10 might have been recruited by participants who engaged in voluntary strategies to select one stimulus dimension before it appeared.

In this view, activation of this region by executive WM is expected, in that these tasks all require processing to be carried out on internal representations of stimuli maintained in WM. Activation of this region in LTM, however, is somewhat less clear-cut. Nonetheless, an explanation of why this region is active in LTM tasks emerges from an early meta-analytic review showing that activation of this region is nearly ubiquitous in recall tasks but frequently absent in recognition tasks (Christoff and Gabrieli 2000). Thus, recognition does not recruit ALPFC because the participant need only evaluate the familiarity of a presented stimulus, whereas during recall tasks the subject must engage in controlled retrieval (presumably subserved by the left frontal operculum, as discussed earlier) and then evaluate whether the retrieved information is in fact task-relevant (i.e., that it was actually learned in the context of the experiment), and this latter process results in activation of ALPFC.

Common activations between emotion and cognitive domains

Anterior Insula

As can be seen in Figure 4–6, a portion of the dorsal anterior insula and underlying frontal operculum was activated in most of the cognitive tasks for which we have meta-analytic data. A complication is that activations in many cognitive studies that report activity in IFG appear to be localized at least partially in the operculum and insula, which are very nearby lateral IFG in three-dimensional anatomic space. It is only by comparing activation coordinates across many studies that the consensus across them becomes appreciable. This consensus is that the centroids of activity across many studies lie in the bilateral folds between the frontal operculum and dorsal anterior insula, and these foci may be separable from those on the lateral surface of the IFG. Individual studies in our laboratory have borne out this conclusion as well: the three response-inhibition tasks studied in Wager et al. (2005) activated various parts of insula and IFG, but the superior insular/opercular junction was the area consistently activated across all three tasks. In addition, activity in this area was consistently correlated with higher behavioral interference costs. Nonetheless, it is possible that some of the IFG-related findings discussed above apply to the insula and/or operculum.

Despite being frequently observed in studies of cognition, activation of the anterior insula has received relatively little attention in the cognitive

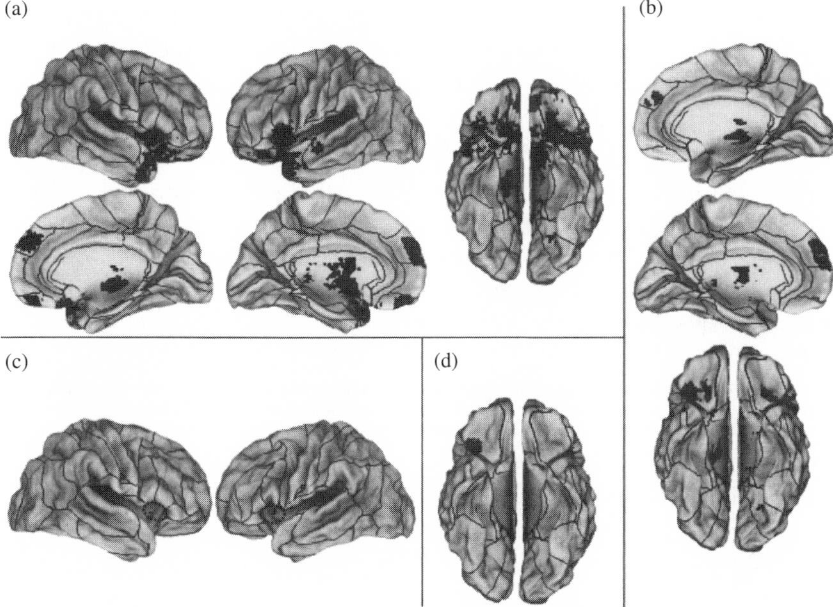

FIGURE 4–6. (a) Regions active in the meta-analysis of experienced emotion. (b) Regions activated during experienced emotion and LTM. (c) Regions active during experienced emotion, LTM, executive WM, and task-switching. The region indicated with a dotted line is the dorsal anterior insula. (d) Orbitofrontal cortex activation observed during experienced emotion, LTM, and executive WM.

literature—perhaps for the reasons mentioned above. Whereas activation of this region is commonly observed in studies of emotion, its role in cognition is not well understood. In our meta-analytic data, however, a common region of the anterior insula is activated during experienced emotion, LTM, task-switching, and WM storage and manipulation (in the left hemisphere, and bilaterally if WM storage is excluded).

One view of anterior insula function that is consistent with the activations observed here is that it serves as an interface between valuations of reward carried out by the OFC (see later) and cognitive control processes carried out by the lateral prefrontal cortex (Wager and Barrett 2004). That is, during the performance of a difficult task, the anterior insula may generate signals that either the wrong task is being performed or that the task is being performed in a suboptimal manner. Thus, in this view the anterior insula "informs" lateral prefrontal regions about which stimuli in the environment should be sought out or avoided based on their motivational salience, as determined by OFC, so that these lateral prefrontal regions can maximize reward by appropriately directing cognition via their roles in task-setting, response selection, and related processes, as discussed previously. In this light, the presence of anterior insula activation in each of the cognitive domains investigated is expected. That such signals would be generated during experienced emotion is also to be expected, in that presumably the experience of a relatively strong affective state would lead to a biasing of cognitive processing toward or away from stimuli or internal representations relevant to the affective state.

Our meta-analytic data suggest that insula activation in response-inhibition tasks appears to be less consistent and right lateralized. If the insula does indeed play a role in signaling motivational salience, then late-stage inhibition tasks in particular may not involve much differential demand on the insula unless there are different stimuli that can be tagged as behaviorally relevant or irrelevant. In Wager et al. (2005), for example, the most insular activity was found in the go/no-go task, in which different stimuli are consistently associated with "go" and "no-go" responses, and the least was found in an S-R compatibility (Simon) task in which a single stimulus is associated with more or less conflict depending on the task instructions.

Orbitofrontal Cortex

Another region commonly activated during the experience of emotion and the performance of some cognitive tasks, in this case executive WM tasks and LTM, is the OFC. A number of authors (e.g., Bechara, Damasio, and Damasio 2000; Barrett, et al. 2007; Coricelli, Dolan, and Sirigu 2007) have suggested that the OFC acts to integrate sensory information and assign value to stimuli in the environment, which then guides decision making. Many studies from the animal and human literature support this broad view. For example, in monkeys damage to the OFC or its connections with the amygdala disrupts updating of the value of reinforcers, causing the animals to continue to overeat liked foods long after intact animals are satiated (Baxter, et al. 2000). The lesions that produce these effects do not disrupt appetitive behavior and satiety generally. Likewise, humans and animals alike show deficits in adjusting behavioral responses after stimulus–reward contingencies change (Wallis, et al. 2001; Fellows and Farah 2003, 2005).

Some of the original descriptions of the effects of PFC damage appealed to accounts of stimulus-driven behaviors. Studies of "utilization behavior" (L'Hermitte, Pillon, and Serdaru 1986) characterized patients as unable to use high-level-context information to avoid making socially inappropriate responses. Other research focused on the inability to flexibly switch strategies after the "correct" stimulus dimension changes in the Wisconsin Card Sorting and related tasks (Milner 1963). It may be that both of these effects, and similar ones on other tasks, are related to OFC damage. OFC and ventromedial prefrontal cortex (VMPFC) damage are apparent in the brains of L'Hermitte patients, for example. In this light, the involvement of OFC in executive WM tasks and LTM tasks can be seen as one of evaluating the motivational relevance of stimuli presented during the task in order to direct cognitive processing by lateral prefrontal regions via the anterior insula and dorsal cingulate cortices. By this account, OFC and VMPFC are involved in using layers of context information to establish higher-order control of behavior, as are other PFC regions; however, OFC/VMPFC are concerned specifically with elements of internal reward value (value to the self) and social context, both of which might be termed internal or motivational context.

This account fits in with other literature that places the OFC and medial prefrontal cortex (MPFC) at the top level of a system for context-based control over adaptive behavioral and physiologic responses. Price (2005), for example, has characterized these regions as "systems for survival" and noted their extensive interconnections with limbic regions and related brain-stem centers. These centers include the insula, amygdala, nucleus accumbens, hypothalamus, and brain-stem periaqueductal gray, and collectively they are critical for adaptive motivational and physiologic regulation. Studies that manipulate affective context by introducing placebo treatments into an ongoing pathophysiologic process have shown that MPFC and OFC are the regions most consistently responsive to placebo (Mayberg, et al. 2002; Petrovic and Ingvar 2002; Lieberman, et al. 2004; Wager, et al. 2004; Petrovic, et al. 2005; Zubieta, et al. 2005; Kong, et al. 2006; Price, et al. 2007; Wager, Scott, and Zubieta 2007). These regions are also critical for other kinds of affective appraisals, including voluntary emotion regulation (Beauregard, Levesque, and Bourgouin 2001; Ochsner, et al. 2002, 2004; Goldin, et al. 2008; Kim and Hamann 2007), reward and punishment prediction and prediction errors (Hornak, et al. 2003; Knutson and Cooper 2005; Tobler, et al. 2006; Jensen, et al. 2007), and valenced emotional responses across a range of stimuli and specific emotion types (Devinsky, Morrell, and Vogt 1995; Baxter, et al. 2000; Hornak, et al. 2003; Wager, et al. 2003; Price 2005; Wager, et al. 2008). They are also altered in structure and/or function in a range of affective disorders, including PTSD (Shin, Rauch, and Pitman 2006; Etkin and Wager 2007) and depression (Drevets 2000; Johansen-Berg, et al. 2007).

Comparing the cognitive meta-analyses discussed above with meta-analyses of emotion (Kober, et al. 2008; Wager, et al. 2003, 2008) can provide insight into which brain regions respond specifically when task demands are relevant to one's internal social and motivational context. As Table 4–1 shows, the OFC and MPFC are activated most consistently by emotion-related tasks, though there is overlap with the most complex and strategy-driven among the cognitive tasks we discuss—LTM and executive WM in particular. This may be either because WM and LTM tasks place greater demand on optimizing motivational settings and performance monitoring or because they require more high-level, task goal–related selection processes.

Dorsomedial Prefrontal Cortex

Notably, experienced emotion and LTM both activate the medial portion of BA 9—the dorsal-most portion of dorsomedial PFC, above the cingulate sulcus and anterior to the typical "cognitive control" DMJ area discussed previously (see Figure 4–6b). Our recent meta-analysis (Kober, et al. 2008) suggests this area is particularly important for the generation and regulation of affective responses, as it was the only cortical area coactivated with both the midbrain periaqueductal gray, a key center for regulating physiologic homeostasis and adaptive emotional reactions, and the hypothalamus, a key area for regulating endocrine and physiologic "stress" responses in the body. This region of the brain has been observed to be active during the active regulation of emotional experience (Ochsner, et al. 2004) and in a number of tasks that involve appraisals of another person's state of mind (e.g., McCabe, et al. 2001; Rilling, et al. 2004), suggesting that it plays a unique role in the interface between social and situational context and motivated behavior in humans.

Putting it together: A modular processing hierarchy in prefrontal cortex

The evidence reviewed here suggests that distinct regions of prefrontal cortex subserve discrete functions in cognition that operate together in a modular manner to allow for the successful performance of a range of cognitive tasks. Admittedly, the evidence presented in this chapter is by no means comprehensive, and the putative functions assigned to the various regions of cortex discussed here are speculative to various degrees. However, the overall picture of prefrontal cortex function presented here leads to a conceptualization of a cognitive processing hierarchy that proceeds along an anterior-to-posterior gradient, from (a) representations of stimulus value in the OFC and rostral MPFC, to (b) processing of internal goal and task-hierarchy representations in the ALPFC, (c) top-down biasing of stimulus representation in posterior cortices by DLPFC, (d) representation and updating of specific S-R mapping rules in IFJ and lateral premotor cortex, (e) the motivated planning of overt motor behavior in pre-SMA and cingulate motor areas, and (f) the actual production of behavior in primary motor cortex. This notion of hierarchy is present in related forms in several current models of prefrontal function (e.g., Koechlin, Ody, and Kouneiher 2003; Christoff and Keramatian 2007).

Of course, any kind of processing hierarchy in prefrontal cortex does not proceed in a truly linear fashion. One way to conceptualize cognitive control in the prefrontal cortex is as proceeding from the result of evaluations about the value of various stimuli or internal representations carried out in OFC. These valuations are then passed through the dorsal anterior insula to lateral prefrontal cortex, wherein DLPFC selects representations in posterior cortical regions that are task relevant and enhances their representation and/or inhibits the representation of task-irrelevant representations. When information needs to be retrieved from LTM, the anterior portion of VLPFC is capable of initiating a controlled retrieval process, and if there are multiple competing active representations, mid-VLPFC is recruited to select between them. The IFJ sets up S-R contingencies based on the current context and directs the development of motor plans in supplementary motor cortex based on these contingencies. If additional processing on activated representations is required, for example the solution of intermediate processing stages or the completion of internally generated subgoals, this is carried out by the ALPFC. Finally, if an incorrect response is generated and detected prior to its execution, the right IFG is brought online to inhibit the actual production of the response, and persistent energization of the entire system is maintained by the DMJ.

Although the putative functions of various regions of prefrontal cortex and their arrangement in a processing hierarchy as outlined above have not been firmly established, one can see that considerable progress in theorizing about the function of human prefrontal cortex has been made since Luria's time. Luria was able to confidently state that patients with lesions to lateral prefrontal cortex suffer from a "...disturbance of selective logical operations" (Luria 1966, p. 287), and we are now able to speculate with considerable specificity about what those operations are and where they are situated in the brain. As with the example of respiration given at the outset of this chapter, the prefrontal cortex is clearly "a complex functional system, effected by a differential dynamic arrangement of nerve cells belonging to different levels of the nervous system," but it is increasingly clear that, much more than being a single functional system, the prefrontal cortex actually subserves a wide array of "atomic" processes that can be flexibly brought to bear depending on the demands of the current situation in order to give rise to an enormous range of human cognitive and affective processes.

References

Anderson, J.R. 1993. *Rules of the Mind.* Hillsdale, N.J.: Lawrence Erlbaum Associates.

Aron, A.R., Fletcher, P.C., Bullmore, E.T., Sahakian, B.J., and Robbins, T.W. 2003. Stop-Signal Inhibition Disrupted by Damage to Right Inferior Frontal Gyrus in Humans. *Nature Neuroscience* 6:115–116.

Aron, A.R., Robbins, T.W., and Poldrack, R.A. 2004. Inhibition and the Right Inferior Frontal Cortex. *Trends in Cognitive Sciences* 8:170–177.

Asaad, W.F., Rainer, G., and Miller, E.K. 2000. Task-Specific Neural Activity in the Primate Prefrontal Cortex. *Journal of Neurophysiology* 84(1):451–459.

Badre, D. and Wagner, A.D. 2005. Frontal Lobe Mechanisms that Resolve Proactive Interference. *Cerebral Cortex* 15:2003–2012.

Badre, D. and Wagner, A.D. 2007. Left Ventrolateral Prefrontal Cortex and the Cognitive Control of Memory. *Neuropsychologia* 45:2883–2901.

Baxter, M.G., Parker, A., Lindner, C.C.C., Izquierdo, A.D., and Murray, E.A. 2000. Control of Response Selection by Reinforcer Value Requires Interaction of Amygdala and Orbital Prefrontal Cortex. *Journal of Neuroscience* 20:4311–4319.

Beauregard, M., Levesque, J., and Bourgouin, P. 2001. Neural Correlates of Conscious Self-Regulation of Emotion. *Journal of Neuroscience* 21(18):RC165.

Bechara, A., Damasio, H., and Damasio, A.R. 2000. Emotion, Decision Making and the Orbitofrontal Cortex. *Cerebral Cortex* 10:295–307.

Botvinick, M.M., Cohen, J.D., and Carter, C.S. 2004. Conflict Monitoring and Anterior Cingulate Cortex: An Update. *Trends in Cognitive Sciences* 8:539–546.

Brass, M. and von Cramon, D.Y. 2002. The Role of the Frontal Cortex in Task Preparation. *Cerebral Cortex* 12:908–914.

Brass, M. and von Cramon, D.Y. 2004. Decomposing Components of Task Preparation with Functinoal MRI. *Journal of Cognitive Neuroscience* 16:609–620.

Braver, T.S. and Bongiolatti, S.R. 2002. The Role of Frontopolar Cortex in Subgoal Processing during Working Memory. *NeuroImage* 15:523–536.

Carter, C.S., Braver, T.S., Barch, D.M., Botvinick, M.M., Noll, D., and Cohen, J.D. 1998. Anterior Cingulate Cortex, Error Detection, and the Online Monitoring of Performance. *Science* 280:747–749.

Chao, L.L. and Knight, R. T. 1998. Contribution of Human Prefrontal Cortex to Delay Performance. *Journal of Cognitive Neuroscience* 10:167–177.

Christoff, K. and Gabrieli, J.D.E. 2000. The Frontopolar Cortex and Human Cognition: Evidence for a Rostrocaudal Hierarchical Organization within the Human Prefrontal Cortex. *Psychobiology* 28:168–186.

Christoff, K. and Keramatian, K. 2007. Abstraction of Mental Representations: Theoretical Considerations and Neuroscientific Evidence. In: S.A. Bunge and J.D. Wallis (eds). *Perspectives on Rule-Guide Behavior*. Oxford: Oxford University Press, pp. 107–126.

Coricelli, G., Dolan, R.J., and Sirigu, A. 2007. Brain, Emtion and Decision Making: The Paradigmatic Example of Regret. *Trends in Cognitive Sciences* 11:258–265.

Curtis, C.E. and D'Esposito, M. 2003. Persistent Activity in the Prefrontal Cortex during Working Memory. *Trends in Cognitive Sciences* 7:415–423.

de Zubicaray, G.I., Andrew, C., Zelaya, F.O., Williams, S.C.R., and Dumanoir, C. 2000. Motor Response Suppression and the Prepotent Tendency to Respond: A Parametric fMRI Study. *Neuropsychologia* 38:1280–1291.

Derrfuss, J., Brass, M., and von Cramon, D.Y. 2004. Cognitive Control in the Posterior Frontolateral Cortex: Evidence from Common Activations in Task Coordination, Interference Control, and Working Memory. *NeuroImage* 23:604–612.

Derrfuss, J., Brass, M., Neumann, J., and von Cramon, D.Y. 2005. Involvement of the inferior Frontal Junction in Cognitive Control: Meta-Analyses of Switching and Stroop Studies. *Human Brain Mapping* 25:22–34.

Desimone, R. 1998. Visual Attention Mediated by Biased Competition in Extrastriate Visual Cortex. *Philosophical Transactions of the Royal Society B* 353:1245–1255.

Devinsky, O., Morrell, M.J., and Vogt, B.A. 1995. Contributions of Anterior Cingulate Cortex to Behaviour. *Brain* 118(Pt 1):279–306.

Drevets, W.C. 2000. Neuroimaging Studies of Mood Disorders. *Biological Psychiatry* 48(8):813–829.

Dum, R.P. and Strick, P.L. 1991. The Origin of Corticospinal Projections from the Premotor Areas in the Frontal Lobe. *Journal of Neuroscience* 11:667–689.

Duncan, J. and Owen, A.M. 2000. Common Regions of the Human Frontal Lobe Recruited by Diverse Cognitive Demands. *Trends in Neurosciences* 23:475–483.

Ekman, P. 1992. Facial Expressions of Emotion: New Findings, New Questions. *Psychological Science* 3:34–38.

Ekman, P., Sorenson, E.R., and Friesen, W.V. 1969. Pan-Cultural Elements in Facial Displays of Emotion. *Science* 164:86–88.

Etkin, A. and Wager, T.D. 2007. Functional Neuroimaging of Anxiety: A Meta-Analysis of Emotional Processing in PTSD, Social Anxiety Disorder, and Specific Phobia. *American Journal of Psychiatry* 164(10):1476–1488.

Barrett, L.F. and Wager, T.D. 2006. The Structure of Emotion: Evidence from Neuroimaging Studies. *Current Directions in Psychological Science* 15:79–83.

Barrett, L.F., Mesquita, B., Ochsner, K.N., and Gross, J.J. 2007. The Experience of Emotion. *Annual Review of Psychology* 58:373–403.

Fellows, L.K. and Farah, M.J. 2003. Ventromedial Frontal Cortex Mediates Affective Shifting in Humans: Evidence from a Reversal Learning Paradigm. *Brain* 126(Pt 8):1830–1837.

Fellows, L.K. and Farah, M.J. 2005. Is Anterior Cingulate Cortex Necessary for Cognitive Control? *Brain* 128(Pt 4):788–796.

Funahashi, S., Bruce, C.J., and Goldman-Rakic, P.S. 1989. Mnemonic Coding of Visual Space during Delayed Response Performance: Neuronal Correlates of Transient Memory. *Journal of Neurophysiology* 61:331–349.

Fuster, J.M. 1973. Unit Activity in Prefrontal Cortex during Delayed Response Performance: Neuronal Correlates of Transient Memory. *Journal of Neurophysiology* 36:61–78.

Fuster, J.M., Bauer, R.H., and Jervey, J.P. 1985. Functional Interactions Between Inferotemporal and Prefrontal Cortex in a Cognitive Task. *Brain Research* 330:299–307.

Garavan, H., Ross, T.J. and Stein, E.A. 1999. Right Hemispheric Dominance of Inhibitory Control: An Event-Related Functional MRI Study. *Proceedings of the National Academy of Sciences of the United States of America* 96:8301–8306.

Goldberg, G. 1985. Supplementary Motor Area Structure and Function: Review and Hypothesis. *Behavioral and Brain Sciences* 8:567–616.

Goldin, P.R., McRae, K., Ramel, W., and Gross, J.J. 2008. The Neural Bases of Emotion Regulation: Reappraisal and Suppression of Negative Emotion. *Biological Psychiatry* 63: 577–586.

Goldman-Rakic, P.S. 1987. Circuitry of Primate Prefrontal Cortex and Regulation of Behavior by Representational Memory. In: F. Plum (ed.). *Handbook of Physiology: The Nervous System* (Vol. 5). Bethesda, Md.: American Physiology Society, pp. 373–417.

Hopfinger, J.B., Buonocore, M.H., and Mangun, G.R. 2000. The Neural Mechanisms of Top-Down Attentional Control. *Nature Neuroscience* 3:284–291.

Hornak, J., Bramham, J., Rolls, E.T., Morris, R.G., O'Doherty, J., Bullock, P.R., and Polkey, C. E. 2003. Changes in Emotion after Circumscribed Surgical Lesions of the Orbitofrontal and Cingulate Cortices. *Brain* 126:1691–1712.

Jensen, J., Smith, A.J., Willeit, M., Crawley, A.P., Mikulis, D.J., Vitcu, I., and Shitij Kapur 2007. Separate Brain Regions Code for Salience vs. Valence during Reward Prediction in Humans. *Human Brain Mapping* 28(4):294–302.

Johansen-Berg, H., Gutman, D.A., Behrens, T.E., Matthews, P.M., Rushworth, M.F., Katz, E., Lozano, A.M. et al. 2007. Anatomical Connectivity of the Subgenual Cingulate Region Targeted with Deep Brain Stimulation for Treatment-Resistant Depression. *Cerebral Cortex* 18: 1374–1383.

Johnson, M.K., Raye, C.L., Mitchell, K.J., Greene, E.J., Cunningham, W.A., and Sanislow, C.A. 2005. Using fMRI to Investigate a Component Process of Reflection: Prefrontal

Correlates of Refreshing a Just-Activated Representation. *Cognitive, Affective, and Behavioral Neuroscience* 5:339–361.

Jonides, J. and Nee, D.E. 2006. Brain Mechanisms of Proactive Interference in Working Memory. *Neuroscience* 139:181–193.

Jonides, J., Lewis, R.L., Nee, D.E., Lustig, C.A., Berman, M.G., and Moore, K.S. 2008. The Mind and Brain of Short-Term Memory. *Annual Review of Psychology* 59:193–224.

Kim, S.H. and Hamann, S. 2007. Neural Correlates of Positive and Negative Emotion Regulation. *Journal of Cognitive Neuroscience* 19(5):776–798.

Knutson, B. and Cooper, J.C. 2005. Functional Magnetic Resonance Imaging of Reward Prediction. *Current Opinion in Neurology* 18(4):411–417.

Kober, H., Feldman Barrett, L., Joseph, J., Bliss-Moreau, E., Lindquist, K., and Wager, T.D. (2008). Functional Groups and Cortical-Subcortical Interactions in Emotion: A Meta-Analysis of Neuroimaging Studies. *Neuroimage* 42, 998–1031.

Koechlin, E., Basso, G., Pietrini, P., Panzer, S., and Grafman, J. 1999. The Role of the Anterior Prefrontal Cortex in Human Cognition. *Nature* 399:148–151.

Koechlin, E., Ody, C., and Kouneiher, F. 2003. The Architecture of Cognitive Control in the Human Prefrontal Cortex. *Science* 302:1181–1185.

Kong, J., Gollub, R.L., Rosman, I.S., Webb, J.M., Vangel, M.G., Kirsch, I., Ted J. Kaptchuk2006. Brain Activity Associated with Expectancy-Enhanced Placebo Analgesia as Measured by Functional Magnetic Resonance Imaging. *Journal of Neuroscience* 26(2):381–388.

L'Hermitte, F., Pillon, B., and Serdaru, M. 1986. Human Autonomy and the Frontal Lobes. Part I: Imitation and Utilization behavior: A Neuropsychology Study of 75 Patients. *Annals of Neurology* 19:326–334.

Lieberman, M.D., Jarcho, J.M., Berman, S., Naliboff, B.D., Suyenobu, B.Y., Mandelkern, M., and Emeran A. Mayer 2004. The Neural Correlates of Placebo Effects: A Disruption Account. *Neuroimage* 22(1):447–455.

Liu, X., Banich, M.T., Jacobson, B.L., and Tanabe, J.L. 2006. Functional Dissociation of Attentional Selection within PFC: Response and Non-Response Related Aspects of Attentional Selection as Ascertained by fMRI. *Cerebral Cortex* 16:827–834.

Luria, A.R. 1966. *Higher Cortical Functions in Man*. New York: Basic Books.

MacDonald, A.W., Cohen, J.D., Stenger, V.A., and Carter, C.S. 2000. Dissociating the Role of the Dorsolateral Prefrontal and Anterior Cingulate in Cognitive Control. *Science* 288:1835–1838.

Mayberg, H.S., Silva, J.A., Brannan, S.K., Tekell, J.L., Mahurin, R.K., McGinnis, S., and Paul A. Jerabek 2002. The Functional Neuroanatomy of the Placebo Effect. *American Journal of Psychiatry* 159(5):728–737.

McCabe, K., Houser, D., Ryan, L., Smith, V., and Trouard, T. 2001. A Functional Imaging Study of Cooperation in the Two-Person Reciprocal Exchange. *Proceedings of the National Academy of Sciences of the United States of America* 98:11832–11835.

Milham, M.P., Banich, M.T., Webb, A., Barad, V., Cohen, N.J., Wszalek, T., DiGirolamo, Gregory J. et al. 2001. The Relative Involvement of Anterior Cingulate and Prefrontal Cortex in Attentional Control Depends on Nature of Conflict. *Cognitive Brain Research* 12:467–473.

Milner, B. 1963. Effects of Different Brain Lesions on Card Sorting: The Role of the Frontal Lobes. *Archives of Neurology* 9:100–110.

Miller, E.K. and Cohen, J.D. 2001. An Integrative Theory of Prefrontal Cortex Function. *Annual Review of Neuroscience* 24:167–202.

Miller, E.K., Erickson, C.A., and Desimone, R. 1996. Neural Mechanisms of Visual Working Memory in Prefrontal Cortex of the Macaque. *Journal of Neuroscience* 16:5154–5167.

Morecraft, R.J. and van Hoesen, G.W. 1998. Convergence of Limbic Input to the Cingulate Motor Cortex in the Rhesus Monkey. *Brain Research Bulletin* 45:209–232.

Nee, D.E., Wager, T.D., and Jonides, J. 2007. Interference Resolution: Insights from a Meta-Analysis of Neuroimaging Tasks. *Cognitive, Affective, and Behavioral Neuroscience* 7:1–17.

Nelson, J.K., Reuter-Lorenz, P.A., Sylvester, C.-Y.C., Jonides, J., and Smith, E.E. 2003. Dissociable Neural Mechanisms Underlying Response-Based and Familiarity-Based Conflict in Working Memory. *Proceedings of the National Academy of Sciences of the United States of America* 100:11171–11175.

O'Reilly, R.C., Noelle, D.C., Braver, T.S., and Cohen, J.D. 2002. Prefrontal Cortex and Dynamic Categorization Tasks: Representational Organization and Neuromodulatory Control. *Cerebral Cortex* 12:246–257.

Ochsner, K.N., Bunge, S.A., Gross, J.J., and Gabrieli, J.D. 2002. Rethinking Feelings: An FMRI Study of the Cognitive Regulation of Emotion. *Journal of Cognitive Neuroscience* 14(8):1215–1229.

Ochsner, K.N., Ray, R.D., Robertson, E.R., Cooper, J.C., Chopra, S., Gabrieli, J.D.E., et al. 2004. For Better or for Worse: Neural Systems Supporting the Cognitive Down-and Up-Regulation of Negative Emotion. *NeuroImage* 23:483–499.

Passingham, R.E., Chen, Y.C., and Thaler, D. 1989. Supplementary motor cortex and self-initiated movement. In: M. Ito (ed.). *Neural Programming*. Basel: S. Karger AG, pp. 13–24.

Pasternak, T. and Greenlee, M.W. 2005. Working Memory in Primate Sensory Systems. *Nature Reviews Neuroscience* 6:97–107.

Paus, T., Koski, L., Caramanos, Z., and Westbury, C. 1998. Regional Differences in the Effects of Task Difficulty and Motor Output on Blood Flow Response in the Human Anterior Cingulate Cortex: A Review of 107 PET Activation Studies. *Neuroreport* 9:R37–R47.

Petrovic, P., Dietrich, T., Fransson, P., Andersson, J., Carlsson, K., and Ingvar, M. 2005. Placebo in Emotional Processing-Induced Expectations of Anxiety Relief Activate a Generalized Modulatory Network. *Neuron* 46(6):957–969.

Petrovic, P. and Ingvar, M. 2002. Imaging Cognitive Modulation of Pain Processing. *Pain* 95(1–2):1–5.

Picard, N. and Strick, P.L. 1996. Motor Areas of the Medial Wall: A Review of their Location and Functional Activation. *Cerebral Cortex* 6:342–353.

Poldrack, R.A., Wagner, A.D., Prull, M.W., Desmond, J.E., Glover, G.H., and Gabrieli, J.D. 1999. Functional Specialization for Semantic and Phonological Processing in the Left Inferior Prefrontal Cortex. *Neuroimage* 10(1):15–35.

Price, D.D., Craggs, J., Verne, G.N., Perlstein, W.M., and Robinson, M.E. 2007. Placebo Analgesia is Accompanied by Large Reductions in Pain-Related Brain Activity in Irritable Bowel Syndrome Patients. *Pain* 127(1–2):63–72.

Price, J.L. 2005. Free will Versus Survival: Brain Systems that Underlie Intrinsic Constraints on Behavior. *Journal of Comparative Neurology* 493(1):132–139.

Ranganath, C. 2006. Working Memory for Visual Objects: Complementary Roles of Inferior Temporal, Medial Temporal, and Prefrontal Cortex. *Neuroscience* 139:277–289.

Ranganath, C. and Blumenfeld, R.S. 2005. Doubts about Double Dissociations Between Short-and Long-Term Memory. *Trends in Cognitive Sciences* 9:374–380.

Raye, C.L., Johnson, M.K., Mitchell, K.J., Reeder, J.A., and Greene, E.J. 2002. Neuroimaging a Single Thought: Dorsolateral PFC Activity Associated with Refreshing Just-Activated Information. *NeuroImage* 15:447–453.

Rilling, J.K., Sanfey, A.G., Aronson, J.A., Nystrom, L.E., and Cohen, J.D. 2004. The Neural Correlates of Theory of Mind within Interpersonal Interactions. *NeuroImage* 22:1694–1703.

Rubia, K., Smith, A.B., Brammer, M.J., and Taylor, E. 2003. Right Inferior Prefrontal Cortex Mediates Response Inhibition While Mesial Prefrontal Cortex is Responsible for Error Detection. *NeuroImage* 20:351–358.

Rypma, B. 2006. Factors controlling Neural Activity during Delayed-Response Task Performance: Testing a Memory Organization Hypothesis of Prefrontal Function. *Neuroscience* 139:223–235.

Rypma, B. and D'Esposito, M. 1999. The Roles of Prefrontal Brain Regions in Components of Working Memory: Effects of Memory Load and Individual Differences. *Proceedings of the National Academy of Sciences of the United States of America* 96:6558–6563.

Shima, K. and Tanji, J. 1998. Role for Cingulate Motor Area Cells in Voluntary Movement Selection Based on Reward. *Science* 282:1335–1338.

Shin, L.M., Rauch, S.L., and Pitman, R.K. 2006. Amygdala, Medial Prefrontal Cortex, and Hippocampal Function in PTSD. *Annals of the New York Academy of Sciences* 1071:67–79.

Smith, E.E. and Jonides, J. 1999. Storage and Executive Processes in the Frontal Lobes. *Science* 283:1657–1661.

Stern, E.R., Wager, T.D., Egner, T., Hirsch, J., and Mangels, J.A. 2007. Preparatory Neural Activity Predicts Performance on a Conflict Task. *Brain Research* 1176:92–102.

Stuss, D.T. and Alexander, M.P. 2007. Is there a Dysexecutive Syndrome? *Philosophical Transactions of the Royal Society B* 362:901–915.

Sylvester, C.-Y.C., Wager, T.D., Lacey, S.C., Hernandez, L., Nichols, T.E., Smith, E.E., John Jonides 2003. Switching Attention and Resolving Interference: fMRI Measures of Executive Functions. *Neuropsychologia* 41:357–370.

Thompson-Schill, S.L., D'Esposito, M., Aguirre, G.K., and Farah, M.J. 1997. Role of Left Inferior Prefrontal Cortex in Retrieval of Semantic Knowledge: A Reevaluation. *Proceedings of the National Academy of Sciences of the United States of America* 94:14792–14797.

Tobler, P.N., O'Doherty J.P., Dolan, R.J., and Schultz, W. 2006. Human Neural Learning Depends on Reward Prediction Errors in the Blocking Paradigm. *Jorunal of Neurophysiology* 95(1):301–310.

Van Essen, D.C. 2005. A Population-Average, Landmark-and Surface-Based (PALS) Atlas of Human Cerebral Cortex. *NeuroImage* 15:635–662.

Van Essen, D.C., Dickson, J., Harwell, J., Hanlon, D., Anderson, C.H., and Drury, H.A. 2001. An Integrated Software System for Surface-Based Analyses of Cerebral Cortex. *Journal of the American Medical Informatics Association* 8:443–459.

Wager, T.D. and Smith, E.E. 2003. Neuroimaging Studies of Working Memory: A Metaanalysis. *Cognitive, Affective, and Behavioral Neuroscience* 3:255–274.

Wager, T.D., Phan, K.L., Liberzon, I., and Taylor, S.F. 2003. Valence, Gender, and Lateralization of Functional Brain Anatomy in Emotion: A Meta-Analysis of Findings from Neuroimaging. *NeuroImage* 19:513–531.

Wager, T.D. and Barrett, L.F. 2004. From Affect to Control: Functional Specialization of the Insula in Motivation and Regulation [Electronic Version]. Retrieved from www.apa.org/psycextra/on, 2005. http://www2.bc.edu/~barretli/pubs/2004/Wager_Edfest_submitted_copy.pdf

Wager, T.D., Jonides, J., and Reading, S. 2004. Neuroimaging Studies of Shifting Attention: A Meta-Analysis. *NeuroImage* 22:1679–1693.

Wager, T.D., Rilling, J.K., Smith, E.E., Sokolik, A., Casey, K.L., Davidson, R.J., Kosslyn, S.M., et al. 2004. Placebo-Induced Changes in FMRI in the Anticipation and Experience of Pain. *Science* 303(5661):1162–1167.

Wager, T.D., Jonides, J., Smith, E.E., and Nichols, T.E. 2005. Toward a Taxonomy of Attention Shifting: Individual Differences in fMRI During Multiple Shift Types. *Cognitive, Affective, and Behavioral Neuroscience* 5:127–143.

Wager, T.D., Sylvester, C.-Y.C., Lacey, S.C., Nee, D.E., Franklin, M., and Jonides, J. 2005. Common and Unique Components of Response Inhibition Revealed by fMRI. *NeuroImage* 27:323–340.

Wager, T.D., Lindquist, M., and Kaplan, L. 2007. Meta-Analysis of Functional Neuroimaging Data: Current and Future Directions. *Social, Cognitive, and Affective Neuroscience* 2:150–158.

Wager, T.D., Scott, D.J., and Zubieta, J.K. 2007. Placebo Effects on Human μ-Opioid Activity During Pain. *Proceedings of the National Academy of Sciences of the UNited States of America* 104(26):11056–11061.

Wager, T.D., Hernandez, L., Jonides, J., and Lindquist, M. 2007. Elements of Functional Neuroimaging. In: J.T. Cacioppo, L.G. Tassinary and G.G. Berntson (eds). *Handbook of Psychophysiology* (4th ed.). Cambridge: Cambridge University Press, pp. 19–55.

Wager, T.D., Barrett, L.F., Bliss-Moreau, E., Lindquist, K., Duncan, S., Kober, H., et al. (2008). The Neuroimaging of Emotion. In: M. Lewis (ed.), *Handbook of Emotions*, 3rd Edition. The Guilford Press: New York.

Wallis, J.D., Dias, R., Robbins, T.W. , and Roberts, A.C. 2001. Dissociable Contributions of the Orbitofrontal and Lateral Prefrontal Cortex of the Marmoset to Performance on a Detour Reaching Task. *European Journal of Neuroscience* 13(9):1797–1808.

Weissman, D.H., Warner, L.M., and Woldorff, M.G. 2004. The Neural Mechanisms for Minimizing Cross-Modal Distraction. *The Journal of Neuroscience* 24:10941–10949.

Wheeler, M.E. and Buckner, R.L. 2003. Functional dissociation among components of remembering: Control, perceived oldness, and content. *The Journal of Neuroscience* 23:3869–3880.

Zubieta, J.K., Bueller, J.A., Jackson, L.R., Scott, D.J., Xu, Y., Koeppe, R.A., Nichols, T.E., et al. 2005. Placebo Effects Mediated by Endogenous Opioid Activity on μ-Opioid Receptors. *Journal of Neuroscience* 25(34):7754–7762.

5

Neuropsychological Foundations of Human Personality and Luria's Legacy

George P. Prigatano

Successful neuropsychological rehabilitation is in part determined by the patient's personality (Prigatano, et al. 1986). In his early writings on rehabilitation, Luria (1948/1963) stated: "As a rule in clinical practice, there are two main factors determining inequality in restoration of function in different cases; differences in the nature of the wound, and the premorbid features of the personality" (p. 223). Yet, Luria never developed (or at least published) his ideas regarding the neuropsychology of human personality. Only in the discussion of how the preliminary conversation with the patient should proceed does Luria (1966) specifically talk about the importance of the patient's personality for diagnosis. He emphasizes the need to elucidate "... the effects of the disease on the patient's personality and emotional reactions and of his attitude toward illness" (p. 319). He goes on to say, however, that when the patient declares himself "more irritable" or "more emotionally upset," it has no localizing value. He later notes, however, that "... unawareness of one's own deficits is one of the classic symptoms of a lesion of the frontal lobes" (p. 321).

In his last book, *The Making of Mind: A Personal Account of Soviet Psychology*, Luria (1979) makes reference to the writings of Sigmund Freud, Alfred Adler, and C.G. Jung as holding some promise for explaining "... the origins of complex human needs in terms of natural science" (p. 23). He later writes, however, "... that I frankly concluded that it was an error to assume that one can deduce human behavior from the biological "depths" of mind, excluding the social "heights" (p. 24). Whether these statements were based on clinical and scientific observations or influenced by political motivations, we will never know.

Yet Luria's (1966) legacy has been profound in neuropsychology, and it may be worthwhile to consider what present-day studies tell us about the neuropsychology of emotion and motivation and how those studies relate to Luria's (1966) views regarding the organization of higher cortical functions in man. Collectively, these insights give us a beginning understanding of what might be broadly described as the neuropsychological foundations of human personality.

Higher cortical functions and the affective neurosciences

In his 1966 book, Luria presented his definition of the higher cortical functions. He states:

> From the point of view of modern psychology, the higher human mental functions are complex reflex processes, social in origin, mediate in structure, and conscious and voluntary in mode of function.
>
> (p. 32)

Elsewhere, I have commented on this definition and attempted a modest expansion of it based on clinical practice (Prigatano 1999, pp. 42–45). At the core of Luria's (1966) definition, complex reflex (i.e., biological) processes form the basis of later thinking. This type of concept can be found in other theorists' writings. Freud (1924) theorized (also see Pribram and Gill 1976) that the emergence of ego processes (which includes consciousness) evolved to solve problems necessary for adaptation that the infant cannot master without dealing with the external world (i.e., the reality principle). Though the terms are different, he places the beginning stage of thinking in the expression of biological needs that "force" consciousness and problem-solving into existence, thereby allowing the child a way of organizing their responses in an adaptive (meaningful) way to the environment. From this perspective, all thinking begins because of unmet biological needs of the infant. Environmental influences, however, shape the form of the emerging problem-solving capacities of the child. The details of how this is actually accomplished have never been explained by any theorist.

The contents of consciousness, and therefore approaches to problem-solving, were described by Luria as "social in origin." The environment shapes the development of personality just as it influences language development. Yet, the most complex and interesting aspect of Luria's definition is his notion that the higher cortical functions are "mediate in structure." By this Luria meant that "something stands" for "something else" in the brain and this mediates the learning process. How this is accomplished is also an unresolved issue in the neurosciences (Fuster 2003). How does a learning experience, be it a conditioned response or an operant behavior, result in something standing for something else?

Fuster (2003) approaches this problem with the concept of *cognits*. He states that the brain develops in a way that experiences lead the individual to learn "if this, then that and if that, then this." These contingences are mediated by cognits, the construction of which is based on patterns of neuronal firing. This concept is at its roots a Hebbian notion (1949). Neurons that fire together form a closer synaptic bond than do neurons that do not. This may be the basis of habit formation and the underlying neurobiological processes necessary for learning.

How different symbols emerge from different social environments to guide emotional and motivational responding also remains a mystery. Many have noted, however, the power of symbols to guide human behavior with both positive and negative outcomes (Jung 1964). The symbols of Christ suffering on the cross allow Christians to find meaning in their suffering and reach out to the suffering of others (e.g., the work of Sister Theresa). Other symbols can have devastating effects on our survivability. Note the example of the highest ranking naval officer who had indicated that he had received two Vietnam War combat ribbons representing valor in combat. When it was discovered that he had never seen combat in Southeast Asia, this gentleman could not simply apologize or explain his behavior to his co-workers. His failure to live up to that symbol resulted in him taking his life (*New York Times* May 17, 1996).

This sad, but not uncommon scenario leads us to another important observation about human personality that has never been adequately discussed by any neuropsychological theorist but is at the core of many psychodynamic theorists: Human beings will frequently behave in a self-destructive manner that results in devastating consequences for them and others. Why is this? If evolution is geared to helping us learn to adapt to the environment and to solve problems for survival (Darwin 1872), why is it that we may function in a way that is antithetical to evolutionary influences? Is this evolution's way of "thinning out humanity" or "weeding out the less fit?" This would be a hard argument to defend because some of the most innovative and creative thinkers have been known to engage in self-punitive behavior and behavior that has caused a considerable amount of harm for others (i.e., the personal life of John F. Kennedy: Hersh 1997).

We are faced, therefore, with the notion that not all human behavior is "rational" in nature (Hebb 1974). This irrational side of human behavior, in addition to the rational side, which Luria refers to as conscious and voluntary in nature, forms the basis of human personality. Luria (1966) did not discuss the irrational side of human personality, and therefore we need to go beyond his definition of higher cortical functions and develop a broad model to help explain it.

The emergent field of affective neurosciences (Panksepp 1998; Davidson, Scherer, and Goldsmith 2003) explores the neurocircuitry of emotion and motivation. The recent *Handbook of Affective Sciences* (Davidson, Scherer, and Goldsmith 2003) presents an impressive array of chapters that summarize hundreds of studies dealing with the neurobiological underpinnings of emotion and motivation. Topics range from the psychophysiology of autonomic nervous system responses to the "genetics" of emotional development. The discussion of neuropsychology of emotion and motivation is also considered, but this area of study remains limited. In their introductory chapters, the editors make the rather poignant statement that:

> . . . the classic concept of the "limbic system" as being the seat of emotion has now effectively been challenged [see LeDoux 1987]. . . . modern research illustrates how there is no single region of the brain dedicated to emotion but, rather, different aspects of emotion processing are distributed in different brain circuits.
>
> (p. 5)

This statement is, of course, decidedly Lurian in nature. It emphasizes the importance of interacting subsystems of the brain to carry out the basic emotional and motivational responses that make up an individual's personality. Yet, within the study of the affective neurosciences, the "irrational" side of human personality is not directly addressed. Explicit attempts to relate Freudian concepts with Lurian ideas also have not adequately addressed this problem (Kaplan-Solms and Solms 2000). As will be discussed later, studies on the neuroimaging correlates of dreaming may provide some insight. For now, however, a review of selected studies and ideas will be presented that relate brain function to overlapping interactive subsystems that are observed in the study of emotion and motivation.

Brain functions and interacting subsystems

For Luria and John Hughlings Jackson before him, the higher integrative (or cortical) brain functions are a result of various interacting subsystems working together at different levels of the nervous system to accomplish such complex tasks as auditory comprehension, speaking, remembering conversations, and carrying out mental arithmetic operations. They must also be involved in such complex tasks as thinking through the theory of relativity and planning the destruction of the World Trade Center towers. Luria remarks, "The most significant feature of a functional system is that, as a rule, it is based on a complex 'constellation' of connections, situated at different levels of the nervous system, that, in the performance of the adaptive task, may be changed when the task itself remains unchanged" (p. 24).

If modern functional neuroimaging studies of brain activity have done anything, they have added considerable support for Luria's (1966) contentions. An example can be seen in a recent study on the neural correlates of motor recovery after stroke (Ward, et al. 2003). Eight patients who suffered hemiparesis resulting from cerebral infarction that spared the primary motor cortex were followed longitudinally with functional magnetic resonance imaging (fMRI) studies. The task presented to each patient was to perform a dynamic isometric hand-grip task using the impaired hand. Whereas the task remained the same over various testing sessions, the pattern of brain activation observed changed as the subject recovered. Good behavioral recovery in patients was associated with a *decrease* of activation throughout the brain and a return to a pattern commonly seen in four normal controls. The patterns of activation were, as Luria would predict, at the level of the cortex, thalamus, basal ganglia, and cerebellum among other areas. These observations would lead us to the proposition that there may be a natural pattern of activation involved when the human brain begins to experience a feeling that could be described later as an emotion or a motivation. There is considerable evidence that deep brain structures involving the hypothalamus, thalamus, and various limbic structures may be crucial for the initial experience of affect that lays the foundation for the later evolution of complex feeling states known as emotions or motivations (MacLean 1973; Prigatano, et al. 1986).

Kagen and Snidman (2004) argue that there are two polar inherent biological features of temperament that can be identified in children. They note that infants can be described as "high reactives" versus "low reactives." The former tend to be "shy and timid children" (i.e., inhibited). The latter (low reactives) tend to be "bold and sociable-uninhibited." Kagen and Snidman (2004) relate these two temperamental differences to the amygdaloid complex. They argue that the amygdaloid complex, which is a set of neurocircuits (the amygdaloid complex involves the amygdala, hippocampus, hypothalamus, and a variety of limbic connections) modulates these two temperamental styles. High-reactive children show high autonomic nervous system arousal (which is mediated by the complex) when presented with an unfamiliar environment or stimulus due to a failure of inhibitory control. Low-reactive children respond with low autonomic arousal due to too much inhibitory control. These biologically inherited temperamental styles help determine if the child will be interested in exploring the environment or will tend to withdraw from the environment when it is unpredictable and unfamiliar.

Labar and LeDoux (2003) have summarized a large literature on the neurocircuitry involved in the conditioned fear response. Figure 5–1 taken from their work highlights the neurocomplexity involved in a "simple" fear reaction.

The amygdala plays a key role, but its input is modified by many variables. Note in Figure 5–1 that an environmental stimulus is needed for setting forth a cascade of neurophysiologic activity involving multiple overlapping systems within the brain when fear is experienced. Although numerous deep brain structures are involved in this emotional response (e.g., the lateral hypothalamus), cortical appraisal of the stimuli is also crucial.

An important aspect of human personality that is not necessarily reflected in the Labar and LeDoux (2003) figure is that these responses may change in their complexity over the course of a lifetime. The notion of whether or not there are critical periods in the life of the organism that guide personality development has not been adequately addressed by neuroscientists. Freud (1924) and

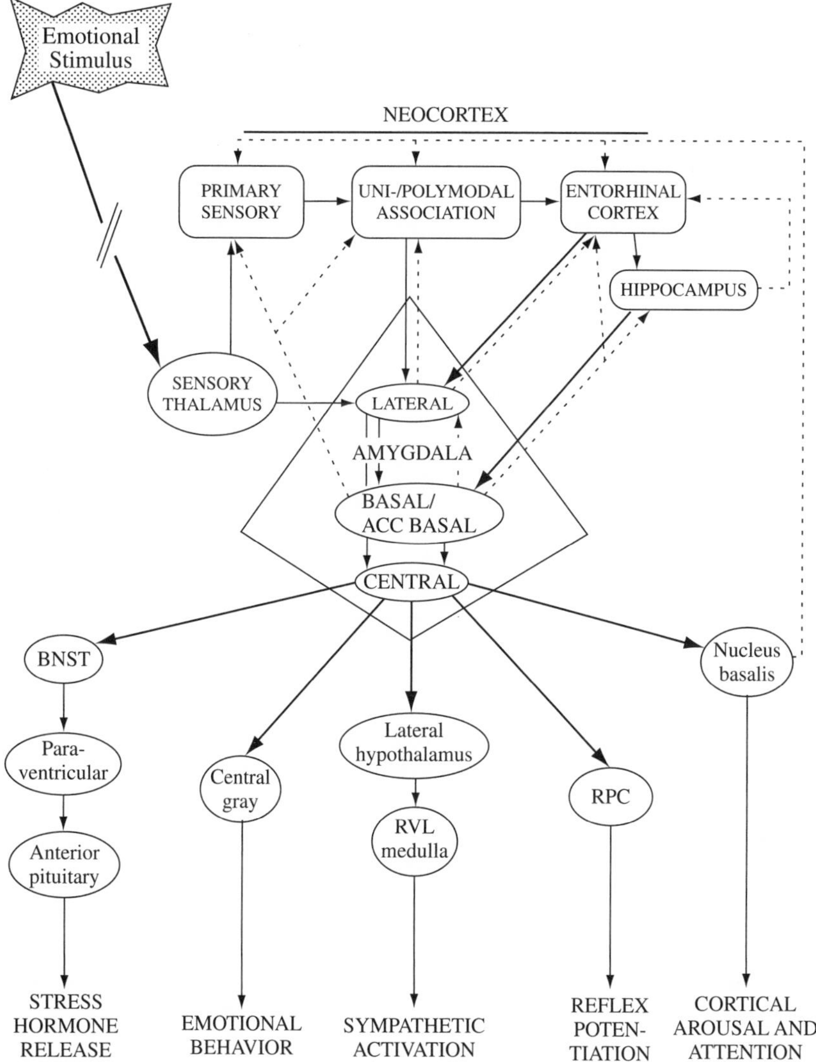

FIGURE 5–1. Neocortex. Reprinted with permission from Davidson, Scherer, and Goldsmith, 2003. ACC, accessary basal nuclei of the amygdale; BASAL, basal nuclei of the amygdale.

others (see Tinbergen 1953; Lorenz 1966), however, were especially interested in how certain life experiences at certain key points of development seemed to put into place a pattern functioning to form the basis of human personality (also see Erik Erikson's work summarized by Hall and Lindzey 1978). In this way, past experiences continue to influence current perceptions of emotional stimuli and responses to them. Psychoanalysts are fond of saying that the "past is alive in the present" (Prigatano 2008). This may be precisely because of the connections of amygdala–hippocampal interactions, which allow learning to occur and influence the learning process throughout the life span.

Sensorimotor development and personality

Children enjoy moving and manipulating objects in their environment (Montessori 1908/1965). Many theorists have noted a connection between the sensorimotor exploration of the environment and the child's later cognitive and affective development (Wadsworth 1984). Children often smile or laugh as they rapidly crawl across the floor. They, and others around them, may express considerable joy in their motor accomplishments. By the second year of life, parents are frequently confronted with the reality that children want to do things for themselves and will become angry if the mother or father tries to help them. This is especially true for "toddlers" who want to walk down a few stairs despite attempts to assist them. Also during the first years of life, one can readily observe that the infant will extend the index finger of one of their hands to touch objects that hold a special interest or appeal for them. What is the connection between these early sensorimotor explorations of the environment and the later development of personality?

Schmahmann and Sherman (1998) have described a cerebellar cognitive affective syndrome. They argue that the inputs from the cerebellum to frontal areas are not only rich, but reciprocal. They note that cerebellar lesions can produce a dissociation of thinking and feeling, which may be in part related to a disturbance of normal regulation of affect and motor control. It is not uncommon to see a patient who has a cerebellar lesion have difficulty controlling the volume of his or her voice when either becoming happy or angry. The modulation of one's linguistic output appears to be mediated by these cerebellar–limbic–frontal connections.

A child who is free to move and explore may well develop a secure sense of who they are and experience the joy of learning. This was in essence the argument that Montessori made more than 100 years ago when she described the importance of having the child have freedom to explore the environment without the adults abandoning the child (Montessori 1908/1965). Recent research has supported Montessori's contentions that the development of social skills using this method may well be superior to normal educational experiences (Lillard 2007).

Perhaps a negative corollary to this observation can be observed when motor activity becomes restricted as a result of a brain disorder. Patients with Parkinson's disease not only have slow motor responses but also have a disturbance in the initiation of thought (Starkstein, et al. 1996). Many of them appear to be depressed, and some, surprisingly, develop substantial changes in personality (Aarsland, et al. 1999). Pribram and McGuinness (1975) suggested years ago that there are important overlapping circuits between the basal ganglia and the frontal regions of the brain. These circuits allow for the initiation and maintenance of behavior when effort is required. Thus, multiple overlapping systems at different levels within the brain are necessary for the complex processes known as "motivation" to occur. Individuals differ in terms of their ease of activation and clearly differ in terms of the effort they are capable of putting forth to achieve certain goals.

Autobiographical memory and personality

The initial learning processes and their relationship to emotional experiences are crucial for setting down early patterns of behavior, which form the basis of human personality. The amygdala and hippocampal circuitry seems to be crucial for the basic bond between emotion and later memory and learning (Squire 1987). In addition to the laying down of these early memories, it is also important to note that the capacity of the human brain to sustain an ongoing conscious representation of who one was in the past is crucial for a sense of who one is in the present. One could refer to this as the capacity for autobiographical memory, that is, memories of the self over many years.

Recently, a 35-year-old woman suffered dense amnestic syndrome secondary to herpes simplex encephalitis. The MRI scan of her brain showed mesial sclerosis in both hippocampal regions. The patient recognized the examining neuropsychologist but could not place how she knew the person. She asked the examining neuropsychologist not only who he was, but also what was her relationship to him in the past. She was unsure if it was a personal or business relationship. She would spontaneously and repetitively ask, at least during the early stages: "Who am I and who was I before?" Without this ability to retrieve long-term information about the self, one clearly would have a fragmented sense of who one is in the here and now.

Bonding/attachment and the thalamic–cingulate connection

Although the amygdala and the "amygdaloid complex" are crucial for the development of basic "emotion" and perhaps form the basis of an individual's temperament, a key aspect of animal behavior is how the animal relates to its mother in order to increase the chances of survival. MacLean's (1985) extraordinary work on the relationship of brain evolution to behavior has not been adequately appreciated by neuropsychologists. Like Luria, MacLean (1985) emphasized that the interaction of various brain systems is necessary to accomplish important behavioral responses necessary for survival. In this regard, his work on the "separation cry" is of considerable interest in the neuropsychology of personality. MacLean (1987) noted that audio-vocal communication is necessary for mammalian maternal–offspring contact. The thalamic–cingulate connection may be crucial for this behavior. He further speculates that the "pain of separation" experienced by mammals may be mediated by the thalamic–cingulate division of the limbic system. The desire for social affiliation is crucial for mammals to survive, and cutting the thalamic–cingulate connection may not only suppress the separation cry but also the desire for such contact. He further speculates that drug addiction (and perhaps many other forms of addiction) may be secondary to feelings of isolation and alienation resulting from a basic disturbance of thalamic–cingulate connection (MacLean 1987).

Bowlby (1983) has studied the attachment behavior of non-human primates as well as that of children. His approach was initially driven by psychoanalytic theory, but his methods of assessment were decidedly behavioral and observational (i.e., empirical) in nature. He makes observations that are quite compatible with MacLean's (1987) conclusions. Bowlby notes that between the ages of 6 months and 6 years, separation of the infant or child from the mother not only produces a "separation cry" (i.e., protest), but also it can be followed by despair and then detachment (p. xxix). He notes that ". . . a tendency to make excessive demands on others and to be anxious and angry when they are not met" (p. xxix) can be a long-term residual of severe disturbances of attachment or bonding. He further notes that a complete "blockage in the capacity of making deep relationships" can ultimately lead to "affectionless and psychopathic personalities" (p. xxx). These observations help us see that early disturbances of thalamic–cingulate connections, driven by experience, may set in motion the first early experiences of irrational (i.e., self or other punitive) behavior. The fact that the child shows detached feelings toward the mother after the initial despair response is not adaptive for the infant. The infant needs to maintain attachment in order to ensure survival.

Als and colleagues (2004) have convincingly shown that early life experiences of premature infants can alter brain function and structure. A systematic program of reducing the distress that premature infants may experience resulted in improved motor and cognitive scores compared with those of matched controls. Additionally, some infants evidenced increased myelinization in deep frontal and subcortical structures.

Frontal lobe lesions, decision making, and changes in human personality

Davidson, Scherer, and Goldsmith (2003), citing their own and others' research, have argued that the prefrontal cortex plays an especially important role in the conscious representation of goals. Damage to this region, therefore, will impair motivation. Citing Damasio's work (see Damasio 1993), Davidson also notes that the ventral prefrontal cortex seems to guide, from an emotional perspective, decision making. Thus, orbital frontal, ventral medial, and dorsal lateral regions of the frontal lobe play an exquisitely important role in what we call human personality, because they underlie the motivations and the goal representations for a person. Recently, a university professor with Pick's disease (frontal temporal dementia) showed a total absence of emotional reaction as he had to vacate his university office and his previous papers were destroyed. His wife experienced a tremendous amount of sadness and pain over these events. When the patient was asked if he had any emotional reaction, he looked blank. When asked if he was sad or neutral about what occurred, he responded "neutral."

Numerous clinicians, including Kurt Goldstein (1952), have noted that damage to the frontal lobe has an extraordinarily negative effect on personality of the individual. The frontal lobes have been hypothesized to play a crucial role in the development of plans and the capacity to initiate actions to achieve goals, which is the core of what we mean by human personality (see Prigatano 1999). Thus, damage to the frontal lobe directly impacts personality.

The anterior cingulate, of course, lies mesial and directly posterior to the prefrontal region. Thayer and Lane (2000) argue that damage to the anterior cingulate disrupts the connection between attention and emotion and therefore also will result in a disorganization of the personality.

Recent research on self-reflection (Johnson, et al. 2002) further notes that the mesial portion of the frontal lobe seems to be extremely important for self-reflection. However, the story does not stop there. Activation of the posterior cingulate and the thalamus are also involved in such activities. The implication again is that the activation of various brain subsystems or overlapping neurocircuits are important for self-reflection and ultimately human consciousness.

Given that the frontal lobes are important for "abstract reasoning," it is no surprise that the ability of human beings to relate to certain symbols is highly connected to frontal lobe activity. Symbols represent or portray a meaning only within a context (Prigatano 1989). In contrast, signs have the same meaning irrespective of the context. For example, the *No Smoking* sign means the same thing irrespective of the culture in which it is observed. However, the picture of Christ on the cross or the Buddha in the lotus position may mean different things within different cultural experiences. Both refer to holy men but one implies that one man was God and the other was a messenger of God. Thus, the ability to guide behavior is very much influenced by frontal lobe functioning via symbols and the emergence of human consciousness. Mesulam (2000) has noted that large regions of the frontal lobe represent heteromodal cortex. These regions play an important role in "integrating thinking with feeling," which is necessary for problem solving, and therefore may be crucial in the emergence of consciousness (Prigatano 1999).

Syndromes of posterior parietal heteromodal cortex

Mesulam (2000) notes: "The posterior parietal heteromodal cortices (Broadmann's area [BA] 7, 39, 40) of the human brain provide sites for multimodal interactions related to praxis, language, visuomotor integration, generation of motor plans, and spatial attention" (p. 39). These abilities are crucial for problem solving. Mesulam (2000) goes on to note that "lesions to the parietotemporal cortex also yield perturbations of mood and motivation" (p. 40). Clinically, this is frequently observed. With more posterior lesions involving the inferior parietal cortex, the patient may show indifference to impairments and sometimes frank anosognosia. Mesulam (2000) also notes that lesions in the posterior–parietal–temporal regions of the right hemisphere at times can lead to psychotic reactions. He further notes that patients who have Wernicke's aphasia are also prone to mood alterations ranging from anger to paranoia. Years earlier, Goldstein (1952) noted that damage to the parietal lobes and to the insula resulted in important changes in personality. Goldstein (1952) and Mesulam (2000) both suggest that these regions are important areas for integrating sensorimotor information that is necessary for understanding "what is real" and knowing how to deal with the environment in the most basic adaptive fashion.

Temporal heteromodal cortex and personality

A number of theorists have noted that lesions to deep brain structures involving the hypothalamus and certain portions of the temporal lobe are associated with psychotic reactions (Lishman 2002). Clinically, we have observed individuals who have temporal lobe lesions who later go on to develop paranoid ideation. They often have a difficult time understanding what is being said and using language to describe what is real. Prigatano and Weinstein (1996) noted that Sapier's early observation was that language not only describes experience, but also it defines experience. Thus, any disturbance in language function puts the individual at risk for knowing what is real, and this may be at the basis of some of the psychotic processes that are observed.

Mesulam (2000) further notes that the "heteromodal cortices in the middle temporal gyrus [represented by area T in Figure 1–11b in his book] may therefore act as transmodal gateways for linking the visual representation of faces with the additional associations (such as the name, voice, and personal recollections) that collectively lead to recognition" (p. 34). Prolonged recognition deficits of any type will clearly influence one's sense of reality, and therefore this may be the basis for psychotic reactions frequently seen with lesions in heteromodal–temporal regions of the brain.

Insular cortex and emotion

The insular cortex is often referred to as the "fifth lobe" of the brain. Although Goldstein (1952) suggested that damage to this region might also result in changes in personality, there have been few studies that have followed up on this clinical observation.

Recent neuroanatomic studies have emphasized the importance of the insula in perceiving changes of temperature and pain. The insula, of course, receives direct input from the thalamus. In addition to perceiving changes in temperature and pain, the insula is extremely important in perceiving subtle tactile changes that are necessary for survival (Jones and Lederman 2006). Craig (2008) has made a convincing argument that the insular cortex plays a major role in emotional behaviors. He notes that "emotional behaviors evolve as energy efficient means of producing goal-directed actions that fulfill homeostatic and social needs." He specifically argues that there is convergent evidence to suggest that the anterior insula plays an important role in all subjective feeling states. His empirical and theoretical work argues that there is indeed a close connection between the regulation of homeostatic functions and the person's subjective emotional state. Damage to this region, therefore, may well produce disturbances in personality that have been ill-defined, but nevertheless may be more common than has been previously recognized, again as Goldstein noted in his earlier (1952) work.

A proposed set of subsystems underlying human personality

From the above discussion, it is clear that the neuropsychological study of emotion and motivation (and therefore personality) is far from being complete. Yet the current data emphasize that complex overlapping neurocircuitry may be at the basis of various subsystems underlying human personality. Given the studies reviewed, it is suggested that there are at least five subsystems that are important to this process. Figure 5–2 summarizes these proposed subsystems. Figure 5–3 outlines the underlying brain structures that are necessary for each subsystem to

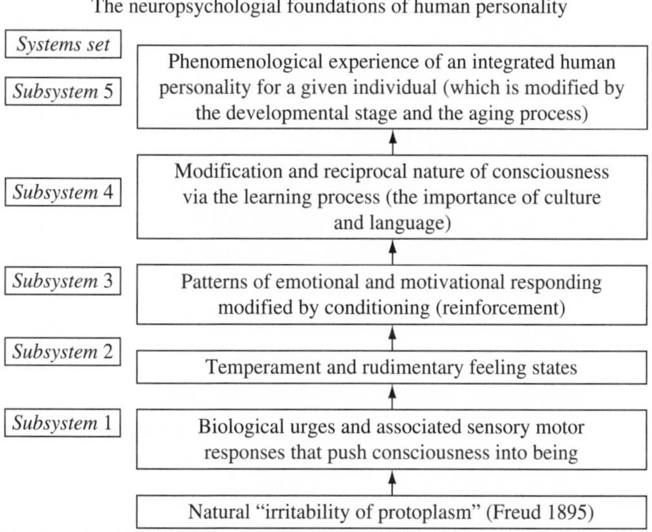

FIGURE 5–2. A proposed theoretical model which outlines 5 subsystems which form the basis of human personality.

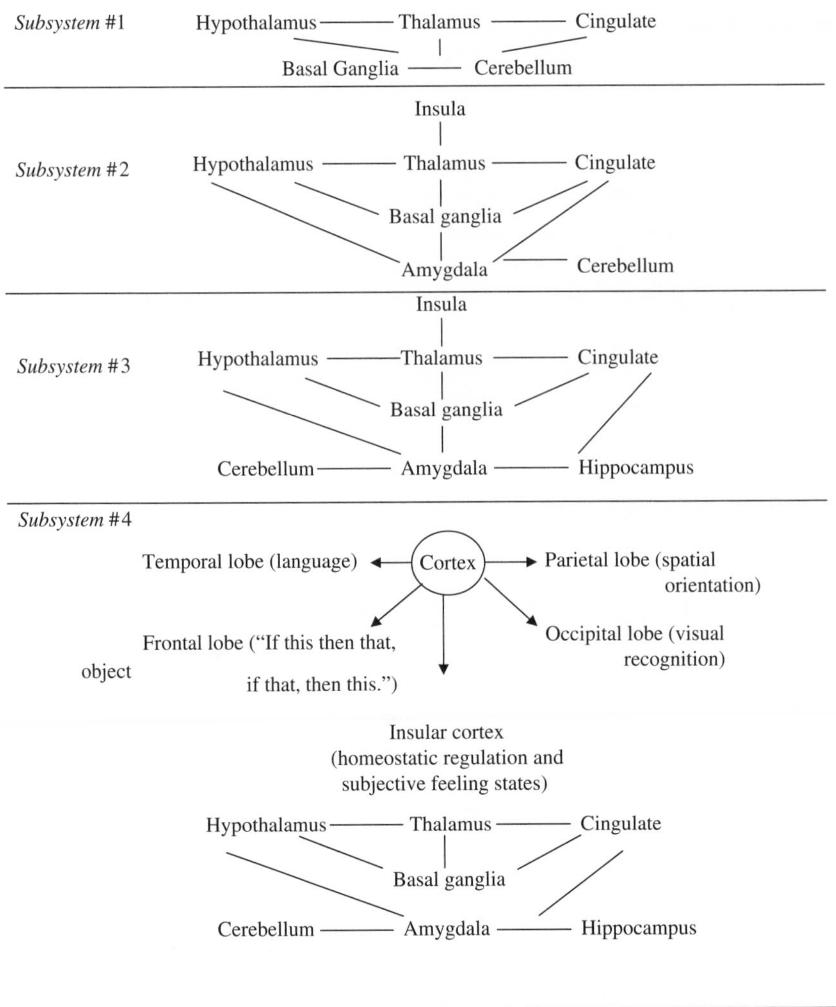

FIGURE 5–3. Proposed relationship between various brain regions that must interact to allow each functional system to operate effectively. With this model each subsystem is dependent on the preceding subsystem to function effectively.

be optimally functional. These latter ideas are heavily based on MacLean's (1973, 1985) work.

The first subsystem is responsible for basic feeling states that encourage human beings to "move" and to explore their environment from a sensory perspective. The biological urge to do so is based on the fact that the infant cannot get their needs met and reduce states of discomfort without effectively interacting with the outer world. Not only are basic structures involved in balance and movement necessary (basal ganglia and cerebellum), but also there must be some sensory representation and feeling state experience (thalamus, cingulate, and ultimately the insular cortex). The hypothalamus is crucial for the early detection of disorders of homeostasis necessary for basic survival.

Subsystem 2 (which is based on Subsystem 1) suggests that there are biologically based differences in temperament and physiologic reactivity. Subsystem 2 is dependent on the amygdaloid complex and may be responsible for individual differences in temperament and how rudimentary feeling states are experienced by the infant.

Subsystem 3 allows for the emergence of conditioning (basic learning) that ultimately molds the various patterns of emotional and motivational responses that seem most adaptive for an individual child. The role of learning and the development of memory systems is vital to the child's being able to parsimoniously confront different situations that have similar properties to past experiences. Hippocampal and mesial temporal lobe structures would seem crucial for this subsystem to effectively work.

Subsystem 4 emphasizes the importance of language and the use of cultural symbols to modify the learning process. Self-reflection, as a rudimentary level of consciousness, is mediated via what the individual says to himself or herself. This is perhaps the most complex of all of the subsystems because it now requires cortical input. Luria's (1966) appreciation of how different zones of the cortex may provide specific and important types of information that allow for different types of problem-solving is relevant here. A summary of the brain structures involved in Subsystem 4 is depicted in Figure 5–3, which is, of course, highly incomplete. It highlights, however, the interaction between multiple brain systems that allow for the beginnings of an integrated personality.

Subsystem 5 remains an enigma from a neuropsychological perspective. Subsystem 5 refers to the phenomenological state of the individual; that is, his or her ability to have a conscious representation of himself or herself and conjointly a psychological representation of others. It is the basis of all existential questions that the individual may pose about their and others' existence. The actual brain structures that allow for human consciousness and the phenomenological state to emerge has remained to this date unanswerable. Undoubtedly, it must depend on the underlying subserving systems, but exactly how it emerges cannot be outlined.

Can these rather broad neuropsychological and neurobiological ideas be mapped onto modern theorists' ideas about human personality? Mayer (2005) has recently summarized a framework for studying personality that can be related to constructs in both psychology and neuropsychology. He suggests that all major theories of personality include four key components or constructs. These constructs are "the conscious executive," "the social actor," "the knowledge works," and "the energy lattice." Note that these constructs are not only embedded in the work of Freud (1924) and Jung (1963), but in one way or another have been addressed by modern neuroscience research.

Figure 5–4, taken from Mayer's work (Mayer 2005, p. 300), suggests that "knowledge works" relies on working memory, verbal intelligence, spatial intelligence, and the capacity to have autobiographical memory (i.e., a life story memory). Damage to frontal-parietal and temporoparietal areas undoubtedly affects knowledge works.

The "social actor" refers to the capacity of the individual to perceive others' intentions, a recognition of what is socially appropriate behavior, and the

PERSONALITY: *Major psychological* subsystems

CONSCIOUSNESS & ATTENTION
Pure awareness
Direction of attention

SELF AWARENESS
Conscious self-control
Self-attention & self-monitoring
Dynamic reevaluations of self

SOCIAL SKILLS
Strategic self-presentation
Acting ability

DEFENSE & COPING
Suppression
Rationalization
Repression

MODELS OF THE SELF
Self-concept
Life-story memory
Self-related aspects of long-term memory

SOCIAL ROLE KNOWLEDGE
Role knowledge
Social relationship enactment

MODELS OF THE WORLD
Beliefs, attitudes, & attributions
Expectancies & predictions
Central knowledge in long-term memory

ATTACHMENT SYSTEM
Expectations & blueprints for interacting with others

COGNITIVE INTELLIGENCES
Verbal intelligence
Perceptual-organizational intelligence
Spatial intelligence

IMAGINATION
Daydreaming
Fantasizing

MOTIVATIONAL & SOCIO-EMOTIONAL EXPRESSIONS
Extroversion & socializing
Dominance & control
Coordination & grace

EMOTION SYSTEM
Constructed emotions
Basic emotinal responses and emotional expressions

HOT INTELLIGENCES
Creativity
Emotional intelligence
Social intelligence

WORKING MEMORY
Short-term memory
Span of apprehension

MOTIVATION SYSTEM
Constructive channeling of motives
Basic biologically-based & learned motives

Note: Each psychological subsystem in the diagram is depicted with a few examples of its possible parts. Each subsystem performs a unique set of psychological functions. Systems related to the external aspects of personality are to the right, those related to internal processing are to the left, More complex, learned systems are forward the top; smaller, more specific systems are lower in the diagram. Related systems were placed, as much as was possible in two dimensions, close to each other. These systems blend into one another and often operated in parallel with one another. Adapted from Figure 2 in "Classifying Change Techniques According to the Areas of Personality They influence: A Systems Framework Integration, " by J. D. Mayer, 2004, *Journal of Clinical Psycholoty*, 60, p. 1299.

FIGURE 5–4. Dividing personality into its key areas can facilitate its study. Reprinted with permission from Mayer, 2005.

ability to make attachments or bonding with others that make mutually interacting social behaviors reinforcing. The social behavior of an individual may, therefore, be clearly damaged if frontal lobe lesions occur later in life or there is an early disturbance of thalamic–cingulate connections in life. It is of some significance that socially inappropriate behavior is frequently one of the most common consequences of early brain disorders (Anderson, et al. 2000).

The "energy lattice," which Mayer (2005) refers to as being dependent on the basic biological and learning motives, would clearly involve the hypothalamus, the thalamus, the amygdaloid complex, as well as upper brain stem and numerous limbic structures. Disturbances to any of these areas affect arousal, effort, and activation as Pribram and McGuinness (1975) noted several years ago.

The "conscious executive" has two components to it. One is conscious awareness as a mediator that directs the attention of the person in the here and now. The other component reflects nonconscious (or unconscious) awareness of information or knowledge that may guide attention and coping processes throughout a given time period. The terms repression and suppression have been used by different theorists to reflect coping processes that remain outside of awareness but nevertheless serve an adaptive function. This model hints at the fact that there may well be emotional and motivational responses that have profound impact on the person's behavior but remain outside the realm of logic.

A return to the problem of irrationality and human personality

The earlier discussion on the "separation cry" in mammals (MacLean 1987) and disturbances of attachment in children (Bowlby 1983) suggest that disturbances that impact deep brain structures (thalamus and hypothalamus) may play an exceedingly important role in how a primate experiences affect in response to others. In humans, we are fond of thinking that our rational capacities guide those emotions and let us get along with one another in a harmonious way. A sad fact of life, however, is that human beings continually respond to each other in a fairly irrational way, which carries with it at times devastating social consequences.

The study of dreaming using positron emission tomography (PET) provides perhaps additional insights as to what occurs in the brain when the individual experiences reality in an illogical manner and does not seem to be bothered by it. Studies by Macquet and colleagues (Macquet, et al. 1996, 1997; Macquet, 1999) demonstrate for the first time that when individuals are dreaming, frontal and parietal areas of the brain appear to become hypometabolic, whereas the brain stem (particularly the rostral brain stem) and the thalamus and portions of the limbic system including the cingulate may become hypermetabolic. What these changes represent is difficult to know, but one possibility is that during the dreaming state, limbic structures become more activated and produce images that are not modulated or controlled or interpreted by higher cortical centers. Thus, one can experience images that are by their nature contradictory or bizarre and yet during the dreaming state accept them to be real.

Everyone has examples of personal dreams that highlight this basic reality. Let me describe a recent dream that I had that highlights this point. To provide background for the context of the dream, recently I was contacted by a neighbor who indicated that I had a substantial leak underneath my driveway at a second home in California. I calmly listened to what he had described concerning the nature of the leak and rationally took steps to have the problem solved (i.e., contacting a plumber/contractor to deal with the problem the next day). I also logically and calmly contacted the department of water works to clarify the nature of the problem and to understand what would have to be done to rectify the problem. Although I knew the project would be expensive, I recognized (again logically) that I had the financial resources to solve the problem. I did not appear to be especially bothered by it, although I was legitimately thinking about this issue at bedtime.

During my night's sleep after this event, I dreamt that there was a huge tidal wave of water that engulfed not only my driveway but also large parcels of land to the right and left of me. In my dream I recalled walking up my driveway and having a huge wave begin to crash on me. While somewhat concerned with this obviously menacing image, I quickly walked up the side of the driveway and avoided being washed away. When I entered my front door, I saw several large leaks of water with the carpeting being pulled back and multiple areas of the house being damaged. I became understandably worried and concerned but accepted all of these images as if they were "true" (and logically occurring). When I awoke, I had recognized that the calm that I had expressed during my earlier dealing with the problem was not in fact reflected in my dream, where there was considerable turmoil that I accepted as being natural or okay.

The point of this personal vignette is that in dreams, we often experience a level of emotionality over an event that we do not experience when we are using our higher cortical functions to deal with problems in an adaptive way.

Recent research on functional imaging correlates of hysterical sensory motor loss also relate to this important problem. Vuilleumier et al. (2001) recently demonstrated that "psychogenic" sensory motor loss was paralleled by a decrease of regional cerebral blood flow in the thalamus and the basal ganglia contralateral to the sensorimotor deficit. After treatment, there was a return to normal activation in the thalamus and basal ganglia. Their findings also suggest that mechanisms such as repression, which are thought to be important in hysterical sensorimotor loss, may somehow be mediated by some basic gating mechanism that is precisely at the level of subcortical structures.

Collectively, these findings suggest that both conscious and nonconscious emotional and motivational reactions of individuals are mediated by a complex network of interacting systems. Deep brain systems involving the limbic structures may be important in allowing nonconscious emotional and motivational conflicts to be experienced, even though cortical inputs apparently are deprived of their influence.

If this is the case, one could consider that more basic instinctual or self-protective mechanisms have "lives of their own" that are frequently modified by cortical inputs, but not always. This is what makes human beings at times dangerous to themselves and others. It may also be the basis of considerable creativity and problem solving. Neuropsychologists need to further study and perhaps recognize that the higher cortical or higher integrative brain functions may be less integrated than we think, particularly in some individuals.

Freud (1924) argued that an "unconscious" existed and that repressed conflicts indeed influenced behavior. No theorist has yet been able to explain what the unconscious is from a neuropsychological point of view and where it may be distributed in the brain. If we assume for a moment that the unconscious represents the impact of learned experiences that remain out of conscious awareness, it would seem more likely that the unconscious "resides" in the heteromodal cortical structures that make consciousness a reality in the first place (a theoretical proposition suggested by Prigatano 1999).

A related but different component to the problem of irrationality in human behavior centers around the basic ambivalence of human emotions as Freud initially described it (Freud 1924). Rizzolatti and Craighero (2004) note that in primates, the same neurons fire when the animal is carrying out a given task, as when observing that same task being performed by another. Although this may be the neurophysiologic basis of imitation learning, it may also explain why different types of movies are exciting and reinforcing to watch. Actually seeing the image on a screen may activate the same neuronal networks that would be involved if the individual was doing what they saw. It would come as no surprise to anyone that movies that challenge traditional beliefs of morality and impulse control are frequently sought after by the movie-going public. It is precisely this ambivalence of wanting to follow the rules of civilization and yet wanting to be free of them at the same time that produces a state of internal tension for individuals that Freud noted many years ago in his book *Civilization and its Discontents* (1930/1961).

These basic tendencies of emotion and motivation can produce a fair amount of subjective or psychological pain for individuals that they deal with by whatever cognitive structures are available. Perhaps the construction of art best reveals how the thought process attempts to control or manipulate disturbing affective experiences that may dominate an individual's life at any given point. A number of individuals have noted throughout history that some of the best art seems to emanate from individuals who struggle with depression and even psychotic experiences (e.g., the paintings of Van Gogh). Recently, an artist provided for me a series of paintings reflecting her struggle dealing with depression associated with what appears to be a mild but nevertheless significant brain injury (Prigatano 2007). Those paintings allowed the individual to make a graphic image of multiple feelings that she was experiencing. The process in itself appeared to be psychotherapeutic in nature and hearkens back to Dora Kalff's (1980) insightful observation that when the inner problem is made exterior, it points to the next step in the psychological development for the individual. Perhaps here we have another insight as to the nature of the neuropsychological foundations of human personality. Whereas the higher cortical functions in man may evolve for problem solving, they often are insufficient for dealing with the instinctual, biological needs of the individual. It is perhaps the eternal (or bitter life) struggle between these two forces that ultimately guide the emergence of human personality in a given individual. This reality has been described by numerous scientists, psychoanalysts, artists, and philosophers.

Summary and conclusions

Numerous studies have appeared on the neurobiological and neuropsychological aspects of emotion and motivation. Luria's (1966) notion (and John Hughlings Jackson before him) that the brain carries out all of its functions as a result of overlapping brain functional subsystems has garnered considerable empirical support over the past 50 years. Neuroimaging studies of various types have perhaps been most helpful in this regard.

Although Luria's (1966) concept of the higher cortical functions in man does not directly address how a human personality emerges, it would postulate that overlapping functional subsystems must be involved in how a personality emerges, much like how language would emerge in a given individual within a given culture or society.

In this brief (and admittedly biased) review of selected papers and ideas, I have presented a model that suggests there are at least five overlapping brain subsystems that underlie the development and emergence of human personality. When these subsystems are disturbed at different times of development or during adulthood by various forms of brain injury, significant but complicated disturbances of emotion and motivation emerge. Whether Luria would agree with this model is, of course, difficult to know. However, I suspect that he would agree with the primary premise of this chapter that the neurosciences have provided much insight as to the underlying, overlapping neurocircuitry of the brain responsible for emotions and motivations. I also suspect that he would agree with the second premise of this chapter that the irrational side of human personality has never been adequately dealt with by neuropsychological theorists. Yet, studies from animal behavior and psychoanalytic and analytic psychology provide some interesting suggestions.

Luria (1979) explicitly states in his last book: "I wanted a psychology that could apply to real people as they live their lives, not an intellectual abstraction in a laboratory" (p. 22). As such, he would be interested in knowing how information coming from the neurosciences helps us explain a given person's struggle to meet their needs within a given environment while at the same time allowing for the emergence of their own individuality (personality) to flourish. Although disturbances of personality may not have localizing value (in the sense of identifying lesion location), Luria would be especially interested in this type of information because it touched on the core issue that got him into psychology in the first place. Luria also notes in his last book the importance of not taking a reductionistic view when understanding psychological phenomena. His discussion of "classical" versus "romantic" science highlights this point of view. He specifically refers to his book *The Man with a Shattered World* (1972) as an effort to recognize the whole person while still understanding the underlying deficits produced by a specific brain lesion. Although he was keenly aware of the limits of any scientific model to explain the uniqueness of a given human personality, he was nevertheless eager to obtain knowledge from any area that would help us explain human behavior, even though those models would remain imperfect.

Acknowledgments

An earlier, brief presentation of several of the ideas outlined in this chapter was presented by this author as a part of the Luria Lectureship sponsored by Kliniken Schmeider Konstanz and the University of Konstanz on August 15, 2005 in Konstanz, Germany. Funding via the Newsome Chair allowed time to prepare this manuscript.

References

Aarsland, D., Larsen, J.P., Lim, N.G., Janvin, C., Karlsen, K., Tandberg, E., and Cummings, J.L. 1999. Range of Neuropsychiatric Disturbances in Patients with Parkinson's Disease. *Journal of Neurology, Neurosurgery, and Psychiatry* 67:492–496.

Als, H., Duffy, F.H., McAnulty, G.B., Rivkin, M.J., Vajapeyam, S., Mulkern, R.V., et al. 2004. Early experience alters brain function and structure. *Pediatrics* 113(4):846–857.

Anderson, S.W., Damasio, H., Tranel, D., and Damasio, A.R. 2000. Long-term Sequelae of Prefrontal Cortex Damage Acquired in Early Childhood. *Developmental Neuropsychology* 18(3):281–296.

Bowlby, J. 1983. *Attachment and Loss, Volume I: Attachment.* New York: Basic Books.

Craig, A.D. (2008). Introception and Emotion: A Neuroanatomical Perspective. In: M. Lewis, J.M. Haviland-Jones, and L.F. Barrett (eds). *The Handbook of Emotion* (3rd ed.). New York: Guilford Publications, Inc., pp. 272–289.

Damasio, A.R. 1993. *Descartes' Error: Emotion, Reason, and the Human Brain.* New York: Putnam.

Darwin, C. 1872. *The Expression of the Emotions in Man and Animals.* (1965 reprint). Chicago: University of Chicago Press.

Davidson, R.J., Scherer, K.R., and Goldsmith, H.H. (eds.). 2003. *Handbook of Affective Sciences.* New York: Oxford University Press.

Freud, S. 1924. *A General Introduction to Psychoanalysis* (24th ed.). New York: Simon and Schuster.

Freud, S. 1930/1961. *Civilization and its Discontents*, J. Strachey (ed.). New York: W.W. Norton.

Fuster, J.M. 2003. *Cortex and Mind: Unifying Cognition.* New York: Oxford University Press.

Goldstein, K. 1952. Effect of Brain Damage on the Personality. *Psychiatry* 15:245–260.

Hall, C.S. and Lindzey, G. 1978. *Theories of Personality* (3rd ed.). New York: John Wiley & Sons.

Hebb, D.O. 1949. *The Organization of Behavior*. New York: Wiley.

Hebb, D.O. 1974. What Psychology Is About. *American Psychologist* 29(2):71–79.

Hersh, S.M. 1997. *The Dark Side of Camelot.* Boston: Little, Brown and Company.

Johnson, S.C., Baxter, L.C., Wilder, L.S., Pipe, J.G., Heiserman, J.E., and Prigatano, G.P. 2002. Neural Substates of Self-Reflective Thought. *Brain* 125:1808–1814.

Jones, L.A. and Lederman, S.J. 2006. *Human Hand Function.* New York: Oxford University Press.

Jung, C.G. 1963. *Memories, Dreams, Reflections.* A. Jaffe (ed.). London: Collins and Routledge and Kegan Paul.

Jung, C.G. 1964. *Man and His Symbols.* New York: Doubleday Windfall.

Kagan, J. and Snidman, N. 2004. *The Long Shadow of Temperament.* Cambridge, Mass.: The Belknap Press of Harvard University Press.

Kalff, D.M. 1980. *Sandplay: A Psychotherapeutic Approach to the Psyche.* Santa Monica, Calif.: Sigo Press.

Kaplan-Solms, K. and Solms, M. 2000. *Clinical Studies in Neuro-Psychoanalysis: Introduction to a Depth Neuropsychology.* London: Karnac Books.

LaBar, K.S. and LeDoux, J.E. 2003. Emotional Learning Circuits in Animals and Humans. In: R.J. Davidson, K.R. Scherer, and H.H. Goldsmith (eds.). *Handbook of Affective Sciences.* New York: Oxford University Press, pp. 52–65.

LeDoux, J.E. 1987. Emotion. In: F. Plum (ed.). *Handbook of Physiology. 1: The Nervous System. Vol. V. Higher Functions of the Brain.* Bethesda, Md.: American Physiological Society, pp. 419–460.

Lillard, A.S. 2007. *Montessori: The Science Behind the Genius.* New York: Oxford University Press.

Lishman, W.A. 2002. *Organic Psychiatry: The Psychological Consequences of Cerebral Disorder* (3rd ed.). Boston: Blackwell Science Ltd.

Lorenz, K. 1966. *On Aggression.* New York: Harcourt, Brace and World.

Luria, A.R. 1948/1963. *Restoration of Function After Brain Trauma* (in Russian). Moscow: Academy of Medical Science 1948; London: Pergamon, 1963.

Luria, A.R. 1966. *Higher Cerebral Functions in Man.* New York: Basic Books.

Luria, A.R. 1972. *The Man with a Shattered World.* Cambridge, Mass.: Harvard University Press.

Luria, A.R. 1979. *The Making of Mind: A Personal Account of Soviet Psychology.* M. Cole and S. Cole (eds.). Cambridge, Mass.: Harvard University Press.

MacLean, P.D. 1973. A Triune Concept of the Brain and Behavior. Lecture I. Man's Reptilian and Limbis Inheritance; Lecture II. Man's Limbic Brain and the Psychoses; Lecture

III. New Trends in Man's Evolution. In: T. Boag and D. Campbell (eds.). *The Hincks Memorial Lectures*. Toronto: University of Toronto, pp. 6–66.

MacLean, P.D. 1985. Brain Evolution Relating to Family, Play, and the Separation Call. *Archives of General Psychiatry* 42:405–417.

MacLean, P.D. 1987. The Midline Frontolimbic Cortex and the Evolution of Crying and Laughter. In: E. Perecman (ed.). *The Frontal Lobes Revisited*. New York: IRBN, pp. 121–140.

Macquet, P. 1999. Brain Mechanisms of Sleep: Contribution of Neuroimaging Techniques. *Journal of Psychopharmacology* 13(4 Suppl 1):S25–S28.

Macquet, P., Degueldre, C., Delfiore, G., Aerts, J., Peters, J.M., Luxen, and Franck, G. 1997. Functional Neuroanatomy of Human Slow Wave Sleep. *Journal of Neuroscience* 17:2807–2812.

Macquet, P., Peters, J.M., Aerts, J., Delfiore, G., Deguedre, C., Luxen, A., et al. 1996. Functional Neuroanatomy of Human Rapid-Eye-Movement Sleep and Dreaming. *Nature* 383:163–166.

Mayer, J.D. 2005. A Tale of Two Visions: Can a New View of Personality Help Integrate Psychology? *American Psychologist* 60(4):294–307.

Mesulam, M.-Marsel. 2000. *Principles of Behavioral and Cognitive Neurology* (2nd ed.). New York: Oxford University Press.

Montessori, M. 1908/1965. *Spontaneous Activity in Education*. New York: Schocken Books.

Panksepp, J. 1998. *Affective Neuroscience: The Foundations of Human and Animal Emotions*. New York: Oxford University Press.

Pribram, K.H. and Gill, M.M. 1976. *Freud's "Project" Reassessed*. New York: Basic Books.

Pribram, K.H. and McGuinness, D. 1975. Arousal, Activation and Effort in the Control of Attention. *Psychological Review* 82(2):116–149.

Prigatano, G.P. 1989. Work, Love, and Play after Brain Injury. *Bulletin of the Menninger Clinic* 53(5):414–431.

Prigatano G.P. 1999. *Principles of Neuropsychological Rehabilitation*. New York: Oxford University Press.

Prigatano, G.P. 2007. *Barrow Quarterly* 23(3):9–10.

Prigatano, G.P., Fordyce, D.J., Zeiner, H.K., Roueche, J.R., Pepping, M., and Wood, B.C. 1986. *Neuropsychological Rehabilitation after Brain Injury*. Baltimore: The Johns Hopkins University Press.

Prigatano, G.P. and Weinstein, E.A. 1996. Edwin A. Weinstein's Contributions to Neuropsychological Rehabilitation. *Neuropsychological Rehabilitation* 6(4): 305–326.

Prigatano, G.P. (2008). Neuropsychological Rehabilitation and Psychodynamic Psychotherapy. In: J. Morgan and J. Ricker (eds.). *Textbook of Clinical Neuropsychology*. New York: Taylor and Francis, pp. 985–995.

Rizzolatti, G. and Craighero, L. 2004. The Mirror-Neuron System. *Annual Review of Neuroscience* 27:169–192.

Schmahmann, J.D. and Sherman, J.C. 1998. The Cerebellar Cognitive Affective Syndrome. *Brain* 121:561–579.

Squire, L.R. 1987. *Memory and Brain*. New York: Oxford University Press.

Starkstein, S.E., Sabe, L., Petracca, G., Chemerinski, E., Kuzis, G., Merello, M., and Leiguarda, R. 1996. Neuropsychological and Psychiatric Differences between Alzheimer's

Disease and Parkinson's Disease with Dementia. *Journal of Neurology, Neurosurgery, and Psychiatry* 61:381–387.

Thayer, J.F. and Lane, R.D. 2000. A Model of Neurovisceral Integration in Emotion Regulation and Dysregulation. *Journal of Affective Disorders* 61:201–216.

Tinbergen, N. 1953. *Social Behavior in Animals*. London: Methuen.

Vuilleumier, P., Chicherio, C., Assal, F., Schwartz, S., Slosman, D., and Landis, T. 2001. Functional Neuroanatomical Correlates of Hysterical Sensorimotor Loss. *Brain* 124:1077–1090.

Wadsworth, B.J. 1984. *Piaget's Theory of Cognitive and Affective Development, Third Edition*. New York: Longman.

Ward, N.S., Brown, M.M., Thompson, A.J., and Frackowiak, R.S.J. 2003. Neural Correlates of Motor Recovery after Stroke: A Longitudinal fMRI Study. *Brain* 126:2476–2496.

6

Studies in the Neuropsychology of Attention

Allan F. Mirsky and Connie C. Duncan

In this chapter, we review the history of the development of current measures used to assess attention, with special emphasis on sustained attention. Every competent neuropsychological assessment should include measures of attention. Many of the methods currently in use (e.g., the Sunrise System Continuous Performance Test, the Connors Continuous Performance Test, the Test of Variables of Attention (TOVA), the Integrated Visual and Auditory Continuous Performance Test (IVA), and the Gordon Diagnostic System) are derived from a measure developed originally to address neuropsychiatric needs arising during wartime. A parallel need arose from a human factors concern related to the newly developed radar instrumentation. We review, as well, efforts to relate states of altered attention to neurologic, neurophysiologic, and, above all, to neuropsychological concepts. For one on us (A.F.M.), an encounter with Professor Alexander Luria in the 1950s had a very salutary effect on the future course of this research, and it is likely that it would have proceeded in a different direction had that encounter not taken place.

We begin the chapter with a discussion of how wartime injuries and military needs during World War II served as a stimulus to the development of measures to assess alterations in attention.

The continuous performance test (CPT) and the clock test: 1939–1945 and beyond

The clinical data that stimulated the development of the attentional measures used in our research stemmed initially from observations of men injured in wartime. As a psychologist in the Canadian army during World War II, Rosvold observed that many head-injured men exhibited brief periods of inattention, or "microsleeps." However, the available, somewhat meagre armamentarium of psychological test instruments was typically unable to detect these episodes. Later, Rosvold and colleagues developed a technique—the Continuous Performance Test, or CPT—that had sufficient sensitivity to detect these brief lapses. The secret lay in having a target detection task and an appreciable test duration to capture the elusive microsleeps (Rosvold, et al. 1956). The test thus presented letters of the alphabet one-at-a-time in a visual display and required the subject to respond to a specified target (i.e., the letter "X"). The task duration was 7–10 minutes. Figure 6–1 illustrates a recent version of the CPT apparatus.

It should be noted, as well, that Mackworth, working with the British military, was endeavoring to discover how to predict the length of time a person could monitor a radar oscilloscope without making significant errors. Radar was developed during World War II, and the *human factors* aspect of performance had been little studied. Mackworth developed the clock test, which required the operator/subject to monitor the hand of a clock that usually moved in one-step increments (Mackworth 1948). At random intervals, the clock hand moved two steps, and the subject had to note these and respond when they occurred. Both the CPT and the clock test were measures of vigilance that were developed to measure human performance that had been altered either by injury or fatigue.

This history is reminiscent of the way in which Luria's observations of Russian soldiers injured in World War II led to the illumination of the role of the frontal

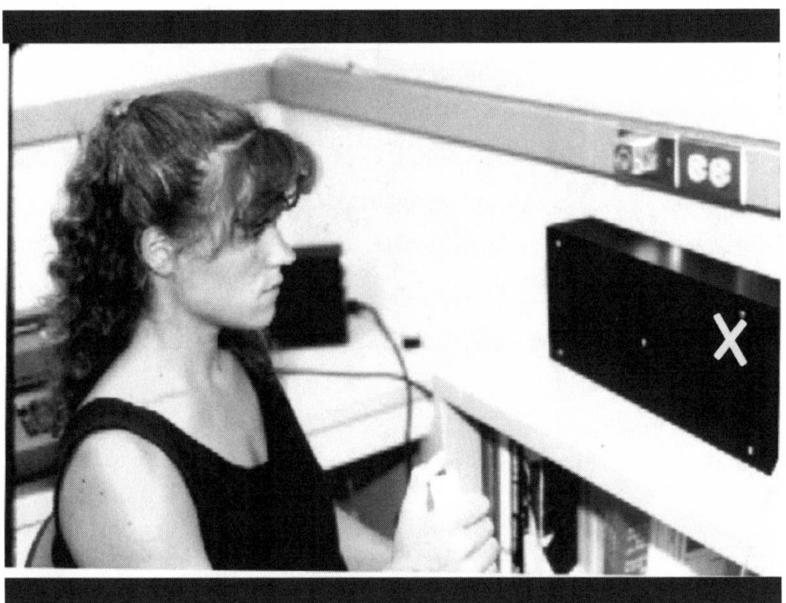

FIGURE 6–1. CPT apparatus.

lobe in the regulation and modulation of executive functions. Thus, men with frontal lobe injuries were frequently unable to initiate an action, but once started, they were unable to stop. Luria described the man who not only cut through a board in the occupational therapy workshop but also continued to saw through the work table (Luria 1980).

To bring these historical vignettes together, as a graduate student, A.F.M. worked with Rosvold and others at Yale to develop the first version of the CPT and to test Rosvold's hypothesis that brain-damaged persons would exhibit response failures on a sustained attention task. Rosvold was correct, of course (Rosvold, et al. 1956). Somewhat later, as a young investigator at the National Institute of Mental Health (NIMH), A.F.M. had the opportunity to meet with Luria in the late 1950s. He was on a tour of research laboratories in the United States and because of his reputation and prestige was one of the relatively few Russian scientists allowed to travel to the West. The National Institutes of Health (NIH), fortunately for A.F.M., was one of the stops on the tour. Luria was shown some of the data in which EEG had been recorded simultaneously with the CPT in a patient with absence epilepsy. In the sample tracing, it was evident that there was a coincidence of omission errors and a burst of three-per-second spike-wave activity (the signature EEG marker of absence epilepsy; Figure 6–2). Luria was

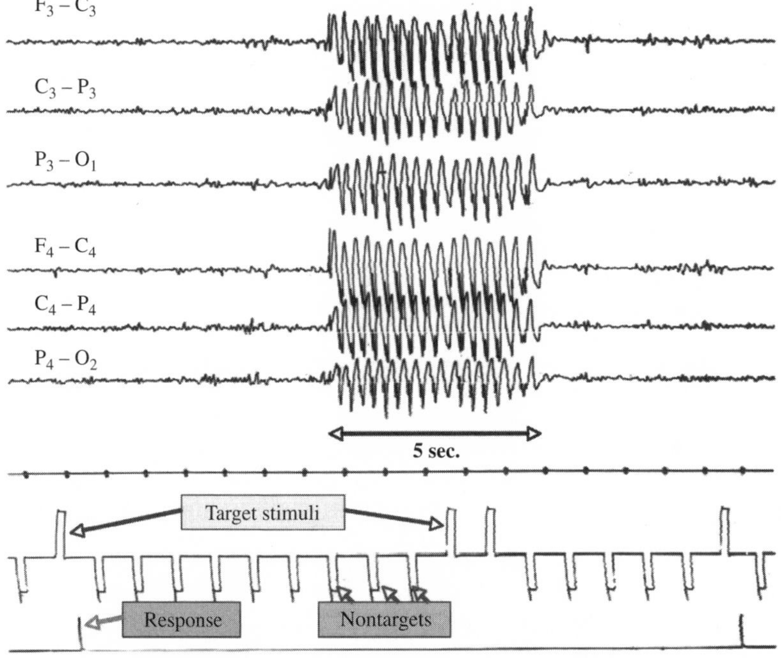

FIGURE 6–2. Simultaneous recording of EEG, CPT targets (letter X) and patient responses. During 5 second spike-wave burst, patient failed to respond to two targets. F3, C3, P3, O1, F4, C4, P4, O2, P3 refer to scalp locations in "10–20" system.

FIGURE 6–3. Luria and his daughter Elena.

very supportive of the work and exclaimed, "And there are people who claim that there is no relation between brain activity and behavior!" (or words to that effect). This vote of confidence from such an eminent, world-famous academician was electrifying and reinforced the feeling that A.F.M. was doing the right thing. Figure 6–3 is a photograph of Luria and his daughter Elena, given to me by her. The photograph is undated but was taken at approximately the time that he visited NIH.

Studies of sustained attention in neuropsychiatric disorders

The Investigation of Seizure Disorders: Idiopathic Epilepsies of the Absence Type

Our early findings demonstrated that patients with absence epilepsy performed significantly worse than did patients with other types of seizure disorders (Mirsky, et al. 1960). The pathophysiology of the disorder thus became a focus of our work, and we became interested in the possible critical role of brain-stem pathophysiology in absence seizures. This was stimulated by the research stemming from the Montreal Neurological Institute, led by Penfield and Jasper. In their overview of a number of human clinical investigations and animal model studies of absence epilepsy, they theorized that dysfunction in a deep subcortical system (i.e., the centrencephalon), with widespread connections to the forebrain, underlies the symptoms of absence epilepsy. Hence, they coined the terms *centrencephalic epilepsy* (Penfield and Jasper 1954) or *cortico-reticular epilepsy* (Gloor 1988) as replacements for the ancient term *petit mal epilepsy*. Patients with this disorder have brief interruptions of consciousness or attentiveness in conjunction with a characteristic EEG pattern (as had been demonstrated to Professor Luria in the late 1950s).

The EEG pattern comprises a bilaterally synchronous and symmetric three-per-second spike-and-wave discharge (Figure 6–2), which is seen more-or-less uniformly over the scalp.

Whether or not they are displaying the spike-and-wave EEG pattern and/or "clinical" signs (e.g., elevation of the eyes or fluttering of the eyelids [Penfield and Jasper 1954]), absence patients have a specific deficit in sustained attention: As noted above, they can be distinguished reliably from patients with other seizure disorders on the basis of performance on tests of visual and/or auditory sustained attention, such as the CPT (Figure 6–4) (Mirsky, et al. 1960; Lansdell and Mirsky 1964; Mirsky and Van Buren 1965; Fedio and Mirsky 1969; Duncan 1988). In each of these studies, spanning a period of nearly 30 years, patients with absence epilepsy were found to perform significantly worse on the CPT than did patients with focal seizure or healthy controls.

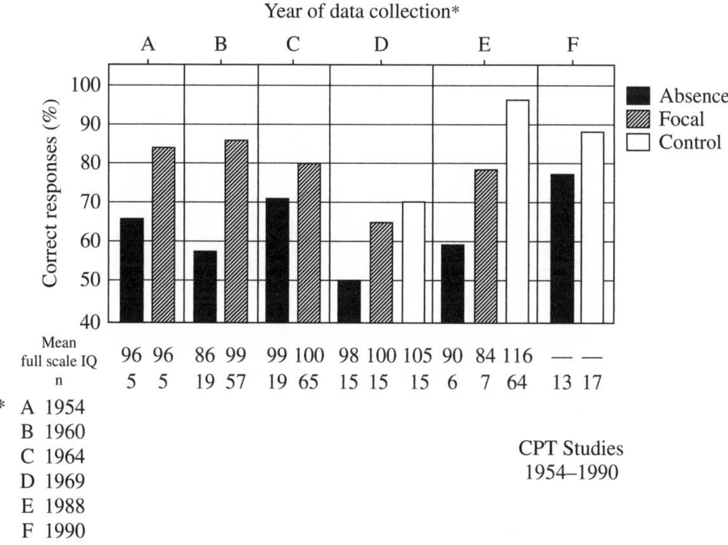

FIGURE 6–4. CPT studies, 1954–1990, showing consistently poorer performance of absence patients in comparison to focal controls and healthy controls.

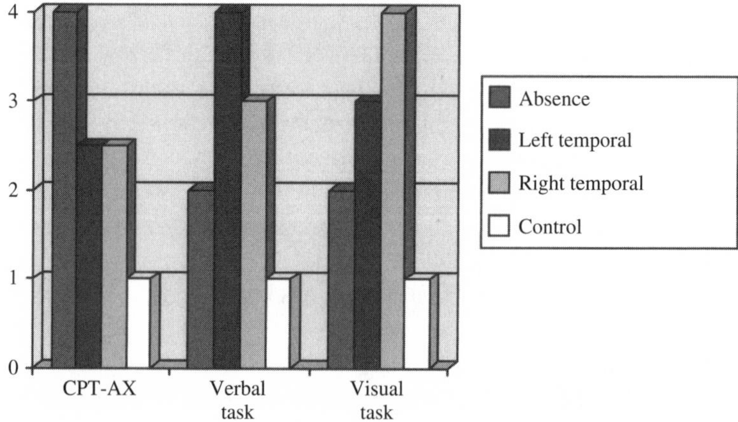

FIGURE 6–5. Comparison of three groups of seizure disorder patients, and healthy controls, on three different tasks (from Fedio and Mirsky, 1969).

Moreover, the absence patients are not simply more uniformly impaired than other patients; Figure 6–5 shows the relative rank of impairment of three groups of seizure patients (those with left temporal foci; right temporal foci; absence patients) and controls on three tasks: the AX task of the CPT, a verbal learning task; and a visual-spatial recall task. The AX task requires the subject to press the response key for the letter X if it follows the letter A. A rank of 1 indicates the least impaired group on a task; a rank of 4 indicates the group with the most impairment on that task. The absence patients were most impaired on the CPT task, whereas the left and right temporal lobe foci patients were most impaired, respectively, on the verbal learning and visual-spatial tasks (Fedio and Mirsky 1969).

Schizophrenia and Vulnerability to Psychosis

Kraepelin noted the poor attention in patients with schizophrenia as early as 1919 (Kraepelin 1919). Other alienists remarked on this symptom as well, including Shakow, who wrote extensively on the inability of patients to maintain a "set" to respond (Shakow 1962). Zubin summarized the disordered attention in patients with schizophrenia by noting that they had difficulty focusing on some event in the environment, they could not sustain a focus once it was achieved, and they had difficulty in shifting a focus in an adaptive, flexible manner (Zubin 1975). This observation resembles closely the attention "elements" we identified in 1991 (Mirsky, et al. 1991). Our list of attentional elements includes the ability to *sustain* attention, to *focus* on some aspect of the environment and *execute* responses efficiently, to *encode* information, to *shift* attentional focus easily and adaptively, and to maintain a *stable* and efficient response to stimuli.

TABLE 6–1. Etiology of disorders of attention: A proposed nosology

I. Familial/Genetic
   a. Absence epilepsy, other forms of idiopathic generalized epilepsy*
   b. Schizophrenia*
   c. Autism
   d. Attention deficit disorder, with or without hyperactivity*
   e. Narcolepsy

II. Metabolic
   a. Phenylketonuria*
   b. Uremia*

III. Environmental
   a. Malnutrition*
   b. Lead intoxication*
   c. Pregnancy/birth complications
   d. Fetal alcohol (cocaine) syndrome/effect*
   e. Neurocysticercosis/other parasitic infections*
   f. Lack of intellectual stimulation

IV. Other
   a. Cerebral insult, including traumatic brain injury*
   b. Cerebral infections/tumors*
   c. Sleep breathing disorders*
   d. Eating disorders*

Source: From Mirsky, A.F., Duncan, C.C., 2001. A nosology of disorders of attention. In: J. Wasserstein, L. Wolff, and F.F. LeFever (eds.). *Adult Attention Deficit Disorder: Brain Mechanisms and Life Outcomes*, Vol. 931. New York: New York Academy of Sciences, pp. 17–32 Adapted with permission of the authors.

* Impaired CPT performance was seen in these disorders; for the others, there are either no published studies using the CPT or no CPT impairment was found. References are listed in the Mirsky and Duncan (2001) N.Y. Academy of Sciences publication.

The inability of patients with schizophrenia to sustain attention, especially under conditions of distraction, has been studied with versions of the CPT by many investigators (e.g., Stammeyer 1961; Wohlberg and Kornetsky 1973, Erlenmeyer-Kimling and Cornblatt 1992; Mirsky, et al. 1995; Seidman, et al. 1998). It is clear that the test is sensitive to the disorder, although poor CPT performance is not specific to patients with schizophrenia (as seen in Table 6–1).

Although mindful of the graveyard full of anatomists who had hopes of discovering the cerebral basis/cause of schizophrenia, we assert with some temerity that the same—or a similar—subcortical disturbance that underlies the poor attention in patients with absence epilepsy is responsible for this negative symptom in schizophrenia.

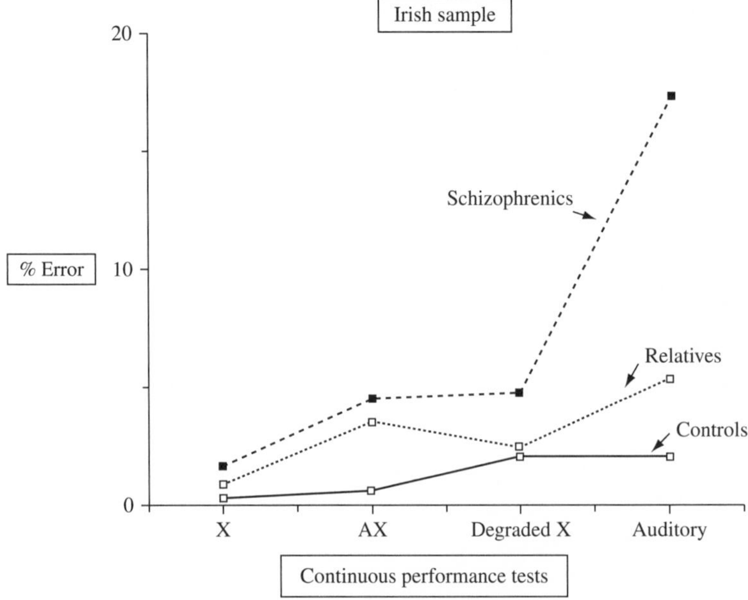

FIGURE 6–6. Comparison of error percentages on four CPT tasks in schizophrenia patients, their first-degree relatives and controls. From Mirsky, A.F., Yardley, S.L., Jones B.P., Walsh, D., and Kendler, K.S. 1995. Analysis of the Attention Deficit in Schizophrenia: A Study of Patients and Their Relatives in Ireland. *Journal of Psychiatric Research* 29:23–42.

Figure 6–6 (from Mirsky, et al. 1995) displays the impaired performance on four versions of the CPT in a group of patients with schizophrenia, their first-degree relatives, and a group of normal controls. The auditory version of the task was particularly difficult for the patients and their relatives. In this regard, it is of interest that Duncan et al. (2005) have reported greater impairment of auditory than visual information processing after closed-head injury. They have proposed that this finding is due to the greater vulnerability of the auditory system than that of the visual system to trauma. Mirsky and Duncan (2004) have suggested that this vulnerability may have implications for the auditory-related symptoms of schizophrenia.

The Role of Environmental Factors in Schizophrenia

In addition to a genetic diathesis, a number of environmental risk factors for developing schizophrenia have been proposed. These include pregnancy and birth complications, winter or spring births, viral infections, and low social class/urban residence. The effect of such injuries lies in a diminished capacity for sustained attentive behavior, with deleterious effects on both the capacity to learn and the

TABLE 6–2. Deleterious environmental effects associated with poverty

ENVIRONMENTAL EFFECT	REPRESENTATIVE REFERENCES
Fetal alcohol (cocaine) syndrome/effect	Streissguth, et al. 1994 Connor, et al. 1999 Bandstra, et al. 2001
Pregnancy/birth complications	Chamberlain, et al. 1975 Chamberlain, et al. 1978
Malnutrition	Levav, et al. 1995a Levav, et al. 1995b
Lead intoxication	Needleman, et al. 1995 Mirsky, et al. 2001
Parasitic infections	Levav, et al. 1995b Cruz, et al. 1993 Marmor, et al. 1987
Lack of intellectual stimulation	Bahrudin and Luster 1998 Mirsky, et al. 1995 Mirsky, 1995

Source: From Mirsky, A.F., Duncan, C.C., 2001. A nosology of disorders of attention. In: J. Wasserstein, L. Wolff, and F.F. LeFever (eds.). *Adult Attention Deficit Disorder: Brain Mechanisms and Life Outcomes*, Vol. 931. New York: New York Academy of Sciences, pp. 17–32 Adapted with permission of the authors.

ability to interact socially (summarized in Mirsky and Duncan, 2004). The conditions associated with increased vulnerability to a schizophrenia spectrum disorder may share common neurodevelopmental effects, and many of them are associated with growing up in an impoverished environment (Table 6–2). Specifically, these effects may all, in some way, alter the brain-stem–forebrain system(s) that underlie sustained attention.

Specifically, they may all act in some way to compromise brain-stem–forebrain systems

A particularly clear example is provided by the results of the experimental asphyxia studies in monkeys of Myers and co-workers (Myers 1972; Mirsky, et al. 1979). They showed that both acute total asphyxia and prolonged partial asphyxia (corresponding with two types of difficult labor and delivery in humans) are accompanied by damage to brain-stem structures. The damaged brain-stem structures include the inferior colliculus, the superior olivary complex, and other regions of the mesencephalon (Duncan, et al. 2005).

Myers' work presents a model for the effects of perinatal brain damage in humans. In a genetically vulnerable individual, such damage could foster the development of a schizophrenic disorder by compromising the integrity of the

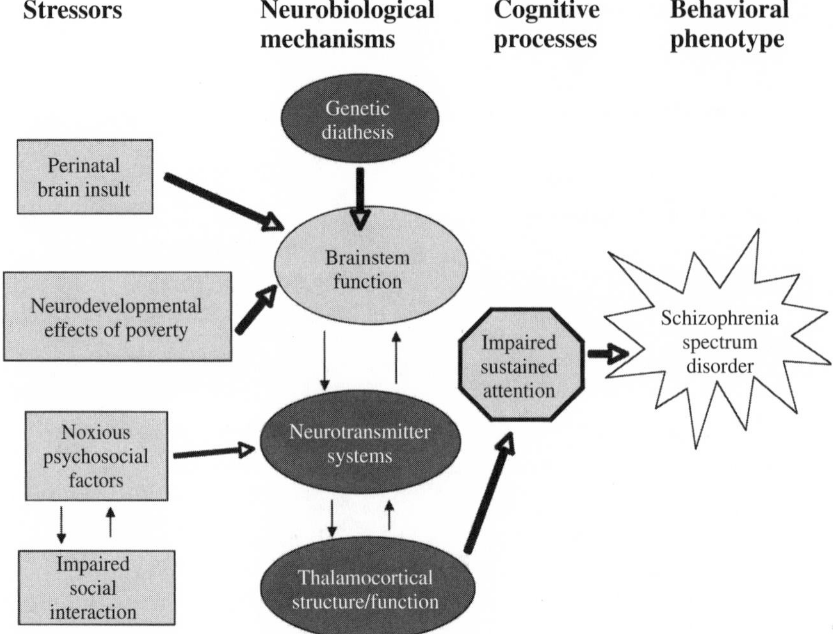

FIGURE 6–7. Schematic model of role of heredity, environment and neurobiological factors in the etiology of schizophrenia spectrum disorders (from Mirsky and Duncan, 2004).

brain stem and the critical behavioral functions it supports. A schematic model of this proposal is presented in Figure 6–7. This illustrates how environmental stressors such as perinatal brain insult, the neurodevelopmental effects of poverty, noxious psychosocial factors, and impaired social interaction can alter neurobiological mechanisms. The end result is to produce impaired sustained attention and ultimately, in a vulnerable individual, a schizophrenic spectrum disorder.

Other Disorders

Impaired attention is a symptom of many neuropsychiatric disorders. In an effort to classify the putative causative factors underlying the disorders, we proposed a preliminary classification of etiologies (Mirsky and Duncan 2001). This nosology or classification is presented in Table 6–1.

We note that none of the etiologies may be exclusive and that genetic and environmental factors interact to produce the disease phenotype in many, if not all, of these disorders. Moreover, genetic influences may be discovered for many of the disorders listed under other headings in the table.

Impairment in attention characterizes all of the disorders listed in Table 6–1, evidenced in most instances by poor performance on the CPT. We assert that these disorders (indicated by* in Table 6–1) involve either genetically and/or environmentally induced compromise (including trauma) of the brain-stem component of a brain-stem–cortical system (BRAS) that supports sustained attention (Mirsky and Duncan 2001). Some of the mechanisms by which this compromise or injury may occur are discussed later, as well as in Mirsky and Duncan (2001, 2004). The latter reference deals with neuropsychological perspectives on genetically high-risk children and has special relevance to the etiology of schizophrenia discussed later; see also Figure 6–6.

ADHD (Attention Deficit Hyperactivity Disorder)

The impaired attention of children and adults with this diagnosis gives rise to the eponymous diagnosis. The evidence that brain-stem pathology is implicated in the disorder is inferential but reasonably convincing. Gruber et al. (2000) have shown that children with ADHD have profound sleep disturbances, with many awakenings, and difficulty in reaching the deeper stages of sleep. Further evidence of BRAS involvement in ADHD, based on analysis of neurotransmitter function, was provided by the PET (Positron Emission Tomography) study of Ernst et al. (1999). These authors reported dopaminergic abnormalities, as measured by a radiolabeled tracer ([^{18}F]DOPA) in the midbrain of children with ADHD. This abnormality in dopamine activity may be involved in the poor sleep regulation of patients with ADHD. The disorder would therefore be interpreted as a disturbance of the normal regulation of functions supported by structures within the BRAS.

Narcolepsy

Narcolepsy is a disorder characterized by excessive sleepiness and abnormal manifestations of rapid eye movement (REM) sleep (Aldrich 1991). In his review article, Aldrich notes that neurochemical studies suggest that deficits in noradrenaline availability in specific brain regions (the locus coeruleus of the brain stem?) may account for much of the pathophysiology in this disorder. Further, the genetic susceptibility to the disorder is apparently closely linked to a region of chromosome 6p that has been implicated in other disorders marked by attention impairment. We shall return to this theme later.

Sleep Breathing Disorders

Groups of patients (N = 328) with sleep breathing disorders were observed to have mean scores on the CPT (in the range 50% to 70% correct responses) as low as those seen in patients with untreated absence epilepsy or severe schizophrenia (Regestein, et al. 2001, unpublished manuscript). The disordered sleep from which these patients suffer is presumably a reflection of some dysfunction of the regulatory mechanisms in the BRAS, which is also reflected in their poor performance on the CPT.

Uremia

An early study by Murawski (1970) indicated that patients with severe uremia (kidney failure) were impaired in sustained attention and that their need for dialysis could be monitored with the CPT. More recently, Burns and Bates (1998) reported similar findings in a review article.

> Patients (with end-stage uremia) show significant deviations in areas of attention/response speed . . . choice reaction time, which measures sustained attention . . . may be the most useful test to determine subtle cognitive impairment in uremia . . . Bilateral spike and wave complexes have been reported in up to 14% of patients with chronic renal failure.
>
> (pp. 814, 816)

The obvious implication of this finding is that the same disorder of the cortico-reticular system implicated in absence (centrencephalic) epilepsy is involved in severe uremia and generates similar attentional symptoms and electrographic signs. An additional finding of considerable interest for this line of reasoning is the recent identification of a genetic defect for severe polycystic kidney disease (Guaywoodford, et al. 1995; Alvarez, et al. 2000) at possibly the same location on chromosome 6p that has been identified for juvenile myoclonic epilepsy (Greenberg, et al. 1988). Juvenile myoclonic epilepsy is a form of idiopathic generalized (absence-type) epilepsy that may show the same type of EEG patterns seen in Figure 6–3.

Correlated Behavioral and Electrophysiologic Investigations of Attention: The Relationship Between Attention Test Performance and Paroxysmal EEG Activity

Figure 6–2 provided a striking example of the co-occurrence of errors on the CPT and the paroxysmal spike-wave EEG discharge. This was a somewhat more sophisticated replication of a study published in 1939 by Schwab (1939). Schwab recorded EEG and reaction time simultaneously in a group of patients with absence epilepsy and found that patients responded more slowly or not at all if there was a coincidence of the imperative stimulus and a spike-wave burst. Mirsky and Van Buren (1965) confirmed and extended Schwab's results. They found that although there was a strong association between performance and EEG bursts (i.e., the bilaterally synchronous and symmetrical three-per-second spike-and-wave activity), the two phenomena were, in fact, to some degree independent. Thus, some patients were able to attend and respond to task stimuli in the presence of spike-wave bursts, whereas others could not respond at such times. The capacity for response was affected by such factors as degree of left–right symmetry in the EEG paroxysm, burst length, and time of occurrence of the stimulus during the burst (i.e., beginning vs. end). Moreover, Mirsky and Van Buren (1965) found that even when those errors in performance associated with bursts were excluded, patients with idiopathic generalized seizures made more errors in the interictal periods than did controls.

Attention Test Performance Between Seizures in Patients with Idiopathic Generalized Seizures: Analysis of the EEG

The finding that patients with generalized seizures tended to make more errors in the interictal periods than did controls led to an intensive study of the EEG of such patients. This work involved not only analysis of the power spectrum (amount of "power" in various EEG frequencies) between seizures in such patients (Siegel, et al. 1979, 1980; Grady 1982; Mirsky and Grady 1988), but also studies of the capacity for information processing, as measured with event-related brain potentials (ERPs). The major finding of the interictal power spectrum studies was that in persons with idiopathic generalized seizures, there is a more-or-less continuous subclinical abnormality in the brain's electrical activity that erupts from time to time into EEG paroxysms. Figure 6–8 (from Mirsky and Grady 1988) shows the buildup in power in the frequency of 3.5 cps

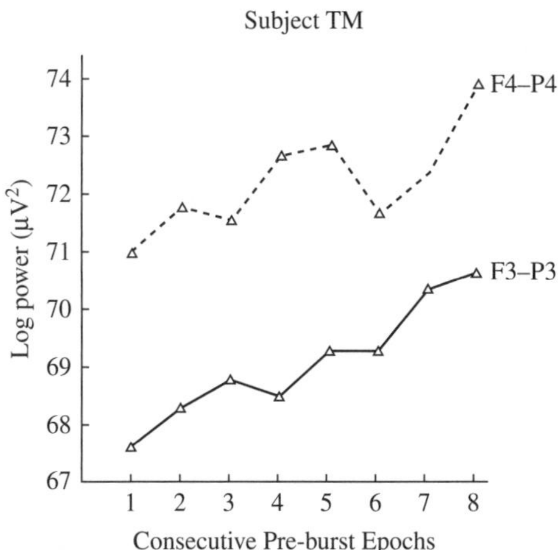

Mean total power at the best discriminating frequencies (3,5, 5.5, 12.5, and 24.2 cps) plotted against preburst values for 8 successive 2.56-sec epochs for subject T. M. Epoch 8 is closest to burst. (Grady, 1982)

The Continuous Presence of Absence Pathophysiology Between Spike-Wave Bursts (Power Spectrum Analysis)

FIGURE 6–8. Buildup of low frequency power in patient's EEG prior to burst of spike-wave activity. F4, P4, F3, P3 refer to scalp locations in "10–20" system (from Mirsky and Grady, 1988).

in subject K.G. prior to the eruption of a burst of 3-per-second spike wave activity.

This buildup is not evident from visual inspection of the EEG. Our assumption is that the tendency for patients with generalized seizures to make errors in attention tasks between seizures is a reflection of this subclinical, subcortically driven brain activity.

Duncan provided direct evidence of the impaired capacity for mobilizing attention in the interictal period in patients with absence epilepsy; these patients show reduced amplitudes of ERP components associated with the mobilizing of attentional resources, such as the P300 and slow wave component, as elicited by performance on the AX task of the CPT. Such reductions (Figure 6–9) appear more pronounced in the processing of auditory than visual task stimuli. Moreover, patients with focal, temporal lobe seizures do not show the type of reduction in P300 and slow wave amplitude seen in patients with idiopathic generalized seizures (Figure 6–9).

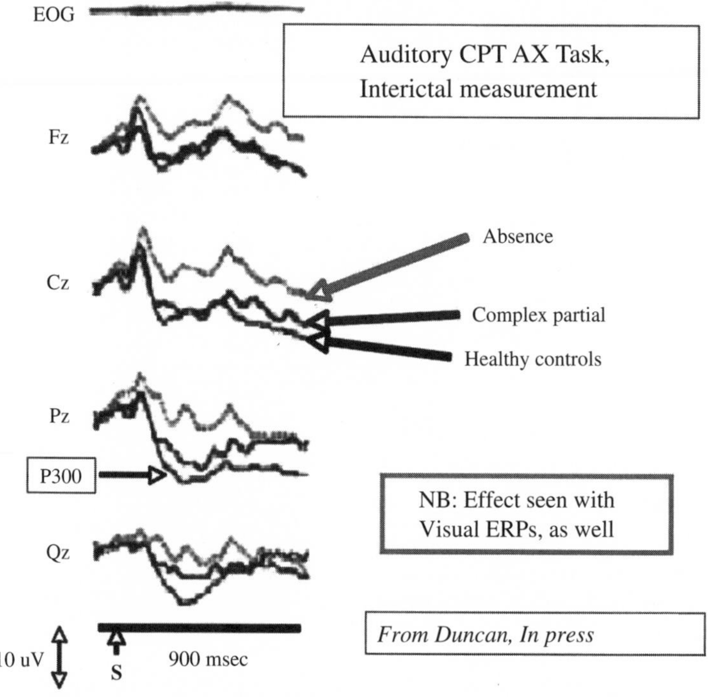

FIGURE 6–9. Reduced P300 component in absence patients, in comparison to seizure and healthy controls in interictal period. Fz, Cz, Pz, Oz refer to scalp locations in "10–20" system (from Duncan et al., in press).

Correlated Behavioral and Electrophysiologic Investigations of Attention: Schizophrenia and Closed-Head Injury

To review in depth all of the studies that have shown the profound alterations of basic attentive processes in schizophrenia and closed-head injury (CHI) would increase many-fold the length and depth of this chapter. In lieu of this, we refer to the publications of Duncan and colleagues that have shown the profound changes in information processing seen in patients with schizophrenia (Duncan, et al. 1987; Duncan 1988, 1990; Egan, et al. 1994) and CHI (Duncan, et al. 1995, 2003). To summarize, the P300 component of the ERP has shown significant reductions in both of these neuropsychiatric disorders; moreover, there is a greater impairment evident in auditory than in visual processing. Duncan has speculated that altered *visual* information processing may be a state variable in schizophrenia, as patients who respond well to medication will show considerable normalization of the P300/attention component of the ERP. In contrast, altered *auditory* information processing may qualify as a trait variable of the disorder, as reductions in P300 are less likely to normalize after medication. The greater alteration in aspects of the auditory than in the visual ERP in CHI may reflect the greater vulnerability of the auditory system to traumatic injury (Duncan, et al. 2005).

Summary and conclusions

We have provided a brief historical account of studies of the neuropsychology of attention that were stimulated by the sequelae of the war in Europe during the period 1939–1945. During the 50 years since that event, research on attention has grown from a consideration of brain-injured soldiers and fatigued radar operators to investigations of seizure disorders, schizophrenia spectrum disorders, ADHD, infections, pregnancy and birth complications, effects of maternal substance abuse, kidney disease, and a number of other conditions. The effects on attention of all of these may eventually be included under the rubric of injury to a mesencephalic–thalamic–frontal system with the responsibility of maintaining an attentive attitude in the organism. It is our hope that this review will do honor to Alexander Luria and Anne-Lise Christensen and remind others of the significant antecedents of the methods currently in use to assess disorders of the brain.

References

Aldrich, M.S. 1991. The Neurobiology of Narcolepsy. *Trends in Neurosciences* 14: 235–239.

Alvarez, V., Malaga, S., Navarro, M., Espinosa, L., Hidalgo, E., Badia, J., Alvarez, R., Coto, E. 2000. Analysis of chromosome 6p in Spanish families with recessive polycystic kidney disease. *Pediatric Nephrology* 14:205–207.

Baharudin, R., Luster, T. 1998. Factors related to the quality of the home environment and children's achievement. *J. Fam. Issues* 19: 375–403.

Bandstra, E.S., Morrow, C.E., Anthony, J.C., et al. 2001. Longitudinal investigation of task persistence and sustained attention in children with prenatal cocaine exposure. *Neurotoxicol. Teratol.* 23: 545–559.

Burns, D.J. and Bates, D. 1998. Neurology and the kidney. *Journal of Neurology, Neurosurgery and Psychiatry* 65:810–821.

Chamberlin, R., Chamberlin, G., Howlett, B., et al. 1975. *British births 1970*, Vol. 1, London: Heineman Medical Books.

Chamberlin, R., Chamberlin, G., Howlett, B., et al. 1975. *British births 1970*, Vol. 2, London: Heineman Medical Books.

Connor, P.D., Streissguth, A.P., Sampson, P.D., et al. 1999. Individual differences in auditory and visual attention. *Alcohol. Clin. Exp. Res.* 23: 1395–1402.

Cruz, M.E., Levav, M., Ramirez, I., et al. 1993. *Niveles de nutricion y rendimiento en pruebas neuropsicologicas en ninos escolares de una comunidad rural andina.* Academia Ecuatoriana de Neurosciencias. Quioto, Ecuador.

Duncan, C.C. 1988. Application of Event-Related Brain Potentials to the Analysis of Interictal Attention in Absence Epilepsy. In: M.S. Myslobodsky and A.F. Mirsky (eds.), *Elements of Petit Mal Epilepsy*. New York: Peter Lang, pp. 341–364.

Duncan, C.C., Kosmidis, M.H., Mirsky, A.F. 2005. Closed Head Injury-Related Information Processing Deficits: An Event Related Potential Analysis. *International Journal of Psychophysiology* 58:133–157.

Duncan, C.C. and Mirsky, A.F. 2004. The Attention Battery for Adults: A Systematic Approach to Assessment. In: G. Goldstein, and S.R. Beers (eds.). *Comprehensive Handbook of Psychological Assessment*, Vol. 1. Intellectual and Neuropsychological Assessment. New York: Wiley, pp. 263–276.

Erlenmeyer-Kimling, L. and Cornblatt, B.A. 1992. Summary of Attentional Findings in the New York High Risk Project. *Journal of Psychiatry* 26:405–426.

Ernst, M., Zametkin, A.J., Matochik, J.A., Pascualvaca, D., Jons, P.H., and Cohen, R.M. 1999. High Midbrain Accumulation in Children with Attention Deficit Hyperactivity Disorder. *American Journal of Psychiatry* 156:1209–1215.

Fedio, P. and Mirsky, A.F. 1969. Selective Intellectual Deficits in Children with Temporal Lobe or Centrencephalic Epilepsy. *Neuropsychologia* 7:287–300.

Gloor, P. 1988. Neurophysiological Mechanism of Generalized Spike and Wave Discharge and its Implication for Understanding the Absence of Seizures. In: M.S. Myslobodsky and A.F. Mirsky (eds.). *Elements of Petit Mal Epilepsy*. New York: Peter Lang, pp. 159–209.

Grady, C.L., 1982. *The Prediction of Spike-Wave Bursts in the Electroencephalogram by Power Spectrum and Coherence Analysis*. Unpublished Ph.D. dissertation, Boston University.

Greenberg, D.A., Cayanis, E., Strug, L., Marathe, S., Durner, M., Pal, D.K., Alvin, G.B. et al. 2005. Malic Enzyme 2 May Underlie Susceptibility to Adolescent-Onset Idiopathic Generalized Epilepsy. *American Journal of Human Genetics* 76:139–146.

Gruber, R., Sadeh, A., Raviv, A., 2000. Instability of sleep patterns in children with attention-deficit/hyperactivity disorder. *Journal of American Academy of Child and Adolescent Psychiatry* 39:495–501.

Guaywoodford, L.M., Muecher, G., Hopkins, S.D., Avner, E.D., Germino, G.G., Guillot, A.P., Herrin, J. et al. 1995. The Severe Perinatal Form of Autosomal Recessive Polycystic Kidney-Disease Maps to Chromosome 6p21.1-p12-implications for Genetic Counseling. *American Journal of Human Genetics* 56:1101–1107.

Kraepelin, E. 1919. Dementia Praecox and Paraphrenia (Trans. R.M. Barclay). *International Journal of Psychoanalysis.* New York: Robert E. Krieger.

Lansdell, H. and Mirsky, A.F. 1964. Attention in Focal and Cetrencephalic Epilepsy. *Experimental Neurology* 9:463–469.

Levav, M., Cruz, M.E., Mirsky, A.F. 1995. EEG abnormalities, malnutrition, parasitism and goiter – A study of school children in Ecuador. *Acta Paediatrica.* 84: 197–202.

Levav, M., Mirsky, A.F., SCHANTZ, PM., et al. 1995. Parasitic infection in malnourished school children – effects on behaviour and EEG. *Parasitology* 110: 103–111.

Luria, A.R. 1980. *Higher Cortical Function in Man* (2nd ed.). New York: Basic Books.

Mackworth, N.H. 1948. The Break Down of Vigilance during Prolonged Visual Search. *Quarterly Journal of Experimental Psychology* 1:6–121.

Marmor, M., Glickman, L., Shofer, F., et al. 1987. Toxocara-canis infection of children. *Amer. J. Pub. Hlth.* 77: 554–559.

Mirsky, A.F., Anthony, B.J., Duncan, C.C., Ahearn, M.B., and Kellam, S.G. 1991. Analysis of the Elements of Attention: A Neuropsychological Approach. *Neuropsychology Review* 2:109–145.

Mirsky, A.F. and Duncan, C.C. 2001. A Nosology of Disorders of Attention. In: J. Wasserstein, L.E. Wolff, and F.F. Lefever (eds.). *Adult Attention Deficit Disorder: Brain Mechanisms and Life Outcomes,* Vol. 931. New York: New York Academy of Sciences, pp. 17–32.

Mirsky, A.F., Fantie, B.D., Tatman, J.E. 1995. Assessment of attention across the lifespan. In: R. I. Mapou and J. Spector (eds.) *Clinical Neuropsychological Assessment: A Cognitive Approach.* Plenum: New York, pp.17–48.

Mirsky, A.F. 1995. Perils and pitfalls on the path to normal potential: The role of impaired attention. *J. Clin. Exp. Neuropsychol.* 17: 1–17.

Mirsky, A.F. and Grady, C.L. 1988. Toward the Development of Alternative Treatments in Absence Epilepsy. In: M.S. Myslobodsky and A.F. Mirsky (eds.). *Elements of Petit Mal Epilepsy.* New York: Peter Lang, pp. 285–310.

Mirsky, A.F., Kellam. S.G., Pascualvaca, D., et al. 2001. Bone lead level and sustained attention—a longitudinal study. *Clin. Neuropsychol.* 15: 265.

Mirsky, A.F., Orren, M.M., Stanton, L., Fullerton, B., Harris, S., and Meyers, R.E. 1979. Auditory Evoked Potentials and Auditory Behavior following Prenatal and Perinatal Asphyxia in Rhesus Monkeys. *Developmental Psychobiology* 12:369–379.

Mirsky, A.F., Primac, D.W., Ajmone Marsan, C., Rosvold, H.E., and Stevens, J.A. 1960. A Comparison of the Psychological Test Performance of Patients with Focal and Nonfocal Epilepsy. *Experimental Neurology* 2:75–89.

Mirsky, A.F. and van Buren, J.M. 1965. On the Nature of the "absence" in Centrencephalic Epilepsy: A Study of Some Behavioral, Electroencephalographic and Autonomic Factors. *Electroencephalography and Clinical Neurophysiology* 18:334–348.

Mirsky, A.F., Yardley, S.L., Jones B.P., Walsh, D., and Kendler, K.S. 1995. Analysis of the Attention Deficit in Schizophrenia: A Study of Patients and their Relatives in Ireland. *Journal of Psychiatric Research* 29:23–42.

Murawski, B.J. 1970. The Continuous Performance Test: A Measure of Sustained Attention in Human Uremics. In: R.B. Coletti and K.K. Krueger (eds.). *Proceedings of the Workshop on Bioassays in Uremia.* Washington, D.C.: U.S. Government Printing Office, pp. 72–73.

Myers, R. 1972. Two Patterns of Perinatal Brain Damage and their Conditions of Occurrence. *American Journal of Obstetrics and Gynecology* 112:246–276.

Needleman, H.L., Reiss, J.A., Tobin, M.J., 1995. Bone lead levels and delinquent behavior. *J. Amer. Med. Assn.* 275: 363–369.

Penfield, W. and Jasper, H. 1954. *Epilepsy and the Functional Anatomy of the Human Brain.* Boston: Little, Brown.

Regestein, Q., Pavlova, M., and Gleason R. 2001. Vigilance Testing in Patients Referred for Sleep Breathing Disorder. Unpublished manuscript.

Rosvold, H.E., Mirsky, A.F., Sarason, I., Bransome, E.D., Jr., and Beck, L.H. 1956. A Continuous Performance Test of Brain Damage. *Journal of Consulting Psychology* 20:343–350.

Schwab, R.S. 1939. Method of Measuring Consciousness in Attacks of Petit Mal Epilepsy. *Archives of Neurology Psychiatry* (*Chicago*) 41:215–217.

Seidman, L., Van Manen, K.J., Gamser, D.M., Faraone, S.V., Goldstein, J.M., and Tsuang, M.T. 1998. The Effects of Increasing Resource Demand on Vigilance Performance in Adults with Schizophrenia or Developmental Attentional/Learning Disorders: A Preliminary Study. *Schizophrenia Research* 34:101–112.

Shakow, D., 1962. Segmental set: a theory of the formal psychological deficit in schizophrenia. *Archives of General Psychiatry* 6:17–33.

Siegel, A., Mirsky, A.F., and Grady, C.L. 1979. A Predictor of Spike-Wave Bursts in Petit Mal EEG. *Electoencephalography of Clinical Neurophysiology* 46:8.

Siegel, A., Mirsky, A.F., and Grady, C.L. 1980. A Predictor of Spike-Wave Bursts in Petit Mal EEG II. *Electoencephalography of Clinical Neurophysiology* 49:24–25.

Stammeyer, E.C. 1961. *The Effects of Distraction Performance in Schizophrenic Psychoneurotic, and Normal Individuals.* Unpublished doctoral dissertation, Catholic University of America, Washington D.C.

Streissguth, A.P., Sampson, P.D., Carmichael Olson, H., et. al. 1994. Maternal drinking during pregnancy. *Alcohol. Clin. Exp. Res.* 18: 202–218.

Wohlberg, G.W. and Kornetsky, C. 1973. Sustained Attention in Remitted Schizophrenics. *Archives of General Psychiatry* 28:533–537.

Zubin, J. 1975. Problem with Attention in Schizophrenia. In: M.L. Kietzman, S. Sutton, and J. Zubln (eds.). *Experimental Approaches to Psychopathology.* New York: Academic Press, pp. 139–166.

7

The Neuropsychology of Epilepsy: An Application of Luria's Concepts

William B. Barr and Luba Nakhutina

The work of Alexander Romanovich Luria encompassed many topics, and his ideas have influenced many in the field of neuropsychology and beyond. However, it is impossible for one man's work to have had direct implications for every known neurologic condition. It is also unreasonable to assume that the work of such an important historical figure would have anticipated the directions the field of neuropsychology has taken since his passing. This brings us to the topic of epilepsy, which forms the subject matter of this chapter. In examining his written works, it is apparent that Luria was clearly familiar with epilepsy as a condition and its influence on behavior. Whereas he alluded to epilepsy in his writings, he never provided a comprehensive clinical approach to this condition or an outline of its relationship to his theories. The goal of this chapter is to demonstrate how some of the central concepts from Luria's theories are relevant to the neuropsychological study of epilepsy.

Epilepsy is a condition affecting approximately 1% of the general population and is characterized by recurring seizures. The majority of patients with epilepsy achieve adequate control of their seizures through medical management with antiepileptic drugs. However, approximately 20% to 30% of these patients do not respond to standard medical treatments and may be considered for epilepsy surgery (Lardizabal 2008). Up to 60% to 80% of those patients undergoing surgical treatment for partial epilepsy with a well-defined seizure focus are known to become seizure-free (Wiebe, et al. 2001). It is also known, however, that 25% to 40% of these individuals will also experience a postoperative decline in memory, language, or some other aspect of cognitive functioning (Barr 2008). Over the past 50 years, neuropsychologists have learned to use their knowledge of the brain and behavior to guide surgical teams in making a decision whether or not to perform a surgical resection of abnormal brain tissue on a given patient. Helping to understand, evaluate, and prevent these postoperative changes in language and cognitive functioning has become an important task for the field of neuropsychology.

Traditional approaches to neuropsychological assessment of epilepsy surgery candidates have been based primarily on two simple theoretical concepts, both of which were developed on the basis of some of the earliest cases to have undergone surgical treatment. The first concept is based on the observation that patients undergoing surgical intervention on the language-dominant (usually left) hemisphere of the brain developed specific difficulties with processing and retaining verbal material, whereas patients having surgery on the opposite side of the brain often demonstrated analogous problems with material presented in different modalities that was not easily verbalized. The second concept developed after observations that patients undergoing surgical resection of the temporal lobes and/or adjacent structures, including the hippocampus, amygdala, parahippocampal gyrus, and entorhinal cortex will experience an inordinate decline in memory relative to other cognitive functions. Accordingly, it is posited that those undergoing surgical resection of the frontal lobes develop specific difficulties with executive functions, including initiation, reasoning, and set-shifting, with inordinately less effect on memory.

What the field of neuropsychology developed in the West in the 20th century was a quadrant-based approach to the brain, based on the existence of two separate "double-dissociations" in functioning. A disorder of verbal memory was largely considered to be associated with left hemisphere dysfunction, whereas a disturbance in nonverbal recall was associated with an abnormality of the right hemisphere. Additionally, disorders of executive functions were related to an exclusive disturbance of the frontal lobes, whereas memory functions were localized to the temporal lobes and associated structures, including the hippocampus, fornix, and thalamus. The mnestic abilities of the temporal lobes were characterized as separate and distinct from the frontal lobe's executive functions.

In this chapter, we will demonstrate how neuropsychological approaches to the study of epilepsy developed in the West can be expanded and refined with the aid of some of central concepts from Luria's theories. We will begin by providing a historical context on the study of epilepsy in Russia before and during the time that Luria was developing his theories.

Epilepsy in Russia

The modern study of epilepsy in Russia began at the end of the 19th century with neurophysiologic investigations of epileptic excitation by Ivan Pavlov

(Kandel 1990). A contemporary of Pavlov, Vladimir Bechterev, the famous Russian neurologist, psychiatrist, and academician, described the various forms of epilepsy, detailing their pathogenesis and clinical presentation.

Whereas many consider surgery for epilepsy to have originated in the West with Victor Horsley in England and Wilder Penfield in North America, it is known that surgical treatment for this condition in Russia dates back to the 1890s (Kandel 1990). The first neurosurgical department was organized by Bekhterev in St. Petersburg, where his disciple, Ludwig Puusepp, began to operate on patients, including those with epilepsy (Kandel 1990; Lichtermann 1993). In 1908, Bekhterev and Puusepp published *Surgery in Mental Diseases*, presenting much of the original data on the surgery of epilepsy (Bekhterev and Puusepp, 1908). The first stage of development of surgical treatment for epilepsy focused on patients with lesional epilepsy and traumatic epilepsy, resulting from open skull injuries and penetrating bullet wounds (Ugriumov and Shefer 1967; Zemskaya and Ryabukha 1976).

The number of patients with brain injuries rose precipitously during World War I and the Russian Civil War (Ugriumov and Shefer 1967). Surgical interventions during this period included resections of cortical lesions, cysts, and epileptogenic zones of the cortex, as well as sectioning of subcortical pyramidal tracts (Polenov and Babchin 1954; Zemskaya and Ryabukha 1976). The latter procedure was first proposed in 1928 by Andrei Polenov, the prominent physician and scientist (Kandel 1990). In the 1930s, attention was also devoted to the study of one particular variant of epilepsy, epilepsia partialis continua, initially described by the Russian neurologist Kojevnikov. This form of epilepsy, also known as Kojevnikov syndrome, was discovered to result from tick-borne encephalitis and was initially treated by surgical resections in the area of epileptogenic focus. Although this treatment was relatively effective, it often resulted in paralysis, speech problems, and other deficits (Ugriumov and Shefer 1967).

In the first decades of Soviet rule, neurosurgical departments were organized within the various institutes of traumatology where traumatic epilepsy patients were treated (Ugriumov and Shefer 1967). The Central Neurosurgery Institute was founded in 1934 by Nikolai Burdenko, surgeon-in-chief of the Red Army, the same year that the Montreal Neurological Institute was established by Wilder Graves Penfield. Lichterman (2004) reviewed archival sources and witness accounts and raised a question whether the establishment of these institutes in the same year was a mere coincidence. He wrote that during the Cold War era, Penfield was one of very few channels of communication between the neuroscience communities of the USSR and the West (Lichterman 2004). In 1943, Penfield visited Soviet Russia for the first time within the British–American–Canadian surgical mission. He spent time in Moscow and its vicinity and became a personal acquaintance of Burdenko (Lichterman 2004). Penfield visited again in 1955, giving lectures in Moscow and Leningrad, and a few years later, he was elected a foreign member of the Academy of Sciences of the USSR. His major texts, including *Epilepsy and the Functional Anatomy of the Human Brain*, were translated into Russian in 1958.

Also, in the 1950s, two Soviet neurosurgeons, Aleksandra Zemskaya and Yuri Savchenko, traveled to Canada and spent several months at the Montreal Neurological Institute. When they returned to the USSR, they introduced Penfield's approaches to epilepsy surgery to their home institutions in Leningrad and Omsk and became leading figures in this field. Penfield also corresponded with Boris Egorov, director of the Burdenko Neurosurgery, as the Central Neurosurgery Institute was renamed after the death of Burdenko in 1946 (Lichterman 1998, 2004). Because of the centralized structure of the Soviet health care system, Burdenko Institute began to specialize in the most complex cases, which were referred to the institute from all over the USSR (Lichterman 1998).

During World War II and in the postwar years, more cases of traumatic epilepsy emerged as combatants developed seizures from penetrating missile injuries. This led to a wider spread of the application of surgical treatment across the various hospitals in the USSR and to extension of these techniques to other forms of epilepsy (Ugriumov and Shefer 1967). Typical procedures included resection of cortical lesions, meningio-encephalolysis, and correction of skull bone defects, conducted in stages. Proposed surgical interventions for the treatment of epilepsy included decompressive trephination of the skull, fastening of vertebral artery, cervical sympathectomy, desympathization of cervical blood vessels, ovariectomy, removal of adrenal glands, and thyroidectomy. All these were subsequently deemed ineffective and abandoned. The resection of epileptogenic focus, introduction of alcohol into the epileptogenic zone, coagulation of blood vessels in this zone, sectioning of the subcortical pyramidal tracts, and meningio-encephalolysis proved more effective, with positive effect reported in 73% of patients at 15-year follow-up (Arendt and Leibson, 1965 as quoted by Ugriumov and Shefer 1967). In addition, improved therapeutic effect was seen with a procedure involving suctioning of cortical tissue, sometimes with the white matter, in the epileptogenic zone.

In addition, prefrontal leukotomy was introduced as a treatment for some epilepsy patients in the late 1940s, although this technique was most frequently used with chronic and incurable schizophrenic patients, as it was in the United States, to reduce psychomotor agitation and affective disturbance. However, in 1950, the therapeutic effects of prefrontal leukotomy were said to be unproved, and this technique was prohibited by a special order of the Soviet Union's Ministry of Health. The prohibition against this technique lasted for 30 years and is considered to have had a negative impact on the development of psychosurgery in Russia (Lichterman 1993).

Increased efficacy in treatment of epilepsy was achieved with further development of electrophysiologic techniques that took place in the 1950s. In addition to these methods, comprehensive investigations including neuropsychological and neuroophthalmological exams, pneumoencephalography, and angiography used at this time further extended indications for surgery to other forms of epilepsy (i.e., nontraumatic, however, typically cortical and focal) (Zemskaya and Ryabukha 1976). Repeated electrophysiologic investigations with the use of functional tasks (e.g., photostimulation, hyperventilation), as well as intraoperative electrocorticography and electrostimulation allowed more precise localization of the epileptogenic zone (Ugriumov and Shefer 1967; Zemskaya and Ryabukha 1976).

Long-term monitoring of subcortical structures with subsequent electrolysis was also used (Zemskaya and Ryabukha 1976). For temporal lobe epilepsy patients, resection of anterior temporal lobe, and resection of hippocampus and amygdala, while sparing temporal cortex were conducted (Ugriumov and Shefer 1967). In the absence of focal findings, surgical intervention involved the destruction of commissural and projection fibers along which seizures were thought to generalize (Zemskaya and Ryabukha 1976). Finally, advances were made also in the treatment of Kojevnikov epilepsy. In the 1960s, stereotactic destruction of the ventrolateral nucleus of the thalamus in Kojevnikov epilepsy patients was reported to be effective, whereby the hyperkinesias disappeared in half of the cases and diminished in the rest (Kandel 1990).

In terms of pharmacologic treatment, in addition to anticonvulsant agents, medications included antibiotics, vitamins, and sedatives (Remezova 1964). For epilepsy patients with psychological disturbances, nonpharmacologic treatments were often recommended, which included psychotherapy and hypnosis (Boldirev 1986). Psychotherapy programs were developed based on personality and cognitive characteristics, as assessed by tests, including the Wechsler measures, Minnesota Multiphasic Personality Inventory (MMPI), Eysenck's questionnaire, and learning and memory tasks (Gromov and Yakunina 1978). Others described treatment of epilepsy patients that strived toward the "elimination of unfavorable psychogenic influences and creation of the most satisfactory social environment" (Remezova 1964).

Neuropsychological approaches to epilepsy

The goal of this chapter is to discuss how Luria's theoretical concepts can enhance our understanding of the neuropsychological basis of epilepsy. As stated, Luria never provided a comprehensive account of his approach to epilepsy, although through his work at the Burdenko Institute in Moscow, he clearly must have been exposed to much of the work that is listed above. As is well known, Luria developed complex theories of memory and executive functions through observations developed on a number of other patient populations.

In his writing about the neuropsychology of memory in particular, Luria acknowledged the important contributions of many scientists in the West who studied epilepsy, including Scoville and Milner, Talland, Warrington and

Weiskrantz, and Penfield. However, in his view, their findings left many important questions unsolved. Namely, the contribution to the memory process of different parts of the brain extending beyond the temporal lobes, physiologic mechanisms underlying the loss of memory, and the types of memory deficits observed in patients with other types of brain lesions. For Luria, answers to these questions could be obtained only after a careful "psychological qualification" of the memory disturbances observed in patients with local brain lesions (Luria 1973b).

Before beginning our discussion of popular Western approaches to the neuropsychology of epilepsy, it is important to provide a brief introduction and review of Luria's concept of a functional system. Luria regarded all higher cortical processes as *complex functional systems* organized by "a dynamic constellation of collectively working parts of the brain," where every area of the brain contributes in a *specific* and unique way to the operation of the functional system (Luria 1966). According to this approach, a brain lesion can disrupt the functional system at any point; however, the nature of the disturbance will differ qualitatively, depending on the particular location of the lesion. Luria quoted Pavlov in explaining that older notions, both localizationism and antilocalizationism, attempted to "superimpose the nonspatial concepts of contemporary psychology on the spatial construction of the brain" (Luria 1978). He stressed that instead of "localizing" a complex function in a limited part of the brain, attempts should be made to "discover how a functional system is distributed in different brain regions, and the role that every part of the brain plays in the realization of the whole functional system" (Luria 1973a). We now provide the contrasting Western approaches to localization, as they are relevant to epilepsy.

Material-specific memory disorders

Early studies of surgical samples in the West found that unilateral removal of the medial temporal region, including the hippocampus, failed to produce the severe amnesic disturbance seen after bilateral lesions. Findings from research pioneering the use of sensitive neuropsychological tests, however, did show that more mild and specific disturbances of memory resulted from unilateral lesions (Milner 1967). Selective removal of the left medial temporal region resulted in a specific disturbance of verbal memory, regardless of whether the information was presented in an auditory or visual modality. Right medial temporal lobe damage, in turn, was found to be associated with a preservation of verbal memory, while the ability to process and remember nonverbal material, including tones, melodies, and nonsense designs, was impaired (Milner 1971). This observation of an apparent double dissociation between verbal and nonverbal memory and the functions of the left and right medial temporal lobe formed the basis of what was termed as a material-specific model of lateralized memory function.

Although the earliest observations of this phenomenon were based on temporal lobectomy samples, observations of less severe but functionally similar disturbances were observed in nonsurgical samples consisting of patients with partial epilepsy involving unilateral medial temporal regions (Milner 1975). Since the publication of the initial findings, there has been strong and consistent support for the existence of a relationship between verbal memory and the left temporal lobe region. A number of studies have found that patients with left temporal lobe impairment exhibit disturbances in recall of verbal material, whether presented in narrative passages, supraspan lists, or word pairs, both before and after surgery (Delaney, et al. 1980; Hermann, et al. 1987; Loring, et al. 1991). Identification of this verbally based memory disturbance is now considered one of the primary aims in the neuropsychological evaluation of presurgical candidates (Jones-Gotman 1991).

Most of the available evidence indicates that surgical resection of the right medial temporal region produces impairment in memory for material that is not easily verbalized, labeled, or coded into words (Smith, 1989). The findings are observed most frequently with use of visual material, though similar findings have been observed on tasks using auditory and tactile stimuli (Corkin 1965; Zatorre 1985). There are some indications that the right medial temporal lobe may be particularly important for spatial learning and memory (Kessels, et al. 2001). There are also consistent findings suggesting that this region may be particularly important to processing and retaining information regarding human faces (Milner 1968; Barr 1997; Kanwisher and Yovel 2006).

Although it is clear that a number of different tasks might be sensitive to dysfunction in the right medial temporal region, there remains no larger theoretical basis by which to classify these tasks. Support for the relationship between nonverbal memory and the right medial temporal region has been far less consistent than have the findings associated with left hemisphere dysfunction. It is clear that the concept of a nonverbal memory system, in its most simplified terms, does not account for the range of empirical findings. A number of studies have failed to replicate earlier results using measures of visual and spatial memory (Barr, et al. 1997). Many psychometric studies using groups of tests fail to distinguish a visual memory factor (Larrabee, et al. 1985; Roid, et al. 1988; Smith, et al. 1992).

It has been suggested that nonverbal memory is a circular concept that defies any specific definition. A theoretical approach to classifying this "other" type of memory would provide a significant contribution to the field. There is a possibility that the critical difference between left and right temporal lobe memory functions may reside more in stages of processing than in the type of material that is used (Pillon, et al. 1999). The observed differences between verbal and nonverbal material may also be a secondary effect of more basic differences in hemispheric functioning. There has been little emphasis on developing experimental memory tasks to study alternative conceptions of hemispheric functioning, including analytic/holistic (Levy-Agresti and Sperry 1968), sequential/simultaneous (Gates and Bradshaw 1977), or categorical/coordinate (Kosslyn 1994) modes of processing. Little attention has focused on demonstrations of the right hemisphere's role in processing novel information (Goldberg and Costa 1981). Newly developed clinical tests of memory remain firmly entrenched in the use of the verbal/nonverbal dichotomy without signs of incorporating any new theoretical developments (Wechsler 2009).

An alternative approach to cerebral laterality is provided in Luria's work. When considering the functional role of the two hemispheres, Luria held the view that higher psychological processes are not "localized" in any one hemisphere but take place with the participation of both hemispheres, each of which makes its own "specific contribution" to the performance of a psychological function (Luria 1966). He stressed that this view is contrary to the opinion held by most of his contemporaries who in their research attempted to relate each complex psychological process to a particular brain *location*.

Luria argued that while it is known that the dominant (left) hemisphere is responsible for the learning and use of the codes of language, and the nondominant (right) hemisphere does not have this role, "it by no means follows that all components of speech are 'localized' in the dominant hemisphere, and all the components of visual sensory experience are 'localized' in the nondominant hemisphere." Based on theories of development of higher psychological processes described by Vygotski, Luria contended that such processes are constructed as a synthesis of impressions or traces of experience and their organization with the use of language. Given this inseparability between the verbal–logical activity and its basis (i.e., visual impressions), all complex psychological processes "depend on functional interaction between the two hemispheres" (Luria 1966).

Using this principle, Luria investigated the specific role of each hemisphere in enabling the performance of various complex psychological processes, including speech, writing, reading, and mnestic abilities. Particular attention was paid to memory functioning, where Luria distinguished two main types of memorizing and suggested that each hemisphere made a unique contribution at a different level of this process. The dominant hemisphere was viewed as responsible for *voluntary* memorizing, a form of conscious activity where the material to be memorized was organized through the use of logical and often linguistic codes, whereas the role of the nondominant hemisphere was in the *involuntary* or unpremeditated "background" process of imprinting and storing of traces. His investigations of patients with unilateral lesions supported this dissociation and demonstrated that both hemispheres have a role in the memorization of verbal information at different levels of this process (Luria and Simernitskaya 1977).

Luria and Simernitskaya (1977) examined memory deficits resulting from unilateral lesions using a list of words that the patients were instructed to memorize (i.e., voluntary memory) and another series of words where they were asked to perform a letter-counting task. In the latter condition, any retained information was considered a "by-product" of the counting activity (i.e., involuntary memory). Their results supported dissociation between impairment of voluntary memory, associated with lesions of the dominant hemisphere, and involuntary memory, associated with lesions of the nondominant hemisphere, demonstrating that "both hemispheres are active in the memorization of verbal material, being perhaps responsible for different levels of this psychological process" (Luria and Simernitskaya 1977).

Based on Luria's conceptualization of the interhemispheric interaction in enabling complex psychological processes, such as mnestic abilities, the finding of impairment on the Rey–Osterrieth Complex Figure Test frequently observed in patients with right hemisphere dysfunction may be thought of as reflective of the disruption at the level of involuntary trace retention, given that the nature of the task is that of incidental learning. This conceptualization is unlike the one based on the hypothesis posited by Penfield and Milner, whereby poor performance on this task would be attributed to "material-specific" impairment or a *nonverbal* memory deficit. It should be noted, however, that Luria did not view the hypothesis about "material-specific" memory processes—that is, lesions in the left temporal region resulting in *verbal memory* deficits, whereas lesions in the right temporal region resulting in *nonverbal memory* deficits (e.g., Milner 1968)—as contrary to the idea of "modality-specific" organization of memory functions that he laid out. He suggested that these two hypotheses may be dealing with memory processes occurring at different stages. Namely, if memory process is viewed as taking place in stages, one can suppose that the connection between memory and linguistic functions is established at a certain level in the process and that at a lower level in the hierarchy of information processing, a memory function may be defined with one sensory system (Luria 1975).

Distinctions between frontal and temporal lobe functions

Neuropsychological studies of epilepsy played a major role in Western distinctions between the functions of the frontal and temporal lobes. The popular conception is that the frontal lobes are intrinsically involved in executive functions, whereas the temporal lobes are particularly important for memory.

Central to this view is the notion that the hippocampus is the brain structure most involved in the processes of learning and memory. The presumed role of this structure has undergone a number of transformations over the past 100 years. Owing to its anatomic placement, it was once thought to have its functions limited to olfaction. It was later recognized to play a role in mediating complex emotional states (Papez 1937; MacLean 1952). Interest in a hippocampal model of memory did not develop until the 1950s, when the detailed observations of profound memory disturbance resulting from surgical removal of both medial temporal lobe regions were made. Studies on patient H.M. demonstrating the existence of a severe and persistent amnesia, unaccompanied by obvious deficits in other higher-intellectual functions, provided the primary source for a new interest in developing neuroanatomic models of memory (Scoville and Milner 1957). Although surgery on this patient included resection of the hippocampus and several other medial temporal lobe structures, including the amygdala and parahippocampal gyrus, it was assumed as a result of subsequent work that removal of the hippocampus provided the lesion that was critical for producing the memory disturbance (Penfield and Milner 1958).

Initial descriptions of amnesic disturbance resulting from surgery to bilateral medial temporal lobe regions were supported by findings of more specific and less severe memory disturbance resulting from unilateral temporal lobe resection (Milner 1958). More support for the role of the hippocampus originated from findings that the degree of memory disturbance observed in these cases was related to the extent of the hippocampal resection (Milner 1967). Findings from additional studies indicated that the memory disturbance observed after temporal lobe resection contrasted with the range of cognitive deficits observed after surgical removal of other cortical regions. These studies included the well-known work contrasting the effects of frontal and temporal lobe resection in performance on measures such as the Wisconsin Card Sorting Test (Grant and Berg 1948). The report of a double dissociation between card sorting and memory performance in frontal lobe subjects and controls undergoing hippocampectomy formed the basis of popular conceptions regarding the functional capacity of these two brain regions and the independence of neural systems underlying memory and those abilities typically subsumed under the label of executive functions (Milner 1964).

The proposed links of the hippocampus with memory functions were met with some early resistance. Many questioned this functional relationship as a result of numerous studies failing to find a relationship between hippocampal lesions and memory defects in nonhuman animals (Isaacson 1972). Some investigators argued against the specificity of the lesions producing the findings in human subjects, indicating that the crucial lesion may be the result of destruction to other areas in the medial temporal lobe (Horel 1978; Mishkin 1978). Others developed theories that the hippocampus may be responsible for a host of functions extending beyond learning and memory. Some proposed that the hippocampus may, in fact, play a more general role in monitoring or and inhibiting behavioral responses (Douglas 1967; Gray 1982). In other views, it was portrayed as providing a link between perception and action (Pribram and McGuiness 1975). In these more extended views, a lesion to the hippocampus would be predicted as resulting in defective performance on memory tests, in addition to more wide-ranging disturbances on tasks requiring shifting or alternating response sets, which are tasks that are commonly classified as functions of the frontal lobes.

Over the past 30 years, there have been numerous studies failing to demonstrate dissociation of memory and executive functions associated with the frontal lobe (Barr and Goldberg 2003). Many consider this region to be critically involved in performance on working memory tasks (Goldman-Rakic 1987; Fuster 1996). It is also well known that patients with frontal lobe dysfunction may experience difficulties in performance on tests of episodic memory, particularly when organization and sequencing of the material is required (Wheeler, et al. 1995; McDonald, et al. 2001).

Deficits on tests of executive functions have been demonstrated in epilepsy patients with hippocampal dysfunction, both before and after surgery. A number of studies have shown that these patients are prone to exhibit perseverative responding on the Wisconsin Card Sorting Test, which is similar in nature to the pattern of performance observed in frontal lobe patients (Hermann, et al. 1988; Trenerry and Jack 1994; Martin, et al. 2000; Horner, et al. 1996). Some have posited that the findings in hippocampal patients are the result of remote effects on the frontal lobes (Hermann and Seidenberg 1995; Corkin 2001) or the effects of an underlying memory disturbance (Giovagnoli 2001). Others have suggested that the findings are a direct result of the cognitive effects of hippocampal dysfunction (Upton and Corcoran 1995). Relations between the hippocampus and frontal lobe functions have also been found in other patient groups. It has been demonstrated that Magnetic Resonance Imaging (MRI) volumes of the hippocampus in schizophrenic patients are more related to scores on measures of executive functions than they are to scores from tests of memory (Bilder, et al. 1995).

In most modern theoretical accounts, the hippocampus is recognized as part of a larger medial temporal lobe system of related structures extending to adjacent anatomic regions, which include the entorhinal, perirhinal, and parahippocampal cortices (Squire and Zola-Morgan 1991). The system is considered to be crucially involved in encoding and retrieving information from declarative memory. In most current accounts, the hippocampus is viewed in terms of mediating large-scale associative networks involving other brain regions. Squire (1992) considers it as responsible for binding together distributed sites in the neocortex. Others consider it important for facilitating relational or integrative functions involved in both encoding and retrieving episodic information (Eichenbaum and Bunsey 1995; Gluck and Myers 1995). Most continue to view the hippocampus and frontal lobes as separate, in spite of attempts by many well-respected theorists to account for these structures together in terms of an integrated functional system (Nauta 1964; Pribram 1986). There appears to be little interest in developing theories viewing the role of the hippocampus as extending to executive functions, in addition to episodic memory.

Many in the West acknowledge that Luria played a major role in advancing neuropsychology's appreciation of the role that executive functions play in complex behavior. Based on Luria's clinical investigations and on ideas expressed previously by Bekhterev, Pavlov, and others who made detailed observations of the frontal lobe functions, he concluded that frontal lobes play an important role in "organization and control of complex forms of programmed conscious behavior" (Luria 1973b). With a foundation based on ideas formulated by Vygotsky, he described behavioral programs being formed with the intimate participation of external or internal speech, and subsequent actions being subordinated to these programs. The behavior gains its selective character as the system of connections evoked by the program becomes dominant, and irrelevant connections are inhibited (Luria 1966).

Contrary to early work in the West, Luria did not limit his concepts regarding the frontal lobes to those involved in executive functions. He provided clear descriptions on the distinct character with which memory deficits of frontal lobe patients manifest. Analyses of difficulties experienced by these patients when performing memory tasks, such as a word list learning test, revealed a profound disturbance in the structure of mnestic activity, whereby it ceases to be an active and goal-directed process. Unlike normal subjects who make a comparison of their recall and the actual series and pay attention to the missed items, steadily increasing their recall, patients with a frontal syndrome memorize a few items and repeat the same items on subsequent trials without making such a comparison and without correcting their errors. They do not demonstrate an active attempt to increase the number of memorized items, and their plateau-like learning curve reflects the inactive character of the memorizing process (Luria 1966).

Luria was able to further specify the character of the mnestic disturbance in frontal lobe patients when he examined the level of *aspiration* made by these patients on memory tasks (Luria 1966). He noted that the patients did not formulate a reasonable level of aspiration for memorization on subsequent learning trials taking into account the results of their previous attempts. Other pathologic features emerged when a second series of words was introduced. The patients were found to demonstrate notable difficulty recalling the new series, as the traces of the previously presented information were "pathologically inert," interfering with new information and manifesting in perseveration. Also evident in these patients was the influence of irrelevant associations, leading to "contamination" of information recalled and confabulation. Luria believed that these patterns of performances resulted from loss in "selectivity of mental traces" and a breakdown in "closed logical systems," which are then replaced by "systems open to every influence—the influence of immediate impressions, inert stereotypes, and outside associations" (Luria 1973b). This disturbance in selectivity of mnestic processes was also evident in patients' inability to use logical connections as aids to memorizing, as these auxiliary connections did not prove helpful in restoring the required information and instead acted as a source of irrelevant associations.

Investigations of higher cortical functioning in frontal lobe patients led Luria to differentiate between the lateral frontal syndrome, where the memory functions remain relatively intact, and the mediobasal frontal syndrome, which leads to a dysregulation of nonspecific activation processes through close connections with the limbic system, thalamic nuclei, and reticular formation, and where patients' symptoms tend to include affective and memory disturbances. He observed that the memory deficits described above were particularly pronounced in patients with lesions in the medial zones of the frontal brain region or with lesions extending to fronto-temporal and fronto-diencephalic regions. Also noted in patients with mediobasal frontal syndrome was impulsive and fragmentary responding when recalling information or performing other cognitive tasks (Luria 1966).

Similarly, Luria's analyses of neuropsychological deficits exhibited by patients with temporal lobe lesions shed light on differentiated roles in memory processes played by convexial and mesial temporal brain regions. Luria described acoustic-mnestic disturbances that arise in patients with lesions of the extraauditory divisions of the left temporal region. Patients were observed to have difficulty recalling acoustically presented information, such as a paragraph-long story. Although they were often able to grasp the general meaning of the story, demonstrating preservation of the "program," they omitted details, replaced words, and were often unable to recall the first story after the second has been read to them. In contrast, intact performance was observed when the same material was presented visually or if visual stimuli, such as geometric figures, were introduced. Luria suggested that the mechanisms that lie at the basis of these disturbances include a weakening of the audioverbal traces and susceptibility of the weakened traces to interference (Luria 1966).

Whereas lesions in posterior parts of convexial brain regions result in *modality-specific* memory disturbances (e.g., acoustic, verbal, spatial), lesions in deep regions of the brain, including thalamic nuclei, hypothalamus, and hippocampus, lead to *modality-nonspecific* deficits, or general deficits that are observed uniformly in different modalities. Luria noted that the hippocampus, other limbic structures, and the closely connected regions of the frontal lobe "appear to work as a single system." In discussing the specific nature of the disturbances caused by lesions in medial zones of temporal lobe, Luria concluded that these regions belong to a system that "regulates the state of activity of the animal and its emotions" and that they play "an important role in processes responsible for the preservation and activation of traces of impressions from the outside world." He found that the observations of temporal epilepsy patients reported by Penfield and his colleagues, whereby stimulation of the medial temporal zones in these patients gave rise to general affective changes and special states of consciousness, and not so much to audioverbal disorders, confirmed these conclusions (Luria 1966).

Luria suggested that memory deficits in patients with lesions of the medial temporal zones and adjacent formations appeared to reflect insufficiently firmly established traces, which disappeared after a short period of time (Luria 1971).

He referred to the classic studies by Milner and her collaborators for descriptions of memory disorder in patients with mesial temporal lesions (Milner, et al. 1968). His own work allowed him to further qualify the nature of these memory disturbances. For example, he noted that although such patients could correctly repeat a series of words presented to them and do so without inaccuracies often observed in patients with lesions in the lateral temporal zones, if asked to recall the same series of words after a brief time delay, they were unable to do so and often did not remember having taken part in a test. In patients with a mild general (or modality-unspecific) memory disorder, retrieval of well-organized information (e.g., story) was intact, whereas severe general memory disorder disrupted memory functioning at all levels of semantic organization.

When mesial temporal lesions were confined to hippocampus, memory deficits were not associated with deterioration of consciousness or confabulation. However, when lesions were massive and involved thalamic, hypothalamic, or mesial regions of frontal lobes, disorientation, confusion, and confabulation was sometimes observed, as the process of "active remembering" was disrupted and "selectivity of mental traces" lost.

Deficits in select aspects of executive functioning were also observed in patients with lesions of the lateral zones of the left temporal region. Whereas many of the fundamental operations of abstract intellectual activity (e.g., spatial analogies) are largely preserved, deficits may be observed in performance of logical problems that are mediated by speech. Luria suggested that underlying such deficits is the disturbance in audioverbal processes and the associated mental activity, which lead to a patient's inability to retain traces of word associations and sequence. He described examples of patients who demonstrated considerable difficulty when required to sort pictures telling a story when he or she was not allowed to touch the pictures. Similar disruptions were sometimes observed when patients were asked to solve logical problems that are wholly dependent on speech or perform a series of successive mental arithmetic calculations with some of the results to be kept in mind (Luria 1966).

Conclusions

The goal of this chapter was to demonstrate how an application of Luria's theories would enhance our understanding of the neuropsychological basis of epilepsy. The conclusion is that a neuropsychological approach to epilepsy, based on Luria's concept of functional systems, extends our knowledge of cognitive deficits in epilepsy well beyond the constraints introduced by continued use of a quadrant-based approach to the brain. Luria's concepts are particularly relevant at this time as neuropsychology evolves further from an emphasis on lesion-based studies to a more network or systems-based approach to brain functioning, as necessitated by the requirements of modern-day neuroimaging.

It may be surprising to some that the surgical treatment of epilepsy developed in Russia at the same time it developed in the West. One can state with confidence that epilepsy was a topic of active investigation in Russia during the 20th century and continued strongly during the era of Soviet rule. Although Luria is not known to have provided any extended writings on epilepsy, he and his colleagues were very familiar with others' work on this disorder, especially that conducted by Penfield and his colleagues from Canada, but he made it clear in his writings that there were limitations to these authors' conclusions regarding higher cortical functions.

Luria's approach to functional systems allowed him to view brain–behavior relations on a continuum, within an integrated system. As a result, he did not portray one type of memory or another as "localized" to a specific hemisphere or lobe, but rather provided a view that each hemisphere is involved in a particular stage of functioning for each psychological task. The result is that hemispheric differences in memory processing become more an issue of processing styles, rather than focusing on what type of material is remembered. The frontal lobes are appreciated for how they contribute to performance on all psychological tasks as opposed to being limited to those labeled by investigators as assessing executive functions. It is our hope that Luria's ideas will continue to live on with each new application and to have a lasting influence on the neuropsychology of epilepsy.

References

Barr, W.B. 1997. Examining the Right Temporal Lobe's Role in Nonverbal Memory. *Brain and Cognition* 35(1):26–41.

Barr, W.B. 2008. Neuropsychological Outcome. In: H.O. Luders (ed.). *Textbook of Epilepsy Surgery*. London: Informa UK, Ltd.

Barr, W.B. and Goldberg, E. 2003. Pitfalls in the Method of Double Dissociation: Delineating the Cognitive Functions of the Hippocampus. *Cortex* 39:153–157.

Barr, W.B., Chelune, G.J., Hermann, B.P., Loring, D.W., Perrine, K., Strauss, E., Trenerry, M.R., et al. 1997. The Use of Figural Reproduction Tests as Measures of Nonverbal Memory in Epilepsy Surgery Candidates. *Journal of the International Neuropsychological Society* 3(5):435–443.

Bekhterev, V.M. and Puusepp, L.M. 1908. *Obozrenie Psychiatrii, Neurogii i Experimentalnoy Psychologii* [Surgery in Mental Diseases] 208–227 [in Russian].

Bilder, R.M., Bogerts, B., Ashtari, M., Wu, H., Alvir, J.M., Jody, D., Reiter, G., et al. 1995. Anterior Hippocampal Volume Reductions Predict Frontal Lobe Dysfunction in First Episode Schizophrenia. *Schizophrenia Research* 17(1):47–58.

Boldyrev, A.I. 1986. Onekotorich storonach lecheniya bolnich epilepsiyei. [Various Aspects of the Treatment of Epilepsy Patients.] *Zhurnal Nevropatologii i Psychiatrii Imeni S.S. Korsakova* 86(6):867–871 [in Russian].

Corkin, S. 1965. Tactually-Guided Maze-Learning in Man: Effects of Unilateral Cortical Excisions and Bilateral Hippocampal Lesions. *Neuropsychologia* 3:339–351.

Corkin, S. 2001. Beware of Frontal Lobe Deficits in Hippocampal Clothing. *Trends in Cognitive Sciences* 5:321–323.

Delaney R.C., Rosen A.J., Mattson, R.H., and Novelly, R.A. 1980. Memory Function in Focal Epilepsy: A Comparison of Non-surgical, Unilateral Temporal Lobe and Frontal Lobe Samples. *Cortex* 16:103–117.

Douglas, R.J. 1967. The Hippocampus and Behavior. *Psychological Bulletin* 67:416–442.

Eichenbaum, H. and Bunsey, M. 1995. On the Binding of Associations in Memory: Clues from Studies on the Role of the Hippocampal Region in Paired-Associate Learning. *Current Directions in Psychological Science* 4:19–23.

Fuster, J.M. 1996. *The Prefrontal Cortex: Anatomy, Physiology, and Neuropsychology of the Frontal Lobe*. New York: Raven Press.

Gates A. and Bradshaw, J.L. 1977. The Role of the Cerebral Hemispheres in Music. *Brain and Language* 4:403–431.

Giovagnoli, A.R. 2001. Relation of Sorting Impairment to Hippocampal Damage in Temporal Lobe Epilepsy. *Neuropsychologia* 39:140–150.

Gluck, M.A. and Myers, C.E. 1995. Representation and Association in Memory: A Neurocomputational View of Hippocampal Function. *Current Directions of Psychological Science* 4:23–29.

Goldberg E. and Costa L. 1981. Hemisphere Differences in the Acquisition and Use of Descriptive Systems. *Brain and Language* 14:144–173.

Goldman-Rakic, P.S. 1987. Circuitry of the Primate Prefrontal Cortex and Regulation of Behavior by Representational Memory. In: F. Plum and V. Mountcastle (eds.). *Handbook of Physiology, Volume 5, The Nervous System*. Bethesda, Md.: American Physiological Society.

Grant, D.A. and Berg, E.A. 1948. A Behavioral Analysis of Degree of Impairment and Ease of Shifting to New Responses in a Weigel-type Card Sorting Problem. *Journal of Experimental Psychology* 39:404–411.

Gray, J. 1982. *The Neuropsychology of Anxiety*. Oxford: Oxford University Press.

Gromov, S.A. and Yakunina, O.N. 1978. Ob Osobennostyach Izmeneniya Lichnostei i Psychoterapii Bolnich Epilepsiei (Clinicopsychologicheskoe Isledovaie). [Personality Changes and psychotherapy of epileptic patients (clinicopsychologic study).] *Zhurnal Nevropatologii i Psychiatrii Imeni S.S. Korsakova* 78(4):583–586 [in Russian].

Hermann, B.P. and Seidenberg, M. 1995. Executive System Dysfunction in Temporal Lobe Epilepsy: Effects of Nociferous Cortex Versus Hippocampal Pathology. *Journal of Clinical and Experimental Neuropsychology* 17:809–819.

Hermann, B.P., Wyler, A.R. and Richey, E.T. 1988. Wisconsin card Sorting Test Performance in Patients with Complex Partial Seizures of Temporal Lobe Origin. *Journal of Clinical and Experimental Neuropsychology* 10:467–476.

Hermann, B.P., Wyler, A.R., Richey, E.T., and Rea, J.M. 1987. Memory Function and Verbal Learning Ability in Patients with Complex Partial Seizures of Temporal Lobe Origin. *Epilepsia* 28(5):547–554.

Horel, J.A. 1978. The Neuroanatomy of Amnesia: A Critique of the Hippocampal Memory Hypothesis. *Brain* 101:403–445.

Horner, M.D., Flashman, L.A., Freides, D., Epstein, C.M., and Bakay, R.A. 1996. Temporal Lobe Epilepsy and Performance on the Wisconsin Card Sorting Test. *Journal of Clinical and Experimental Neuropsychology* 18:310–313.

Isaacson, R.L. 1972. Hippocampal Destruction in Man and Other Animals. *Neuropsychologia* 10:47–64.

Jones-Gotman, M. 1991. Localization of Lesions by Neuropsychological Testing. *Epilepsia* 32(Suppl. 5):S41–S52.

Kandel, E.I. 1990. Soviet Investigations in Epilepsy. *Acta Neurochirurgica Suppl.* 50:136–141.

Kanwisher, N. and Yovel, G. 2006. The Fusiform Face Area: A Cortical Region Specialized for the Perception of Faces. *Philosophical Transactions of the Royal Society of London* 361:2109–2128.

Kessles, R.P., de Haan, E.H., Kappelle, L.J., and Postma, A. 2001. Varieties of Human Spatial Memory: A Meta-Analysis on the Effects of Hippocampal Lesions. *Brain Research Brain Research Reviews* 35(3):295–303.

Kosslyn, S.M. 1994. *Image and Brain: The Resolution of the Imagery Debate*. Cambridge, Mass.: MIT Press.

Lardizabal, D.V. 2008. Medical Intractability in Epilepsy. In: H.O. Luders (ed.). *Textbook of Epilepsy Surgery*. London: Informa UK, Ltd.

Larrabee, G.J., Kane, R.L., Schuck, J.R., and Francis, D.J. 1985. Construct Validity of Various Memory Testing Procedures. *Journal of Clinical and Experimental Neuropsychology* 7:239–250.

Levy-Agresti, J. and Sperry, R.W. 1968. Differential Perceptual Capacities in the Major and Minor Hemispheres. *Proceedings of the National Academy of Sciences* 61:1151.

Lichterman, B.L. 1993. On the History of Psychosurgery in Russia. *Acta Neurochirurgica (Wien)* 125:1–4.

Lichterman, B.L. 1998. Roots and Routes of Russian Neurosurgery (from Surgical Neurology towards Neurological Surgery). *Journal of the History of the Neurosciences* 7(2):125–135.

Lichterman, B.L. 2004. Wilder Penfield and Soviet Neuroscience. Abstract. Ninth Annual Meeting, International Society of the History of the Neurosciences.

Loring, D.W., Lee, G.P., Meador, K.J., Smith, J.R., Martin, R.C., Ackell, A.B., Flanigin, H.F., et al. 1991. Hippocampal Contribution to Verbal Recent Memory Following Dominant-Hemisphere Temporal Lobectomy. *Journal of Clinical and Experimental Neuropsychology* 13(4):575–586.

Luria, A.R. 1966. *Higher Cortical Functions in Man.* New York: Basic Books.

Luria, A.R. 1971. Memory Disturbances in Local Brain Lesions. *Neuropsychologia* 9: 367–375.

Luria, A.R. 1973a. Neuropsychological Studies in the USSR. A Review (Part I). *Proceedings of the National Academy of Sciences* 70(3):959–964.

Luria, A.R. 1973b. Neuropsychological Studies in the USSR. A Review (Part II). *Proceedings of the National Academy of Sciences* 70(4):1278–1283.

Luria, A.R. 1975. *Brain and Memory.* Moscow: Press Moscow University.

Luria, A.R. 1978. The Localization of Function in the Brain. *Biological Psychiatry* 13(6):633–635.

Luria, A.R. and Simernitskaya, E.G. 1977. Interhemispheric Relations and the Functions of the Minor Hemisphere. *Neuropsychologia* 15:175–178.

MacLean, P.D. 1952. Some Psychiatric Implications of Physiological Studies on Frontotemporal Portion of the Limbic System. *Electroencephalography and Clinical Neurophysiology* 4:407–418.

Martin, R.C., Sawrie, S.M., Gilliam, F.G., Palmer, C.A., Faught, E., Morawetz, R.B., and Kuzniecky, R.I. 2000. Wisconsin Card Sorting Performance in Patients with Temporal Lobe Epilepsy: Clinical and Neuroanatomical Correlates. *Epilepsia* 41:1626–1632.

McDonald, C.R., Bauer, R.M., Grande L., Gilmore, R., and Roper, S. 2001. The role of the Frontal Lobes in Memory: Evidence from Unilateral Frontal Resections for Relief of Intractable Epilepsy. *Archives of Clinical Neuropsychology* 16:571–585.

Milner, B. 1958. Psychological Deficits Produced by Temporal-Lobe Excision. *Research Publications Association for Research in Nervous and Mental Disease* 36:244–257.

Milner, B. 1964. Some Effects of Frontal Lobectomy in Man. In: J.M. Warren and K. Akert (eds.). *The Frontal Granular Cortex and Behavior*. New York: McGraw-Hill, pp. 313–334.

Milner, B. 1967. Brain Mechanisms Suggested by Studies of Temporal Lobes. In: F.L. Darley (ed.). *Brain Mechanisms Underlying Speech and Language*. New York: Grune and Stratton, pp. 122–145.

Milner, B. 1968. Visual Recognition and Recall after Right Temporal-Lobe Excision in Man. *Neuropsychologia* 6:191–209.

Milner, B. 1971. Interhemispheric Differences in the Localization of Psychological Processes in Man. *British Medical Bulletin* 27(3):272–277.

Milner, B. 1975. Psychological Aspects of Focal Epilepsy and its Neurosurgical Management. *Advances in Neurology* 8:299–321.

Milner, B., Corkins, S., and Teuber, H. 1968. Further Analysis of the Hippocampal Amnestic Syndrome: 14 Year Follow-Up Study of H.M. *Neuropsychologia* 6: 215–234.

Mishkin, M. 1978. Memory in Monkeys Severely Impaired by Combined but not separate Removal of Amygdala and Hippocampus. *Nature* 273:297–298.

Nauta, W.J.H. 1964. Some Efferent Connections of the Prefrontal Cortex in the Monkey. In: M. Warren and K. Akert (eds.). *The Frontal Granular Cortex and Behavior*. New York: McGraw-Hill.

Papez, J. 1937. A Proposed Mechanism of Emotion. *Archives of Neurology and Pathology* 38:725–743.

Penfield, W. and Milner, B. 1958. Memory Deficit Produced by Bilateral Lesions in the Hippocampal Zone. *Archives of Neurology and Psychiatry* 79:475–497.

Pillon, B., Bazin, B., Deweer, B., Ehrle, N., Baulac, M., and Dubois, B. 1999. Specificity of Memory Deficits after Right or Left Temporal Lobectomy. *Cortex* 35(4):561–571.

Polenov, A.L. and Babchin, I.S. (eds.). 1954. *Osnovi prakticheskoj nejrokhirurgii*. [Fundamentals of Practical Neurosurgery.] Leningrad [in Russian].

Pribram, K.H. 1986. The Hippocampal System and Recombinant Processing. In: R.L. Isaacson and K.H. Pribram (eds.). *The Hippocampus*. New York: Plenum Press.

Pribram, K.H. and McGuiness, D. 1975. Arousal, Activation, and Effort in the Control of Attention. *Psychological Review* 82:116–149.

Remezova, E.S. 1964. The Social and Medical Services for the Epileptic Patient in the Soviet Union. *Epilepsia* 5:201–208.

Roid, G.H., Prifitera A., and Ledbetter M. 1988. Confirmatory Analysis of the Factor Structure of the Wechsler Memory Scale – Revised. *The Clinical Neuropsychologist* 2:116–120.

Scoville, W.B. and Milner B. 1957. Loss of Recent Memory after Bilateral Hippocampal Lesions. *Journal of Neurology, Neurosurgery and Psychiatry* 20(1):11–21.

Smith, G.E., Malec, J.F., and Ivnik, R.J. 1992. Validity of the Construct of Nonverbal Memory: A Factor-Analytic Study in a Normal Elderly Sample. *Journal of Clinical and Experimental Neuropsychology* 14:211–221.

Smith, M.L. 1989. Memory Disorders Associated with Temporal Lobe Lesions. In: F. Boller and J. Grafman (eds.). *Handbook of Neuropsychology*. Amsterdam: Elsevier. Vol. 3, pp. 91–106.

Squire, L.R. 1992. Memory and the Hippocampus: A Synthesis from Findings with Rats, Monkeys, and Humans. *Psychological Review* 99:195–231.

Squire, L.R. and Zola-Morgan, S. 1991. The Medial Temporal Lobe Memory System. *Science* 253:1380–1386.

Trenerry, M.R. and Jack, C.R. 1994. Wisconsin Card Sorting Test Performance Before and After Temporal Lobectomy. *Journal of Epilepsy* 7:313–317.

Ugriumov, B.M. and Shefer, D.G. 1967. Problemi Chirurgicheskogo Lecheniya Epilepsii v Sovetskoi Neurochirurgii. [Problems in the Surgical Treatment of Epilepsy in Soviet Neurosurgery.] *Voprosi Neurochirurgii* 31(5):30–34 [in Russian].

Upton, D. and Corcoran, R. 1995. The Role of the Right Temporal Lobe in Card Sorting: A Case Study. *Cortex* 31:405–409.

Wechsler, D. 1987. *Wechsler Memory Scale – Revised Manual.* New York: Psychological Corporation.

Wechsler, D. 2009. *Wechsler Memory Scale – Fourth Edition.* San Antonio, TX: Pearson Corporation.

Wheeler, M.A., Stuss, D.T. and Tulving, E. 1995. Frontal Lobe Damage Produces Episodic Memory Impairment. *Journal of International Neuropsychological Society* 1:525–536.

Wiebe, S., Blume, W.T., Girvin, J.P., and Eliaszw, M. 2001. A Randomized, Controlled Trial of Surgery for Temporal-Lobe Epilepsy. *New England Journal of Medicine* 345:311–318.

Zatorre, R. 1985. Discrimination and Recognition of Tonal Melodies after Unilateral Cerebral Excisions. *Neuropsychologia* 23:31–41.

Zemskaya, A.G. and Ryabukha, N.P. 1976. N.N. Burdenko I Nekotorie Aspecti Razvitiya Otechestvennoi Neurochirurgii. [N.N. Burdenko and Some Aspects of the Development of National Neurosurgery.] *Vestnik Khirugii Imeni I. I. Grekova* 116(5):10–15 [in Russian].

8

When East Meets West: Systematizing Luria's Approach to Executive Control Assessment

Kenneth Podell

I had the good fortune and opportunity to train with Elkhonon Goldberg during the first few years of my graduate training. That relationship continues today. While my classmates were learning to administer the Wechsler Instruments and other standardized measures, I, on the other hand, was learning the protocol put together by Dr. Goldberg. And as the saying goes, the apple did not fall far from the tree. It included portions of *Luria's Neuropsychological Investigation*, questions and items designed by Dr. Goldberg while studying with Luria, and occasionally a few standardized measures. I can remember talking with my classmates and comparing notes and thinking to myself how different my training was from that of everyone else. I must admit that at first it felt odd, and I thought how could these simple tasks and questions be as powerful as the standardized instruments that my peers were learning? Well, it did not take long for me to become a "convert" to Luria's techniques. I had the opportunity to watch Dr. Goldberg examine patients and to see the power of Luria's technique in the hands of a skilled neuropsychologist. The ability of these techniques to draw out the cognitive and behavioral components of neuropsychological deficits and identify areas of CNS dysfunction was utterly fascinating.

I can still recall the very first patient (Pick's disease) I tested on my own. Seeing the executive deficits, particularly their productive features, manifest themselves was fascinating. I remember at the end of the first testing session the patient had completed a precursor of the Graphical Sequences Test (Goldberg, et al. 2000); a measure of graphomotor perseverations (see Goldberg and Tucker 1979;

Luria 1980). When I came back the next morning to finish testing, the unit nurse met me at the station and promptly took me into the group room where the patient was at a blackboard intently drawing the stimuli she had drawn for me the day before. The nurse informed me that other than eating and sleeping a few hours, this was all the patient had been doing since I left the day before.

In the example above, imagine if the last test I gave during the first testing session was the Wisconsin Card Sorting Test (Heaton, et al. 1993). Would I have still seen the same type of behavior the next day? Probably not. This example highlights the essence of this chapter; that being the richness of qualitative, productive symptomatology in clinical neuropsychology. In this chapter, we will discuss the nature of productive symptomatology, how it was integral to Luria's techniques, how it differed from the West's reliance on psychometrics, and our attempt to incorporate the two through the development of The Executive Control Battery (Goldberg, et al. 2000).

Introduction

If you were to take a poll, it is likely that you will find that A.R. Luria's work is most associated, if not synonymous, with executive control functions, or as he described it, the functions of the "anterior frontal cortex." Although Luria's legacy covers many different areas of research (see Cole 1990), his work in executive control functions is often considered his best and most productive area, at least in the Western Hemisphere. In fact, this is rather apparent just looking at his most seminal work, *Higher Cortical Functions in Man* (Luria 1966/1980). Luria devoted more than twice the number of pages to describing "disturbances of higher cortical functions with lesions of the frontal region" than he did for any other cortical area/lobe. Granted the frontal lobes are larger than any other area and contain both motor and executive functions, Luria's descriptions of deficits were predominately about executive deficits; but mostly with a motor component. This is not surprising because Luria first described anterior cortical lesions as producing deficits in "successive synthesis" of movement and organized action (see Tueber in Luria 1966, *Human Brain and Psychological Processes*) and that the frontal lobes perform a "universal function of general regulation of behavior" (p. 89, Luria 1973a from Stuss and Benson).

When reviewing Luria's research on executive deficits, one can notice two interesting patterns. First, he primarily described and discussed effects from a dorso-lateral lesion with much less exploration of orbito-frontal effects, and second he most often described productive symptomatology and deficits rather than negative (or inability type) deficits. By *productive*, we refer to those types of impairments that alter or introduce an added component or stimuli to the subject's response. Predominately, Luria described variations of perseverations and sequencing impairments. Perhaps the best examples for this would be the graphomotor perseverations described by Luria (1966/1980) and then systematized by others (Goldberg and Tucker 1979; Goldberg, et al. 2000). These types of productive perseverations "reflects an impairment in inertia which leads to the intrusion of previous, external or irrelevant actions on current actions" (Goldberg, et al. 2000, p. 43). They are very striking to see and differ from negative or absent types of perseverations where the subject cannot respond correctly; for example, perseverative responses on the Wisconsin Card Sorting Test (WCST; Milner 1963). For the WCST, the difficulty lies in understanding the cause of the perseveration. There are times when the subject is clearly perseverative and "stuck-in-set," but other times it is very difficult to know why they are responding in this fashion (i.e., poor conceptualization rather then being stuck in set where the patient reverts back to the last known response set because they cannot figure out how to respond differently).

The distinction between assessing productive versus inability does not simply boil down to a qualitative versus quantitative distinction. The difficulty is in being able to quantify the productive symptomatology in a standardized and reliable fashion. It is much easier to accurately and consistently measure a subject's inability to answer or respond to questions on tests such as the WCST or Category Test because in essence it is a binary decision (correct or incorrect). Now, some tests can then quantify the incorrect response to a greater detail, but the true flavor of "why" they responded in that way is lost. As subsequent research has shown (Goldberg, et al. 1994; Goldberg and Podell 1995, 2000), the essence of prefrontal functions is not necessarily in its ability to find correct answers but rather in how the problem is approached (style of response).

Productive symptomatology is much harder to accurately and consistently record, yet it is something we observe all the time during neuropsychological evaluations. Given that productive features can have a much greater number of probable responses, one needs to have a more complex scoring method. The more complex the scoring method in neuropsychological testing, the harder (and longer) it is to score the test, invariably leading to poorer interrater reliability and making it less likely to be adopted in North America. However, productive features are extremely rich in information and can be very enlightening in characterizing the neuropsychological status of our patients.

One other distinction we see in the productive versus negative deficit approach is in test administration. The typical negative deficit assessment test is often highly structured and given in the same fashion all of the time. The classic example is the Halstead–Reitan Battery (HRB). Such tests can be easily administered by technicians. Although the technician can be highly skilled in test administration, he or she does not need to know much about brain–behavior relationships to administer the tests and does not need to report productive deficits in that they would not affect test scores. In stark contrast, assessing qualitative and productive symptomatology and deficits (via Lurian techniques) requires a high degree of neuropsychological expertise for test administration to be able to know how to elicit possible productive features, identify them when they occur, and know how to use them to direct the evaluation.

Luria's techniques, which were painstakingly developed and refined over the years, have often been mistaken for being loose, unsystematic, or nonstandardized. What many fail to realize is that Luria's approach (and logic) was rooted in well-established brain–behavior relationships and offered a logically organized and highly systematic branch-tree logic methodology/hypothesis testing that allowed one to fully explain and understand what the deficits were with a richness and level of detail that was not possible using standardized assessment techniques (Goldberg 1990). In many ways, it served as the precursor to the "process approach" later developed by Edith Kaplan.

What few people realize is that Luria was not primarily interested in assessment techniques per se. His assessment techniques were created to allow him to develop rehabilitation techniques, which were his primary interest in neuropsychology (Goldberg 1990). In contrast, formalized quantitative assessment techniques were designed specifically for diagnostic purposes.

When east meets west

Luria is considered one of, if not the first, to develop a qualitative approach to neuropsychological assessment. One can understand how Luria developed this approach when you consider his methods of research. Rather then applying classic experimental group design and studying large groups of patients with the same lesion on one test, Luria took the exact opposite approach and studied individual patients in excruciating detail. The advantage of this method was that it allowed for a more thorough understanding of the underlying function of the lesional area. The symptom or deficit served as the starting point for Luria to investigate and not the end point, which was the goal of quantitative approaches (e.g., HRB). This allowed Luria to fully appreciate and explore the subtle intricacies and nuances of the behavioral and cognitive effects of focal lesions and to note the exquisitely rich qualitative features associated with frontal lesions, for example. Not only did Luria do this to fully elicit the signs and symptoms associated with that particular lesion but also to develop tests and techniques to better understand the underlying mechanism (i.e., the normal role of the damaged area) (see Tueber in Luria 1966, *Human Brain and Psychological Processes*). Luria refined and perfected this approach and his various techniques during the 1940s and 1950s in his laboratory in the Bourdenko Neurosurgical Hospital (Christensen 1990). This was in stark contrast with the techniques being developed in the United States (i.e., HRB) where the goal was to develop statistically reliable and valid techniques for predicting the presence of dysfunction, and if present, its location and type (e.g., focal or diffuse; Wheeler and Reitan 1963). Luria extracted the data through observation and challenging the patient through hypothesis testing "using a flexible but systematic set of tests" (Luria and Majovski 1977, p. 962). For Luria and other Russian neuropsychologists, the assessment of each patient was "... a theoretically based dynamic experiment on the behavioral effects accrued from a disturbance in the brain" (Luria and Majovski 1977, p. 962). They did not believe that comparison with the mean was appropriate in understanding the deficits of an individual because each individual was not average. Thus it appears that the original goals of the two techniques were different—almost opposite ends of the same continuum. The American or Western approach was more clinically diagnostic (looking for *what* was impaired), and the Russian or Eastern approach was more experimental and explanatory in nature (*why* was it impaired).

Anne-Lise Christensen is credited with introducing the West to Luria's approach to neuropsychological assessment. After studying with Luria first in 1970 and then later in 1972, she published *Luria's Neuropsychological Investigation* in 1975. Christensen (1990), true to Lurian ideology, described the need to look at each assessment as an "exploratory clinical investigation" (p. 133) of the individual and the need for each and every interaction to be scrutinized. This mandates an individual *dynamic* approach with each patient because every patient and their situation is different. Even use of the word *investigation* in the title of the test connotes the importance of qualitative features. By investigating the patient, one must take a very individualized (that is, flexible) but systematic approach and analyze each piece of information within the context of the situation and the question being asked.

Thus far, the point of this introduction is to familiarize the reader with some of the conceptualization behind different approaches to studying brain–behavior relationships in neuropsychology. However, the object of this chapter is not to advocate strictly one method over the other. As both have evolved over time and have been shaped by others, we find merit and value in both approaches. It has been our experience that the clinical question (and even setting) can determine the weight of one approach over the other. There are times when a more Lurian approach to assessing neuropsychological status is more informative (e.g., hospital bed-side evaluation, focal lesions, or when productive symptoms are evident), and there are times when a strictly quantitative approach is probably better (e.g., forensics, mild levels of impairments such as MCI). Often, I combine the two approaches starting off or ending with Lurian techniques and supplementing it with quantitative data.

The next section will discuss Elkhonon Goldberg and his co-workers' adaptation of Lurian techniques for assessing productive aspects of executive impairment using a more quantitative approach.

Executive Control Battery

The Executive Control Battery (ECB; Goldberg, et al. 2000) is modeled after Luria's approach and techniques developed by Professor Luria and Elkhonon Goldberg while studying patients with focal prefrontal lesions in Luria's laboratory. The goal of ECB was to develop and adapt a more rigorous methodical assessment of "... the qualitative type of error analysis inherent in the Lurian tradition of Neuropsychology" (Goldberg, et al. 2000, p. 2). We strived to maintain the qualitative richness often found in patients with executive deficits without sacrificing systemic assessment, administration, and scoring.

ECB constitutes a major and innovative departure from the traditional psychometric approach in that it does not rely upon strictly comparing the deficit of the patient group to a normative group for which the phenomenology that is specific to the given patient population is absent in reference populations. In other words, the types of errors or productive symptoms elicited by the ECB are nearly absent from the normal population (Table 8–1). By using qualitative error analysis, we are better able to explain the underlying deficit, but at the same time we applied standard testing procedures and well-operationalized scoring systems to quantify the level of impairment.

TABLE 8–1. Mean and standard deviation* for ECD subtest error scores in healthy control, focal frontal, schizophrenic, and traumatic brain–injured male and female subjects.

	N	GRAPHICAL SEQUENCES	MANUAL POSTURES	COMPETING PROGRAMS	COMPETING PROGRAMS
		PERSEVERATIONS	MIRRORING	MIRRORING	PERSEVERATIONS
Male					
Healthy control	23	2.5 (2.1)	1.4 (1.8)	0.5 (0.1)	0.1 (0.3)
Left frontal	7	15.3 (5.2)	4.1 (3.8)	3.4 (3.3)	1.0 (1.4)
Right frontal	6	8.7 (9.4)	9.0 (7.1)	4.8 (7.5)	0.3 (0.5)
Bifrontal	4	5.8 (4.2)	4.3 (4.3)	0.5 (1.0)	0.3 (0.5)
Schizophrenic	21	9.1 (7.1)	4.9 (3.9)	5.6 (7.4)	1.1 (1.0)
Traumatic brain injury	29	5.2 (5.6)	4.3 (4.0)	4.4 (5.0)	0.8 (0.81)
Female					
Healthy control	9	3.7 (2.0)	0.7 (0.7)	0.2 (0.4)	0.0 (0.0)
Left frontal	4	5.0 (11.8)	3.0 (3.2)	4.3 (7.5)	2.0 (2.0)
Right frontal	4	6.8 (3.7)	1.8 (1.3)	2.0 (1.7)	2.0 (1.9)
Schizophrenic	8	15.6 (11.1)	9.0 (1.9)	7.2 (6.1)	0.8 (0.8)
Traumatic brain injury	18	2.9 (2.5)	3.7 (3.9)	4.2 (4.2)	0.8 (1.1)

Source: From Goldberg, et al. 2000. Reproduced with permission of PsychPress, Melbourne Australia.
*Standard deviations occur in parentheses.

The ECB is designed to identify unambiguously qualitative and phenomenological aspects of executive dyscontrol in a quantified fashion. This is accomplished through systematic assessment using standardized administration and scoring procedures of the various qualitative features often associated with executive dyscontrol, which includes perseverations, echopraxia, "field-dependent" behavior, inertia of initiation and/or termination of activity, stereotypies, impulsivity, and omission of passive responses. It produces quantifiable scores in each of these domains and compares them with normal controls and various clinical populations.

Executive deficits are consistent with, but not pathognomonic of, prefrontal lesions (Luria 1980; Goldberg and Bilder 1987). Although prefrontal lesions are sufficient in producing executive control deficits, they are not a necessary condition, and prefrontal systems functions are vulnerable to effects from a wide variety of diffuse CNS dysfunction. However, oftentimes there are clear distinctions between the qualitative features of executive deficits after prefrontal versus nonprefrontal lesions. Prefrontal lesions will produce "horizontally" pervasive executive deficits such that the executive deficit can be elicited across most, if not all, cognitive domains. However, nonfrontal focal lesions can produce domain-specific executive deficits that are "vertically" pervasive within the cognitive domain affected (Goldberg 1986; Goldberg and Bilder 1987). Also, nonfocal or diffuse lesions or encephalopathic states can mimic frontal lesions causing severe and horizontally pervasive executive deficits.

The productive features of executive deficits follow a hierarchical pattern in the breakdown of a cognitive domain (Goldberg and Costa 1981). Within a given domain, the executive deficit can express itself at various levels of that domain's hierarchical arrangement. The breakdown is often most evident at the top of the cognitive hierarchy as the most complex components are the most sensitive to dissolution (Goldberg and Bilder 1987). This has been demonstrated in graphomotor perseverations (Goldberg and Tucker 1979) and language (Barr, et al. 1989), for example.

The qualitative, productive executive deficits are most readily apparent in the motor domain, which is to be expected given the physical proximity and interconnectedness of the prefrontal cortex with premotor and motor cortices (Goldberg 1990, 1989), but clearly do not have to be limited to it. However, ECB took advantage of this, and all of its subtests require a motoric output. Initially, other tests were considered during the development of the battery (e.g., verbal memory test) but were ultimately dropped due to difficulties with response and scoring standardizations.

The ECB consists of four subtests (Table 8–2), each designed to assess a wide variety of executive dyscontrol, both negative and productive. This unique feature is uncommon among some of the more popular tests of executive control (e.g., WCST and Category Test). In fact, ECB is one of the few, if not

TABLE 8–2. Description of the four subtests of the ECB

1. **The Graphical Sequences Test**
   The Graphical Sequences Test involves drawing graphical sequences after verbal commands under time pressure. The task is designed to elicit perseverations of four types and various behavioral stereotypies (Goldberg and Tucker 1979). The four persistent types are

   (a) hyperkinetic motor perseverations
   (b) perseveration of elements
   (c) perseveration of features
   (d) perseveration of activities

   The task takes 15–20 minutes to administer.

2. **Competing Programs Test**
   The Competing Programs Test consists of executing various responses after commands whose physical characteristics are "in conflict" with desired responses. Two types of sequences are employed:

   (a) conflict visual version
   (b) "go/no-go" version

   The task is designed to elicit various types of echopraxia, behavioral stereotypies, and disinhibition (Luria 1980). The task takes 12–15 minutes to administer.

3. **Manual Postures Test**
   The Manual Postures Test, a more elaborate variant of the test developed by Henry Head (see Luria 1980, pp. 418–420), involves imitations by the patient of various asymmetric static manual postures (both unimanual and bimanual) produced by the examiner who is facing the patient. The task assesses the patient's ability to relate egocentric and allocentric spaces. This ability has been demonstrated to be severely impaired after dorsolateral prefrontal lesions in monkeys (Rosenkilde 1979) and in humans (Semmes, et al. 1963). The task is designed to elicit various types of echopraxia and "mirroring" (Luria 1980). The task takes 10–15 minutes to administer.

4. **Motor Sequences Test**
   The Motor Sequences Test requires rapid alternation of both simple and complex unimanual and bimanual motor sequences. Six types of such sequences are employed:

   (a) unimanual two-stage movement
   (e) unimanual two-stage movement reversal
   (b) unimanual three-stage movement
   (c) bimanual (reciprocal) coordination: distal
   (f) bimanual (reciprocal) coordination: proximal
   (g) bimanual (reciprocal) coordination: mixed

   The task is designed to elicit various types of motor perseverations, stereotypies, and other deficits of sequential motor organization (Luria 1980). The task takes 10–15 minutes to administer.

Source: Adapted from Goldberg, et al. 2000. Reproduced with permission of PsychPress, Melbourne Australia.

the only, executive control measure that systematically assesses environmental/field-dependency via echopraxia. Additionally, another unique feature of ECB is its use of patient feedback and understanding of instructions after producing executive deficits. For all of the subtests, the patient is asked to repeat the instructions after making an executive deficit to ensure they understood the task requirements but were unable to follow them correctly because of the executive deficit. This dissociation of knowing from doing is a hallmark example of executive impairment after prefrontal lesions in patients described by Luria (1980). We find this a very powerful way of "proving" that the response deficit was truly due to an executive deficit rather than to a misunderstanding or forgetting of the instructions. For example, one of our personal experiences in clinical work is that perfectly intact patients (in terms of executive control) have failed the WCST because of overstrategizing about how to respond and not because of true perseverative responding, per se.

We believe that the ECB constitutes a major and innovative departure from the traditional psychometric approach in the following sense: the standard psychometric approach entails documenting and measuring the decrement of a certain index of performance in a patient group compared with that of a reference group. It does not, however, make use of the phenomenology that is specific to the given patient population and is absent in reference populations. The traditional psychometric approach is limited because every appreciably complex cognitive function or behavior can deteriorate for any number of reasons, and the specific reason cannot be identified by documenting the decrement alone. To identify the underlying cause of the deficit, one needs to take productive errors into account. Our approach overcomes this limitation by introducing fine qualitative error analysis. At the same time, it approaches such qualitative error analysis with standard procedures and well-operationalized scoring systems.

Graphical Sequences Test

The Graphical Sequences Test (GST) is designed to elicit graphomotor perseverations that occur during drawing or writing. Luria (1965 and 1980) first described these types of perseverations (for examples, see Luria 1980, pp. 298–306). Goldberg and Tucker (1979) then developed a taxonomy for describing these types of perseverations, which was adopted for ECB. In this model, the graphomotor component can break down at different levels of the graphomotor hierarchy causing different types of perseveration. The following is a description of the four types of graphomotor perseverations described by Goldberg and Tucker:

1. Hyperkinetic Perseveration: Hyperkinetic perseverations make up the base or elemental component of the graphomotor hierarchy. It is defined as an inability to stop a single elementary graphomotor component such as drawing a circle

or straight line. Luria described it as where "...the task of drawing a simple figure is easily interrupted by the revival of elementary motor automatism; having started to perform a particular task, the patient is unable to give up, and the performance of the action is interrupted by bursts of uncontrollable automatisms" (Luria 1980, p. 298). Here the patient literally continues to draw a circle or straight line over and over (see Figure 8–1 for examples). Luria associated hyperkinetic perseverations with involvement of the basal ganglia.

2. Perseveration of Elements: The next level of perseveration in the hierarchy has to do with perseveration of the element of the stimulus unit such as a circle, square, or symbol whereby the basic elemental unit of drawing (straight or curved line) is intact but the perseveration involves aspects of the discreet element or object. In this case, there is an addition or substitution of a previously occurring element or elements (entire element or portion of one) that intrude upon the current response. It can either be a replacement of the current correct element with

Hyperkinetic perseverations – an inability to stop a single elementary graphomotor component such as drawing a circle or straight line.

Perseveration of elements – the basic elemental unit of drawing (straight or curved line) is intact. However, there is an addition or substitution of a previously occurring element or elements (entire, portion of one) that intrude upon the current response.

Substitution of the entire element

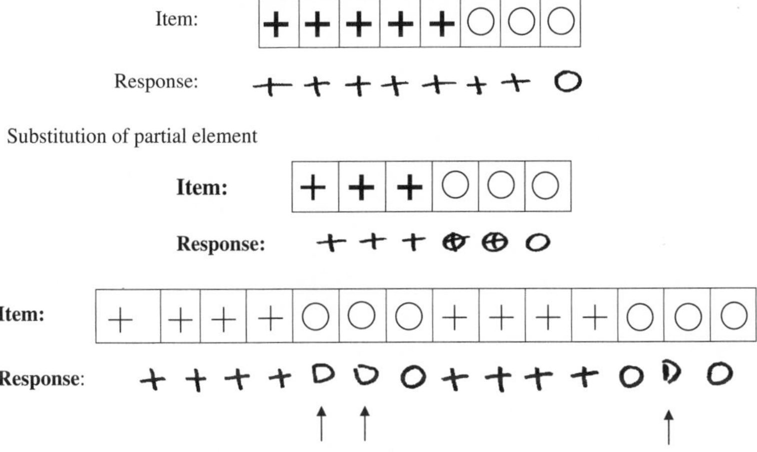

FIGURE 8–1. Examples of graphomotor perseverations from the Graphical Sequences Test: hyperkinetic perseverations and perseveration of elements. (From Goldberg, et al. 2000. Reproduced with permission of PsychPress, Melbourne Australia.)

an entire previous element or it can fuse to form a hybrid response of the current and a previous element (Figure 8–1).

3. Perseveration of Features: The next level of perseveration within the graphomotor neurocognitive hierarchy is when specific characteristics or features of the element, rather then parts or the entire element itself, intrude upon the current response. For example, geometric figures have parameters of openness/closeness, orthogonality/nonorthogonality or straightness/curvedness, and number of elementary components used to draw the object. As with the previous perseveration types, one or multiple features can be perseverated, as seen in Figure 8–2.

4. Perseveration of Activities: Perseveration of activities are at the highest level of the neurocognitive hierarchy of graphomotor activity and *occur when there is an intrusion between semantic categories such as drawing pictures versus geometric designs or writing of letters and words.* Perseverations at this level occur when there is perseveration of the prior type of activity upon the current and different type of activity; for example, when asked to draw something, the patient writes it out in words or the reverse (Figure 8–3).

Manual Postures

Luria (1980) credits the famous English neurologist Henry Head with being the first to recognize that frontal lobe patients "mirror" the movements of examiners. This has been referred to as field-dependent responding, "echo" behavior, or "stimulus-boundedness." The patient has conflicting information coming in through multiple modalities and becomes fixated or dependent upon responding to one modality that is incorrect according to the instructions. Echopraxia and echolalia are common examples of this. Echopraxia is actually a rather common phenomenon that we have all experienced or committed at some point. For example, how many times have you been walking when another person is walking directly toward you and you both move in the same direction to avoid each other? A similar example of this is what can be called the aerobics phenomenon. Here, the instructor, who is facing the class, says, "move toward your right," and when he or she moves to the right, everyone mirrors and moves to their left because the visual image was powerful enough to pull them in the same direction as that of the instructor rather than listening and following the directions. Various forms of field-dependency and echo behaviors are common in various disorders and have been reported in patients with frontal lesions (Luria 1980; Lhermitte 1983; Goldberg 2001), Tourette's syndrome (Lees, et al. 1984; Sacks 1989, 1992; Berthier, et al. 1996) and schizophrenia (Chapman 1964; Ford 1991), for example.

The Manual Postures (MP) subtest, to our knowledge, is the first systematic examination designed to elicit pathologic echopraxia. It is also designed to measure spatial errors where the subject has difficulty reproducing the vertical, horizontal, distal, and proximal directions of basic hand movements. The test is preceded by a pretest to ensure the subject understands basic egocentric and allocentric space through assessing the patient's understanding of their

Perseverations of features – specific characteristics or features of the element, rather then parts or the entire element itself, intrude upon the current response.

A. Parameter of Closeness/Openness

Open figures, when they follow closed figures, may adopt the quality of closeness.

Example:

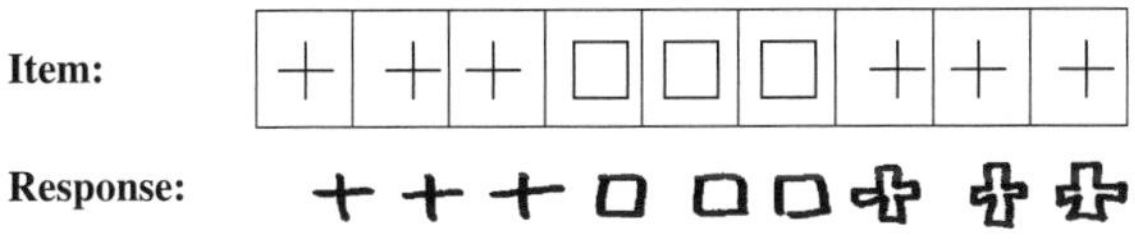

Item:

Response:

Example:

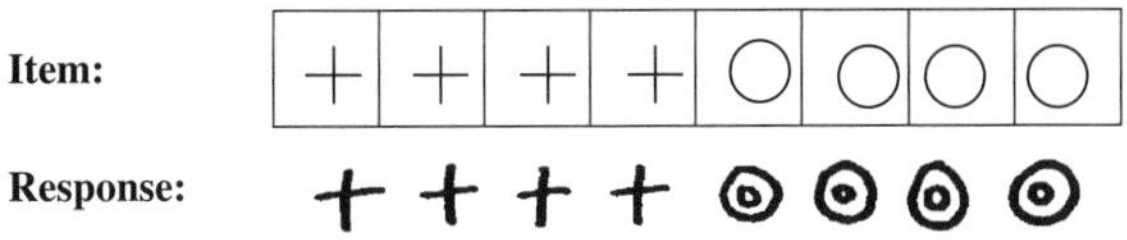

Item:

Response:

B. Parameter of number of elementary components

This parameter refers to the graphical components in drawing an element. For example, a cross has two elementary components: one horizontal, one vertical. The letter M has four elementary components.

Example:

Item: Draw two L's, three N's and an M.

Response: LL NNN MMMM

The L's and N's were elicited with the same frequency as each letter's respective elementary components. This parameter was then perseverated in drawing 4 M's instead of one. An alternative explanation for this error is that the subject may have perseverated on the stereotypic features of numerosity, i.e. that the elements were requested in groups of two, then three and then one, while the subject produced groups of 2, 3 and 4. The true explanation for this error can not be determined from the subject's response, but the scoring would be the same in both cases.

C. Parameter of Straightness/Curvedness

The feature of curvilinearity can affect a straight-line figure:

Example:

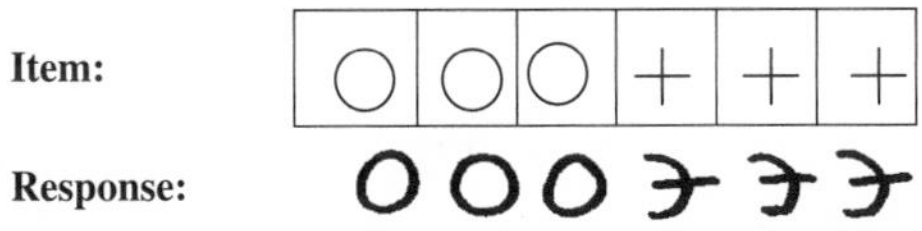

Item:

Response:

FIGURE 8–2. Examples of graphomotor perseverations from the Graphical Sequences Test: perseveration of features. (From Goldberg, et al. 2000. Reproduced with permission of PsychPress, Melbourne Australia.)

The effect of straightness upon curvilinearity can also be observed.

Example:

Item: | 2 | + | □ | 2 |

Response:

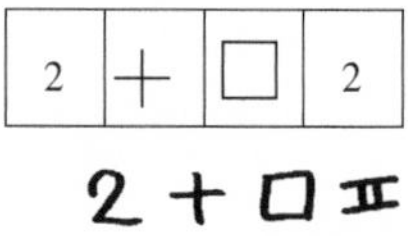

D. Parameter of Orthogonality/Nonorthogonality

Graphically, this perseveration takes the form of confusions of diagonal versus right angular lines with respect to the page orientation. For example, the diagonal lines of a triangle intrude upon the right angles of a square.

Example:

Item: | △ | △ | △ | □ | □ | □ |

Response:

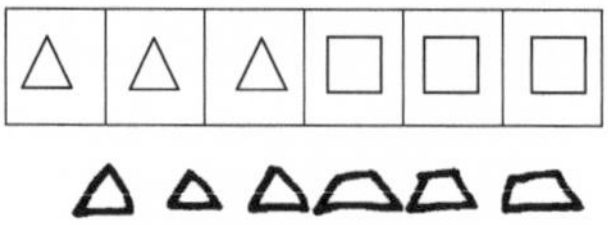

It is also possible for more than one feature to intrude upon an item simultaneously. The following example illustrates a perseveration of orthogonality/nonorthogonality together with closeness/openness.

Item: | △ | △ | △ | + | + | + |

Response:

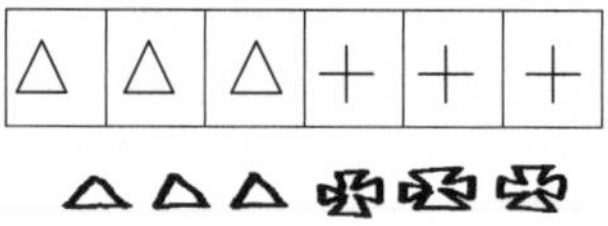

FIGURE 8–2. (*continued*)

individual and examiner's left and right orientation. Next, the subject is asked to replicate simple unimanual and bimanual hand postures of the examiner sitting directly in front of the patient making sure that they place their right and left hands in the same positions as those of the examiner's right and left hands.

This method allows for a direct "conflict" between the visual image and the instructions, which require mental rotation of right and left. Patients with pathologic echopraxia will "mirror" the examiner placing their right and left hands in the same positions as those of the examiner's left and right hands, respectively. After every third mirroring error, the patient is asked to repeat the instructions. True to Luria's classic description of the prefrontal patient's dissociation of knowing and doing, patients with pathologic echopraxia will give the correct instructions, indicating they *know* what they need to do, but on the very next trial revert to "mirroring" the examiner. If the patient maintains correct left/right orientation but commits errors in placing the hands in the correct spatial orientation, parieto-occipital dysfunction is considered.

Perseveration of Activities – occur when there is an intrusion between semantic categories such as drawing pictures versus geometric designs or writing of letters and words.

The following is an example of switching between semantic sets with a perseveration of activities

1. **Item:** Write the following sentence in words: "A cross to the left of a square".
   Response:
   A cross to the left of a square.

   Item: Draw four circles.
   Response: Draw four circles.

2. **Item:** Write the following sentence in words: "A cross to the left of a square".
   Response:
   A + to the left of a □

Note: While this response could be due to the subject's use of a shorthand rather than a perseveration, items from a pretest serves to minimize this source of false positive scoring by giving the examiner the opportunity to correct this type of response.

3. **Item:** Draw four L's, three M's and 2 H's

   Response a: 4 L's , 3 M's and 2 H's

   Response b: 4 LLLL 3 MMM 2 HH

4. **Item:** Draw three K's, two T's and an F.
   Response:
   3 KKK 2TT FFF

The F was repeated three times, a perseveration of the features of elementary components

5. **Item:** Draw a small flower to the right of a big house.

   Response: The subject draws an extensive landscape scene including, but far exceeding, that requested.

FIGURE 8–3. Examples of graphomotor perseverations from the Graphical Sequences Test: perseveration of activities. (From Goldberg, et al. 2000. Reproduced with permission of PsychPress, Melbourne Australia.)

Competing Programs

These tasks are based on the patient's ability to respond to the examiner's command that "competes" or is in conflict with the desired response. In Competing Programs (CP), the subject can have five types of executive deficits: (1 and 2) perseverations in the form of stereotypies or interminability, (3) echopraxia, (4) disinhibition (either through premature reaction or impulsive disinhibited responding), (5) omission of passive movement (when the patient consistently does not lower his or her hand/arm or finish the movement by relaxing). All of these have been described after prefrontal lesions (Luria 1980).

There are two CP tasks: a simple go/no-go and a simple conflict reaction, which have been shown to be sensitive to the effects of prefrontal lesions in humans (Luria 1980; Oscar-Berman, et al. 1991) and animals (for a review, see Fuster 1997). The simple go/no-go task is designed to measure all of the above types of executive deficit features. The simple conflict reaction is designed to assess mainly perseverations, echopraxia, and omission of passive movement but can measure other aspects, as well.

Each CP task has four parts: a training session and Runs A, B, and C. The training task is used to teach the correct responses. For example, the examiner might say, "If I do this (knock once on the table), you (the patient) knock twice." Then the examiner would say, "If I knock twice, you (the patient) do nothing, don't knock." This is reviewed one more time or up to four more times to train. In our experience, you can almost always get the patient trained on these very simple instructions. Run A is a pseudorandom combination of alternating actions by the examiner. Runs B and C have two blocks each of 10 trials. In Run B, the examiner gives nine consecutive commands of the same type and then switches on the 10th trial to the opposite command. This sets up a critical response to see if the patient can appropriately switch response set. If the patient does not switch and continues with the same response as in the previous nine responses, we consider that a stereotypic perseveration. The patient can also be echopraxic on any trial as well as have an omission of passive movement, premature reaction, and interminability of response (gives more responses then required; i.e., four knocks when only asked to give two). As with all of the other ECB tasks, the patient is asked to repeat the instructions if any errors were made. If the subject gives back a reasonable description of the task instructions, you have yet another example of the dissociation of knowing from doing, which solidifies the fact that the deficits were executive in nature. However, if the patient cannot give the correct instructions and only says, for example, "Do what you did," then it is not as clear that the deficit was executive in nature and it could have been due to poor understanding or a memory problem. The simple go/no-go task uses one knock/two knocks or two knocks/no knocks as conflicts, and the simple conflict reaction task uses palm/fist and fist/palm conflicts.

Motor Sequences

Luria was aware of the need to parcel out the effects of lesions in various parts of the frontal lobe and developed techniques that would distinguish between prefrontal and premotor lesions. Luria (1980) demonstrated that lesions of the premotor region disrupted "the dynamic organization of the motor act" (Luria 1980, pp. 421–424). The breakdown of the kinetic organization of motor acts occurs when an individual is incapable of smoothly transitioning between different simple motor acts. In more severe impairments, the subject tends toward stereotyped perseverations of one motor component. Also, patients may have difficulties "switching" or reversing the kinetic motor movements and perseverate on the one motor sequence.

The best way to assess this, according to Luria, was through tasks "... in which the patient is required to smoothly perform a simple series of movements, whose components follow in connected sequence" (Luria 1980, p. 421). Luria believed that bimanual tasks were best at eliciting this type of impairment but he developed unimanual assessment techniques as well. Luria's bimanual "test of reciprocal coordination" (p. 421), which he attributed to Ozeretskii (1930), was his preferred method for assessing this. However, he also developed and used unimanual tasks. Luria's two-stage "fist-ring" test with reversal (1980, pp. 422–423) is an adaptation to a task originally described by Eidinova and Pravdina-Vinarskaya (1959). Here the patient unimanually bends his arm at the elbow and alternates making a ring (with the thumb and index finger) when flexed to an open palm when the arm is extended. Luria noted that lesions of the premotor region prevent the smooth transition between the two individual motor acts while leaving the individual motor acts (motor cortices) intact. Additionally, the patient is then asked to reverse the task, that is to make an open palm when the elbow is flexed and a ring when the elbow is extended. Here patients with prefrontal lesions would perseverate and revert back to the actions of the first part of the test, whereas premotor lesions would cause an impairment in the transition between motor acts.

One can even make the task more difficult by having three motor acts to coordinate. Luria's famous "fist-palm-edge" or three-stage motor task (1980, pp. 423–224) was designed to be a more complex measure of the dynamic organization of the motor act. Luria noted that at first even healthy individuals require practice to learn the task but with only a few trials of practice easily master the task. Patients with prefrontal lesions, though being able to perform each of the three components individually, cannot establish a "kinetic melody" and become "increasingly nonautomatic" in their motoric output where they lose the proper sequence, perseverate positions, or develop inertia of movement.

Motor sequences has seven component tests derived from two components: dynamic praxis and bimanual coordination. Dynamic praxis has two parts; unimanual two-stage and unimanual two-stage reversal movements (for both the right and left upper extremities) and the more familiar unimanual three-stage motor sequencing task for each hand. The second component consists of bimanual coordination consisting of three levels of difficulty: proximal, distal, and mixed.

It is very important that the examiner is fluent in performing these motor techniques such that they become rote motor skills. Otherwise it is difficult to perform these tasks, talk, and note the patient's performance simultaneously. The patient should keep both hands and arms on the table in plain view. Pathologic motor overflow and synkinetic movements are likely to occur during these tasks.

Making sure one can see the patient's legs is also important, as overflow can easily occur in the feet and legs.

Before the administration of any of the components, a simple pretest is recommended where the patient is asked to perform each of the individual motor tasks *without* having to invoke dynamic organization of the motor act. So the pretest dynamic praxis tests consists of simply asking the patient to make a "ring" with his or her index and thumb, show the examiner his or her palm with the fingers straight, and make the action of a "knife" on the table. While this seems mundane to do, it demonstrates that the inability to do the task is not because of any primary motor or kinesthetic deficit (true to the Lurian tradition). Also, it will alert you to any problems that may arise because of paresis or peripheral factors such as arthritis.

All of the tasks follow the same pattern of administration:

1. Demonstration: The examiner demonstrates 10 repetitions while the patient watches.
2. Imitation: The patient simultaneously copies the examiner's movements for 20 repetitions.
3. Continuation Without Model: The patient continues the motor sequence for 20 repetitions after the examiner stops.

Dynamic Praxis. For the unimanual two-stage task, the patient is asked to place his or her forearm on the table (start with the dominant side) with the fingers clenched into a fist and the palm facing down. The patient is then shown how to bend his or her arm to be vertical with the table while straightening the fingers so his or her palm is showing and the fingers are pointing straight up. The important key here is to have a smooth simultaneous transition of the fingers while bending the elbow. Bending the elbow and then switching the fingers sequentially to either a palm or a fist is considered a pathologic error of asynchrony, for example. After doing this with each arm and hand, the reversal component is administered. Here the movements are the same *except* now the palm and fist are reversed (palm flat facing down when the forearm is parallel to the table and then making a fist when the elbow is flexed and the arm is vertical to the table). See Goldberg et al. (2000) for a more detailed description.

The types of pathologic tendencies that can be elicited on the unimanual two-stage task consist of:

1. Distal or proximal position fixed: The patient does not switch hand positions when moving their arm through the range of motion.
2. Distal or proximal position reversed.
3. Asynchrony of proximal or distal dimension: Here the patient switches hand positions sequentially after moving the arm rather than simultaneously as requested.

4. Amplitude decrease: Here the patient goes through a progress decline in the range of motion between the two positions such that they no longer flex the elbow as much as when they started or no longer return the arm to the original resting position on the table.
5. Overflow movement/synkinesis: The patient moves body parts that are not required during the task.

The two-stage and two-stage reversal tasks are followed by the three-stage component. For the three-stage component, the subject rests both arms and elbows on the table. After administering a demonstration in the same order as the two-stage tasks, with model and without model conditions are administered for both hands with the dominant hand first.

The types of pathologic tendencies that can be elicited on the three-stage movement task consist of:

1. Sequencing errors: Not only does this include any incorrect order of hand positions (e.g., "knife-fist-palm") but also a reduction in the number of hand positions used as well as a perseveration of one hand position into another (a fusion). An example of the latter is when the "fist" and the "knife" position are fused and the patient places a fist in the position of the knife (a fist with the ulnar side resting on the table).
2. Dysrhythmic response: The flow or transition between individual hand positions is uneven or a lack of smoothness between the "sets" (the three movements) such that the patient does the three movements but has to pause before starting the series again.
3. Amplitude decrease: Movements become smaller or slower over time.
4. Overflow movements/synkinesis: Movements in other body parts not involved in the task that can include mirror movements of the other hand.
5. Upper arm/trunk involvement: Involvement of the same-side shoulder such that the hand and arm performing the task move along the horizontal plane (i.e., back and forth), which serves to help the patient perform the task.
6. Perseveration from prior task: The repetition of a movement from a prior task (i.e., two-stage task).

Bimanual Coordination. The bimanual coordination component of Motor Sequences has three parts: distal, proximal, and mixed. In the distal (or fist/palm) component, the subject alternates switching distal musculature (fingers) between fingers straight and palm facing down and a clenched fist (palm facing down). In the proximal condition (palm up/palm down), the distal musculature is fixed (fingers extended and straight) and only the more proximal musculature of pronating and supinating the forearms is required, causing the palms to alternate between facing up and down. The mixed condition combines elements from both the distal and proximal conditions and is arguably the most complex component. In the mixed condition, you start with one hand clenched into a fist with the palm facing down and the other hand with the fingers straight and the palm facing up. The idea is to switch such that the hand that was in a fist facing down now has the fingers straight with the palm facing up while the other hand that originally had the fingers straight with the palm pointing up is now making a fist with the palm facing down.

The types of pathologic tendencies that can be elicited on the three-stage movement task consist of:

1. Asimultaneity: The changes in positions of the two hands is sequential rather then simultaneous.
2. Upper arm/trunk involvement: The use of the shoulder or upper body to help one or both hands change relative position (a forward or backward movement). This makes it easier to perform the task but is not essential in carrying out the task.
3. Amplitude decrease: The magnitude of the movement of either hand decreases such that the patient does not fully complete a movement (not fully clenching the fist or opening the hand) or a reduction in speed.
4. Unimanual reduction or slowing: The amplitude or size of the movement in one hand decreases such that both hands eventually are performing the same movement simultaneously.
5. Intrusion of other movements: This includes perseverating to other movements from a prior task.

Normative Data

As mentioned above, ECB is designed to measure productive features of the executive deficits that are commonly reported in patients with frontal lesions but do not necessarily occur in the normal population. It is "normal" to make a mistake on occasion, thus "executive slips" are possible. However, because they are not typical of normal behavior, then they are not normally distributed in the healthy population. This fact is both a positive and a negative psychometric by-product. It is a positive in that the presences of productive deficits invariably indicates an executive deficit and minimizes false-positive errors. However, because they are not normally distributed, one cannot have solid psychometric properties (for ECB it is common for groups to have standard deviations larger than the mean; see Table 8–1). This is often frowned upon in North American neuropsychology where psychometric tests rule.

Table 8–3 represents the demographic variables for the healthy control group (HC) and the clinical populations: schizophrenia (SZ), focal frontal lesions (FF), and traumatic brain injury (TBI).

Please see Goldberg et al. (2000) for a more detailed description of the groups. Table 8–1 represents the means and standard deviations for the ECB subtest error

TABLE 8–3. Mean and standard deviation* for demographic variables in healthy controls, focal frontal lesions, schizophrenic, and traumatic brain–injured male and female subjects

	N	AGE	EDUCATION	FULL SCALE IQ[†]
Male				
Healthy control	23	32.0 (6.2)	12.5 (1.4)	101.5 (11.2)
Left frontal	7	41.1 (12.1)	12.3 (3.3)	82.4 (7.1)
Right frontal	6	36.8 (8.4)	11.3 (2.9)	83.0 (8.7)
Bifrontal	4	35.5 (12.4)	15.7 (4.5)	89.5 (19.2)
Schizophrenic	21	31.7 (6.8)	12.5 (2.0)	89.9 (8.8)
Traumatic brain injury	29	28.7 (11.3)	12.0 (1.9)	91.2 (12.5)
Female				
Healthy control	9	30.3 (6.6)	12.8 (2.2)	98.3 (14.7)
Left frontal	4	32.2 (10.9)	14.3 (2.6)	89.3 (17.7)
Right frontal	4	32.2 (5.0)	13.5 (3.0)	94.5 (9.5)
Schizophrenic	8	34.6 (6.1)	11.4 (1.6)	73.1 (10.9)
Traumatic brain injury	18	28.1 (9.9)	13.1 (2.4)	95.1 (18.3)

Source: From Goldberg, et al. 2000. Reproduced with permission of PsychPress, Melbourne Australia.

*Standard deviations occur in parentheses.

[†]Wechsler Adult Intelligence Scale – Revised prorated four subtest Full Scale IQ.

scores for all of the groups. As one can see, HC subjects produce very few errors on ECB. Although the number of errors is much higher in the clinical populations reported to have executive deficits, oftentimes the standard deviations are close to the means. This occurs in the HC and clinical population groups because not all subjects have productive errors, which skews the distribution of most of the groups. This tends to help with classification as there are few, if any, type I errors unlike other standardized tests of executive functions.

Formal test/retest reliability was not performed with any of the ECB tests. The rationale for not doing this is based on the fact that productive executive errors are inherently unstable and patients with frontal lesions are known to have variable performance over time (Stuss, et al. 2003). Similarly, performance on other measures, such as the WCST, does not show good test/retest reliability (Heaton, et al. 1993). Thus, this type of information would not have been helpful in determining the stability of the measures. We did, however, measure interrater reliability for GST and MP. We found very high interrater reliability for two sets of trained raters: Cronbach alpha = 0.94 and 0.98, respectively, for the total number of graphomotor perseverations on GST (Jaeger, et al. 1987). Interrater reliability for the total number of echopraxic errors on MP was perfect. Moreover, we were able to show that the errors from three ECB tests (GST, CP, and MP) group into either perseverative or echopraxic (mirroring) errors using confirmatory (varimax) factor analysis and were highly dissociable (Podell et al. 1993).

	Factor 1 (Perseveration)	Factor 2 (Echopraxia)
Perseverative Responses		
Graphical Sequences	.89	.03
Competing Programs	.76	.35
Mirroring Errors		
Manual Postures	.08	.88
Competing Programs	.26	.85

ECB tests are sensitive in detecting the productive errors found in various clinical populations known to have executive deficits and also have good discriminative properties between healthy control subjects and the clinical groups (Podell, et al. 1992, 1993; Podell and Lovell 1999; Podell, Wisniewski, and Lovell 2000). They have demonstrated that FF and SZ clinical groups are more perseverative than are healthy controls, but with no real difference between the two clinical groups and that FF, SZ, and TBI groups, are more field-dependent (echopraxic) than HC. In fact, Podell et al. (1992) demonstrated that GST is as sensitive as WCST in classifying HC from the clinical groups (FF = 83% and SZ = 85%), but more importantly, GST had 100% specificity whereas WCST did not.

It also appears that mirroring errors are a very prominent feature of executive deficits and sometimes are as accurate or even more accurate in distinguishing a clinical group. Podell and Lovell (1999) showed that mirroring errors from MP were greater in the clinical groups (FF and SZ) and were as accurate as WCST perseverative responses (80% and 81%, respectively) in discriminating between HC and the clinical groups combined. Also, combining WCST variables and MP yielded slightly greater discriminability (84%). Podell et al. (2000) extended this work and demonstrated that field-dependency (as measured by echopraxia on MP) was a prominent feature (as was perseveration) in TBI. However, they went on to demonstrate that (1) the TBI group was relatively more field-dependent than they were perseverative and (2) the MP test was the most (and highly) accurate measure of field-dependency.

We would like to mention again that the discrimination between the different clinical groups was very poor because ECB measures components of a behavior (executive control errors) that are disease or etiology nonspecific. Executive deficits are commonly found in a wide range of disease and pathologic conditions (Goldberg 2001). However, given that type I errors were extremely rare and only found in mild TBI comparisons strongly indicates that impaired performance on ECB tests implies the presence of a true executive control deficit.

We have also been able to study ECB in dementia. Lamar et al. (1997) demonstrated that patients with Alzheimer's disease and cerebrovascular dementia evidenced a high number of perseverations on GST (although they used a slightly different scoring system). Lastly, we have demonstrated a dose-dependent response (severity of dementia as measured by the Mattis Dementia Rating Scale) for the number of mirroring errors on MP in dementia.

Oftentimes, we are asked if ECB can demonstrate laterality effects with frontal lobe lesions. This has not been studied systematically. However, it has been our experience that most clinical measures of prefrontal functions (ECB included) do not distinguish laterality very well (Demakis 2003). However, Stuss' group has shown specific deficit types associated with lesions in specific frontal regions (Alexander, et al. 2007). Goldberg and Podell as well as others have also demonstrated distinct laterality patterns in cognitive abilities using novel, theoretically driven cognitive paradigms (Goldberg et al. 1994; Goldberg and Podell 1995, 2000).

Summary

Two distinct assessment camps exist in clinical neuropsychology: one emphasizing qualitative hypothesis testing exploration at the individual level (Lurian; this much more commonly accepted in Europe), and one emphasizing strict adherence to standardization and psychometric properties at the group level (widely used in North America). Each has its distinct advantages (and disadvantages), and likely a combination of both yields the most powerful data and information about neuropsychological functioning and impairment. Hopefully, we introduced some of the Lurian techniques (that are not commonly used in North America) along with the rationale behind them and the power that they have in demonstrating productive features of neuropsychological deficits (e.g., executive control). The introduction of the ECB is our attempt at standardizing Lurian techniques in such a way that they are more useful and acceptable to the clinician that favors more psychometric-based tests.

References

Alexander, M.P., Stuss, D.T., Picton, T., Shallice, T., Gillingham, S. 2007. Regional Frontal Injuries Cause Distinct Impairments in Cognitive Control. *Neurology* 68(18):1515–1523.

Barr, W. Bilder, R. Goldberg, E. Kaplan, E. and Mukhergee, S. 1989. Neuropsychology of Schizophrenic Language. *Journal of Communication Disorders* 22:327–349.

Berthier, M.L., Campos, V.M., and Kulisevsky, J., 1996. Echopraxia and Self-Injurious Behavior in Tourette's Syndrome: A Case Report. *Neuropsychiatry, Neuropsychology, and Behavioral Neurology* 9(4):280–283.

Cole, M. 1990. Alexandr Romanovich Luria: Cultural Psychologist. In: E. Goldberg (ed.). *Contemporary Neuropsychology and the Legacy of Luria*. Hillside-London: Lawrence Erlbaum, pp. 11–28

Chapman, J. 1994. Echopraxia in Schizophrenia. *British Journal of Psychiatry* 110(466):365–374.

Demakis, G.J. 2003. A Meta-Analytic Review of the Sensitivity of the Wisconsin Card Sorting Test to Frontal and Lateralized Frontal Brain Damage. *Neuropsychology* 17(2):255–264.

Ford, R.A. 1991. Neurobehavioural Correlates of Abnormal Repetitive Behaviour. *Behavioural Neurology* 4(2):113–119.

Fuster, J. 2008. *The Prefrontal Cortex,* Fourth Edition. London: Academic Press.

Goldberg, E. 1986. Varieties of Perseveration: A Comparison of Two Taxonomies. *Journal of Clinical and Experimental Neuropsychology* 8(6):710–726.

Goldberg, E. 1989. Gradiental approach to neocortical functional organization. *Journal of Clinical and Experimental Neuropsychology* 11(4):489–517.

Goldberg, E. 1990. Higher Cortical Functions in Humans: The Gradiental Approach. In: Goldberg, E. (ed.). *Contemporary Neuropsychology and the Legacy of Luria.* Institute for Research in Behavioral Neuroscience. Hillsdale, N.J.: Lawrence Erlbaum Associates, pp. 229–276.

Goldberg, E. 2001. *The Executive Brain: Frontal Lobes and the Civilized Mind.* New York: Oxford University Press.

Goldberg, E. and Bilder, R.M. Jr. 1986. Neuropsychological Perspectives: Retrograde Amnesia and Executive Deficits. In: Poon, L.W., Crook, T., Davis, K.L., Eisdorfer, C., Gurland, B.J., et al. (eds.). *Handbook for Clinical Memory Assessment of Older Adults.* Washington, D.C.: American Psychological Association, pp. 55–68.

Goldberg, E. and Bougakov, D. 2000. Novel Approaches to the Diagnosis and Restoration of Frontal-Lobe Functions. In: Christensen, A.-L. and Uzell, B. (eds.). *International Handbook of Neuropsychological Rehabilitation.* New York: Plenum Press.

Goldberg, E. and Bilder, R.M. Jr. 1987. The Frontal Lobes and Hierarchical Organization of Cognitive Control. In: Perecman, E. (ed.). *The Frontal Lobes Revisited.* New York: The IRBN Press, pp. 159–187.

Goldberg, E. and Costa, L. 1981. Hemisphere Differences in the Acquisition and Use of Descriptive Systems. *Brain and Language* 14:144–173.

Goldberg, E. and Podell, K. 1995. Lateralization in the Frontal Lobes: Searching the Right (and left) Way. *Biological Psychiatry* 38:569–571.

Goldberg, E. and Podell, K. 2000. Adaptive Decision Making, Ecological Validity, and the Frontal Lobes. *Journal of Clinical and Experimental Neuropsychology* 22:56–68.

Goldberg, E., Podell, K., Harner, R., Lovell, M. and Riggio, S. 1994. Cognitive Bias, Functional Cortical Geometry, And The Frontal Lobes: Laterality, Sex and Handedness. *Journal of Cognitive Neuroscience* 6(3): 276–296.

Goldberg, E., Podell, K., Bilder, R, and Jaeger, J. 2000. *The Executive Control Battery.* Melbourne, Australia: PsychPress.

Goldberg, E. and Tucker, D. 1978. Motor perseverations and the levels of encoding a visual form. *Journal of Clinical Neuropsychology* 4:273–288.

Heaton, R.K., Chelune, G.J., Talley, J.L., Kay, G.G., and Curtiss, G. 1993. *Wisconsin Card Sorting Test Manual (Rev.).* Psychological Assessment Resources, Inc.

Jaeger, J., Goldberg, E., Bilder, R., and Podell, K. 1987. The Graphical Sequences Test of The Executive Control battery: Administration, Scoring, Reliability, and Validity. *Journal of Clinical and Experimental Neuropsychology* 9:52.

Lamar, M., Podell, K., Giovannetti, T., Carew, B.S., Cloud, B.S., Resh, R., Kennedy, C., Goldberg, E., Kaplan, E., Libon, D.J. 1997. Perseverative Behavior in Alzheimer's Disease and Subcortical Ischaemic Vascular Dementia. *Neuropsychology* 11:523–534.

Lees, A.J., Trimble, M.R., and Murray, N.M. 1984. A Clinical Study of Gilles de la Tourette Syndrome in the United Kingdom. *Journal of Neurology, Neurosurgery and Psychiatry* 47(1):1–8.

Luria, A. R. 1966/1980. *Higher Cortical Functions in Man.* Basic Books: New York.

Milner, B. 1963. Effects of Different Brain Lesions on Card Sorting. *Archives of Neurology* 9:90–100.

Lhermitte, F. 1983. 'Utilization Behavior' and its Relation to Lesions of the Frontal Lobes. *Brain* 106:237–255.

Oscar-Berman, M., McNamara, P., and Freedman, M. 1991. Delayed-Response Tasks: Parallels Between Experimental Ablation Studies and Findings in Patients with Frontal Lesions. In: Levin, H.S., Eisenberg, H.M., and Benton, A.L. (eds.). *Frontal Lobe Function and Dysfunction*. New York: Oxford University Press, pp. 230–255.

Ozeretskii, N.I. 1930. Technique of Investigating Motor Function. In: M. Gurevich and N. Ozeretskii (eds.). *Psychomotor Functions*. Moscow: Medgiz.

Podell, K. 2000. An Orbito-Frontal Disconnection Syndrome Produced by a Right Thalamic Hemorrhage. Paper presented at The International Neuropsychological Society Annual Meeting, Denver, CO.

Podell, K. and Lovell, M. 1999. The Manual Postures Test: A Clinically Useful Measure of Echopraxia. Paper presented at The International Neuropsychological Society 27th Annual Meeting.

Podell, K., Wisniewski, K., and Lovell, M. 2000. The Assessment of Echopraxia as a Component of Executive Control Deficit in Traumatic Brain Injury. Poster presented at The 10th Annual Rotman Research Institute Conference.

Podell, K., Zimmerman, M., Menezes, A., and Goldberg, E. 1993. Multidimensional Nature of Executive Control Deficit in Schizophrenia. Paper presented at The International Neuropsychological Society 21st Annual Meeting.

Podell, K., Zimmerman, M., Sovastion, M., Lovell, M., and Goldberg, E. 1992. The Utility of The Graphical Sequences Test in Assessing Executive Deficits. Paper presented at The International Neuropsychological Society 20th Annual Meeting.

Sacks, O.W. 1989. Neuropsychiatry and Tourette's. In: Mueller, J. (ed.). *Neurology and Psychiatry: A Meeting of Minds*. Basel: Karger, pp. 156–174.

Sacks, O.W. 1992. Tourette's and Creativity. *British Medical Journal* 305:1516.

Stuss, D.T. and Benson, D.F. 1986. *The Frontal Lobes*. London: Raven Press.

Stuss, D.T., Murphy, K.J., and Binns, M.A. 2003. Alexander MP: Staying on the Job: The Frontal Lobes Control Individual Performance Variability. *Brain* 126(Pt 11):2363–2380.

Wheeler, L. and Reitan, R.M. 1963. Discriminant Functions Applied to the Problem of Predicting Cerebral Damage from Behavioral Testing: A Cross-Validation Study. *Perceptual and Motor Skills* 16:681–701.

9

VIII Interdisciplinary Approach to Rehabilitation

Klaus R.H. von Wild

> Brain damage has become synonymous with loss of skills, while rehabilitation of brain damaged individuals has become known as a method to reconstruct lives within a social context.
>
> Anne-Lise Christensen 1988 (p. XV)

The desire and requirement for rehabilitation (Latin: "habilis" and "habilitare") in the context of "apt" and "appropriate" is, in terms of the World Health Organization (WHO) ICIDH-2 (International Classification of Impairment, Disability and Handicap, second version) (Stucki, Wert, and Cieza 2003), just as old as the endeavors to heal diseases and injuries and the wish to continue living and working in one's own social environment, already reported as long as 5000 years ago (Thorwald 1962). The obligation of a state to reintegrate the sick and injured into vocational life and the commitment to give these people support and take care of the handicapped was first defined in the French constitution in the wake of the enlightenment of the French Revolution and the accompanying upheavals of social conditions, resulting in the emergence of early models of social medicine in the modern-day sense of the term. In Germany, the first institutions for disabled persons were established at the end of the 18th century, most of them to be converted into military hospitals for invalids during World War II (Goldstein 1919; Kleist 1934; von Wild 2001).

When Anne-Lise Christensen invited me in my capacity as neurologic surgeon to report on my personal view on Luria's legacy in the 21st century and

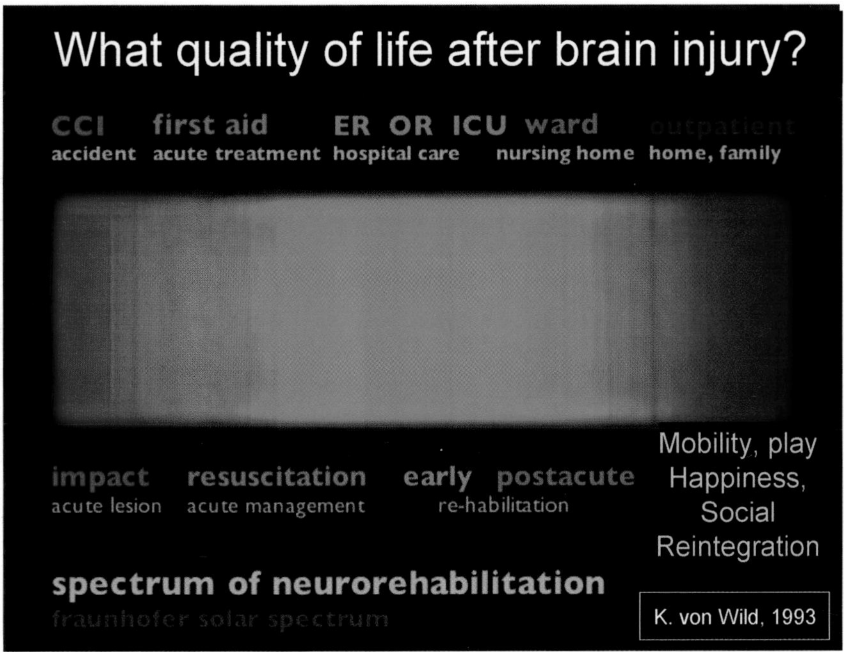

FIGURE 9–1. Spectrum of neurorehabilitation. Similar to the characteristic absorption of Fraunhofer lines in the solar spectrum, there are marks in each individual brain-injured patient, milestones on the road of his recovery progress up to reintegration into society and vocational life, or else determination that there is no more rehabilitation potential at all. This dynamic process runs along a time axis that can extend over several years, depending on the primary impact to the brain and the individual's rehabilitation potential along with the quality and intensity of rehabilitative measures. ENNR is an indispensable component within the ongoing chain of holistic transdisciplinary rehabilitation.

our approach to neurorehabilitation, I felt much honored because she became my teacher in this very complex field of restoration of neuropsychological behavioral functioning after having met at the first conference on early neurorehabilitation in Münster in 1990, a relationship that led to a close and fruitful collaboration. For her it was a challenge to work with neurosurgeons, teaching them Luria's neuropsychological investigation in Aahus (Christensen 1975, 1988; Christensen and Uzzel 2000). As desired I will restrict myself to my personal view on neurologic, neurosurgical, and neuropsychological rehabilitation after acute brain damage and shall divide my comments into past, present, and future. Some preliminary biographical data shall explain why neuroscience at Frankfurt University influenced my approach to the restoration of brain and spinal cord functioning as well as the current status (von Wild, Simons, and Schoeppner 1992; von Wild 2000, 2001, 2002, 2005, 2006; Voss, et al. 2000; von Steinbüchel, et al. 2005; von Wild, et al. 2007). The actual theories of brain protection, brain recovery, and health-related

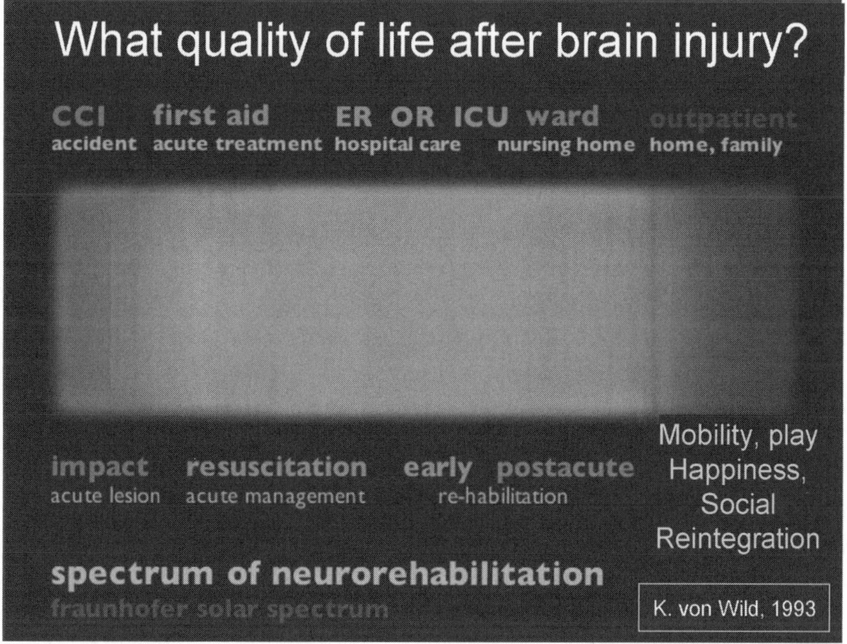

FIGURE 9–1. Spectrum of neurorehabilitation. Similar to the characteristic absorption of Fraunhofer lines in the solar spectrum, there are marks in each individual brain-injured patient, milestones on the road of his recovery progress up to reintegration into society and vocational life, or else determination that there is no more rehabilitation potential at all. This dynamic process runs along a time axis that can extend over several years, depending on the primary impact to the brain and the individual's rehabilitation potential along with the quality and intensity of rehabilitative measures. ENNR is an indispensable component within the ongoing chain of holistic transdisciplinary rehabilitation. (See color insert)

quality of life are described elsewhere (Luria 1963; Boyeson and Jones 1996; Berger, et al. 1999; Lotze, et al. 1999; Sabel 1999; Stein 1998; von Steinbüchel, et al. 2005; Sharma 2007) and will not be discussed here, nor the topic of evidence-based medicine in neurorehabilitation. Most interventions consist of training techniques, and so far there is only little class I or II evidence for both physical motor and mental-cognitive interventions to actively restore impaired higher cortical functioning (Christensen 1988; Christensen and Uzzel 2000; von Wild 2005; Wilson, et al. 2005). Therefore I will describe our concept of early neurologic–neurosurgical rehabilitation (ENNR), which is an example of successful transdisciplinary rehabilitation. It corresponds with the German Guidelines on ENNR quality management (1993) and has been accepted by the German Social Health Authorities. Over the years, it has also been adopted by other German-speaking European countries. ENNR is an important link within the ongoing chain of holistic rehabilitation after brain damage (Figure 9–1) (Ortega-Suhrkamp and von Wild 2001; von Wild 2000; Voss, et al. 2000).

Past

Physical neurologic and neuropsychological rehabilitation has an old tradition in Europe (Prigatano 1999b), especially in Frankfurt am Main, Germany, where I graduated in medicine and qualified as a professor of neurologic surgery in 1977. Frankfurt University has become a renowned center for neurology, psychiatry, neuropsychology, and neurorehabilitation owing to the important work of Ludwig Edinger (1855–1918), Kurt Goldstein (1878–1965), Adhémar Gelb (1887–1936), Karl Kleist (1879–1960), Heinrich Hoffmann (1809–1894), and G. Jacobi and A. Ritz. Hoffmann, a practitioner and neurologist, was director of the Anstalt für Irre und Epileptische (Institution for Mentally Ill and Epileptics) in Frankfurt in 1851 and established the first German psychiatric hospital outside of town in 1864 (people did not want to be in touch with psychiatrically ill individuals). Children around the world got to know Hoffman because of his classic children's story "Struwwelpeter," for example the Story of "Fidgety Philip": Let me see if Philip can be a little gentleman; let me see if he is able to sit still for once at table," and "Pah. . . . See shock-headed Peter, on his fingers rusty, on his tow-head musty, scissors seldom come . . . (Hoffmann 1846). Hoffmann originally dedicated this book to his own children and incorporated illustrations to describe abnormal physical and mental-cognitive behaviors of children in order to influence their understanding by teaching and learning. Pediatric neurology became a well-known field in Europe headed by Jacobi and Ritz, for example regarding epilepsy, head trauma, and the Glasgow Coma Scale (GSC) for children (Ritz, et al. 1982). Together we taught the students inter- and multidisciplinary neurotraumatology in regular seminars.

Edinger, the co-founder of the University of Frankfurt, also created and became first ordinary professor of the neurologic institute, which is the oldest institute for brain research in Germany (Edinger 1900, 1908). Having the vision of combining neuropathology of the brain and neuropsychology, he cooperated in a transdisciplinary way with the independent discipline of psychology.

Kleist, a pupil of C. Wernicke, was ordinary professor of psychiatry and neurology from 1920 to 1950 and director of the Heilanstalt für Epileptische und Irre (Home for Epileptics and Mentally Ill). This name was later changed to Municipal and University Hospital for Psychiatry and Neurology. His main contribution "Gehirnpathologie" ("brain pathology") was based on his neurosurgical experience in a field hospital during World War I (Kleist 1934). His "moderne Hirnkartographie nach Gall" ("localization mapping of brain functioning") became well known (Kleist 1952).

Goldstein, also mentored by K. Wernicke, was the first to establish an exemplary 100-bed military hospital for brain-injured patients (Hirnverletzten-Lazarett) in Frankfurt after World War I (Goldstein 1919). Together with Adhémar Gelb, a psychologist, they saw clients in a special laboratory for psychological testing (Gelb and Goldstein 1920). It was the beginning of holistic rehabilitation when, for the first time, full treatment was offered to the traumatized soldiers comprising transdisciplinary medical, neurologic, psychiatric and neuropsychological, vocational and social rehabilitative therapy. Goldstein described the adjustment problems of patients suffering from brain dysfunction and has drawn attention to the importance of the underlying neurologic factors of their neuropsychological symptoms while relating them to constructs on brain function and dysfunction (Goldstein 1925). He explained patients' enormous emotional crises after severe traumatic brain injury (TBI) as "catastrophic reactions" and introduced neuropsychological therapeutic concepts to create an individual replacement strategy for the disabled patient according to his or her impairments including protected work trials. As Prigatano stressed, Goldstein was "concerned about the entire person" (in contrast with just considering the objective effects of brain lesion behaviour); "... Goldstein provided a human approach to rehabilitation that later reemerged in the work of Luria (1948/1963)" quote Prigatano (1999, p. 14).

Hugo Ruf, previously trained in both neurology and psychiatry, was ordinary professor of neurosurgery between 1953 and 1980 and my teacher in neurologic surgery in Frankfurt. He was a charismatic personality, characterized by his humanity and respect to patients. His clinical evaluation, face to face when assessing the entire individual's impairment of higher brain functioning, was a demonstration of this respect and of his human approach (Teasdale and Jennett 1974). He observed symptoms and psychological reactions (Goldstein 1925), and at the same time he differentiated the symptoms of psychoneurotic behavioral disturbances and paid attention to functional prognostic signs, age, intellect, family, and cultural and social-economic background. He had gained his knowledge from his great experience during World War II when he had to evaluate and diagnose complaints of soldiers who wanted to stay away from the frontiers, like, in the literature, Felix Krull by Thomas Mann (Mann 2000).

I became interested in neurorehabilitation in 1966 at the beginning of my neurosurgical training when I was first confronted with two brain-injured patients in full-stage apallic syndrome (AS) which has been established by Kretschmer in 1940 (Kretschmer 1940), at our intensive care unit (ICU). AS full stage was described by my friend Franz Gerstenbrand in 1967 as "a separate entity of AS, characterized by the classical symptoms and signs of wakefulness without awareness of self and environment and related to signs and symptoms of functional disinhibition of the upper brainstem" (Gerstenbrand 1967; von Wild, et al. 2007). The term *persistent vegetative state* (PVS) was coined only in 1972 by Jennett and Plum (Jennett and Plum 1972).

While Ruf personally took care of one male individual next door, a famous racing cyclist in his twenties suffering from severe subdural hematoma and brain swelling, he asked me to try my best in treating the second patient, a boy of 8 or 9 years with acute epidural hematoma and multiple brain contusions. Computed cranial tomography (CCT), a standard diagnostic procedure of today, was first available in Germany at our clinic in 1975 when I was being trained in neuroradiology. Neurologic monitoring of cerebral functioning was the only way—and still is the best way—to assess impaired brain functioning (Gill-Thwaites, H. and Munday, R. 1999), complemented by electro-neurophysiologic studies, for example, cortical electroencephalogram recording, EEG, evoked spinal, visual, and auditory potentials, and Evoked potentials (EPs) (Dolce and Sannita 1973; Dolce and Künkel 1975; Narayan et al. 1996; Kotchoubey, et al. 2001; Schoenle and Witzke 2004). Young in my job, I was convinced that this boy might have a realistic chance to survive and to become socially reintegrated one day, although in those days patients in AS mainly died after some weeks or months (as happened to the first patient) or ended severely disabled or handicapped. Reviewing the literature, I picked up A.R. Luria's theory of restoration of function after brain trauma (1963) and his concept of pharmacologic stimulation of impaired brain functioning, when in 1969 he described restoration of motor and sensory functioning in brain-damaged patients after neostigmine and eserine injections (see Myers 1974). The rapidity of effects was remarkable, and functions were often restored immediately after first administration of the drug. At that time, treatment of AS was mainly symptomatic as is more or less the case today (Zasler, Kreutzer, and Taylor 1991; von Wild, et al. 2007). Together with nurses and family members, we cared for the boy. The object of our daily visits was to check on the state of the patient's health, documenting the functional impairments as well as any improvements in his condition.

Physical and mental-cognitive, neurobehavioral monitoring had become a reliable and efficient method by means of the 24-point German Coma Remission Scale (CRS) score (von Wild, 2000; Voss, et al. 2000; Stepan, Haidiger, and Binder 2004), which is based on the Glasgow Coma Scale adding neurobehavioral items (Teasdale and Jennett 1974). Even the slightest clinical changes in awareness and motor functions, reported by family members, nurses, or therapists, were important indicators for progressive functional recovery of the patient or else an imminent secondary and tertiary complication, generally involving the respiratory system or being of an intestinal, urologic, neurosurgical, or orthopedic nature, respectively (von Wild 2005). Consequent posturing will help reduce spasticity and enhance the patient's sense of his own body, at the same time promote local blood circulation to prevent common pressure sores. High caloric nutrition was introduced as a routine measure. Spasticity and pathologic ossifications of the major joints were treated together with physiotherapists and orthopedists. Our early rehabilitative measures for the boy at the ICU were performed, reviewed, and discussed with nurses, physiotherapists and physical therapists, the neurologist and his assistant from the electro-neurophysiology laboratory, the neuroradiologist, microbiologist, dietician, friends from internal endocrinology and pharmacology, including the photographer; a neurophysiologist was not yet available (Myers 1974; Hildebrand 1994; Vincent, et al. 1995; Hoffmann 1998; von Wild 2000). The father, a teacher and musician, came twice a day to sit at the bedside and play the guitar, flute, or to sing songs that his son had previously enjoyed. We started auditory stimulation by playing records. For taste and smell the family brought food the boy used to love. Body massage was meant to improve local circulation and to stimulate personal perception. This was the starting point of my multidisciplinary approach (Voss, et al. 2000; Hoffmann, Düwecke, and von Wild 2001; Ortega-Suhrkamp and von Wild 2001; von Steinbüchel, et al. 2005; von Wild, et al. 2005, 2007). Family members and music therapy became part of our rehabilitation program (Aldridge and Dembski 2002; Thaut 2005). The family was always allowed to be around the boy, speaking gently and helping with washing and caring, giving him warmth all the time. Warm baths helped reduce spasticity, although at that time neurologists considered this a clear contraindication of spasticity and changed their mind only recently. The boy was relaxed by the warm bath, and the nurses and therapists were in agreement that the characteristic autonomic vegetative hyperactivity was reduced for 6 to 8 hours without any additional medication. Hence warm baths have been included in our concept until now (Ortega-Suhrkamp and von Wild 2001; von Wild, et al. 2007). The boy survived; his higher cortical functioning improved over months so that he was discharged to a rehabilitation center. About 10 years later, I heard that he underwent several orthopedic procedures to correct for contractions and spastic defective positions, which we do not see anymore nowadays, and that he graduated from secondary school and started his vocational training, corresponding with Glasgow Outcome Score (GOS) grade 4 (Jennett and Bond 1975a, 1975b). In the 1960s, I joined the electrophysiologic experimental group of G. Dolce in our hospital for the evaluation of vigilance-enhancing effects of central-acting drugs on alertness and cognition focused on comatose and apallic patients with the aid of computerized pharmaco-EEG analysis, EPs, and the contingent negative variation (CNV) (Dolce and Sannita 1973; Dolce and Künkel 1975). In the following years, electrophysiology became an important adjunct in neurorehabilitation (Dolce and Künkel 1975; Voss, et al. 2000; Kotchoubey, et al. 2001; Schoenle and Witzke 2004; Crossley, et al. 2005; von Wild, et al. 2007).

Neuromonitoring has the function of acting as a guide in decision-making in terms of differential diagnostic, definition, and therapy planning of pharmacologic intervention for methods of stimulation within the framework of physio-, ergo-, and psychotherapeutic treatment measures (Myers 1974; Zasler, Kreutzer, and Taylor 1991; von Wild, et al. 1992; Cope 1996; Francisco, et al. 2007). Positron emission tomography (PET) and functional magnetic resonance imaging (fMRI) are procedures reserved for scientific queries and specialized centers (Sturm, et al. 1997; Prigatano 1999b; Laureys 2004; Hömberg 2005; Seitz, et al. 2005; Miotto, et al. 2006). In addition to the morphologic imaging of the brain, they allow an insight into the regional quantitative brain functions at the time of examination, which enables a direct portrayal of the neuroplasticity of the human brain (Stein 1998; Sabel 1999).

To summarize, neurorehabilitation in neurotraumatology needs a transdisciplinary approach right after the impact. A-L. Christensen helped us to establish the Euroacademy (EMN) and the World Academy of Multidisciplinary Neurotraumatology (AMN) stressing the importance of neuropsychology (von Wild 2006; Lipovsec and von Wild 2007).

Present

The number of patients with permanent brain damage is growing as a result of the increased survival rate (Murray, et al. 1999; Rickels, et al. 2006). This, however, is achieved in many cases on the cost of suffering long-lasting mental-cognitive impairments (impaired self-awareness) (Prigatano 1999a), behavioral disabilities (Leonardi, et al. 2006), and handicaps (Goldstein 1919; Gelb and Goldstein 1920; Kleist 1952; Jennett and Bond 1975b; Christensen 1988, 1992; Zasler, Kreutzer, and Taylor 1991; Hellawell, Taylor, and Pentland, 1999; Lotze, et al. 1999; Murray, et al. 1999; Christensen and Uzzel 2000; Hoffmann, Düwecke, and von Wild 2001; Mazaux, et al. 2001; Ortega-Suhrkamp 2001; Stucki, et al. 2003; Stepan, Haidiger, and Binder 2004; von Steinbüchel, et al. 2005; Wilson, et al. 2005; Rickels, et al. 2006; Onoso, et al. 2007). When we prospectively analyzed the quality management of TBI in Germany in the years 2000–2002, the incidence was 332 victims per 100,000 population, whereas previous data showed an incidence of severe TBI of 9, 3, and 13, respectively, per 100,000 population (Glasgow Coma Scale score 8 and less) with an overall mortality rate of 46.6% (Rickels, et al. 2006). Forty percent to 55% of severe TBI patients died prior to hospital admission (Baethmann et al. 2000). In our series, 77% of TBI patients were hospitalized. They were assessed as severe (5%), moderate (4%), and mild (91%) brain injuries. Only 4.9% of all hospitalized TBI patients and 3.8% of all acute TBI patients (total of 6783 patients) received some kind of in-hospital rehabilitation (von Wild 2005). No single individual was treated primarily on an out-patient rehabilitation basis (Figure 9–2).

The high number of concomitant extracranial multiple organ lesions and polytrauma (N = 196 of 258) required frequent consultations during rehabilitation (Broos, Stappaerts, and Rommens 1998; Ortega-Suhrkamp 2001; von Wild 2005). They were 118 (60%) ophthalmic, 114 (58%) Ear Nose Throat (ENT) specialist 97 (50%) internal medicine, 103 (53%) microbiology, 73 (37%) neurologic, 40 (20%) neurosurgical, 62 (32%) traumatic, 16 (8%) abdominal, 15 (8%) maxillofacial surgery, 11 (6%) urologic, 6 (3%) pediatric, 2 (1%) gynecologic, and 17 (9%) other causes. Ninety-two of 196 patients (47%) were examined at least once by an ophthalmologist and an ENT specialist, other combinations account for less than 5% of all cases. One third, or 95 patients, suffered from multiple organ lesions, and one third of these (32.6%) experienced multiple complications from different organs, 14 cases only from one organ. Nine patients had respiratory tract, neurologic/neurosurgical, and other complications. Fifty-six patients were transferred to another hospital due to complications, and 16 (28.65%) were polytrauma cases. One-year outcome (N = 176 reviewed for Glasgow Outcome Scale score(GOS) showed GOS 1 = 1.7%, GOS 2 = 1.7%, GOS 3 = 21.6%, GOS 4 = 36%, and GOS 5 = 39%. These data confirm high-quality management in neurorehabilitation (Hoffmann 1998; Hildebrand 1994; von Wild 2005; Voss, et al. 2000). A total of 63% of all acute cases were reviewed after 1 year of which 883 (20.6%) individuals reported some postinjury complaints. These were 90% mild and 5% each moderate and severe TBI as in the beginning. Complaints were 60% headache, 39% each dizziness and impaired concentration, and 19% impaired mobility. Other impairments of speech, hearing, vision, and sense of smell were between 6% and 9%; other complaints were 23%. However, the possibility of out-patient neuropsychological rehabilitation was used in less than 3% of all individuals. When compared with conventional alternatives, our transdisciplinary ENNR services, attached to and part of the general neurosurgical department, show the best functional results (von Wild 2001, 2005; Rickels, et al. 2006). Our data confirm that essential cognitive impairment and neuropsychological disability will ultimately determine the final degree of handicap and performance capacity after brain damage as classified by the WHO ICIDH-2 (Stucki, et al. 2003) and its new definition of disability (Leonardi, et al. 2006).

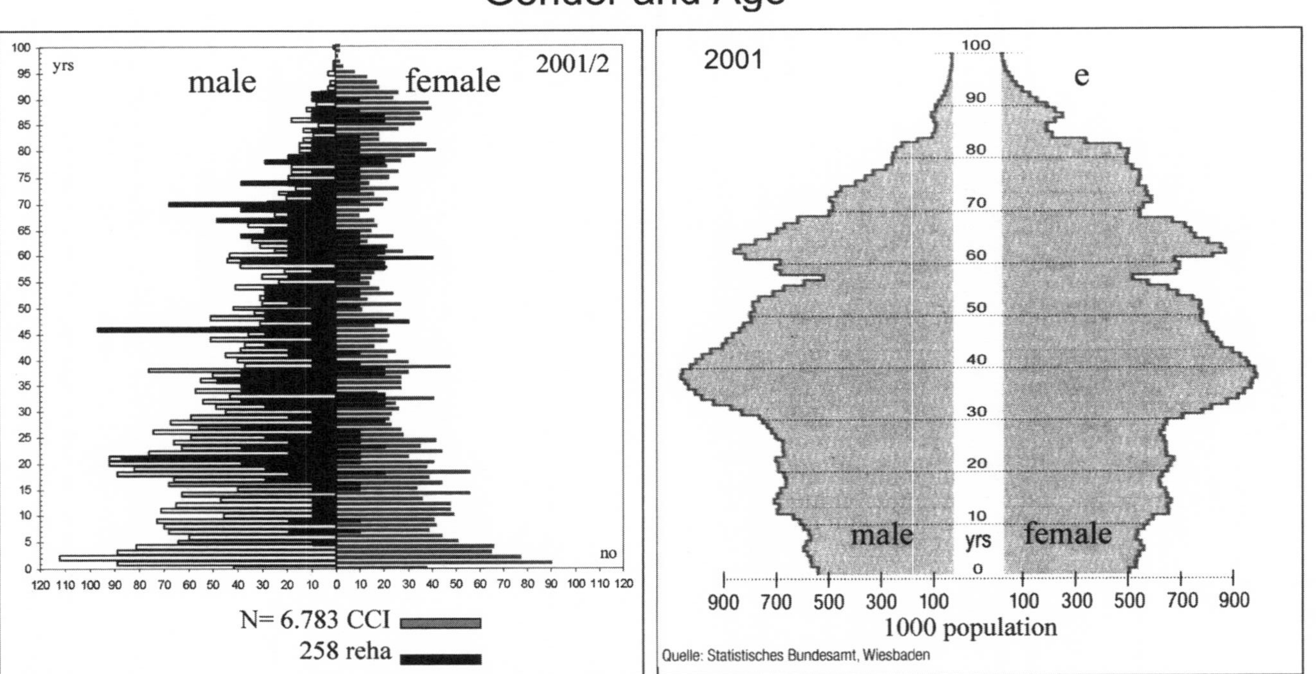

FIGURE 9–2. Age and gender of 6783 patients after acute TBI in comparison with the German population.

Functional rehabilitation has been an original task of neurosurgery from the very onset (von Wild 2001). Our actual ideas on and our concepts of neurosurgical rehabilitation of sensory-motor impairments are essentially based on the fundamental rules as formulated by the neurologist and neurological surgeon Otfried Foerster (1873–1941). He had already expressed the view that reactivation takes place via homolateral motor fields so that he recommended using movements of the healthy side to trigger corresponding movements of the paretic side. Motor skills can be improved only by specifically targeted exercises, for example, constraint induced movement therapy (forced use training), repetitive training, imagery training, functional electrical stimulation (FES), robot-assisted training of limbs, and treadmill training, which have shown high levels of evidence (Elliot et al. 2005; Foerster 1916, 1936; Hömberg 2005; von Wild 2005). Functional neuroimaging procedures give evidence of the importance of the sensory-motor network in the reorganizational ability of the brain, as was already sketched out as a model by Foerster in 1916, in form of a central network of sensitive and motor cerebral fields with diffusely distributed cortical systems of formulation of the will and a spatial presentation on the environment.

Alexander R. Luria, in much the same sense, saw the activity of the nervous system as a social organ with coordinated and adaptable cooperation between various segments of the nervous system, and consequently, constant results should always be reached under varying historical, cultural, and social conditions (Luria 1963, 1980; Christensen 1975; Prigatano 1999b). Neurorehabilitation that respects all aspects of the individual in question with its health-related social, economic, and cultural aspects can successfully be performed by means of an inter-/transdisciplinary team approach (Christensen 1998; Barnes 1999; Prigatano 1999a; Voss, et al. 2000; Stepan, Haidiger, and Binder 2004; Wilson, et al. 2005; von Wild, et al. 2007). By contrast, in emerging countries, these preconditions are still generally lacking. Neurorehabilitative measures there are guided by the given cultural, traditional, and economic situation. To reach such goals, neurosurgeons should start with an interdisciplinary team approach as early as possible after brain damage, working in close collaboration with the neuropsychologist and all other members of the team day by day, as we have been doing since 1993.

For educational purposes, we produced a scientific film on Early Rehabilitation of Higher Cortical Brain Functioning in Neurosurgery, demonstrating our personal team approach of how to humanize human skills after acute brain lesions (Prigatano 1999a), in cooperation with S. Skudelny, Media Faculty University Siegen, and Public Relation specialist F. Hernádez Meyer. This film has been presented and discussed at a number of national and intercontinental conferences. On request it is available on DVD-R (40 minutes; send e-mail to kvw@neurosci.de).

Future

According to Hildebrand (1994) Total Quality Management quote from Board of directors, Klinikum Rupprecht-Karls- University: "The quality of a hospital requires: a vision uniting all contributing agents, measurable aims, the mobilisation of all staff, a carefully co-ordinated plan of action for the hospital as a whole, perspective planning in accordance with the hospital's aims, documentation of such planning and a target-orientated evaluation of results," end of quotation We will have to respect structural and procedural results in the quality management of neurorehabilitation when assessing health-related outcome; not least to get the costly, long-term rehabilitative treatment paid by social health care authorities and care providers. In 1999, our task force including A-L. Christensen started to develop a new disease-specific instrument, the QOLIBRI, to assess cross-culturally health-related quality of life after brain injury in adults within six domains (physical condition, thinking activities, feelings and emotions, functioning in daily life, relationships and social/leisure activities, current situation and future prospects). The QOLIBRI integrates disease-specific issues of TBI individuals in the long run, for example cognition, existential aspects, and so forth, that are missing in generic tools (Berger, et al. 1999; Mazaux, et al. 2001). The validation process of the first version has been completed in 15 countries and 13 languages, demonstrating its efficacy and reliability (von Steinbüchel, et al. 2005). The QOLIBRI will be available for clinical use in 2009.

We have to accept that neuropsychological impairment and disability after brain damage turned out to ultimately define the patient's socioeconomic outcome and so his health-related quality of life. Health and health-related components of well-being are nowadays defined in terms of the World Health Organization International Classification of Functioning (ICF). These domains are described from the perspective of the body, the individual, and the society in the two basic lists: (1) body function and structures and (2) the activities and participations. Theses terms, which replace the formally used terms impairment, disability, and handicap, extend the scope of the classification to now allow positive experience to be described.

Neurorehabilitation means to set the consistent goal of taking into account the individual patient's symptoms and the complexity of the impaired brain functions to restore and humanize human skills (Christensen 1988, p. XV). This, however, will need a multidisciplinary national and intercontinental approach and exchange of knowledge, including philosophers, artists, musicians, poets, and historians like in the World Academy of Multidisciplinary Neurotraumatology (AMN) (Figure 9–3). Based on this concept, we recently established CNM, International Society of Neuro-Musicology (President M. Thaut), to come to a more scientific understanding of music therapy in neurology. We also introduced art into multidisciplinary neurotraumatology at the 5th AMN in Düsseldorf with

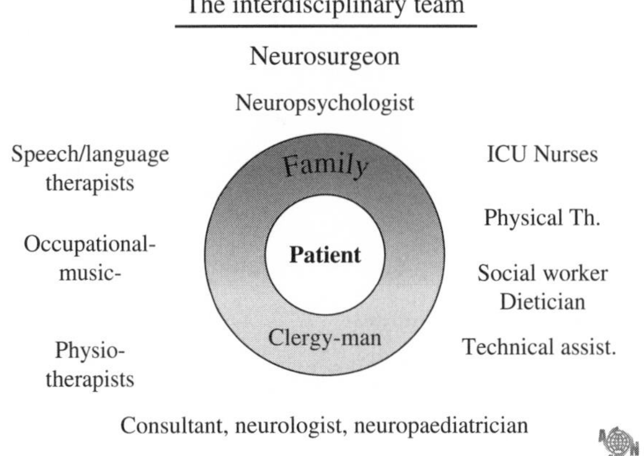

FIGURE 9–3. Interdisciplinary professional team.

lectures on esthetics, language and music, and functional imaging. Our committee of neurorehabilitation and restorative neurosurgery of the World Federation of Neurological Societies (WFNS) (von Wild 2001, 2005), in cooperation with the International Society of Reconstructive Neurosurgery (ISRN) and the "flying faculty" of the World Federation of Neuro-Rehabilitation (WFNR), have already started educational and training programs for physicians and rehabilitation personnel in accordance with the local and national authorities, where hands-on workshops have shown to be most efficient, not only in developing countries. Regular national internal and external postgraduate education specifically for all neurorehabilitation professionals as well as interdisciplinary education is essential for the future. Consequently, neurorehabilitation has to become part of a medical student's education. Neurologists and neurosurgeons, who are at present not too much interested in restoring brain functioning, will then hopefully pick up this challenging field, always respecting the cultural and economic requirements, as we are depending on a trustful cooperation with the public health authorities (Christensen 1992, 1998). The prospects are promising according to our experience. About 70% of all TBI patients can be saved from mental cognitive handicaps and return back to their social environment thanks to an adequate acute therapy and neurorehabilitation.

AMN and EMN offer the unique possibility for a multidisciplinary approach in neurorehabilitation together with neuroscientists from all fields of experimental and clinical neuroscience (von Wild 2005; Lipovsec and von Wild 2007). The aim of the two academies is the advancement of neurotraumatology in research, practical application, and teaching by organizing international congresses and participating in such events, including regional and national workshops as well as educational meetings in all fields of neurotrauma. They are committed to excellence in education through the organization of workshops and intensification of cooperation with scientific academies, societies, associations, as well as research institutions and companies who are concerned with questions related to this complex issue. The proceedings of our academies are all designed to achieve this target (von Wild 2006) (for reference, see www.world-amn.com. and www.EMN cc).

Progress in biotechnology is a challenge for future neurorehabilitation, for example neuroimplants, FES, robots, personal computer training, multisensorial stimulation procedures, nanotechnology, and gene biotechnology. We will have to take all this into consideration, inviting the representative neuroscientists to share with us their experiences and results by using our multidisciplinary approach. Preventive programs to protect from stroke, TBI, and spinal cord damage have been demonstrated to be most efficient as long as they are adapted to the cultural behaviors.

Explicatory Case Histories

Case Study 1: In 1973, during my additional training in neuroradiology in our neurosurgical clinic in Frankfurt, a very pretty private patient in her early twenties was transferred to us as an emergency with the suspected diagnosis of paraplegia, which had occurred suddenly the same day with no apparent cause. She was accompanied by her lover, the junior manager of a well-known European-wide enterprise with seat in Frankfurt. This gentleman, deeply worried, had arranged the transport of his beloved by plane from the Côte d'Azur to his hometown to have access to the diagnostic and therapeutic possibilities of a university clinic. A number of specialists awaited them accordingly. Professor Ruf was away on leave that day and was represented by the consultant on call. He as well as the neurologist confirmed the diagnosis of paraplegia with retention of urine, flabby paralysis of both legs, and complete anaesthesia corresponding to T11/12 ventral, dorsal intermittently. It was agreed to perform immediately a lumbar myelography, thus gaining cerebrospinal fluid (CSF) for the diagnosis, also a computed tomography scan of the entire spinal canal to exclude or confirm an acute inflammation, an acute episode of multiple sclerosis (MS), or a spinal extra- or intramedullary space requirement. This was when I met the young woman who seemed strangely indifferent and who suffered all examinations and possible pain with patience. Contrary to her lover, she was not surprised when I told her that we had not found any pathology, but would keep her in hospital for further observation. Already 24 hours later—nothing new had been detected clinico-neurologically—a consultant neurosurgeon appeared at the bedside, summoned from the United States for his expert opinion, also known to me for his great experience in the field of spinal neurosurgery. He examined the patient thoroughly, first in the supine position, then in the lateral and finally neurologically in the prone position: physiologic and pathologic reflexes, holding test of both legs, checking of spontaneous and nonspontaneous force of the pelvis, the pelvic floor and lower extremities musculature, and all aspects of superficial sensory function and proprioception as well as coordination. Thereafter, he had a long personal talk in private with the patient concerning her relation to the concerned businessman, with further particulars of their holiday and their sexual life. Then he outstretched his hand to help her getting up from bed, as he told us. Standing with support and the first cautious steps in front of the bed were suddenly possible by the relieved and smiling patient. It was "only" the question of a typical defense reaction of a young woman toward a co-dependent sexual relationship inconvenient to her during a luxurious holiday, an alarm reaction that had to be interpreted by her environment, showing signs of reactive somatized, neurotic, hysterical behavior. This was possible owing to our special experience in the treatment of such neurobehavioral disturbances, and appreciating the situation we could help the patient in a gentle and caring manner to solve her problems. To the astonishment of her partner, she severed their relation, and "solo" again she could leave the hospital alone and in a good mood after a few days.

Case Study 2: In the middle of the 1970s, during the weekly clinical visitation of the head physician to the men's ward of not privately insured patients, Prof. Ruf together with the other doctors observed the gait and symptoms of a middle-aged man who demonstrated a lopsided, bent-forward gait with a painfully distorted face, limping heavily and dragging the right leg with the left leg showing spastic circumduction, a combination of flabby paralysis and spasticity that did not appear to be explicable from a neurologic point of view. Because of the seemingly great back pain, the gait disturbance, and suspicion of urine retention, the admitting doctor during the night had probably suspected an upcoming so-called caudal paralysis, that is, functional disorder of certain nerve fibers descending from the spinal canal and connected with high risk and sequelae in the sense of an atypical acute disk prolapse or bleeding, and had consequently initiated the entire invasive emergency diagnostics after duly having equipped the patient with a draining bladder catheter. The lumbar ascending contrast-enhanced radiographic examination of the spinal canal and the needle of electroneurophysiologic examinations, however, did not reveal any pathologic findings including CSF diagnosis. When the ward physician underlined the discrepancy between the objective unobtrusive results of the examinations on the one hand and the complaints demonstrated out of bed on the other hand, Prof. Ruf, who had seen the x-ray images already, gave us a lesson in neurologic behavioral diagnostics. In his own, unforgettable manner and with his great experience as a neurologist and psychiatrist from World War II, when he had to examine soldiers who were simulating neurologic and psychiatric symptoms—like Felix Krull—because they could not return to the front, they did not want to go back there for anything in the world. Ruf, with his systematic way of examining, always conveyed the feeling that he took the displayed symptoms seriously, without rendering the patient ridiculous or letting him appear not trustworthy in front of others when uncovering obviously feigned functional disorders. But his way of targeted questioning and the way in which he influenced the neurologic movement and course of examination taught me, who had become experienced over the years but was still ready to learn, to esteem this knowledgeable person and his insight into pretended neurotic, hysterical misposture according to a given situation. With the patient in bed again, Prof. Ruf sat down at the bedside, in his typical way of personal attention to the patient, and questioned him calmly about his profession, his income and living, his family, his wishes and hopes, and of course the particular circumstances of his emergency admittance. The patient obviously had financial problems. He was the driver of a big truck, which he had to drive regularly from the former Eastern Block through the Iron Curtain to the Federal Republic of Germany and The Netherlands carrying different kinds of goods and then back again with industrial goods. What had happened? At a control point when going through the Austrian customs, a considerable amount of drugs had been detected among the loaded goods. They had immediately confiscated the truck and the goods, but due to his heavy pain and signs of paralysis, they accepted his plea and allowed him to travel to Frankfurt for an operation. Demonstration as cry for help. We kept him in the hospital until the smoke had cleared, "protected" and cared for him, and finally the patient could be dismissed free of complaints and with social reintegration.

Case Study 3: The 43-year-old man had a serious car accident in early winter when driving at night from his hometown Münster to Brandenburg on the then still bad country road (former GDR). The Audi overturned several times and crashed into a tree, with total damage. The patient, according to the description of his colleagues, was a highly intelligent judge at the Higher Regional Court and had been transferred from Münster to Cottbus in the wake of the reunification in the framework of cooperation between the authorities to develop a new constitutional state. Intensive medical emergency care and computed tomography examination was performed for the primarily still responsive but disoriented patient, corresponding with Glasgow Coma Scale (GCS) score 10, at the clinic in Brandenburg. One hour after admission he became unconscious, hemiplegic, pupil disturbance, GCS5. Transport by helicopter to our clinic in Münster as requested by the family was possible only at daylight. Because of brain contusion with multiple bleeding in the right frontal lobe, traumatic subarachnoid and subdural hemorrhage, and "midline shift" of 15 mm right fronto-parietal temporal decompression, removal of the bleeding and the bled brain tissue was performed immediately. A second brain surgery for decompression the following day due to rising brain pressure under intracranial pressure monitoring solved the obvious pathophysiologic problem. A third surgery was performed after 2 weeks with plastic reconstruction of the cranial vault in combination with operative treatment of the left acromioclavicular fracture (a consequence of the safety belt that has saved his life). After short- and long-term rehabilitation—consequent adjuvant outpatient neuropsychological therapy was not successful due to lack of special experience of the institution—stepwise professional reintegration (1/3 position) was attempted 9 months after the accident at the court in Münster. He himself overlooked the remarkable change of his behavior while his colleagues noticed the personality changes from the psychological consequence of his right frontal lobe damage and left frontal lobe contusion. Three years after the accident, the patient was working full-time again as prosecutor but in a sheltered way as he continued to lack insight about the extent of his residual disorders, for example, of learning and memory, of attention and concentration, of planning and goal-directed activities, judgment and perception, and sometimes losing his way. This was when he fell on his head while skiing and suffering brief unconsciousness. The observed tongue biting led to the suspicion of a first epileptic seizure but no increased readiness for cerebral seizure was noticed thereafter. Four years after his trauma, an appeal was filed to the social court against the allocation of only 50% handicap. Five years after the TBI, a university professor of neurology was asked for a social expert opinion. To me, the patient had appeared uncritical and overburdened because of his inevitable cognitive and behavioral disturbances and manifest symptoms of depression. Notwithstanding my recommendation to admit the patient first to an in-patient neurorehabilitative treatment of several weeks in a different region of Germany for his individual and detailed neuropsychological diagnostics and therapy his doctors neither cared about his needs nor provided him any chance for social reintegration. Although he passed the expert opinion as being classified as to remain in employment as a judge he had to go into retirement and his long time companion left him.

Ten years later, upon my telephone inquiry about his quality of life and social reintegration, Mr. M. said, "They dismissed me after the expert's report [socio-medical opinion] and sent me home!", which means the federal state of North-Rhine-Westphalia had no longer accepted him as a judge in public service due to his posttraumatic brain disorders, declared him unable to work, and sent him on premature retirement. In view of this, I approached Prof. H.C. Diener, the reviewing neurologist, who answered as follows: "I last reviewed Mr. M in 2002. To the employer I recommended professional reintegration of Mr. M. Why this opinion was not followed, I don't know." His companion had left him and over the years his friends and colleagues at court had turned away from him. He was living alone now in his old flat, self-sufficient, and was allowed again to drive a car himself. In playing golf—which he started after his retirement—and watching television, he finds relaxation and some pleasure in life.

I asked myself: Did all our intensive efforts for a holistic rehabilitation fail? Yes and no. What is good health-related quality of life (HRQoL)? So far there has been no specific adequate assessment tool for patients after TBI. Together with neurologists, neuropsychologists (in the beginning with Anne-Lise Christensen), medical rehabilitation and social specialists, human biologists and an epidemiologist, we neurosurgeons developed a special questionnaire in 1999 that was registered as QOLIBRI, which is the abbreviation of "quality of life following brain injury." The patient concerned is questioned personally; the first part of the questionnaire assesses satisfaction with HRQoL issues, while the second part is devoted to bothered questions. Only based on the responses to this questionnaire should future HRQoL after TBI be evaluated as the patient personally experiences it over the years.

Case Study 4: A 65-year-old, very successful businessman, a very circumspect, solicitous, and energetic kind of person, patriarchically determining the fate of his worldwide enterprise and his family, suffered a spontaneous hypertonic mass bleeding in the left cerebellar hemisphere with infiltration into the fourth ventricle and consecutive obstructive hydrocephalus (emergency CCT, neurologic clinic). He was immediately referred to the neurosurgical department of the University Clinic Münster (UKM). After exclusion of a vessel anomaly (by means of angio-CCT), an external ventricular drainage (right frontal) was immediately set in place for 7 days. During intensive medical treatment, a discrete cerebellar symptomatology (left) with continuing impairment of conscientiousness scores and mental-cognitive functions (loss of orientation to person, place, and time) was observed. Therefore I was asked by the wife, initially at a loss, for a consiliar examination with the express consent of my colleague, Prof. Hansdetlef Wassmann, the director of the clinic. My friendly relationship with the patient originated through the common interest of our two families in contemporary art. The patient collected with large expert knowledge informal paintings of the Münster artist Wolfgang Troschke, who had meanwhile become a close friend of the family. On the evening of the operation, the patient did neither recognize me in the ICU nor his wife. Apart from typical neck stiffness and distinct bewilderment and drowsiness, I did not find further functional disorders. It was however remarkable that above the patient, in his field of vision, a typical Troschke aquarelle painting (approximately 50 × 40 cm) in wonderfully bright colors had been hung up by the wife, suspended from the metal frame for fixing infusion bottles. It was one of the favorite paintings of the patient. And in fact, the first signs of orderly orientation by the patient appeared 2 days later, triggered by recognizing this aquarelle painting, and only through this picture, a little deferred in time, he also recognized his wife sitting up with him. Knowing her husband well, she had wisely relied on the awakening effect of a cherished work of art in the strange environment of an intensive care unit, which he might at first perceive as chaotic, and the organizing force of targeted emotions. I confirmed the instituted therapy and after the acute treatment of the cognitive disorders recommended early neurosurgical rehabilitation in my special department, but this was first refused by the patient.

Four weeks after the event, I saw the patient in my office, accompanied by his wife. He reported a 2-week retrograde amnesia; he appeared depressive, full of anxiety, depressed, and disconcerted. Orientation, drive, and affective behavior at the family level were reported normal. I could persuade the patient to undergo a first neuropsychologic examination by Ms. Birgit Kemper, PhD, the head neuropsychologist of my special department for early rehabilitation in neurosurgery that I had developed in Germany in 1993. Whereas other rehabilitation attempts, which had been proposed at remote places for personal reasons, could not be realized, the patient finally accepted an out-patient treatment by Dr. Kemper. Below is her medical evidence and treatment report, and herewith I wish to express my sincere thanks to her for the professional management of this patient. Owing to her help and patience, the patient today after 10 years is still optionally active in his company by word and deed, and is rejoicing in his health-related quality of life by actively participating in his social environment including critical observation of the art market.

The following is Dr. Kemper's report:

After discharge from hospital he experienced unanticipated difficulties at his work. He needed more time for doing routine activities. He complained of forgetting names of well-known customers. He could not remember telephone conversations in detail. He had difficulties in understanding newspaper articles and complained of attention problems in longer conversation with customers. He began to observe every bodily change and feared to suffer again a sudden cerebral haemorrhage. He could not stop to ponder about his health and his future, felt very ashamed of his failures, tried to hide his difficulties and avoided to meet people. He stopped his manifold social activities as a respected businessman in his field and asked himself if life was still meaningful. He could not understand the reasons for the decline of his intellectual capacities and his limited toughness. In summary, the clinical interview (HAMD) and the self-rating of the patient (BDI) showed considerable *depressive symptoms of clinical relevance and moderate problems in psychosocial adjustment.*

The patient underwent a brief neuropsychological examination. During assessment he realized his cognitive deficits and showed a catastrophic reaction. The patient's speech was fluent. An aphasia screening (token-test) showed no abnormal test result, but he had definite difficulties in the word fluency task (Benton). Subtests of the German Aachener Aphasia test battery (AAT) revealed no difficulties in naming, reading and writing. The premorbid IQ measured by a vocabulary (MWT-B) test ranged within normal limits. The application of a computerized basic attention diagnostic (TAP) primarily demonstrated slow reaction times in the alertness and go/no-go test. The patient was not able to perform a complex divided attention task. Tests of memory function revealed normal results in verbal span forward and backward. The results of the auditory verbal (AVLT) and non-verbal learning test (DCS) demonstrated severe deficits in all test parameters. The patient already showed severe impairments in learning the memory materials and in visual retention (Benton-Test). After the patient received feedback about the test results some weeks later he agreed to an out-patient neuropsychological therapy. The patient was very outspoken about his problems, but he could not believe that the kind of therapy we recommended might really help him.

Attention and memory problems were the most prominent cognitive deficits. Because of the striking depressive symptoms and problems in psychosocial adjustment, first of all we focus on a psychotherapeutic approach in order to develop a therapeutic alliance and to allow the patient to experience his personal suffering, sadness, frustration and ambivalence towards the therapy. The genesis of the patient's cognitive problems was discussed. He began to speak about his social fears and his tendency to social isolation, which was unusual for him. He described himself as a communicative and always socially engaged personality. He mentioned his questions whether he really had a life worth living, but he hesitated to engross these thoughts during psychotherapeutic sessions. He developed an interest in improving cognitive abilities, because he realized charges and restriction during his work in his company. A computerized cognitive rehabilitation program motivated the patient to deal with his cognitive problems. Realizing intact cognitive functions, the therapist could encourage him to speak more openly about his cognitive problems in activities of daily living. He developed a better acceptance to learn compensation techniques (e.g., use of a memory notebook, use of memo held during speeches and conferences, computerized working schedule) and was more motivated to implement these techniques in his everyday life. The entire therapy took about 6 months. It was remarkable that the patient kept all appointments with the therapists in spite of his beginning ambivalence. The challenge for the therapist was to manage the patient's avoidance to speak about his emotional state. We believe that the acceptance of his avoidance, which is a kind of self-protection from emotional overwhelming and the supporting character of psychotherapeutic interventions without time pressure, enabled the patient to participate in the therapy for 6 months. Although he still struggled with cognitive deficits after finishing therapy, he had an eye for his preserved abilities. From the background of his life achievements in his business career and his family life, he began to accept a reduced workload and level of competency in his older age. He was successful in changing his lifestyle to be compatible with his cognitive impairments and realized that he can do things which make his life worth living.

This case is an exemplary demonstration of the fact that we neurosurgeons should be aware that good neurologic recovery of motor functioning after acute brain lesions is not at all equivalent to normal functioning of the brain.

All four patients illustrate my neurosurgical approach of today for rehabilitation of neuropsychological behavioral disorders. The personal talk, with calm and if possible in private, as well as the thorough anamnesis is the key to a comprehensive diagnosis by the experienced doctor. Neurorehabilitation involves many professionals from different fields of experimental research and clinical application. Only a transdisciplinary approach will help reach the target of restoring impaired higher cortical brain functioning to humanize human skills in the sense of Luria and A-L. Christensen, the voice of our days, stressing the importance of neuropsychology.

References

Aldridge, D. and Dembski, M. (Hrsg) 2002. *Music Therapy World Musiktherapie – Diagnostik und Wahrnehmung*. Private Universität Witten-Herdecke GmbH.

Baethmann, A., Wirth, A., Chapuis, D., Schlesinger-Raab, A., and Study Group. 2000. A System Analysis of the Pre- and Early Hospital Care in Severe Head Injury in Bavaria. *Restorative Neurology and Neuroscience* 16:173.

Barnes, M.P. 1999. Rehabilitation after Traumatic Brain Injury. *British Medical Bulletin* 55(4):927–943.

Berger, E., Leven, F., Pirente, N. Boullion B, Neugebauer E. 1999. Quality of Life after Traumatic Brain Injury: A Systematic Review of the Literature. *Restorative Neurology and Neuroscience* 14:93–102.

Bouillon, B., Raum, M., Fach, H Buchheister, B., Lefering, R., Menzel, M., and Klug, N. 1999. The Incidence and Outcome of Severe Brain Trauma Design and First Results of an Epidemiological Study in an Urban Area. *Restorative Neurology and Neuroscience* 14:85–92.

Boyeson, M.G. and Jones, J.L. 1996. Theoretical Mechanisms of Brain Plasticity and Therapeutic Implications. In: Horn, L.J. and Zasler, N.D. (eds.). *Medical Rehabilitation of Traumatic Brain Injury*. Philadelphia: Hanley and Belfus Inc, pp. 77–102.

Broos, P.L., Stappaerts, K.H., Rommens, P.M. 1998 Polytrauma in Patients of 65 and Over: Injury Patters and Outcome. *International Surgery* 73(2):119–122.

Christensen, A.-L. (ed.). 1975. *Luria's Neuropsychological Investigation. Manual and Test Materials*. New York: Spectrum.

Christensen, A.-L. 1988. Preface. In: Christensen, A.-L. and B. Uzzell (eds.). *Neuropsychological Rehabilitation*. Boston, Dordrecht, London: Kluwer Academic Publishers, p. XV.

Christensen, A.-L. 1992. Outpatient Management and Outcome in Relation to Work in Traumatic Brain Injury Patients. *Scandinavian Journal of Rehabilitation Medicine – Supplement* 26:34–42.

Christensen, A.-L. 1998. Sociological and Cultural Aspects in Postacute Neuropsychological Rehabilitation. *Journal of Head Trauma Rehabilitation* October; 13(5):79–86.

Christensen, A.-L. and Uzzel, B. (eds.). 2000. *International Handbook of Neuropsychological Rehabilitation*. New York, Boston, Dordrecht, London, Moscow: Kluwer Academic/Plenum Publishers.

Cope, D.N. 1996. Psychopharmacological Aspects of Traumatic Brain Injury. In: Horn, L.J. and Zasler, N. (eds.). *Medical Rehabilitation of Traumatic Brain Injury*. Philadelphia: Hanley and Belfus Inc., pp. 573–612.

Crossley, M., Shiel, A., Wilson, B. 2005. Monitoring Emergence from Coma Following Severe Brain Injury in an Octogenarian Using Behavioural Indicators, Electrophysiological Measures, and Metabolic Studies: A Demonstration of the Potential for Good Recovery in Older Adult. *Brain Injury* 19(9):729–737.

Dolce, G. and Künkel, H. 1975. CEAN Computerized EEG Analysis. Stuttgart: Fischer.

Dolce, G., Sannita, W. 1973. CNV-like Negative SHIFT in Deep Coma. *Electroencephalography and Clinical Neurophysiology* 34:647–650.

Elliott, L., Coleman, M., Shiel, A., Wilson, B.A., Badwan, D., Menon, D., Pickard, J., 2005. Effect of Posture on Levels of Arousal and Awareness in Vegetative and Minimally Conscious State Patients: A Preliminary Investigation. *Journal of Neurology, Neurosurgery and Psychiatry* 76:298–299.

Edinger, L. 1900. Hirnanatomie und Psychologie. *Berliner Medizinische Wochenschrift* 37:561–564; 600–604.

Edinger, L. 1908. *Der Anteil der Funktion an der Entstehung der Nervenkrankheiten.* Wiesbaden: J.F. Bergmann.

Foerster, O. 1916. Therapie der Motilitätsstörungen bei den Erkrankungen des zentralen Nervensystems. In: Vogt, H. (ed.). *Handbuch der Therapie der Nervenkrankheiten, Bd 2. Symptomatische Therapie und Therapie der Organneurosen. Krankheitsbilder und deren Behandlung.* Jena: Fischer, pp. 860–940.

Foerster, O. 1936 Übungstherapie. In: Bumke, O. and Foerster, O. (eds.). *Handbuch der Neurologie Bd. 8.* Berlin: Springer, pp. 316–414.

Francisco, G.E., Walker, W.C., Zasler, N.D., and Bouffard, M.H. 2007. Pharmacological Management of Neurobehavioral Sequelae of Traumatic Brain Injury: A Survey of Current Physiatric Practice. *Brain Injury* 21(10):1007–1014.

Gelb, A. and Goldstein, K. (eds.). 1920. *Psychologische Analysen hirnpathologischer Fälle.* Leipzig: J.A. Barth.

Gerstenbrand, F. (ed.). 1967. Das Traumatische Apallische Syndrom. *Klinik, Morphologie, Pathosphysiologie und Behandlung.* New York: Springer-Verlag Wien.

Gill-Thwaites, H. and Munday, R. 1999. The Sensory Modality Assessment and Rehabilitation Technique (SMART): A Comprehensive and integrated assessment and Treatment Protocol for the Vegetative State and Minimally Responsive Patient. *Neuropsychological Rehabilitation* 9(3/4):305–320.

Goldstein, K. (ed.). 1919. *Die Behandlung, Fürsorge und Begutachtung der Hirnverletzten (Zugleich ein Beitrag zur Verwendung psychologischer Methoden in der Klinik).* Leipzig: FCW Vogel.

Goldstein, K. 1925. Das Symptom, seine Entstehung und Bedeutung für unsere Auffassung vom Bau und von der Funktion des Nervensystems. *Archiv für Psychiatrie und Nervenkrankheiten* 76:84–108.

Hellawell, D.J., Taylor, R.T., and Pentland, B. 1999. Cognitive and Psychological Outcome Following Moderate or Severe Traumatic Brain Injury. *Brain Injury* 13(7): 489–504.

Hildebrand, H. 1994. Total Quality Management, quote from Board of directors, Klinikum Rupprecht-Karls- University. Published by Vorstand der Rupprechts-Karl.Universität of Heidelberg.

Hömberg, V. 2005. Evidence Based Medicine in Neurological Rehabilitation—a Critical Review. *Acta Neurochirurgica* (Suppl) 93:3–14.

Hoffmann, B., Düwecke, C., and von Wild, K.R.H. 2001. Neurological and Social Long-Term Outcome After Early Rehabilitation Following Traumatic Brain Injury. 5 Years Report on 240 TBI Patients *Acta Neurochirugica* (Suppl) 79:37–39.

Hoffmann, H. 1846. *Struwwelpeter.* German first edition 1846; First English edition 1948. Germany: Universitätsbibliothek Frankfurt am Main.

Hoffmann, H. 1998. Leitlinien in der Medizin (eine vornehme, aber risikobehaftete Aufgabe der medizinischen Fachgesellschaften). *Arzt und Krankenhaus* 9:193–201.

Jennett, B. and Bond, M. 1975a. Assessment of Outcome after Severe Brain Damage. A Practical Scale. *Lancet* 1(7905): 480–484.

Jennett, B. and Bond, M. 1975b. Outcome after Severe Brain Damage. A Practical Scale. *Lancet* I:634–637.

Jennett, B. and Plum, F. 1972. Persistent Vegetative State after Brain Damage. A Syndrome in Search for a Name. *Lancet* 1:734–737.

Kleist, K. 1934. Gehirnpathologie. *Vornehmlich auf Grund der Kriegserfahrungen.* Leipzig: Johannes Ambrosius Barth.

Kleist, K. 1952. Brain and Psyche. *Journal of Nervous and Mental Diseases* 116:776–782.

Kotchoubey, B., Jetter, U., Lang, S., Baales, R., Semmler, A., Mezger, G., Schmalohr, D., Schneck, M., Birbaumer, N. 2001. Brain Potentials in Human Patients with Extremely Severe Diffuse Brain Damage. *Neuroscience Letters* 301:27–40.

Kretschmer, E. 1940. *Das apallische Syndrom. Zeitschrift für die gesamte Neurologie und Psychiatrie* 169:576–579.

Laureys, S. 2004. Functional Neuroimaging in the Vegetative State. *NeuroRehabilitation* 19:335–341.

Leonardi, M., Bickenbach, J., Ustun, T.B. et al. on behalf of the MHADIE Consortium 2006. The Definition of Disability: What Is in a Name. *Lancet* 368:1219–1220.

Lipovsec, M. and von Wild, K. 2007. *A Brief History of EMN.* China press. Available at zt1611@sohu.com.

Lotze, M., Laubis-Hermann, U., Topka, H., Erb, M., and Grodd, W. 1999. Reorganization in the primary motor cortex after spinal cord injury. A functional Magnetic Resonance (fMRI) study. *Restorative Neurology and Neuroscience* 14:183–187.

Luria, A.R. 1963. *Restoration of Function after Brain Injury.* Oxford, London, Paris: Pergamon.

Luria, A.R. et al. 1969. Quote in Myers, R.D. 1974. *Handbook of Drug and Chemical Stimulation of the Brain.* New York: Van Nostrand Reinhold Company.

Luria, A.R. 1980. *Higher Cortical Functions in Man* (2nd ed.). New York: Basic Books.

Mann, T. 2000. *Bekenntnisse des Hochstaplers Felix Krull.* Frankfurt: Fischer.

Mazaux, J.M., Croze, P, Quintard, B, Rouxel, L., Joseph, P.A., Richer, E., Debelleix, X., et al. 2001. Satisfaction of Life and Late Psycho-Social Outcome after Severe Brain Injury: A Nine-Year Follow-up Study in Aquitaine. *Acta Neurochirurgica* (Suppl) 79:49–51.

Miotto, E.C., Savage, C.R., Evans, J.J., Wilson, B.A., Martins, M.G., Iaki, S., Amaro, E. 2006. Bilateral Activation of the Prefrontal Cortex after Strategic Semantic Cognitive Training. *Human Brain Mapping* 27:288–295.

Murray, G.D., Teasdale, G.M., Braakman, R., Cohadon, F., Dearden, M., Iannotti, F., Karimi, A., et al. 1999. The European Brain Injury Consortium Survey of Head Injuries. *Acta Neurochirurgica* (Wien) 141: 223–236.

Narayan, R.K., Wilberger Jr, J.E, Povlishock, J.T. (eds.). 1996 *Neurotrauma*, Chapters 30–32, *Monitoring and Treatment.* New York: McGraw-Hil Companies Inc., USA, pp. 413–470.

Onoso, G., Ciurea, A.V., Rotarescu, V., Anghelescu, A., Mihaescu, A., Mardare, D.C., Chendreanu, C., Haras, M. 2007. The Clinical Expertise of the Emergency Hospital "Bagdasar-Arseni" in the Complex Rehabilitation of Post-Traumatic Brain Injury Patients. *Romanian Neurosurgery* XIV(1):65–73.

Ortega-Suhrkamp, E. 2001. Early Functional Outcome in Isolated (TBI) and Combined (CTBI) Brain Injury. *Acta Neurochirurgica* (Suppl) 79:31–32.

Ortega-Suhrkamp, E. and von Wild, K.R.H. 2001. Standards of Neurological-Neurosurgical Rehabilitation. *Acta Neurochirurgica* (Suppl) 79:11–79.

Prigatano, G.P. 1999 a *Principles of Neuropsychological Rehabilitation.* New York, Oxford: Oxford University Press, p. 12.

Prigatano, G.P. 1999 b. Working with Interdisciplinary Rehabilitation Teams. In: Prigatano, G.P. (ed.). *Principles of Neuropsychological Rehabilitation.* New York, Oxford: Oxford University Press, pp. 228–243.

Rickels, E., von Wild, K., Wenzlaff, P., Bock, W.J. (eds.). 2006. Schädel-Hirn-Verletzung Epidemiologie und Versorgung. *Ergebnisse einer prospektiven Studie.* München: Zuckschwerdt Verlag.

Ritz, A., Emerich, R., Jacobi, G., and Thorbeck, R. 1982. Prognostische Wertigkeit der Glasgow Coma Scale bei Schädelhirntraumen im Kindesalter (GCS Adopted for Children and Adolescents). In: V. von Loewenich (ed.). *Pädiatrische Intensivmedizin.* Stuttgart: Thieme Verlag, pp. 19–25.

Sabel, B.A. 1999. Neurotrauma and Plasticity. A Conference of the German BMBF-Research Initiative. *Restorative Neurology and Neuroscience* 14:209–236.

Schoenle, P.W. and Witzke, W. 2004. How Vegetative is the Vegetative State? Preserved Semantic Processing in VS Patients – Evidence from N 400 Event-Related Potentials. *NeuroRehabilitation* 19:329–334.

Seitz, R.J., Kleiser, R., and Bütefisch, C.M. 2005. Reorganization of Cerebral Circuits in Human Lesion. *Acta Neurochirurgica* (Suppl) 93:65–70.

Sharma, H.S. 2007. 4th Global College of Neuroprotection and Neuroregeneration. *Expert Review of Neurotherapeutics* 7(6):595–578.

Stein, D.G. 1998. Brain Injury and Theories of Recovery. In: Goldstein L.B. (ed). *Restorative Neurology.* Armonk, N.Y.: Futura Publishing Company, pp. 1–24.

Stepan, Ch., Haidiger, G., and Binder, H. 2004. Problems of Clinical Assessment of Patients with Apallic Syndrome/Vegetative State Represented by Rehabilitation Scores – a Survey. *Journal of Neurology, Neurosurgery and Psychiatry* 5(3):14–22.

Stucki, G., Wert, T., and Cieza, A. 2003. Value and Application of the ICF in Rehabilitation Medicine. *Disablity and Rehabilitation* 25:628–634.

Sturm, W., Willmes, K., DeSimone, A., Hesselmann, V., Specht, K., Herzog, H., Krause, B. 1997. *Funktionelle Neuroanatomie der Aufmerksamkeitsaktivierung (Alterness). Eine PET-Studie.* Magdeburg, März: Jahrestagung der DGNKN.

Teasdale, H. and Jennett, B. 1974. Assessment of Coma and Impaired Consciousness. A Practical Scale. *Lancet* 2:81–84.

Thaut, M.H. 2005. Neurologic Music Therapy (N.M.T.) in Sensory Motor Rehabilitation, pp. 137–164; N.M.T. in Speech and Language Rehabilitation, pp. 165–178; N.M.T. in Cognitive Rehabilitation, pp. 179–201. In: Thaut, M.H. (ed.). *Rhythm, Music, and the Brain. Scientific Foundations and Clinical Application.* New York: Routledge Taylor & Francis Group.

Thorwald, J. (ed) 1962. *Macht und Geheimnis der frühen.* München: Ärzte Droemer.

Vincent, J.L., Bihari, D.J., Suter, P.M. et al. 1995. The Prevalence of Nosocomial Infection in Intensive Care Units in Europe. Results of the European Prevalence of Infection in Intensive Care (EPIC) Study. EPIC International Advisory Committee. *Journal of the American Medical Association* 274(8):639–644.

von Steinbüchel, N., Petersen, C., Bullinger, M. and the QOLIBRI group. 2005. Assessment of Health-Related Quality of Life in Persons after Traumatic Brain Injury—Development of the QOLIBRI, a Specific Measure. *Acta Neurochirurgica* (Suppl) 93:43–49.

von Wild, K , Gerstenbrand, F., Dolce, G., et al. 2007 Guidelines for quality management of Apallic Syndrome/Vegetative State. *European Journal of Trauma and Emergency Surgery* 3:268–292.

von Wild, K., Simons, P., Schoeppner, H. 1992. Effect of Pyritinol on EEG and SSEP in Comatose Patients in the Acute Phase of Intensive Care Therapy. *Pharmacopsychiatry* 25:157–165.

von Wild, K.R.H. 2000 Perioperative Management of Severe Head Injuries in Adults. In: Schmiedek, H.H. (ed.). *Operative Neurosurgical Techniques* (4th ed.). Vol. 1. Philadelphia: W. B. Saunders Company, pp. 45–60.

von Wild, K.R.H. 2001. Neurorehabilitation – a Challenge for Neurosurgeons in the 21st Century – Concepts and Visions of the WFNS-Committee on Neurosurgical Rehabilitation. *Acta Neurochirurgica* (Suppl) 79:3–10.

von Wild, K.R.H. (ed.). 2002. *Functional Rehabilitation in Neurosurgery and Neurotraumatology*. Wien: Springer-Verlag.

von Wild, K.R.H. 2005. Neurorehabilitation following craniocerebral trauma. *European Journal of Trauma* No. 4:344–358.

von Wild, K.R.H. (ed.). 2005. Re-Engineering of the Damaged Brain and Spinal Cord. *Evidence-Based Neurorehabilitation.* Wien: Springer-Verlag.

von Wild, K.R.H. (2006) Multidisciplinary Treatment of Trauma – the AMN. In: Kanno, T. and Kato, Y. (eds). *Minimally Invasive Neurosurgery and Multidisciplinary Neurotraumatology.* Tokyo: Springer, pp. 240–250.

Voss, A., von Wild, K.R.H., and Prosiegel, M. (eds.). 2000. Qualitätsmanagement in der Neurologischen und Neurochirurgischen Frührehabilitation. München, Berne, Wien, New York: W. Zuckschwerdt.

Wilson, B.A., Emslie, H., Quirk, K., Evans, J.J., and Watson, P. (2005). A Randomised Control Trial to Evaluate a Paging System for People with Traumatic Brain Injury. *Brain Injury* 19:891–894.

Zasler, N.D., Kreutzer, J.S., and Taylor, D. 1991. Coma Stimulation and Coma Recovery: A Critical Review. *NeuroRehabilitation* 1:33–40.

10

The Bedside Neuropsychological Examination and Luria's Influence

Anne-Lise Christensen and George P. Prigatano

A "bedside" neuropsychological examination implies that two clinical conditions are present. First, the patient is "in bed" and therefore is during the acute stages after the onset of their neurologic condition. Second, the patient is not in a position to do extensive "testing" and therefore must be examined in a manner that briefly but reliably reveals the nature of their higher cortical (or at least, higher integrative) brain dysfunctions. The information becomes useful for diagnostic purposes as well as for patient management.

Luria's (1966) theoretical perspectives on the higher cortical functions as emergent psychological skills dependent on overlapping functional systems of the brain suggested that focal brain lesions would alter higher cortical functions in fairly predictable ways. This led to examination procedures that were modified to meet the patient's clinical state that were guided by Luria's theoretical understanding concerning the nature of higher cortical functions in man. The examination procedures were first introduced to the neuropsychological community by Christensen (1975). The first part of this chapter provides a historical context for the Luria approach as applied to the bedside neuropsychological examination. Next, a summary description of Luria's model is given concerning three major functional components underlying higher cerebral functions. This is followed by a clinical description of how this model and the examination procedures are then used to provide a *qualification* of disturbed as well as preserved functions in clinical practice.

The next section of this chapter describes how *Luria's Neuropsychological Investigation* (Christensen 1975/1979) influenced the "bedside examination" that is used at the Barrow Neurological Institute at St. Joseph's Hospital and Medical Center in Phoenix, Arizona. This section attempts to describe what could be broadly called one American modification of the Luria approach to the neuropsychological examination procedures. This section introduces the BNI Screen for Higher Cerebral Functions and how information obtained from this screening test provides both qualitative and quantitative information that is helpful for diagnosis and patient management. Examples are given regarding how this information can be used for research purposes. This section also includes a brief discussion of the importance of the preliminary conversation with the patient as Luria first outlined it in his work.

The final section of this chapter includes comments from both authors regarding how the Lurian approach has influenced the clinical neuropsychological examination as practiced in different parts of the world.

The Lurian approach to the bedside neuropsychological examination: Historical context, reflections, and clinical observations

The acceptance of neuropsychology as the profession to illuminate and treat the "Mind" integrated among the professions working in neurologic and neurosurgical university departments has a history evidencing the development toward an accentuated technically complex, multidisciplinary, holistic procedure, which has proved successful in the handling of brain injury. In the first part, the description will mainly concentrate on the development within European countries.

However, the very first and important influence came from the United States, where basic surgical techniques were developed for operating on the brain. The surgeon behind this was Dr. Harvey Cushing, a pupil of William Halstead and later professor at Harvard Medical School, who became the world's leading teacher of neurosurgeons in the first decades of the 20th century. It was under his influence that neurosurgery became a new and autonomous surgical discipline, and it was to his credit that wounded soldiers during World War I could be operated on at the battle frontiers. This was first true for German soldiers who as soon as possible after acute treatment in the battlefields were transferred to the neurologist Kurt Goldstein's Frankfurt hospital for further treatment and rehabilitation, described in his book *Aftereffects of Brain Injuries during War* (1942).

The experiences described in his book were based on collaboration between Kurt Goldstein and the psychologist Adhemar Gelb. The soldiers were examined neurologically and psychologically with tests, developed specially for the purpose of detecting organic disturbances after which their rehabilitation took place either in a school or a workshop that were part of the hospital. Kurt Goldstein also collaborated with the members of the contemporary influential psychoanalytic school in Frankfurt in his attempts to understand the behavior and functioning of the brain-injured persons and to support them in regaining abilities of living their lives. He described the behavioral problems he observed as "protective mechanisms" developed in the organism's attempts to overcome an anxiety so overwhelming that it had the character of a catastrophe (Goldstein 1934/1995, 1983).

The action of the British team during World War II followed the same procedure. Hugh Cairns, who had worked with Cushing, was the neurosurgeon operating at the frontier and Ritchie Russell and Freda Newcombe the neurologist and the neuropsychologist performing the examinations and the rehabilitation at Radcliffe Infirmary in Oxford. The long-term results of their work were published by Freda Newcombe in the article "Very Late Outcome after Focal Wartime Brain Wounds" (1996).

In the Soviet Union, also during World War II, A.R. Luria was appointed the director of a rehabilitation hospital in the Urals, where he made use of experiences from his early work at the Bourdenko Neurosurgical Institute in his development of rehabilitation programs for the soldiers, described in his books *Restoration of Function After Brain Injury* (1963), *Traumatic Aphasia* (1947/1970), and the case history *A Man with a Shattered World* (1972).

In the years after the great wars, the needs for neurosurgical intervention in cases of brain injury became manifested in the growing amount of casualties from traffic accidents being referred to neurosurgical departments. The lives of these patients were saved, the neurosurgical departments were filled up, resulting in needs for a prolonged intensive care treatment, causing a general interest in the patients' prospects for early and effective improvement of their functional abilities.

> It was in the late eighties and early nineties that the increasing morbidity and mortality of Traumatic Brain Injury (TBI) together with the growing complexity of management compelled some neurosurgeons in Germany to assemble a group of professionally oriented individuals with an interest in the problem. The idea was to deal with all facets of brain injury at an academic level involving not only medically trained people but also any other experts who, by the nature of their work, had a certain relevancy in the field of neurotrauma—a project which could only be done through a holistic approach. (Lipovsek and von Wild 2007)

The quotation above stems from the statement that defined the founding of the Euroacademy for Multidisciplinary Neurotraumatology (EMN), which was established in 1994 with Prof. Klaus von Wild as its first president. There were no neuropsychologists among the founders of the society but some neurosurgical departments, among them the one developed by Prof. Richard Malmros at the University Hospital in Aarhus, Denmark, established the first position in 1961 for a neuropsychologist who became an important partner in the team taking part in the clinical practice of the departments; the benefits of the neuropsychological expertise became evident and resulted in a very fruitful collaboration regarding both clinical practice and research (Christensen 2002).

The domain of EMN was described: "From the site of the accident to the reintegration of the patient." In the following years, countries outside Europe expressed interest in joining the society leading to the founding in 1998 of the World Academy of Multiprofessional Neurotraumatology (AMN) including Asia and North and South America; the first president of this society was the neuropsychologist Prof. George P. Prigatano.

For the neuropsychologist participating as a member of the brain-injury team, this meant further possibility to develop new approaches, such as various evaluation scales, the first developed specifically for brain injury, The European Brain Injury Questionnaire (EBIQ; Teasdale, et al. 1997), but also new methods, such as to perform evaluations already at the patient's bedside, thereby contributing to earlier and more specialized treatment.

Luria's methodology as used at the bedside

The following is a description of the bedside examination focusing on the Luria methodology, which in the neurosurgical department at Aarhus University Hospital proved its special value in the evaluation of patients at a very early state, in line with the statement by Luria that it had been a central theme in his development as a psychologist (1) to take part in the creation of an *objective* approach to behavior, emphasizing real-life events and (2) to solve the central theme: the conflict between the explanatory, physiologic psychology and the descriptive, phenomenological psychology of the higher psychological functions.

Performing an evaluation during the early stage, when the patient may be barely conscious, is based on Luria's basic notion of brain function as related to a unity of three major functional components, in Vygotsky's term "units" (Luria 1970).

The first unit regulates the general activity of the cortex in accordance with the actual demands confronting the organism much in correspondence with Moruzzi and Magoun's earlier publication (1949); it is located in the reticular formation and other parts of the brain stem. If injury occurs to some part of this structure, a marked diminution of wakefulness can be observed together with a disruption of the ability of the cortex to respond selectively to the stimuli impinging on the brain. The inclusion of the medial zones of the cerebral hemispheres in this unit also means that inclinations and emotions are controlled from this unit and consequently may be affected.

The second major functional division of the brain is located in the posterior parts of the cortex, behind the postcentral gyrus. It processes and stores information. The systems of this second unit include the primary areas for sensory information for visual (occipital), auditory (temporal), and general sensory (parietal) regions. Also, a secondary zone exists, analyzing the information further, as well as a tertiary zone where the data from different sources are combined, building various more specific organizations.

The third major division, the unit comprising the frontal lobes, is involved in the formation of intentions and programs or plans for behavior.

All three units are hierarchical in structure. In the second and third units, at least three cortical zones are built one above another, the primary zone of each receiving impulses from or sending impulses to the periphery, spreading excitation gradually and thus modulating the whole state of the nervous system. The secondary zone processes information or prepares programs, and the tertiary zone carries out and controls the program and is therefore responsible for the most complex forms of mental activity.

Each unit has special systems belonging to it. In the first unit, disturbances in the systems of instinctive "food-getting" and sexual behavior may be due to lesions in the brain stem and archicortex. These are considered to be the first and most fundamental source of activation of the brain; the second source has to do with the orienting reflex. For example, disturbances that have the character of a generalized lack of tonus are attributable to the lower regions of the reticular formation, whereas phasic disturbances are connected with higher regions of the brain stem. The third source of activation has to do with the coordinated movements and actions made possible by the descending and ascending connections of the powering system of the reticular formation of the brain stem, with the thalamus and the higher levels of the cortex responsible for the formation of intentions and plans.

The disturbances in consciousness related to disturbances in the central medial and lower parts of the brain are accompanied by varying degrees of affective, emotional, and motivational changes and characteristic defects of memory. A general asthenia is present; reactions become slow, fatigue develops rapidly; the voice may become "aphonic"; the emotional tone is depressed or indifferent. Sometimes anxiety develops and can take an acute course, at times leading to catastrophic proportions, earlier described as an essential element in Goldstein's *The Organism* (1934/1995).

The basic knowledge of these three units, their primary and secondary areas, and their implications for the behavior and reactions of the patient creates the background for the clinical observation of the brain-injured person, a knowledge that is of utmost importance for the examiner at the early state where the patient is confined to bed.

In Luria's last book, *The Making of Mind*, published posthumously by Cole and Cole (1979), he describes the basis of scientific observations: "the object of observation is to ascertain a network of important relations. When done properly, observation accomplishes the classical aim of preserving the manifold richness of the subject," where the statement "done properly" (p.178) is used in the sense "to view an event from as many perspectives as possible. The eye of science does not probe 'a thing,' an event isolated from other events or things. Its real object is to see and understand the way a thing or event relates to other things or events. It seeks out the most important traits or primary, basic factors that have immediate consequences, and seeks out the secondary or 'systemic' consequences of these underlying factors."

When examining the patient, the task of the neuropsychologist is to obtain knowledge of the contributions of each part of the brain, the component named by Joaquin Fuster (Fuster 2003) as the *cognit* relating it to the organization of the *function* or the *functional system*, and this can only be obtained by way of a thorough analysis of the whole system delineated by the observation.

Thus the performance of an examination of this kind implies knowledge of the brain and experienced observations by the person performing the tests or tasks, included in what henceforth will be named *the investigation*. However, also Luria's and Vygotsky's basic statement, that *the higher cortical functions* are social in their genesis, created by the experiences through the life of the individual and the culture in which he or she is brought up, mediated by the development of language in their structure, and conscious in their performance needs to be taken into consideration. Consequently, the characteristics of the individual patient's cultural, psychosocial, and educational state are the traits that have to be elucidated in order to obtain the insight searched for. Finally, and also referring to Luria's basic conviction, the investigation has to be carried out in a phenomenological collaboration between the neuropsychologist and the patient.

Originally, referring to Jaspers (1963), the phenomenological approach was conceived of as a descriptive catalogue of symptoms and experiences. The German phenomenologist Thomas Fuchs (2002) has expanded this description to include the person as the proper subject of experience. To Fuchs, much in correspondence with Luria's and Vygotsky's basic ideas, meaning is not located somewhere in the brain but only in the interaction between the living human being and his natural and social environment: "The neurocognitive system exists enmeshed in the world, in which we move, behave and live with others through our bodily existence."

Monitoring patients in intensive care in the attempt to build up a state of expectancy of stimuli in the patients waking up from unconsciousness can be obtained by regular daily visits to the bedside, accompanied by the reassuring information that the patient is (aware of being) in a hospital and that everyone around them is knowledgeable of his or her condition and will do the best to understand and provide the right kind of treatment to speed up the improvement. Such kind of recurring information has been shown not only to calm down agitated patients and make the nursing care easier but also to have a reassuring effect, coming to the fore in the patient's relationship to their families, and it creates a base for the bedside evaluation.

On the whole, the presence of the neuropsychologist in the acute care, being the main contact to the family members, has opened possibilities to learn more about the patient's premorbid situation and personality, valuable for the multiprofessional team in their diagnostic work. It has further made it easier to be informed about the patient's social situation, friends, colleagues, and workplace along with the progression of the patient's recovery.

The presence of the neuropsychologist as part of the clinical team not only makes it possible to start evaluation earlier but also makes it possible to perform the evaluation more closely in stages, little by little, during states of decline or progress.

The choice of tests to use from *Luria's Neuropsychological Investigation* (Christensen 1979) during this very early phase of the investigation depends on a combination of all medical information, including findings from the objective examinations of the brain and from the discussions about the team members' observations at the daily conferences, integrated in the neuropsychologist's observation of the patient's behavior, orientation, education, cultural and social background, all obtained through observation and through what Luria called "the preliminary conversation," the first part of the investigation. On this background, the evaluation can be directed in accordance with the three units described by Luria, first clarifying awareness, orientation regarding time, place, and person, energy level, emotion, and motivation; secondly investigating cognition (perception, language, thinking, and concept formation); and finally, the patient's higher cortical functions, the abilities to plan and to control reactions and behavior.

For all tests selected, it is important to know their component parts and in accordance with this to *analyze* the patient's performance in detail.

Usually, this initial testing taking place at the bedside must be short, due to the low tone characterizing the first unit at this stage after the patient's injury, when lack of energy, or easily provoked tiredness, can be expected. If this is not taken into consideration, false conclusions may be drawn, and a secondary disturbance may be distinguished as the primary defect.

On the whole, the reliability of the investigation must be ensured. How consistent and reliable, in fact, are the findings? When tests have been administered only a few times, the number being limited by the necessity of a short duration of the examination, the findings may be unclear. If the same experiment on the other hand is repeated for too long, the observations may differ; actually, the results of each individual test during this kind of evaluation of a patient are highly questionable. The reliability of the results can, however, be ensured by syndrome analysis; that is, the *comparative analysis* of the results of a group of assorted tests and the determination of general signs among these results, grouped together into a unified syndrome. This is so because the presence of a primary defect, interfering with the proper function of a given part of the brain, inevitably leads to disturbances of a group of functional systems; that is, to the appearance of a symptom-complex, or syndrome, composed of externally heterogeneous but, in fact, internally interrelated symptoms. For instance, writing, like the pronunciation of words, has as one of its components the reception of acoustic elements of speech. Operations involving spatial relationships or calculation, externally very different functions, also possess a common link—simultaneous spatial analysis and synthesis.

The reliability of the neuropsychological investigation—carried out under such clinical conditions—thus has to be obtained not only by way of distinguishing the underlying defect but also by demonstrating how this defect manifests itself through changed activity, coming to the fore in the complex system of disturbances that arises. Hence, if the results obtained in different tests are compared, and a common type of disturbances affecting different forms of activity is observed, the results of the investigation are reliable and acquire clinical significance. In this line of thought, Hans Lukas Teuber's "double dissociation of symptoms" can serve as verification: "A strategy for inferring an underlying mechanism from behavioral symptoms, i.e. in cases of double dissociation, one symptom is found with one particular lesion but not with a contrasting lesion and thereby suggesting separable mechanisms" (Milner and Teuber 1968).

The demands of the skills of the neuropsychologist performing a bedside examination are many, but what can be obtained is an insight in the functioning of the individual patient, more enlightening than the technical illustrations of a scan, be it a functional magnetic resonance imaging (fMRI) or a positron emission tomography (PET) scan, whereas the neuropsychological investigation and the scan may serve to complement each other (see Chapter 3 in this volume).

An important objective of the bedside evaluation obtained by specific information of this kind can be useful for the nursing staff as well as the relatives staying with the patient regarding the understanding of the anxiety and fear the patient is experiencing, causing his or her reactions and behavior. The neuropsychological interpretation may not only have a reassuring effect but also lead to improved interactions between the patient and the family members and thereby even help improve the patient's own insight.

During the testing period, it is important to observe the patient's reactions, that is, how additional support, such as giving the patient more time or repeating the tasks within short intervals, may change the patient's behavior, preferences, or adaptive skills.

The final aim is an integration of all observations, so that the patient's condition at this early stage can be described and evaluated with respect to possibilities of improvement and future development. Reports from patients at a later stage in the course of their recovery have often given evidence of the importance of such early stimulation and support.

The preliminary conversation with the patient is the first stage of the examination. Stage two is *the preliminary investigation*: the tests are short and standardized at a level that anyone who does not have an organic brain lesion can perform them—including people with a poor educational background. At this stage, the primary aim is to discover the status of the individual analyzers (visual, auditory, kinesthetic, and motor) which provide information about the major areas in the second unit, responsible for registration, analysis, and memorization of information—abilities located in the primary areas in the occipital, temporal, and parietal lobes of the cerebral cortex. Simple sensory motor tasks are relevant as a start, together with tests from the primary perception areas, the visual, auditory, and kinesthetic; the demand on the neuropsychologist is to get as close to obtaining insight in the processes by which the patient is attempting to solve the tasks. The third stage is *the selective individualized investigation* in any groups of mental processes in which the preliminary tests have detected the presence of definite defects. The tests included in this part of the investigation examine speech, writing, and reading.

These tests involve secondary and tertiary areas of the second functional unit, and the task of the neuropsychologist is to follow the steps of reasoning, make inquiries, and *analyze* the components of the process.

The first test/task in *Luria's Neuropsychological Investigation* (LNI) of the evaluation of learning process, "Series of unrelated words," may be illustrative as an example (Table 10–1).

The observation or what in this context should be termed the analysis of patients' behavioral reactions may reveal different patterns; some patients strive to learn the words in a particular order, paying attention each time to the words

TABLE 10–1. Results of a Learning Experiment

SERIAL NO.	LEVEL OF ASPIRATION	ACTUAL RESULT	HOUSE	FOREST	CAT	NIGHT	TABLE	NEEDLE	PIE	BELL	BRIDGE	CROSS
1	–	6	1	2	3	–	4	–	–	–	5	6
2	8	7	1	2	3	–	4	5	–	–	6	7
3	8	8	1	2	3	4	5	6	–	–	7	8
4	10	9	1	2	3	9	4	5	–	6	7	8
5	10	10	1	2	3	9	4	5	10	6	7	8
–												
–												
–												

The patient is presented with a series of unrelated words too long to memorize and asked to reproduce them in any order, usually 10 to 12 words. In the case of a bedside evaluation, the number should be adapted to the situation and the individual patient. After he or she has said aloud the words retained, the results are plotted in a table by the neuropsychologist and the series is given again. Again the results are recorded. The procedure is repeated at most 8 to 10 times. During the memorizing, the patient may be asked how many words he or she believes it will be possible to memorize when the series is next repeated, and the answers given are compared with the actual results as shown in the table.

that he or she could not remember last time. However, if a new group of words is remembered, this may be linked to leaving out the group previously memorized. The patient makes few mistakes, and the same mistake is not made many times in succession. These traits show that the patient is aware of the task he or she is performing and trying hard to control what is taking place, but where the scope is limited, the performance most possibly is pointing to a defective functional system caused by lesions in the posterior divisions of the brain (the second unit). In another pattern, where the learning is slow, where only a few words are remembered and where the patient is easily fatigued, and the performance declines very soon or after the fourth or fifth repetition, the cause may be ascribed to general changes in cerebral activity, corresponding with the first unit. However, if the patient does not evaluate his or her performance realistically, if he or she cannot predict how many elements of the series may be repeated, or if inertly a low number is predicted, even after the actual result has been better, and the words are produced in random order, or there is lack of attention to words previously forgotten, together with a stereotyped continuation of the same words and mistakes, all these traits will be pointing to a functional system located in anterior (frontal) lesions, the third unit.

The most important aspect of the test can be summarized as an analysis of the systems at work, the methods used to increase the volume of retained material, the influence of the aspiration level, and the patient's reaction to mistakes. The process thus may show valuable results for the clinical study of local brain lesions: with which methods is the patient being investigated, which material is retained, and how does the patient react to mistakes?

Depending upon the location of the injury, varying numbers of words will be retained, as illustrated by the curve representing the course of memorizing of the individual patients, and their levels of aspiration and fatigue (Figure 10–1). Such factors can be calculated and compared, used quantitatively as well as qualitatively, not only in the test described but also in a number of other tests employed as tools in the course of the neuropsychological investigation.

The fourth stage is *formulation of a clinical neuropsychological conclusion* based on an integration of the results obtained and the comparative analysis of the data.

From a phenomenological point of view, the more supportive the professional approach, the better is most often the compliance of the patients. Making the patients repeat the information they are given at different time intervals may also show how it is received, how it is recalled, and for how long it is kept in mind; providing reassurance, rather than causing insecurity and anxiety, showing trust in the patients' performance, along with continuous feedback and support, all seem to be effective approaches.

At this early stage, it may also prove successful and lead to change in the performance to provide information to the patient instead of asking questions, which

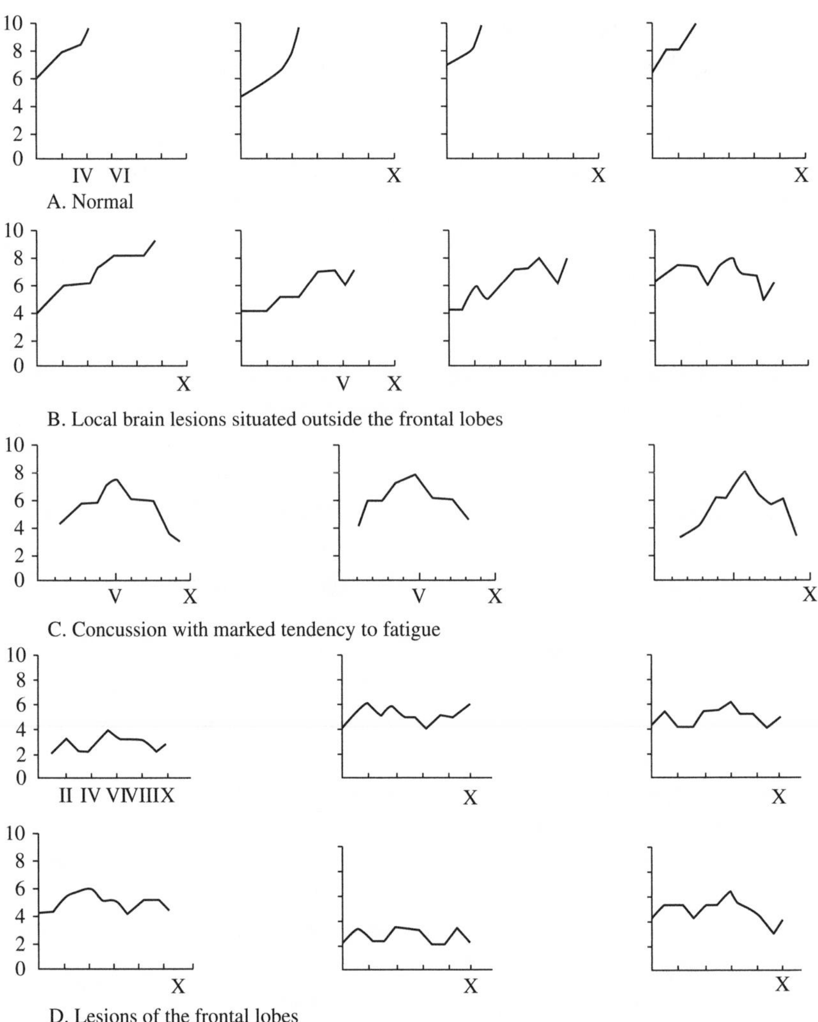

FIGURE 10–1. Memorizing curves in normal subjects and in patients with lesions of the frontal lobes and of other parts of the brain.

in a sense reminds us of what is described as "errorless learning" (Baddeley and Wilson 1994).

Conclusion of the Luria approach

Awareness the complexity of brain functioning is an important prerequisite for all professions working together being responsible for diagnostics and in rehabilitation of patients with brain injury. Clinical neuropsychology performed by the neuropsychologist in accordance with Luria's theories and methods, and further elaborated by Elkhonon Goldberg's hemispheric interaction (Goldberg 2005), has achieved becoming a highly needed and appreciated partner in the team, playing an important role among the other disciplines involved. The correspondence of Luria's theories with the newest achievements within cognitive neuroscience, the theories of Joaquin Fuster (2003) and Gerald M. Edelman (2004), and the confirmative results in neuroimaging, all have contributed to a growing attention to the area. Luckily, seen from a clinical and social point of view, it has also changed attitudes toward brain injury.

Brain injury can no longer be considered without hope; the insight obtained within scientific, technical, and practical approaches seems to point to a future where effective early treatment and rehabilitation provided by professionals from all the areas involved, based on the latest neuroscientific knowledge, collaborating as a team, will in a great many cases lead to a much wanted regaining of the injured patient's mental capacity and at the same time add to the scientific understanding of the brain's capacity to self repair and restoration.

An American modification of the Lurian approach to the bedside neuropsychological examination and the development of the Barrow Neurological Institute Screen for Higher Cerebral Functions

The LNI (Christensen 1979) is an extraordinary approach to understanding the neuropsychological syndromes patients may demonstrate when certain regions of the brain have been rendered dysfunctional via various neuropathologic processes. Its goal is not to obtain quantitative estimates of how certain "abilities" may be differentially affected. Rather, it strives to reveal how the higher cortical functions (or mental processes) are specifically negatively affected in a given individual. If this can be done, it provides indispensable information for how to approach a given patient from a rehabilitation point of view. The examining procedures naturally flow from the neurologic examination and are used in concordance with Luria's (1966) theoretical ideas concerning the organization of higher cortical functions in man.

Many who attempt this type of examination are humbled by their lack of knowledge concerning the organization of brain–behavior relationships, which is absolutely necessary to guide this examination process. This reality has moved many of us to examination procedures that reflect our limitations as neuropsychologists but draw on our strengths as clinical psychologists trained in the psychometric tradition.

What I (G.P.P.) will outline below is my approach to the "bedside examination," which has been influenced by my understanding of the writings of Luria

(1966), Ward Halstead (1947), Goodglass and Kaplan (1983), De Renzi and Vignolo (1962), Rapaport, Gill, and Schafer (1968), and Kurt Goldstein (1942). It has also been influenced by a practical problem. Namely, could we obtain both qualitative and quantitative information about a person's higher integrative brain functions in both a reliable and brief manner? Brevity is often necessary because of the patient's clinical condition (i.e., they may fatigue easily) and the numerous time pressures clinicians face. There is also another related, but different practical problem. How does a clinician establish adequate rapport with a patient in the examination process and in so doing obtain a overview of their higher cerebral functions (and dysfunctions) that raise hypotheses regarding differential diagnosis and areas to examine in detail as the neuropsychological assessment process continues? These two questions resulted in the establishment of the Barrow Neurological Institute Screen for Higher Cerebral Functions (BNIS) (Prigatano 1991). An outline of the examination procedures and how they are currently used will be discussed.

Barrow Neurological Institute Screen for Higher Cerebral Functions

Luria (1966) noted that tumors of deep brain structures involving the upper brain stem and thalamus may compromise a person's level of arousal/alertness and therefore their cooperation level. The same could be said of persons who suffer severe traumatic brain injury (Jennett and Teasdale 1981) or large cerebral infarctions (Prigatano and Henderson 1996). The first step in a bedside examination is to determine (and thereby rate) the level of consciousness/alertness. The BNIS provides for initial screening of this dimension and records the capacity of the person to orient and respond to the examiner's questions (Prigatano, Amin, and Rosenstein 1995). The second step in the initial screening process is to determine if basic language functions are adequate for assessing a number of other abilities. Again, a 3-point rating scale is used. The third step in the initial evaluation of the patient is a determination of the patient's cooperation level. Whereas most patients are cooperative, there are some who are not. If the patient makes derogatory comments to the examiner or to the examination process and/or is slow in responding, but is not aphasic or hypoaroused, the examiner should evaluate whether or not the patient is putting forth adequate effort in the examination. This is perhaps the most difficult area to estimate, but some estimation of cooperation level is necessary in order to draw conclusions about what will be observed from the patient's later performance.

Once the patient meets minimum standards for demonstrating adequate arousal/alertness, language skills, and cooperation, the examiner can begin to inquire as to the patient's current clinical state and whether the patient is aware of any limitations in their functioning. Luria (1966) emphasized this as the preliminary conversation and noted its importance when later interpreting neuropsychological test findings. Later in this chapter, I (G.P.P.) will discuss in more detail how the initial interview with the patient might proceed. For the purposes of the bedside examination, however, the point that needs to be emphasized is that the examiner simply inquires as to the patient's awareness of any functional limitations that are of concern to him or her.

After this is done, the examiner explains that he will ask the patient to carry out a series of tasks, some of which may seem extremely simple, whereas others may appear to be challenging. The examiner emphasizes that it is not important that the patient "pass" each item, but that it is the pattern of findings that may be most helpful to the examiner in having a better understanding of the patient's current clinical condition.

Luria (1966) emphasized, as did Goldstein (1942), Goodglass and Kaplan (1983), and Rapaport, Gill, and Schafer (1968), that what the patient says and how he or she says it has important diagnostic implications. The examining clinician, therefore, must listen very carefully to the patient's beginning utterances and determine if the patient's speech is fluent, dysarthric, or shows any signs of paraphasic errors. This information has obvious diagnostic significance when evaluating aphasic syndromes and syndromes that affect articulation secondary to upper motor neuron disease.

The formal examination process begins by showing the patient a 3 inch × 5 inch card that has different colors of circles and squares on it. The patient is asked to simply touch the yellow circle to determine if there is any color blindness. The patient is then asked to touch the small red circle and the large white square. The instruction can be given a second time if necessary. The purpose is to evaluate the patient's auditory comprehension skills using items adapted from the Token Test (DeRenzi and Vignolo 1962).

Once it is established that the patient can understand what is being asked of him or her, a series of language tests are given to assess difficulties in naming, sentence repetition, reading, writing, and spelling. Visual representation of two common objects is also presented to determine if visual object agnosia is present. Though a rare condition, it can exist after significant bilateral temporal–occipital lobe disturbances (Blumenfeld 2002).

After speech and language functions are briefly assessed, the patient's orientation is determined. The patient is asked to state the date (the month, the year, the day of the week) and their location (the city and the name of the building in which they are examined). Right–left orientation is also assessed.

The patient is then asked to carry out a variety of tasks that include constructional praxis, arithmetic, and attention/concentration skills. Visuospatial problem-solving abilities are then assessed by tasks that sample visual sequencing as well as visual scanning. The patient is asked to copy a pattern and to detect the underlying pattern. This latter task was inspired by Luria's observation that patients who make perseverative errors will have difficulties accurately copying a repetitive pattern.

The patient's ability to learn and remember information is then assessed. A unique aspect of the BNIS is that the individual is asked to learn a series of number–symbol associations and is specifically told that they could use paper and pencil to aid them in the memory process. The goal is to determine if the patient spontaneously uses compensatory techniques to solve a memory problem.

An important component to this examination is asking the patient to remember three words with distraction and to predict the number of words they believe they will be able to recall when they are called upon to do this task. This again was inspired by Luria's (1966) approach when asking patients to remember a list of words read to them. He would read the list of words to the patient and record their response. He would then tell them how many words they recalled on that trial and ask them to predict what they think they would be able to do on the second trial. He noted that a failure to integrate information about current performance with future performance may reflect some disturbance in self-awareness and associated underlying frontal lobe pathology. Thus, embedded in the process of assessing learning and memory capacity, one also attempts to assess the patient's awareness of limitations they may have in memory performance.

A final component of the BNIS that is not included in the Luria (1966) examination or in any other bedside examination is a brief assessment of the patient's capacity for affect expression and the perception of affect. The patient is asked to generate in a happy or angry tone of voice the sentence, "They won the game." In addition, the patient is shown three drawings of facial affect. The first have to do with anger and happiness, which most brain-dysfunctional patients can easily pass. The third face is more vague and represents either an individual who is fearful or surprised. It has turned out that this has become an exceptionally useful projective measure. Some brain-dysfunctional (and psychiatric) patients will describe a mildly ambiguous face as confused. Others may describe the face as uncertain, and still others might describe the face as reflecting a neutral reaction. The face is normally described as one of fear or surprise. The patient's response to these stimuli may provide insight into their phenomenological state when approaching a problem-solving task.

A final aspect of the BNIS is to determine if one can stimulate spontaneous affect in the individual. Two stimulus cards are used for this purpose. Luria (1948/1963) and others have noted that significant lesions of the frontal lobes may produce a blunting of affect, and yet this part of the examination has never been formalized. The BNIS attempts to rectify this problem (see Prigatano, Amin, and Rosenstein 1991).

From qualitative to quantitative information

The BNIS is constructed so that passing all items correctly produces a score of 50 out of 50 points. The score can then be transferred into an age-adjusted T score. In addition, there are seven BNIS subtests that can be calculated. These subtests are Speech and Language Function, Orientation, Attention and Concentration, Visuospatial and Visual Problem-Solving, Memory, Affect, and Awareness versus Performance.

These quantitative scores have been shown to be useful in cases of differential diagnosis (Rosenstein, Prigatano, and Nayak 1997) and for predicting the capacity of patients to achieve inpatient rehabilitation goals (Prigatano and Wong 1999). Moreover, the test has been shown to be useful in detecting both cognitive and affective sequelae during the early stages after traumatic brain injury (Borgaro and Prigatano, 2002). Recently, the test has been cross-validated on a Swedish population (Denvall, Elmstahl, and Prigatano 2002) and has been shown to discriminate control subjects from patients on an inpatient neurorehabilitation unit (Hofgren, et al. 2007a). Another investigation has used it to measure recovery after stroke in a Swedish population (Hofgren, et al. 2007b).

These observations reinforce the notion that one can obtain both qualitative and quantitative information regarding patients in a brief but reliable fashion. This information is helpful for a variety of practical clinical purposes. Although this approach does not fully reveal the underlying neuropsychological syndrome of a patient, it provides information that helps classify the severity of neuropsychological disturbance of a patient and reveals patterns of disturbed abilities after various forms of brain injury.

Examples of the research utility of the BNIS

A brief clinical neuropsychological examination not only should help evaluate a given patient's neuropsychological status, but also information should be obtained that is relevant for rehabilitation. Prigatano and Wong (1999) assessed how performance on different aspects of the BNIS related to the achievement of inpatient rehabilitation goals. They demonstrated that impairments in both cognitive and affective areas, as sampled by the BNIS, helped predict what patients went on to achieve their rehabilitation goals. In that study, they reported that less than 20% of inpatients with brain dysfunction could accurately predict their capacity to retrieve three words with distraction when first admitted to the rehabilitation unit. However, they noted that those patients who were able to accurately predict if they could recall three words with distraction (irrespective of the number of words they were able to recall) at time of discharge achieved rehabilitation goals more frequently than did patients who could not accurately predict their performance at time of discharge (see Figure 10–2).

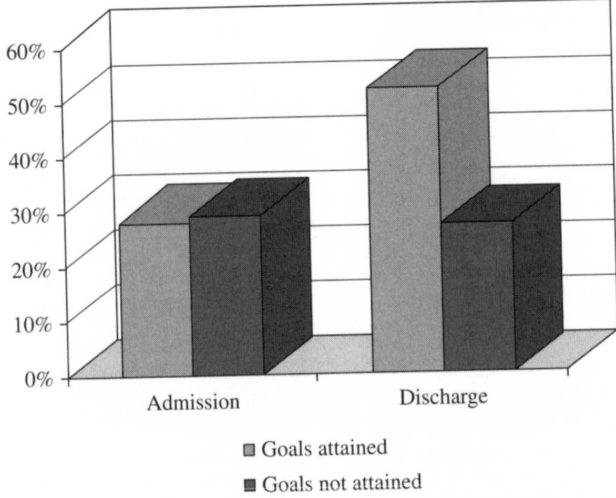

FIGURE 10–2. Percentage of patients who could accurately predict the number of words they would recall on the BNIS. Scores were obtained at time of admission and at discharge. Those patients who were able to accurately predict their ability to recall three words tended to achieve their goals at a higher percentage than that of patients who were not able to accurately predict.

A return to the preliminary conversation

One of Luria's (1966) most important insights was that how the patients view their clinical condition has important diagnostic implications. Far too few clinical neuropsychologists discuss the importance of the clinical interview for establishing rapport for the patient, adequately engaging the patient in the neuropsychological examination, and using this information for differential diagnosis. In this context, it is important to consider how the preliminary conversation should be approached, both during the bedside examination as well as when the patient is sitting face-to-face with the neuropsychologist in his or her office during the post–acute period.

Bedside Preliminary Conversation

Early after the onset of a brain disorder, patients are often fatigued, irritable, hypoaroused, and show significant language disturbance. It is not possible, therefore, to conduct a thorough preliminary conversation during the acute stages of any brain injury. What should be done, however, in the initial stage is to explain to the patient who the examiner is and why they are seeing the patient. This should be brief and to the point. For example, the examiner might introduce themselves as "I am Dr. Prigatano, a clinical neuropsychologist at the Barrow Neurological Institute." The next statement should be along the lines of "Your doctor, Dr. Smith, has asked that I see you today in order to determine how you are doing and whether or not you are experiencing any notable problems in memory or thinking."

The examiner would then politely ask the patient whether or not they notice any change of their abilities. The examiner should determine whether or not the patient appears confused with this question or if they can give a sensible answer to what is being asked.

During this preliminary interview, the examiner should ask the patient if they would be willing to carry out a few simple tasks so that the examiner could better determine whether, in fact, there are any areas of difficulty that need further medical/rehabilitation attention. It is important that the examiner emphasizes to the patient that he or she is asking permission to do this and that he or she will appreciate whatever effort the patient puts forth. As has been described elsewhere (Prigatano 1999), the first goal in the contact with the patient is to reduce the patient's confusion and frustration so that his or her needs are met in as reliable and effective a fashion as possible at whatever stages they are in the recovery process.

It is against this background that the individual conducts the BNIS as noted above and specifically observes whether or not the patient overestimates or underestimates his or her memory capacity and whether or not the patient recognizes their need to use compensatory techniques when carrying out a memory task. This can have important implications for how the patient is actually helped to make a transition to the rehabilitation environment.

The Preliminary Conversation During the Post–Acute Phase

Once the patient leaves the hospital and is able to function in a home or rehabilitation environment, the patient may be able to engage in a more complete discussion of his or her current functioning and to be asked specific queries that would help the examiner determine the level of insight the patient has into his or her difficulties, as well as the level of insight that family members have. This is an aspect of the preliminary conversation that has not been specifically addressed by the previous work of Luria, Goldstein, and others. That is, when faced with the rehabilitation of brain-dysfunctional patients and/or their management, it is important to understand how family members actually perceive the patient and whether their judgments appear to be valid (Prigatano and Gray, 2008). If they are not, the examining clinician has two tasks. One is to establish a working relationship with the patient and help him or her make decisions that are in his or her best interest. Next, the clinician needs to establish a good working relationship with family members and help them become realistic about the patient without losing hope for the patient's future.

How should the examination thus be conducted during the post–acute phase? The procedure used is as follows. When the appointment is made to see the patient, a request is also made that a family member or significant other attend the initial clinical interview.

When both arrive for the interview, the examining neuropsychologist greets the patient first and then greets the family member that is attending. They are asked to come into the office of the clinician. It should be emphasized that the clinician goes to the waiting room to find the patient and family member and brings them back to his or her office. The patient is not escorted to the clinician's office. The clinician must show an interest in the patient and family and go the extra effort to welcome them.

The interview thus begins with the neuropsychologist explaining his or her understanding of why the patient is there. The patient should never be put "on the spot" to explain why they are there. Once the examiner gives an explanation, the examiner asks the patient whether or not that is his or her understanding of why they are there. In many instances the patient is on "the same page" and in some instances the patient is not. Clarifying early the purpose of why the patient is being seen is important for having honest dialogue that is the basis of all clinical discussion. The same is also asked of the family member. That is, is the family member in agreement as to why the patient is being seen.

The examiner then asks the patient to describe what, if any, difficulties that he or she may currently experience. Note the examiner does not ask the patient to list "problems." The examiner emphasizes that he or she wants to know what the patient's experience is of day-to-day functioning. After the patient lists whatever difficulties he or she experiences, the examiner turns to the significant others and asks if there is anything that the person wishes to add. If the patient's significant other raises problems that the patient did not mention, it is important to watch the patient's reaction. Does the patient concur readily or does the patient seem perplexed? Again, this provides important diagnostic information.

After this phase of the interview is conducted, the examiner asks the patient to provide information concerning his or her background. This can be brief or extensive, depending on the clinical question that is being asked. Basic information regarding the patient's age, date of birth, handedness, and educational background are minimal information to be obtained. Information concerning job history or marital history is also sampled, again depending on the clinical purpose of the examination and the patient's capacity to cooperate.

Then the patient is asked about sleep, appetite, any sensory or motor disturbances, and whether or not there is a history of smoking or alcohol use. During all of this time, the family member is asked to sit quietly and listen. The patient's responses to these questions, both verbal and nonverbal, provide exceptionally diagnostically important information. Is the family member tolerant of the patient or irritated by the patient? Does the family member start to answer for the patient when the family member was specifically asked to hold his or her comments? This provides extremely important information about the dynamics of the family situation, which again is crucial for patient management and sometimes for differential diagnosis.

After this, the patient is asked to rate on a scale from 0 to 10 (with 0 meaning no difficulty and 10 meaning severe difficulty) his or her level of difficulty in areas of memory, word-finding, concentration, irritability, anxiety, depression, fatigue, and problems with directionality (Prigatano and Borgaro 2004). The patient's ability to follow the instruction and provide ratings is in and of itself important diagnostic information, particularly in the assessment of patients with early Alzheimer's disease. After the patient completes this task, the family member completes the task. The disparity between ratings can provide useful information. In one preliminary study, it has been shown that such information relates to the ultimate diagnosis of the patient (Prigatano and Borgaro 2004).

Time and commitment

The time to conduct a bedside neuropsychological examination may be as brief as 10–15 minutes or as long as 1 hour. The time to conduct an interview and complete the BNIS in the post–acute phase is approximately 1 hour to 1 hour 15 minutes. During this time, the neuropsychologist must be committed to focusing his or her attention on what the patient says, how the patient performs, and how the patient's family members react. With this time and commitment, adequate rapport is often established, and the patient can begin a more comprehensive neuropsychological examination as needed.

Conclusions

The bedside neuropsychological examination is influenced by the patient's clinical state and the theoretical orientation and practical experience of the examining clinician. What is outlined above represents one approach to briefly but reliably and validly assess qualitative and quantitative information that may be helpful to patient diagnosis and management after various brain disorders.

Acknowledgments

Funds from the Newsome Chair allowed time to prepare this chapter. Funds from the Danish Velux Foundation allowed assistance to prepare this chapter.

References

Baddeley, A. and Wilson, B.A. 1994. When Implicit Learning Fails: Amnesia and the Problem of Error Elimination. *Neuropsychologia* 32(1):53–68.

Blumenfeld, H. 2002. *Neuroanatomy Through Clinical Cases*. Sunderland, Mass.: Sinauer Associates.

Borgaro, S.R. and Prigatano, G.P. 2002. Early Cognitive and Affective Sequelae of Traumatic Brain Injury: A Study Using the BNI Screen for Higher Cerebral Functions. *Journal of Head Trauma Rehabilitation* 17(6):526–534.

Christensen, A.L. 1975/1979. *Luria's Neuropsychological Investigation* (2nd ed.). Denmark: Munksgaard.

Christensen, A.L. 1989. The Neuropsychological Investigation as a Therapeutic and Rehabilitative Technique. In: Ellis, D.W. and Christensen, A.-L. (eds.). *Neuropsychological Treatment after Brain Injury*. Dordrecht: Kluwer Academic Publishers, pp. 127–153.

Christensen, A.L. 2002. Lifelines. In: A. Stringer (ed.). *Pathways to Prominence: Reflections of the 20th Century Neuropsychologists*. New York, London, Hove: Psychology Press, pp. 119–137.

Cole, M. and Cole, S. (eds.) 1979. *The Making of Mind. A Personal Account of Soviet Psychology*. A. R. Luria. Harvard University Press.

Denvall, V., Elmstahl, S., and Prigatano, G.P. 2002. Replication and Construct Validation of the BNI Screen for Higher Cerebral Function with the Swedish Population. *Journal of Rehabilitation Medicine* 34:153–157.

DeRenzi, E. and Vignolo, L.A. 1962. The Token Test: A Sensitive Test to Detect Disturbances in Aphasics. *Brain* 85:665–678.

Edelman, G.M. 2004. *Wider than the Sky: The Phenomenal Gift of Consciousness*. New Haven, Conn.: Yale University Press

Fuchs, T. 2002. *The Challenge of Neuroscience: Psychiatry and Phenomenology Today. Psychopathology* 35:319–326.

Fuster, J.M. 2003. *Cortex and Mind, Unifying Cognition*. New York: Oxford University Press.

Goldberg, E. 2005. *The Wisdom Paradox*. New York: Gotham Books.

Goldstein, K. 1934/1995. *The Organism: A Holistic Approach to Biology Derived from Pathological Data in Man*. With a foreword by Oliver Sacks. New York: Zone Books.

Goldstein, K. 1942. *Aftereffects of Brain Injuries in War*. New York: Grune and Stratton.

Goldstein, K. 1983. Effect of Brain Damage on Personality. In: T. Millon (ed.). *Theories of Personality and Psychopathology*. New York: Holt, Rinehart and Winston, pp. 54–62.

Halstead, W.C. 1947. *Brain and Intelligence: A Quantitative Study of Frontal Lobes*. Chicago: The University of Chicago Press.

Hofgren, C., Björkdahl, A., Esbjörnsson, E., and Stibrant-Sunnerhagen, K. 2007a. Recovery after Stroke: Cognition, ADL Function and Return to Work. *Acta Neurologica Scandinavia* 115:73–80.

Hofgren, C., Esbjornsson, E., Aniansson, H., and Stibrant Sunnerhagen, K. 2007b. Application and Validation of the Barrow Neurological Institute Screen for Higher Cerebral Functions in a Control Population and in Patient Groups commonly seen in Neurorehabilitation. *Journal of Rehabilitation Medicine* 39:547–553.

Jaspers, K. 1963. *General Psychopathology*. Chicago: University of Chicago Press.

Jennett, B. and Teasdale, G. 1981. *Management of Head Injuries*. Philadelphia: F.A. Davis.

Lipovsek, M. and von Wild, K. 2007. *A Brief History of the EMN*. Beijing: China Press.

Luria, A.R. 1963. *Restoration of Function after Brain Injury*. Oxford: Pergamon Press.

Luria, A.R. 1966. *Higher Cortical Functions in Man*. New York and London: Basic Books and Plenum Press.

Luria, A.R. 1970: The Functional Organization of the Brain. *Scientific American* 222(3):66–72, 78

Luria, A.R. 1947/1970. *Traumatic Aphasia*. The Hague: Mouton.

Luria, A.R. 1972: *The Man with a Shattered World*. New York: Basic Books.

Luria, A.R. 1979. *The Making of Mind: A Personal Account of Soviet Psychology*. M. Cole and S. Cole (eds.). Cambridge, Mass.: Harvard University Press.

Milner, B. and Teuber, H. L. 1968. Alteration of Perception and Memory in Man: Reflections on Methods. In: L. Weiskrantz (ed.). *Analysis of Behavioural Change*. New York: Harper & Row, pp. 268–375.

Moruzzi, G. and Magoun, H.W. 1949. *Brain Stem Reticular Formation and Activation of the EEG: Electroencephalography and Clinical Neurophysiology* 1:455–473. (Dept. Anatomy, Northwestern University Medical School, Evanston, Ill.).

Newcombe, F. 1996: Very late Outcome after Focal Wartime Brain Wounds. *Journal of Clinical and Experimental Neuropsychology* 1996;February 18(1):1–23.

Prigatano, G.P. 1991. BNI Screen for Higher Cerebral Functions: Rationale and Initial Validation. *BNI Quarterly* 7(1):2–9.

Prigatano, G.P. 1999. *Principles of Neuropsychological Rehabilitation*. New York: Oxford University Press.

Prigatano, G.P. and Wong, JL. 1999. Cognitive and Affective Improvement in Brain Dysfunctional Patients who Achieve Inpatient Rehabilitation Goals. *Archives of Physical Medicine and Rehabilitation* 80:77–84.

Prigatano, G.P. and Borgaro, S.R. 2004. Neuropsychological and Phenomenological Correlates of Persons with Dementia versus Memory Complaints, but no Dementia. *BNI Quarterly* (20)2:21–26.

Prigatano, G.P. and Gray, J.A. (2008). Parental Perspectives on Recovery and Social Integration after Pediatric Traumatic Brain Injury. *Journal of Head Trauma Rehabilitation*.

Prigatano, G.P. and Henderson, S. 1996. Cognitive Outcome after Subarachnoid Hemorrhage. In: J.B. Pederson (ed.). *Subarachnoid Hemorrhage: Pathophysiology and Management*. Lebanon, N.H.: American Association of Neurological Surgeons, pp. 27–40.

Prigatano, G. P., Amin, K., and Rosenstein, L.D. 1995. *Administration and Scoring Manual for the BNI Screen for Higher Cerebral Functions*. Phoenix, Ariz.: Barrow Neurological Institute.

Rapaport, D., Gill, M.M. and Schafer, R. 1968. *Diagnostic Psychological Testing*. New York: International Universities Press.

Rosenstein, L.D., Prigatano, G.P., and Nayak, M. 1997. Differentiating Patients with Higher Cerebral Dysfunction from Patients with Psychiatric or Acute Medical Illness with the BNI Screen for Higher Cerebral Functions. *Neuropsychiatry, Neuropsychology, and Behavioral Neurology* 10(2):113–119.

Teasdale, T.W., Christensen, A.-L., Willmes, K., Deloche, G., Braga, L., Stachowiak, F., Vendrell, J.M., Castro-Caldas, A., Laaksonen, R, and Leclercq, M. 1997. Subjective Experience in Brain Injured Patients and their Close Relatives: A European Brain Injury Questionnaire Study. *Brain Injury* 11:543–563.

Index

Note: Page numbers followed by *f* and *t* indicate figures and tables, respectively.